Conflict Management in the Asia Pacific

Conflict Management in the Asia Pacific: Assumptions and Approaches in Diverse Cultures

edited by

Kwok Leung
Department of Psychology
Chinese University of Hong Kong

and

Dean Tjosvold
Department of Management
Lingnan College, Hong Kong

JOHN WILEY & SONS (ASIA) PTE LTD
Singapore • New York • Chichester • Brisbane • Toronto • Weinheim

Other Wiley Editorial Offices

John Wiley & Sons, Inc.
605 Third Avenue, New York, NY 10158-0012, USA

John Wiley & Sons Ltd
Baffins Lane, Chichester, West Sussex PO19 IUD, England

Jacaranda Wiley Ltd
33 Park Road, (PO Box 1226) Milton, Queensland 4064, Australia

John Wiley & Sons (Canada) Ltd
22 Worchester Road, Rexdale, Ontario M9W ILI, Canada

Library of Congress Cataloguing-in-Publication Data

Conflict management in the Asia Pacific/edited by Kwok Leung and Dean Tjosvold.
p. cm.
Includes bibliographical references and index.
ISBN 0–471–24858–4 (hardcover)
1. Conflict management—Asia. 2. Conflict management—Pacific Area. I. Leung, Kwok, 1958–. II. Tjosvold, Dean.
HD42.C655 1998
658.4'053'095—dc21

98–40355
CIP

Printed in Singapore
10 9 8 7 6 5 4 3 2 1

CONTENTS

CHAPTER ONE

Introduction: Conflict Management in the Asia Pacific

KWOK LEUNG
Department of Psychology, Chinese University of Hong Kong
and
DEAN TJOSVOLD
Department of Management, Lingnan College, Tuen Mun, Hong Kong and Simon Fraser University, Canada

"If it becomes necessary to oppose a ruler, withstand him to his face, and don't try roundabout methods."

Confucius

"When two [persons] in business always agree, one of them is unnecessary."

William Wrigley

To do business is to be in conflict, and doing business in the Asia Pacific is particularly fraught with conflict. Japanese managers in a successful joint venture in Guangzhou, China, confided that they were frustrated that their Chinese employees failed to take the initiative in improving product quality and maintaining a clean, efficient factory floor. Why didn't they concern themselves about the collective good of the company as a whole, not just their own individual interests? Although the company did so much for them, they complained and demanded more for themselves. The Chinese employees were in turn upset that their Japanese managers were tough and impersonal, sometimes even condescending. How could the managers expect them to behave like loyal, life-time Japanese workers, especially when the company was prepared to fire them, even close the factory and move the operations?

Managers working only within their own country and in one organization have been found to spend a quarter of their time managing conflict and a good deal more time avoiding conflict (Thomas and Schmidt 1976). Doing business across organizations and cultures requires even more conflict management. Unmet expectations, unspoken assumptions, fast-paced change, and the stress of working in different environments all give rise to complex conflicts in international business. There is no escape from conflict in Asia Pacific business. However, well-managed conflict can help partners, managers, and employees strengthen their relationships, learn to adapt, and take advantage of change.

This introductory chapter first discusses the prevalence of conflict in organizations in the Asia Pacific. It argues that harmony and the traditional avoidance of conflict are increasingly unrealistic and costly. Conflict and the nature of positive conflict management are defined. A particularly difficult issue for those involved in Asia Pacific business is that they even have conflict over how they should manage conflict. The book's chapters show the diverse assumptions and approaches that Asia Pacific peoples bring to their conflicts. With an understanding and appreciation of this diversity, strategic partners, managers, and employees can together recognize the value of managing their conflicts and develop common values, skills, and procedures that promote their productive conflict management.

CONFLICT IN ASIA PACIFIC BUSINESS

Organizations are networks of interpersonal relationships structured to accomplish goals. They transform inputs into outputs by applying technologies and procedures. The management system is responsible for coordination of the human and technological resources to reach organizational goals. However, all aspects of this management provoke conflict and its international nature magnifies conflict in Asia Pacific organizations.

Strategic partners disagree over goals. The Thai partners value employment for friends and learning advanced skills whereas the American partner seeks market share and profitability. Commitment to common goals cannot be assumed: stakeholders all have their own perspectives and agendas.

Partners are apt to disagree about technology. Local partners want high technology to maximize their learning and improve their standing in the business community, whereas international partners seek to protect their emerging technology. Employees complain that the machinery is unreliable: managers that employees are careless and unskilled.

Relationship issues often divide organizations. Organizational members disagree over the social norms and values that should govern their interaction, they have different assumptions about punctuality and how to show respect. Managers may assume that the role of the employee includes group physical exercise and participation in work improvement teams, whereas employees believe their role is to perform their own individual job. Those with authority and power are in conflict with those subject to power.

Marketing, production, and engineering departments come to see each other as obstacles. One executive explained, 'We are so busy fighting each other that we do not have time to worry about the competition.' Unfortunately, in many strategic alliances one thing partners agree upon is that the other organization is troublesome: 'How come we value quality service but they do not?' 'Why are we willing to sacrifice for the joint venture but they are not?'

In the Asia Pacific, national and cultural differences complicate these divisions. The Thai partners are pitted against the American ones. Japanese managers join together in their complaints against the Chinese workers who get together to complain about their Japanese managers. In these situations, there is often a great deal of pressure and there are meetings after the meeting to keep each side 'together' and to make sure everyone has the same perception and that the 'other side' is to be blamed for any difficulties. Each national group talks in their own language to solidify their grievances against the other.

Historical suspicions further exacerbate these organizational divisions. Malaysian and Indonesian employees are wary that their Singapore managers may consider them unsophisticated. Korean employees are sensitive to the possibility that their Japanese managers may dominate them. Language misunderstandings and communication distance add to the conflict mix.

The Asia Pacific dynamic change intensifies conflict. Those committed to the status quo are in conflict with those who want to change.

Partners and managers disagree about the nature of changes confronting the company, the best strategy to respond to these changes, and the methods of implementing new approaches. Is marketing washing machines domestically a profitable way to adjust to a stronger currency and growing standard of living? Who should seek the necessary government approval and how should the marketing channels be established? Production personnel have opposing views about processes needed to adapt the product to local preferences.

The diversity that makes conflict so prevalent in the Asia Pacific is also a major reason why doing business in the Asia Pacific is so inviting. Each area and country has its distinct, but potentially highly complementary, competitive advantage. High technology companies based in one country develop products in another, and produce them in others, yet market throughout the region. But the coordination needed to realize these competitive advantages requires intense, global conflict management.

Rapid change promotes conflict and business opportunities. Partners and managers disagree about how to respond to emerging markets, recent relaxation of tariffs, currency fluctuations, and rising standards of living. As argued later, discussing conflicting opinions is key to capitalizing on emerging business opportunities.

Illusionary Harmony

Although conflict is built into organizational life, especially in the diverse, ever changing Asia Pacific, the temptation to avoid and smooth over conflict is strong. Perhaps the problem will work itself out naturally or dissipate over time. Might not others find dealing with the conflict awkward, even demeaning? The risks of confronting conflict can seem very real and direct whereas the benefits of discussing conflict are distant and remote.

The pull of avoidance is particularly strong in the Asia Pacific. Discussing conflicts productively is more difficult with people with different values and methods. Western managers can be especially reluctant because they have been told that East Asians are committed to interpersonal harmony. They are advised that they should be careful to protect the face of their East Asian colleagues or risk severe disruptions in their international arrangements (Trompenaars 1993; Tung 1991, 1982).

East Asians are considered collectivist with a strong emphasis on maintaining relationships and harmony (Boisot and Child 1996; Triandis,

McCusker, and Hui 1990). Highly committed to protecting social face, East Asians avoid open, assertive ways of handling frustrations and problems (Hwang 1985; Kim and Nam, in press; Cocroft and Ting-Toomey 1994; Leung 1997). Given their sensitivity to face, they seek harmony, communicate that they respect their partners as capable and worthy, and are hesitant to engage in aggressive interaction that may challenge the face of others. They want to avoid conflict and, once engaged, use compromise and accommodation to deal with it. Avoiding open discussions of conflict is expected to protect social face and thereby promote interpersonal harmony (Ding 1995; Kirkbride, Tang, and Westwood 1991).

However, Western managers are also tempted to avoid conflict (Tjosvold 1991; Walton 1969). Conflicts are generally considered bad and are blamed for organizational disintegration, poor morale, high absenteeism, sabotage, and violence. To many, the productive organization is one without conflict. North American managers have been found to avoid conflicts although the bottom line costs of such avoidance are high (Tjosvold and Janz 1985).

Harmony cannot be imposed. The illusion that people can work without conflict is increasingly unrealistic, especially in the Asia Pacific. Frustrations and problems do not just disappear. They are expressed indirectly, and may persist far longer and at much greater cost than would result from open confrontation and settlement of conflict. Papered over conflicts leave problems unsolved, people frustrated, and relationships fragmented. Conflicts must be discussed so that solutions can be developed and implemented. It is through positive conflict that unity and true harmony can be reached.

Definition of Conflict

The chapters in this edited volume offer various perspectives, but we discern a common framework for understanding conflict. Conflict has traditionally been defined as opposing interests involving scarce resources, goal divergence and frustration. Conflict is often thought to occur in mixed-motive relationships where persons have both competitive and cooperative interests (Bacharach and Lawler 1981; Kochan and Verma 1983; Walton and McKersie 1965). The competitive elements produce the conflict; the cooperative elements create the incentives to bargain to reach an agreement (Deutsch and Krauss 1962).

Although conflict is often defined as incompatible interests and goals, it is now clear from the work of Morton Deutsch, a social psychologist at Columbia University, that a great deal of conflict may occur even when people have highly compatible goals. Deutsch (1973) defined conflict as incompatible activities; conflict occurs when one's actions are interfering, frustrating, obstructing, or in some other way making another's actions less effective. Conflict can occur in both cooperative and competitive settings.

What is crucial about defining conflict as incompatible activities is that it does not equate actions with goals, a confusion often made in the writing and practice of conflict management. Just because people's actions are incompatible does not mean that their desired end-states are. Their goals and aspirations can still be compatible. They can still get where they want to go.

Partners who are both committed to the long-term success of the company may disagree whether that requires a priority on market share or profitability, whether they should focus on the domestic or export market, and whether investment in high technology is effective. Managers and employees who want a productive, learning factory can disagree about whether they should all wear uniforms. Team members arguing different positions all want the solution that will make their team successful, but make contrasting proposals of how to accomplish this compatible goal. Partners, managers, and employees with cooperative, highly overlapping goals can be, and often are, in conflict.

Considering conflict as opposing interests confounds conflict with competition (defined as incompatible goals.) Assuming that conflict derives from competition leads people to consider every conflict as a 'win-lose' fight and act accordingly. This conclusion makes the management of conflict difficult. Considerable research has documented that protagonists with this conclusion try to avoid discussing conflict but, once engaged, use tough bargaining tactics, closed-mindedly reject the opposing position and the other side, and escalate the conflict (Deutsch 1973; Tjosvold 1993, 1985).

Of course, sometimes conflict is such that there are incompatible goals that make mutual benefit unlikely or even impossible. However, this incompatibility should be discovered, not assumed in the definition of conflict.

Chapters in this book illustrate that intercultural conflict may occur when both parties intend to cooperate and their interests are compatible with each other. Because of cultural differences, misunderstanding, misattribution, and miscommunication set in and fuel disputes basically attitudinal in nature that easily lead to 'win-lose' ways of handling conflict and 'lose-lose' outcomes. The conclusion that the conflict is competitive can be avoided if both parties appreciate that each has their own way of trying to manage conflict productively.

The Need to Manage Conflict

Conflict is not only too pervasive to be denied, it can, as recent research has demonstrated, help managers confront reality and create new solutions to tough problems (De Dreu and Van de Vliert 1997). Conflict, when well-managed, breathes life and energy into our relationships and makes us much more innovative and productive. Conflict is necessary for true involvement, empowerment and democracy. Through debating their different perspectives, people voice their concerns and create solutions responsive to several points of view (Deutsch 1994, 1973; Eisenhardt 1989; Peterson and Nemeth 1996; Schweiger, Sandberg, and Rechner 1989; Tjosvold 1985). Then they can become united and committed.

Well-managed conflict also develops our individuality so that we feel more fulfilled and capable (Breger 1974). Conflict is an opportunity to form and express our needs, opinions, and positions. But we should also try to understand the perspectives of others and become less egocentric. Resolving issues leaves people feeling more integrated, adjusted, and competent. Through conflict, people feel unique and independent as well as connected to others.

Positive conflict is an investment in the future. People trust each other more, feel more powerful and effective, and believe their joint efforts will pay off. Feeling more able and united, people are more prepared to contribute to their groups and organizations. Success in turn further strengthens relationships and individuality.

But the power of conflict can be destructive. Conflicts that are avoided or poorly managed can wreak havoc on us and our organizations. Problems fester and obsolete ideas are implemented. People remain aloof, skeptical, and angry; they become rigid, fixated, and ambivalent. Both individuals and their organizations lose.

The potential value of conflict also points to the challenges to manage it well. The consequences of positive conflict—strong relationships, individuality, and productivity—are also needed for it. The more open and united the relationship, the more self-aware and empathetic the individuals, and the greater their ability to solve problems, the more successful the conflict management. There are no simple techniques that transform all frustrations into positive conflict. Managing conflict gives more but requires more.

The prevalence and potential value of conflict have led some people to adopt highly conflict-oriented approaches. They believe that anger is the 'honest emotion' and that every conflict must be dealt with directly and openly. However, this positive conflict view must be tempered with the understanding that it is the appropriate, skilled management of conflict, not conflict itself, that contributes to organizational success.

Well-managed conflict results in strong relationships, mature and competent individuals, and high performance, which in turn foster more effective conflict in a beneficial, reinforcing cycle. Learning to manage conflict is a wise investment for individuals and organizations preparing for the uncertain future.

Positive Conflict for Asia Pacific Business

Conflict is fundamental to doing business in the Asia Pacific. The diversity and rapid development that make the region such an inviting, dynamic place to do business also give rise to a great deal of conflict, much of which is highly complex and challenging to manage. Yet the good news is that this conflict is not an inevitable impediment but can actually be the way to cope with diversity and rapid change.

Managing conflict in the Asia Pacific is rewarding but requires considerable discipline and flexibility. Partners must be disciplined to confront their frustrations and differences directly and use them to promote their mutual interests. They must refuse to be sidetracked by the illusion that major conflicts can be avoided or that they should exploit a conflict for their own benefit. Yet to communicate this intention, maintain relationships, and develop mutually advantageous solutions requires significant flexibility. They must show they are putting themselves in the other's shoes even as they press their own demands. They must challenge common assumptions and accepted ways of working to forge new understandings and create new work forums. And they must be prepared to continue to manage conflict and to learn.

Conflict over Managing Conflict

Asia Pacific people are often in conflict as they negotiate issues, establish ventures, and make organizations work. A fundamental challenge is that they often have different views of how they should manage these conflicts. The ways that seem natural and effective for a North American may seem counter productive and inappropriate for a Japanese. 'Conflict over how to manage conflict' is a central part of doing business in the Asia Pacific. People from its highly diverse countries are often shocked by the others' approaches. More damaging, they may conclude that they cannot manage conflict and do business with people whose values and approaches seem so unfamiliar and complex.

East Asians have been found to prefer less assertive approaches to conflict than North Americans (Tse, Francis, and Walls 1994). The forums and procedures that Chinese managers are accustomed to are different from those familiar to Americans. Every culture has conflicts and has developed its own methods to manage them. The ways conflicts are handled are central expressions of the culture.

What then seems reasonable to one group can well seem odd and peculiar to another. Koreans may favor handling conflict while at their parties and socializing, whereas Singaporeans think formal discussion is appropriate. Given the stress of important conflicts, people are particularly wedded to culturally valued ways of coping.

Confronting a conflict with persons from another culture may therefore seem particularly risky, especially if they seem unreceptive to initial overtures. We may know how to begin a conflict with a fellow national, but be much less certain with someone from another land. Status and other differences may further exacerbate the difficulty. How can an untrained Thai employee voice his underlying concerns to his professional engineer Japanese manager?

Unfortunately, because others do not respond to their gestures, people often conclude that the others are unwilling to deal with conflicts usefully. They want to deal with issues honestly, but feel that the other side does not. The conclusion that there is no effective way to manage conflict can be devastating, and the belief that they cannot deal with obstacles is demoralizing.

Believing that only oneself wants to manage conflict results in self-righteous blaming and a sense of futility, and perhaps the conclusion that partners would be better off without each other. These attitudes exacerbate the conflict and, when they explode into the open, make managing the conflict most difficult. However, as the chapters in this book show, it is much more likely that people in the Asia Pacific have their own ways of managing conflict, not that they are unmotivated to deal honestly with their differences.

Learning to Manage Conflict

Learning to manage conflict involves life-long learning, not the mastery of a simple technique or two. Managing conflict requires a direct expression of feelings, an elaboration of ideas, emphatic understanding of the perspectives of protagonists, creation of alternative solutions, and acceptance of new resolutions. Competence at managing conflict therefore depends upon self-awareness, the skills of rational discourse, an ability to put oneself in another's shoes, creativity and a lack of fixation on original positions, and a willingness to reach integrated solutions. Moreover, managing conflict requires a continued focus to seek mutually beneficial resolutions and avoid the temptation to try to win the conflict (Argyris 1991). Managing conflict requires both open-minded flexibility and discipline.

Managing conflict productively is an even more significant challenge in the Asia Pacific because of the prevalence of conflict and the 'conflict over managing conflict.' It can be tempting to avoid discussing the conflict directly, especially if one has the power to try to win and coerce agreement. But this is not the road to successful managing or learning.

By managing conflict productively in Asia Pacific organizations, partners, managers, and employees have an opportunity to greatly strengthen their conflict competence. As they deal with many complex issues, they become more open-minded and more disciplined in their conflict management. They strengthen their self-awareness and confidence, become more empathetic and creative, and feel more resolved and unambiguous. These central skills in turn foster individuals' psychological competence and well-being and work effectiveness. Learning to manage conflict is an investment in individual development as well as organizational success.

In sum, positive conflict is a foundation for the ongoing learning necessary for conducting business in the dynamic Asia Pacific. It helps partners keep in touch with changes in each other, customers, regulations, and technologies. Through open discussion, they forge new arrangements responsive to these changes. Conflicts help partners keep abreast of the rapid developments in the Asia Pacific and make change welcome and constructive.

The Book's Purposes

Research-based and action-oriented, the present book aims at providing both a conceptual understanding of conflict management and suggests how conflicts can be managed in the Asia Pacific. Since most of the trade in the region is between North America and the Asia Pacific, including Australia and New Zealand, we have invited contributors from these two regions to contribute. However, Central and South America are also becoming prominent in Asia Pacific business. It is interesting to note that the editing of this book represents an international joint venture. Kwok Leung is from Hong Kong and received his doctoral training in the United States, whereas Dean Tjosvold is an American who has for years taught and conducted research in Canada and China.

The book describes the various assumptions, expectations, and values people around the Asia Pacific have about how they work with others and deal with their conflicts. The focus is on doing business internationally and managing conflict with different peoples and countries in the region. The chapters examine the way people in each of the major Asia Pacific countries manage conflict. They focus on the attitudes, assumptions, and self-perceptions of how a country deals with conflict. How people from different countries think about and believe they deal with conflict might be very different from how they actually handle conflict. These self-perceptions impact conflict management especially when dealing with people from other countries.

The authors of the chapters drew upon a wide range of disciplines to document the conflict beliefs of people in their country. In addition to cross-cultural and other behavioral studies, they relied on literature and history to identify how people in their country think about themselves and their neighbors. Chapters refer to business cases in which expectations got in the way, how expectations have helped conflict management, and how people overcame interfering expectations to forge successful business alliances.

Authors explicated the stereotypes of themselves and other countries, not arguing that this is the way that people in their country always manage conflict, but that this is how they expect themselves and others to manage conflict. The book is about doing business globally and the chapters speak not just to the reality that nations manage conflict differently but directly to the issue of managing international business conflict.

Productive conflict can be established and destructive conflict avoided if the protagonists are more informed of each other's preferences and styles. They do not assume that different approaches to conflict mean that they cannot find common ground and resolve their disputes. This book provides the cultural bridge between partners. We want this book to aid better cultural understanding of how Asia Pacific people manage conflict and to contribute to the continued prosperity of the region.

The chapters help partners, managers, and employees to appreciate the variety of methods by which Asia Pacific people manage conflict and to be prepared for this variety. Reading these chapters will reduce both the shock of different conflict management approaches and the temptation to conclude that others are unwilling and unable to discuss their differences honestly and productively. We hope readers will, as a result, become more open-minded and flexible in their own approaches.

REFERENCES

Argyris, C. 1991. Teaching smart people how to learn. *Harvard Business Review*, May-June, 99–109.

Bacharach, S.B. and Lawler, E.J. 1981. *Bargaining: Power, Tactics, and Outcomes*. San Francisco: Jossey-Bass.

Boisot, M. and Child, J. 1996. From fiefs to clans and network capitalism: Explaining China's emerging economic order. *Administrative Science Quarterly*, **41**, 600–28.

Breger, L. 1974. *From Instinct to Identity: The Development of Personality*. Englewood Cliffs, NJ: Prentice-Hall.

Cocroft, B.A.K. and Ting-Toomey, S. 1994. Facework in Japan and in the United States. *International Journal of Intercultural Relations*, **18**, 469–506.

De Dreu, C. and Van de Vliert, E. (eds.), 1997. *Using Conflict in Organizations*. Thousand Oaks, CA: Sage.

Deutsch, M. 1994. Constructive conflict resolution: Principles, training, and research. *Journal of Social Issues*, **50**, 13–32.

Deutsch, M. 1973. *The Resolution of Conflict*. New Haven, CT: Yale University Press.

Deutsch, M. and Krauss, R.M. 1962. Studies in interpersonal bargaining. *Journal of Conflict Resolution*, **6**, 52–76.

Ding, D.Z. 1995. *In Search of Determinants of Chinese Conflict Management Styles in Joint Ventures: An Integrated Approach*. Paper presented at the Thirteenth Annual Conference of the Association of Management, Vancouver, Canada.

Eisenhardt, K.M. 1989. Making fast strategic decisions in high velocity environments. *Academy of Management Journal*, **32**, 543–76.

Hwang, K.K. 1985. Face and favor: the Chinese power game. *American Journal of Sociology*, **92**, 944–74.

Kim, J.Y. and Nam, S.H. (in press). The concept and dynamics of face: Implications for organizational behavior in Asia. *Organization Science.*

Kirkbride, P.S., Tang, S.F.Y. and Westwood, R.I. 1991. Chinese conflict preferences and negotiating behaviour: Cultural and psychological influences. *Organizational Studies*, **12**, 365–86.

Kochan, T.A. and Verma, A. 1983. Negotiations in organizations: Blending industrial relations and organizational behavior approaches. In M. Bazerman and R.J. Lewicki (eds.), *Negotiating in Organizations.* 13–32, Beverly Hills, CA: Sage.

Leung, K. 1997. Negotiation and reward allocations across cultures. In P.C. Earley and M. Erez (eds.), *New Perspectives on International Industrial/Organizational Psychology.* 640–75 San Francisco: Jossey-Bass.

Peterson, R.S. and Nemeth, C.J. 1996. Focus versus flexibility: Majority and minority influence can both improve performance. *Personality and Social Psychology Bulletin*, **21**, 14–23.

Schweiger, D.M., Sandberg, W.R. and Rechner, P.L. 1989. Experiential effects of dialectical inquiry, devil's advocacy, and consensus approaches to strategic decision making. *Academy of Management Journal*, **32**, 745–72.

Thomas, K.W. and Schmidt, W.H. 1976. A survey of managerial interests with respect to conflict. *Academy of Management Journal*, **19**, 315–18.

Ting-Toomey, S. 1988. A face negotiation theory. In Y.Y. Kim and W.B. Gudykunst (eds.), *Theory and Intercultural Communication.* 47–92, Thousand Oaks, CA: Sage.

Tjosvold, D. 1991. *Conflict-positive Organization: Stimulate Diversity and Create Unity*. Reading, Mass: Addison-Wesley.

Tjosvold, D. 1993. *Learning to Manage Conflict: Getting People to Work together Productively*. New York: Lexington Books.

Tjosvold, D. 1985. Implications of controversy research for management. *Journal of Management*, **11**, 21–37.

Tjosvold, D. and Janz, T. 1985. Costing effective vs. ineffective work relationships: A method and first look. *Canadian Journal of Administrative Sciences*, **2**, 43–51.

Trompenaars, F. 1993. *Riding the Waves of Culture*. London: Economist Books.

Tung, R. 1982. *Business Negotiations with the Japanese*. Lexington, Mass: Lexington Books.

Tung, R. 1991. Handshakes across the sea: Cross-cultural negotiating for business success. *Organizational Dynamics*, **14**, 30–40.

Triandis, H.C., McCusker, C. and Hui, C.H. 1990. Multimethod probes of individualism and collectivism. *Journal of Personality and Social Psychology*, **59**, 1006–20.

Tse, D.K., Francis, J. and Walls, J. 1994. Cultural differences in conducting intra- and inter-cultural negotiations: A Sino-Canadian comparison. *Journal of International Business Studies*, **24**, 537–55.

Walton, R. 1969. *Interpersonal Peacemaking*. Reading, MA: Addison-Wesley.

Walton, R. and McKersie, R.B. 1965. *A Behavioral Theory of Labor Negotiations*. New York: McGraw-Hill.

CHAPTER TWO

Conflict Management in Korea: The Wisdom of Dynamic Collectivism

YUNG-HO CHO and HO-HWAN PARK
College of Business Administration, Ajou University, Korea

INTRODUCTION

Conflicting Images of Korea

The Nobel-prize-winning Indian poet Rabindranath Tagore (1861–1941) once described Korea as the 'Land of the Morning Calm', where warmth, friendliness, cooperation, and harmony reigned among the people. Even today this image is shared not only by foreigners but also by Koreans themselves. However, a completely different image is also popular. An American journalist described Korea as the 'Land of Warriors' (Kearney 1991). Interestingly, this picture of contemporary Korea is intended to describe the enormous tensions and competition in the everyday lives of ordinary Koreans rather than the military tension which has continued between North and South Korea since the Korean War.

According to Hofstede's survey data (1991), Korea is one of the most collectivist countries in the world. Other studies also provide data supporting Hofstede's description and we can easily find anecdotes from different sources which help confirm the collectivist propensity of Koreans. However, an individualistic tendency among Koreans is also described by many foreign writers and tourists. Among them, Japanese authors like Hasegawa, Watanabe, and Kusayanagi argue that Koreans are more individualistic than the Japanese, contradicting Hofstede's study [1] (Chang and Chang 1994).

If we take into account the fact that Korea has undergone enormous changes in its economic, social and political life in a very short period of time [2], those conflicting images about Korea and Koreans seem to be true. Korea is the 'Land of the Morning Calm' as well as the 'Land of Warriors'. Koreans are as much individualists as collectivists. The mixture of values of traditional harmony and modern free competition, and the collision of Eastern collectivism and Western individualism are the real faces of Koreans. In certain circumstances harmony and emotional well-being are most valued, whereas in other cases freedom and competition are highly valued—sacrificing harmony. However in general, the two competing values are in operation together in a delicate way. The Korean way of managing conflicts emerges from this complex value system.

Purpose of the Chapter

In this chapter we aim at providing a conceptual model for the understanding of Korean conflict-related behavior and at formulating the basic conflict management norms observed among Koreans. Due to the complex nature of modern Korean society, we need an appropriate perspective to understand delicately disguised social phenomena. We must understand not only the nature of the behavior which handles emerging conflicts but also the general processes which prevent them and treat the byproducts of conflict.

To understand the underlying mechanism of Korean conflict management, we need a cultural approach which postulates that conflict management is subject to the culture within which the protagonists live. Our model stresses organizational culture rather than national culture. While national culture is important in molding human behavior, it is a general factor which does not help us understand the sophisticated behavioral dynamics of the modern business world. We attempt here to describe what the major characteristics of the organizational culture of Korean firms are and how they have been formed.

[1] On Hofstede's individualism scale, Japan was ranked 22nd of 50 countries, while South Korea was ranked 43rd (Hofstede 1991).

[2] For instance, Korea has recorded an annual GNP growth rate of around 8% during the 35 years since 1960 when the First Economic Development Plan was launched.

From these perspectives a cycle of four conflict management norms used by Koreans is proposed: context building, smoothing, forcing, and tension releasing. Context building is concerned with sharing information and building an emotional bond between two groups or among group members. Smoothing comprises avoiding conflict and compromising without disputing or threatening each other's 'face'. Forcing is the use of hierarchical power to resolve conflict. It includes involvement of neutral persons in higher positions. Tension releasing includes all kinds of activities for discharging the negative emotions which have occurred due to conflict situations. These four norms make a unique Korean style of conflict management; competition within harmony or vice versa, and individualism within collectivism, or vice versa.

We have tried to base our argument upon previous academic researches on Korean conflict management behavior. However, we have been unable to collect sufficient research evidence about Korean conflict management and so we rely heavily on non-systematic studies, anecdotal descriptions and our own professional experience.

PERSPECTIVES AND A CONCEPTUAL MODEL

Perspective Shift

Most of conflict management studies done in the western context have focused on specific moments when two persons or parties are facing a certain conflict. A typical research question asks how people handle conflict: do they avoid, cooperate or confront, and which of these various handling styles is effective. However in Asian culture, where human relationships are long-term and the density of social contact is high, this 'segmented' approach might be less meaningful. Conflict management in the Asian context is rather a diffused activity and a long-term business. A specific behavior is just the tip of a huge iceberg and should be interpreted in the broad context of a long-term exchange relationship.

Confrontation or the competitive mode of managing conflict, typically known as a western style of conflict management, could be interpreted as conforming to the Asian harmony-seeking norm when it is used in the situation where the context is mutually understood and a high degree of trust has already been built between people. By the same token, avoiding, generally known as a harmony-seeking behavior, could be interpreted as harmony-threatening when the people concerned already share a strong sense of community. In this situation, hiding problems and holding opinions may be considered harmful to the community.

To fully understand conflict management behavior in collectivist cultures like Korea, we need a perspective shift; from a segmented perspective to a holistic one. Confining our perspective to specific conflict situations is as risky as it is non-profitable. Our vision should be enlarged, enabling us to look at how conflict is prevented and how by-products of conflict are treated.

Thomas (1976, 1992) classified conflict researches into two models, a process model and a structural model. A process model identifies and examines events such as frustration, conceptualization, behavior and outcome within a conflict episode, while a structural model attempts to understand conflict phenomena by studying how underlying conditions shape events. Our approach, mentioned earlier, may belong to a process model. However, we are not attempting here to describe events in a specific conflict. Rather what we are trying to do is understand a broader process of preventing and handling a conflict and treating its by-products.[3] In this regard, our model can be called a general process model of conflict management. Our research question is how do Koreans prevent conflict, how do they handle conflict and how do they treat positive or negative outcomes which occur due to the conflict itself and/or conflict handling processes.

We need another shift of perspective to be able to understand conflict management in a modern business context. Nobody would deny that business-related life has become more important not only within a country but also between countries, particularly after the collapse of the ideology which divided the world into socialist and capitalist camps. It can be assumed that management of business-related conflict can also be understood from the perspective of national culture. Although national culture is an important factor in shaping human behavior, it is too general a concept to explain the dynamic aspect of the business-related conflict handling. A shift from national culture to organizational culture is also needed here.

Organizational culture is generally defined as shared values and norms among members of an organization. Some organizations can have a strong culture with a high degree of sharing and be sharply differentiated from

[3] R. R. Blake and J. S. Mouton who first categorized different conflict management behavior had a close position to ours (*The Managerial Grid III*, 1985). However, they did not deal with the possibility of switching the different strategies in a general process of conflict management.

other organizations. On the other hand, we can find organizations with a weak culture having a low degree of internal sharing and external differentiation. Along with its own history, every organization has its own culture. If someone joins an organization, he or she is more or less influenced by the organizational culture. Because it has a socializing and coercing mechanism, particularly for business-related behaviors, its influence is more direct and sometimes stronger than national culture.

Organizational culture, of course, is not independent of the broader societal culture which is a good source of ingredients and one of the determining factors for organizational culture. However, the two are not the same: organizational culture can be a subset of national culture, while it can sometimes be formed with at least some elements contrary to the existing traditional culture. There is a great possibility that the organizational cultures of Asian firms now have more elements divorced from their traditional culture than they had before industrialization.

The fact that each organization has its own culture does not hinder a generalization for diverse organizations. As we can talk generally about organizational culture of an industry, we can also talk about organizational culture of the Korean firms in general. However, this generalization does not mean that organizational culture can be directly translated into national culture. For the purpose of this chapter, we would like to describe the general organizational culture of big Korean firms and *chaebols* (diversified groups of businesses).

A Conceptual Model

Based upon the perspectives mentioned above, we propose a conceptual model (depicted in Fig. 2.1) for analyzing conflict management in Korea. This model assumes that conflict management in Korean firms is a product of the organizational culture of Korean firms (corporate culture). The model also assumes that Korean corporate culture is formed largely under the influence of the Korean traditional culture (cultural legacy), the leadership of corporate founders (corporate leadership) and a social climate arising from peculiar political conditions (social climate). Furthermore, the model assumes that the Korean style of conflict management has contributed to the high-speed economic growth and emotional stability of the people (outcomes).

Conflict management of Korean firms can be described as a cycle of four norms: context building (contexting), smoothing, forcing and

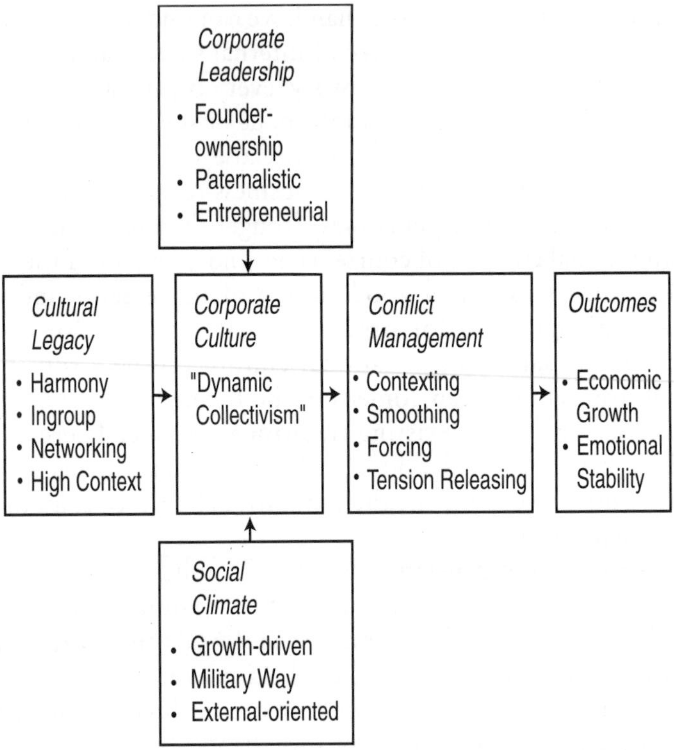

Figure 2.1 A Model for Analysis of Conflict Management in Korea

tension releasing. It means that conflict management in Korea is not a single-shot behavior but a whole dynamic process of organizational life. This particular type of process stems from the corporate culture of Korean firms and can be described as 'dynamic collectivism' (Cho 1995). Collectivism originated in the traditional culture and dynamism derived from the peculiar personalities of the business founders who have pioneered the modern Korean economy and from the social environment characterized as growth-driven and military-led.

In most business scenes in Korea, dynamism and collectivism can be easily observed. While group interest is more respected than individual interest and interpersonal harmony is more valued than interpersonal competition, speedy action, entrepreneurship and change are equally pursued. In this sense, Korean corporate culture has departed from Korea's cultural legacy which is a kind of static collectivism in pursuit of stability rather than dynamic growth and change.

PRECEDENTS OF CONFLICT MANAGEMENT

Cultural Legacy

Collectivism is a culture which puts collective interests over individual ones (Hofstede 1984; Triandis 1995). In this sense, Korea is definitely a collectivist country. Based upon different sources we can list five key concepts characterizing Korean collectivist culture: harmony, hierarchy, differentiation between ingroup and outgroup, networking, and high contexting.

Harmony

While most Asian cultures value harmony, its meaning may vary. According to Alston (1989), even among East Asian countries its meaning is not the same. Japanese harmony (*wa*) emphasizes the group itself, while Chinese harmony (*guanxi*) stresses the relationship (networking) beyond group membership. Korean harmony (*inhwa*), like the Chinese, means the relationship beyond group membership. However, it is different from the Chinese in that the Korean *inhwa* stresses more the emotional aspect of relationship, while the Chinese *guanxi* focuses on the exchange of favors rather than sentiment.

One of the key words one should remember to understand Koreans' behavior is *kibun* (pronounced as kee-boon) which means good personal mood and a general satisfactory state of affairs. Maintaining harmony requires not hurting other's *kibun*, particularly that of personally related people. While harmony contains many philosophical meanings, it has also a socio-psychological meaning of maintaining a peaceful, comfortable atmosphere between known people (Hur and Hur 1988). If it is translated into the public situation, *kibun* means 'face'. Respecting other's personal ego and maintaining a satisfactory mood in public is 'face-saving'.

Hierarchy

Influenced by Confucianism, basic human relationships in Korea are defined not in terms of equals but of unequals determined by gender, age, and position in the society. The language itself reflects the nature of these hierarchical interactions, and social etiquette is highly elaborate between unequal persons, but not between equal persons. Therefore, Koreans often feel embarrassed when two persons meet for the first time as they don't know who is of higher status. A harmonious relationship, in general, emphasizes seniority and loyalty to persons in higher positions.

Differentiation between Ingroup and Outgroup

Triandis (1995) asserted that collectivism does not signify simply putting a group's interest over the individual member's interests, but it means a differentiation between ingroup and outgroup. Koreans have a strong tendency to distinguish 'our' group's members (ingroup) from 'other' group's members (outgroup). For Koreans, a person to whom one has not been introduced, with whom one has had no previous interactions, and with whom one foresees no future relationship, is not considered a person (Hur and Hur 1988).

Therefore, Koreans show collectivist behaviors only to the ingroup, and to the outgroup their behavior becomes rather individualistic. With outgroup members Koreans feel unstable and have difficulties in communication. According to a study done by Gudykunst, Yoon, and Nishima (1987) among Americans, Japanese, and Koreans, Koreans show the greatest differences in communication behavior between ingroup and outgroup. Generally communication is more personalized, smoother (synchronized) and easier with ingroup members than with outgroup members.[4] However the differences between the two groups are sharpest for the Koreans (Table 2.1).

Networking

As already mentioned, Koreans, like the Chinese, like to build personal relationships beyond the organizations to which they physically belong. These kinds of relationships are built principally on blood relations and graduation from the same school. Therefore, informal networks are well developed beyond work groups, and social activities occupy a great part of one's time. Networking not only complements but also hinders formal activities. Chang and Chang (1994) estimated a trust-base scale for Koreans, from which one can easily imagine how Koreans conduct social networking (Table 2.2).

Although it is not surprising that the highest score on the trust-base scale is with blood relations, it is a Korean characteristic that the trust level is very high with school classmates and alumni. Old classmates

[4] Personalized communication relates to the intimacy of communication (e.g. 'We tell each other personal things about ourselves'). Synchronized communication relates to the coordination of communication between parties (e.g. 'Due to mutual cooperation and understanding, our conversation is easy and we don't need effort for good communication.'). Difficult communication relates to barriers to communication (e.g. 'It is difficult for us to know when one of us is serious or sarcastic'). (Gudykunst, Yoon, and Nishima, 1987).

Table 2.1 Differences in Communication Behavior between Ingroup and Outgroup Relationships

Country and Relationship	Personalization		Synchronization		Difficulty	
	Mean	Difference	Mean	Difference	Mean	Difference
United States:						
Ingroup	3.26		4.61		4.84	
Outgroup	2.26		3.80		3.96	
(n=128)		1.00		0.81		0.88
Japan:						
Ingroup	4.24		4.83		5.16	
Outgroup	2.46		3.23		3.69	
(n=130)		1.78		1.60		1.47
Korea:						
Ingroup	5.04		3.58		5.80	
Outgroup	2.85		3.81		3.72	
(n=122)		2.19		1.57		2.08

Note: Each scale ranges from 1 to 7. For personalization and synchronization, the higher the score the more of the quality is perceived. For difficulty, the lower the score, the more the quality is perceived.
Source: Gudykunst, Yoon, and Nishima (1987)

from high school or college, including other alumni, meet regularly or frequently. Their occupations are various. In their meetings, they share any information that each member has. In addition, they express negative emotions toward companies, superiors, and national politics. They enjoy the opportunity to release any kind of satisfaction and dissatisfaction. In contrast to the high trust-base score for blood relations, high school friends, and people from the same region, the trust-base score for strangers and foreigners drops sharply.

High Context

Due to their long history as a relatively homogeneous ethnic group, Koreans have a great deal of common ground in their communication and they therefore communicate rather implicitly. Using Hall's terminology (Hall 1976), Koreans prefer context to content communications. They like to convey information through non-verbal cues embedded in the physical setting or internalized in the person. Therefore, instead of trying to clearly articulate his or her opinion, a typical Korean tries to

Table 2.2 Trust-base Scale

Subjects	Trust-base Scale
Spouse	100
Parents	100
Children	100
Brothers/Sisters	100
Nephews/Nieces	99
Cousins	97
Relatives	96
Classmates from High School	97
Same-church Members	95
People in the Same Job Organization	90
Classmates from College	85
Alumni of High School and College	80
People in the Same Profession	80
People in the Same Religious Denomination	80
People with the Same Family Name	70
People from the Same Region	70
People with the Same Hobbies	70
Neighbors	70
People from a Different Religious Denomination	70
People from Different Regions	60
Classmates from Elementary School	50
People of Different Religions	40
Strangers (Koreans)	5
Foreigners (without any Korean relations)	1

Source: Chang and Chang (1994)

share contextual information with others. He or she is generally very interested in keeping in touch with other people and the outer world which have some relations with them. In this sense, Korea can be called a high context society.

Corporate Leadership

The Korean economy has relied heavily on big business groups called '*Chaebol*', such as Samsung, Hyundai, LG (former Lucky-Goldstar), and Daewoo. Their economic and social power is so huge that the Korean economy itself is often identified with them. Among many features characterizing those *chaebols*, the primordial may be the power and leadership of their founders. The relatively short history of the modern

Korean big firms has permitted the founders to exercise enormous influence as much upon organizational culture as upon business strategy. With Steers, Shin, and Ungson (1989), we can say that the leadership of those founders can be characterized by family control and management, paternalistic leadership, and entrepreneurial orientation.

Family Control and Management

Most big businesses are controlled financially by the founders themselves or by their family members, although the control is not always direct. The founder and his or her brothers, sons, and daughters hold the core positions in the company. This phenomenon contrasts sharply with that of Japanese big groups of businesses.

Paternalistic and Authoritarian

The second feature is that the founder-CEO's leadership is paternalistic and authoritarian. He or she centralizes most decision-making, even for non-critical issues, and emphasizes a strong family-like bond among employees. Therefore, he or she is normally considered as a quasiparent figure and as such has power that is symbolic as well as instrumental. As time passes, this kind of absolute power has become weaker, but his or her successor, often a son, still holds much power. Around this power source an inner circle is formed which has considerable influence on the rest of the organization and sometimes reciprocally on the CEO.

Entrepreneurial Orientation

Like Jung Joo-Young of Hyundai, Lee Byung-Chul of Samsung, and Kim Woo-Jung of Daewoo, the founders are known to have had a distinctive ambition and drive for growth. They set high visions, willingly take risks, and urge employees to work hard. They themselves are more hardworking than other people. Often, this entrepreneurial orientation causes the process of organizational decision-making to be irrational.

Social Climate

Another important source for the formation of the Korean corporate culture is the social climate in general, and this stems largely from Korea's peculiar political situation. After World War II, the Korean peninsula was divided into two parts and a devastating war followed. In that situation, survival was a key issue for the governing institutions as well as for the whole society. From 1961 through 1993, military leadership dominated South Korea. This military leadership has influenced almost every aspect of Korean life.

Growth-Driven

The military government, having succeeded in taking over political power by a coup, started to implement ambitious economic development plans aimed at industrialization and economic growth. The power elite considered that this was the only strategy to cope with survival issues and to acquire political legitimacy from the people. Since 1962, ambitious national growth targets have been set and managed by governmental and civilian leaders. This growth-driven policy has penetrated every aspect of civilian life and is a major influence on the social climate.

Military Way and 'Can-Do Spirit'

The growth-driven social climate has been coupled with a military way of thinking and behaving. Military bodies have great power due to the tension between the South and the North, and former generals and veterans also exercised considerable influence at all levels of society at least until the 1980s. As a result, a military way of life which emphasizes hierarchical command, a result-oriented 'can-do spirit', and aggressiveness has become a part of social life. This influence has produced a lot of functional effects as well as dysfunctional ones.

Dependent upon External Resources

A lack of natural resources, national capital and industrial technology has made Korea turn her eyes toward the outside world. Economic development policy has been dependent upon other industrialized countries, such as the U.S., Japan and Europe. This orientation brought out preference for the Western way of thinking, at least for the people of a higher status.

Organizational Culture: Dynamic Collectivism

The organizational culture of a typical Korean firm is formed from Korea's cultural legacy, corporate leadership, and social climate. While some

Table 2.3 Managerial Values in Korean Business Firms

Managerial Values	% of Firms
Harmony and Unity	46.4
Sincerity and Diligence	44.2
Creation and Development	41.6
Business Credibility	20.8
Productivity and Quality	16.9
Work Responsibility	16.9
Progressiveness	14.3
Social Responsibility	14.3
Scientific Management	10.4
Sacrifice and Service	6.9

Note: Data collected from 87 large Korean firms.
Source: Lee (1989)

elements of those three forces are compatible and reinforce each other, they are not all compatible. The cultural legacy of hierarchy-orientation and the paternalistic leadership of corporate founders are compatible, while the aggressive social climate is apparently incompatible with the cultural legacy of harmony-seeking. Neither is the entrepreneurial element of corporate leadership compatible with that traditional value.

Therefore, the Korean corporate culture can not be unidimensional. It is a mixture of harmony and change, face-saving and aggressiveness, and emotional community and impersonal achievement. This kind of hybrid can be called 'dynamic collectivism' which is composed mainly of three elements; group harmony, progressivism, and hierarchical decision-making.

Group Harmony

Group harmony is still important and is the keystone of the corporate culture. It means that the purposes and interests of a company take precedence over those of individuals, the freedom of an individual is repressed in the name of group cohesiveness, and emotional well-being and face-saving are respected. An empirical survey shows that group harmony is the most important managerial value in Korean firms. Valuing harmony is normally extended to an 'employee-first philosophy' and paternalistic care of employees. A company or colleagues taking care of family matters is a common practice in Korea (Table 2.3).

Table 2.4 Value Orientation of Korean Workers (%)

Value Orientation	Survey for Large Firms (1995)	General Survey (1990)
Collectivism	88.7	68.3
Progressivism	89.3	55.6
Optimism	82.3	71.0

Notes: General survey was administered for a sample of 4,949 employees from 644 large and small firms.
Survey for large firms was conducted for a sample of 933 middle managers in five large firms from different industries.
Source: Cho (1995)

Progressivism and Optimism

Other cardinal elements of Korean corporate culture are progressivism and optimism. An optimistic view of the future and social problems is very common, and making efforts for tomorrow is widely seen as common sense. Almost all companies set high growth targets and have a global vision. Even if they are merely small- or medium-sized companies, they pursue risk-taking. 'Hardwork' is one of the slogans everybody talks about without any reservation. On the other hand, too much progressivism sometimes results in a 'hurry-up' attitude and process-neglecting behavior.

According to a study done by one of the authors (Cho 1995), five big Korean companies in the automobile, electronics, heavy industry, chemical and general trading industries consider progressivism and optimism as important as traditional collectivism. Therefore, we can say that harmony-seeking collectivism and future-oriented optimism co-exist in today's Korean business culture. Even more interesting is that the survey data suggests that the coexistence of the two characteristics is more salient among workers in the big companies than among those in other areas (Table 2.4).

Hierarchical Communication and Decision Making

Reinforced by traditional values and hierarchical leadership patterns, vertical interactions are more valued in organizations, and decision-making by top management is relatively well accepted. Delegation of authority is often formally espoused but not effective in reality. Bottom-up and lateral communication are consistently promoted in most

Table 2.5 Conflict Resolution and Related Concepts in America, Japan and Korea

Items	America (n=227)	Japan (n=291)	Korea (n=177)	Similarity
Conflict Resolution:				
Authoritarianism	3.00	3.42	3.66	(K–J) > A
Advance-Coordination	2.72	3.72	3.12	J > K > A
Confrontation	3.50	3.32	3.07	A > J > K
Decision-making:				
Group Decision	2.98	3.43	2.64	J > A > K
Informal Communication	3.60	3.56	3.44	N.S.

Note: The unit of analysis is the organization. N.S. = not significant.
Source: Chung and Lee (1989)

companies, but fail often. The nature of interactions sharply contrasts to that of neighboring Japan.

BASIC NORMS FOR CONFLICT MANAGEMENT

Empirical Studies

Before discussing conflict management norms in Korea, it is better to look at some suggestive empirical research data, even though they are snap-shots rather than motion pictures.

Chung and Lee (1989) defined three modes of conflict resolution and compared three countries, America, Japan, and Korea to see how these countries use these conflict resolution modes (Table 2.5). The three countries showed significantly different patterns; the Japanese and Koreans used an authoritarian or top-down mode more often than Americans did, Americans preferred confrontation, and the Japanese used advance-coordination or informal coordination before formal decision-making. Regarding decision-making, a concept which is closely related to conflict, the Japanese distinctly preferred group decision-making.

More interesting research was conducted by Ting-Toomey *et al.* (1991), based upon Ting-Toomey's face-negotiation theory. According to Rahim (1983) they classified five different styles of conflict resolution: integrating, or searching for a solution that integrates the differences between the parties in an open environment; obliging, or trying to satisfy the other party's concern at the expense of one's own; dominating, or using

Table 2.6 Face Maintenance and Conflict Styles

	U.S. (n=220)	Japan (n=197)	China (n=117)	Korea (n=207)	Taiwan (n=224)
Face Maintenance					
Self-face	2.69	3.12	2.67	2.38	2.88
Other-face	3.09	2.85	3.71	3.25	3.99
Conflict Styles					
Integrating	3.99	3.38	4.10	3.87	4.40
Obliging	2.85	2.93	3.32	2.64	3.17
Dominating	2.87	2.05	2.63	2.18	2.75
Avoiding	2.88	2.99	3.56	3.02	4.09
Compromising	3.47	3.05	3.45	3.61	4.09
Total Conflict Style Use	16.06	14.40	17.06	15.32	18.50

Note: The last row was calculated and inserted by the authors of this chapter.
Source: Ting-Toomey *et al.* (1991)

power to get one's position accepted; avoiding, or sidestepping the issue and shying away from open discussion; and compromising, or splitting the difference and finding a middle-ground solution.

The data (Table 2.6) showed that the degree of Koreans' concern about self-face was the lowest among five countries; the U.S., Japan, China, Taiwan, and Korea. And the Koreans' concern about other's face was higher than the Americans and Japanese, and lower than the Chinese and Taiwanese. Regarding conflict resolution styles, integrating and compromising were more often used in Korea than obliging, dominating and avoiding. Compared with other countries, Korea's use of dominating style is the lowest, along with Japan, and the use of compromising is the second highest after Taiwan. One thing to be noted, which is not indicated in the original paper, is the fact that the total amount of the use of five styles differs sharply from country to country. Use by Japan and Korea was remarkably low when compared with the other three countries. We think this definitely suggests that in both countries a sixth, hidden, strategy counts more. Koreans, with the Japanese, may not confine conflict management efforts to the behavior used when handling the current conflict.

Lee and Rogan (1991) provide precious evidence about the differences in the conflict handling strategy used for ingroup and outgroup situations, comparing Korean and U.S. cases (Table 2.7). They clustered conflict management behaviors into three styles; (1) a non-confrontational

Table 2.7 Ingroup and Outgroup Difference in Conflict Resolution

Conflict stragery	Korea		U.S.	
	Ingroup	Outgroup	Ingroup	Outgroup
Non-confrontation	3.83	3.77	4.57	5.18
Solution-orientation	5.23	5.12	2.58	2.73
Control	3.02	3.28	5.43	5.44

Notes: The figures represent values measured on a seven-point Likert scale.
Total respondents are 180 employees at the regional banks in the southern part of Korea and the U.S. (90 respondents in each country).
Recalculated based on the data from Lee and Rogan (1991)

style including avoiding, smoothing, and compromising, (2) a solution-orientation style which is comparable to cooperation (Deutsch 1973), collaboration (Thomas 1976), and integration (Rahim 1983), and (3) a control style which is competitive (Deutsch 1973; Thomas 1976) or dominating (Rahim 1983).

According to the survey data for bank employees, Koreans use fewer control strategies and more solution-orientation styles than their American counterparts. Another important finding is that Korean respondents use more non-confrontation strategies in interactions with ingroup members than in interactions with outgroup members, while American respondents showed an opposite tendency, using more non-confrontation strategies with outgroup members. With regard to control styles, Koreans use them slightly more in the outgroup situation, although Americans show no difference in use between groups.

From the above three empirical researches, we can observe the distinctive ways that Koreans behave differently from Westerners and even from other Eastern cultures in coping with conflict situations. Four features can be summarized as follows:

1. Koreans prefer a non-competitive (or non-dominating) strategy in a face-to-face conflict situation.
2. Koreans prefer resorting to a higher position or authoritarian personality to resolve conflict rather than trying to find an integrating solution.
3. Koreans differentiate between ingroup and outgroup situations when handling conflict.
4. Koreans make efforts in managing conflict beyond those used in face-to-face conflict situations.

The first and the third features can be compared to competition and a universal approach in Western culture. The second one can be compared to the Japanese lateral integration effort, and the fourth one can be compared to the Chinese 'confining' approach.

Four Basic Norms for Conflict Management of 'Dynamic Collectivism'

Snap-shotting approaches give useful data for explaining how Koreans handle conflict, but do not provide an insight for understanding the underlying dynamics of the conflict management process. Conflict management is a process of not only handling conflict but also of preventing and managing further problems after the conflict resolution. It is also a process involving not only the persons directly concerned but also others indirectly related according to the nature of the issues.

Korean conflict management cannot be seen independently from the organizational culture of Korean firms. To a great extent, dynamic collectivism influences the process by which conflict is managed within an organization. We suggest that the complex nature of conflict management in Korea can be explained by the following four norms: contexting, smoothing, forcing, and tension releasing.

Contexting[5]

The first conflict management norm is to build a common context or to forge a common understanding about a situation among the organizational members or other persons in the interaction by sharing information and building an emotional bond. Traditionally, Korea is a high context society. Making a high context (common cause) is a very important task even in a highly organized society. To build a common context, sharing information is essential, but the information should include emotional cues concerning other people, because this emotional aspect is very important in Korean social life. If emotional cues are available, one can tell which behavior is good or bad for the other's *kibun* (personal mood), and how

[5] The meaning of contexting is different from contextualization. In a dictionary, contextualization is defined as 'to put (a linguistic element or an action) in a context, especially one that is characteristic or appropriate, as for the purpose of study' (Webster's College Dictionary). By contexting, we mean 'sharing a common context among group members'. Therefore, efficient contexting makes contextualizing unnecessary.

to make harmony in the group. Hereafter trust is built in the organization and between persons in the interaction.

The concrete activities for contexting include, at the individual level, formal and informal meetings, and exchanging calls and letters. At the organization level activities include training and development, information sharing through the media, large group ceremonies, campaigning, collective sports activities, collective hobby-making, and singing and drinking. It is not difficult to understand in Korea why there are so many meetings and activities which are not directly job-related.

Smoothing

If a context is fully shared between different persons, many jobs are achieved without conflict. But in this complex modern society and particularly in Korean business firms pursuing rapid growth, there is inevitably a lot of conflict. The second norm, smoothing, comes next. Smoothing is to try to find a solution without hurting the other's feelings and face. It can be avoiding, obliging, or compromising according to the conventional conflict resolution styles (Blake and Mouton 1964; Thomas 1973; Rahim 1983). The question in smoothing is how to maintain a satisfactory emotional state. The competitive strategy can seldom be included in smoothing, and confrontation or open integrating may not be considered as a smoothing strategy because they can easily contaminate a harmonious relationship and Koreans, in general, are not equipped with lateral communication skills. We chose the term smoothing because Koreans like to use it; probably because the word contains a connotation compatible with that of harmony.

Concrete activities for smoothing include avoiding the conflict situation; waiting for a time when one's interests can more easily get accepted; postponing confrontation hoping that a solution will arise as time passes; conceding one's interests expecting that next time one can get a favor in return; and finding a 'middle road' solution (compromising).

Forcing

When smoothing fails or the problem is very urgent and requires a quick solution, Koreans trigger the third norm, forcing. It indicates using formal or informal hierarchical power to cope with a conflict situation. There are two modes of forcing: one is a direct use of power by a party, and the other is to try to find a higher third party who will enforce a solution or resort to an abstract rule for a solution. One might confuse competition with this situation. However, forcing is not competition since the situation needs a hierarchical power for Koreans. Competition normally means a game between equals.

One may want to know the conditions under which a high-status third party intervenes to resolve a dispute between equals. Based upon our observations, the primary condition is time pressure. When a high-status person judges that he or his company needs a quick response to a problem and his employees cannot agree on a solution, he is very likely to intervene in the dispute. Another important condition is his judgment on whether a dispute among equals remarkably hurts the harmony of the group. In general, the superior is instinctively aware of tension arising from the dispute within his group. As long as the two major conditions are met, the intervention of a senior person is generally accepted as legitimate.

Forcing is not uncommon in Korea and contributes a lot to making Korean firms move quickly. If Korean employees spent a lot of time only in contexting and smoothing, Korean firms could not take risks and achieve a high rate of growth. It is to be noted that forcing is not necessarily harmful to group harmony. With the contexting and smoothing activities, the parties legitimize the forcing situation. The superior who enforces a solution tries to save each party's face. And even if the solution is unfavorable for a party, the loser can console himself because he loses not by his or her equal but by a superior. However, this does not mean that Koreans do not feel frustrated by the forcing process.

For the concrete activities for forcing, we can cite, among others, getting personal access to a power position, using a formal meeting to get a decision from a superior, forming a committee to handle the issue, making rules for certain kinds of solutions, and controlling the budget. One of the reasons why bureaucratic rules flourish in Korea is that this conflict handling strategy is so common.

Tension Releasing

The last norm, tension releasing, means efforts for releasing emotional tension which cumulates in the process of smoothing or forcing. The above mentioned conflict handling activities inevitably produce negative feelings among the parties. Therefore, tension releasing is important to re-establish a trust-based relationship and to maintain group harmony. As far as emotion is important for Koreans, tension releasing is an indispensable process in their social lives. Failure in releasing tension is often considered a serious management fault.

Among the main activities for tension releasing are drinking and singing. Drinking and singing are generally considered an integral part of working life. They are not only personal activities between friends but also department-wide or even company-wide rituals. It is, therefore, not strange to see many '*karaokes*' (singing rooms with accompanying music machines) in cities and even inside some company buildings. Some companies distribute drinking tickets for employees to be able to drink beer and whisky at any time at designated bars.

Conflict Management Norms as a Cycle

The four norms for managing conflict are closely related one to another, forming a cycle as depicted in Fig. 2.2. Contexting starts, followed by smoothing, then by forcing, and then by tension releasing. This tension releasing does not end; it is followed by contexting. This whole cycle forms a Korean style of cooperative conflict management, one which has obviously contributed to the business and economic growth and social stability.

However, the conflict management cycle is not always complete, missing a norm or two. Two typical incomplete cycles deserve some comments. One is a cycle composed of only contexting and smoothing (cycle I in Fig. 2.3). The other is one composed of forcing and tension releasing (cycle II in Fig. 2.3). Cycle I in Fig. 2.3 does not have forcing or, as a result, tension releasing. However, it can not guarantee quick action and high performance. Cycle II with only forcing and tension releasing may result in rapid progress, but it creates difficulty in maintaining employees due to too much accumulated tension. We can call cycle I pure

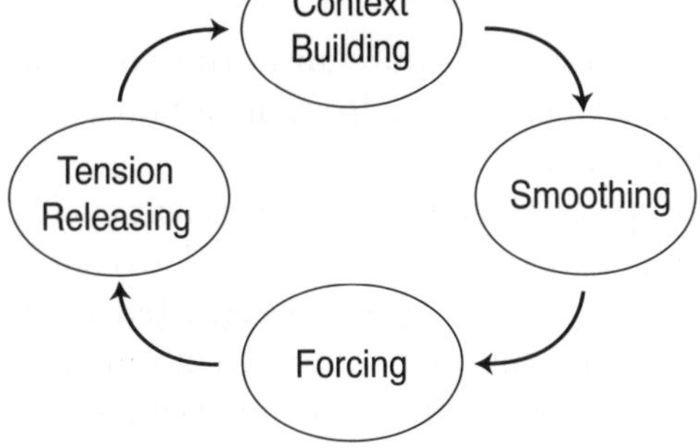

Figure 2.2 Korean Conflict Management Cycle

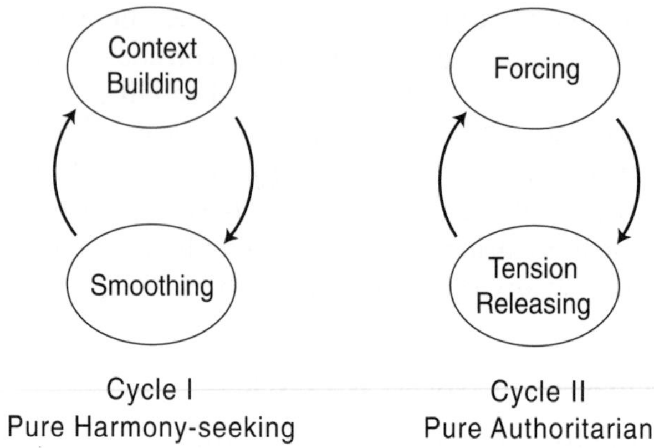

Figure 2.3 Incomplete Conflict Management Cycles

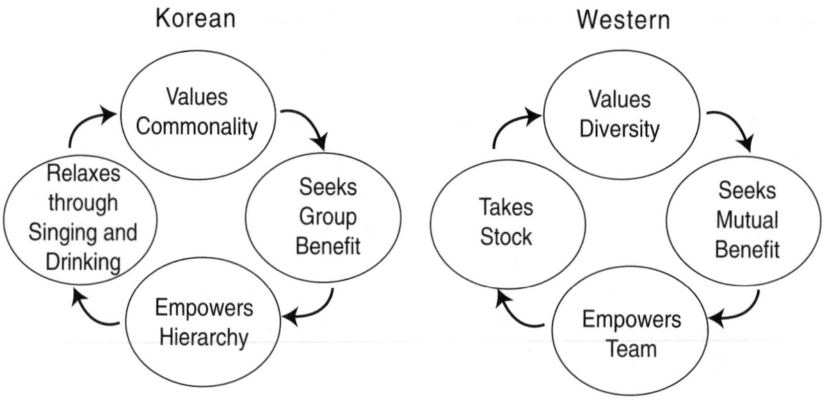

Figure 2.4 Cooperative Conflict Management Cycle: Korean versus Western

harmony-seeking and cycle II pure authoritarian. The complete cycle containing all four elements is needed to maintain a group harmony and achieve a high performance.

The Korean cooperative conflict management cycle is comparable to the Western cooperative cycle suggested by Tjosvold (1991) in Fig. 2.4. Based upon Deutsch's theory, Tjosvold suggested a Western style cooperative conflict management cycle composed of valuing diversity, seeking mutual benefit, empowering the team and taking stock. Our model for Koreans can be expressed in a similar way as valuing commonality (contexting), seeking group benefit, empowering hierarchy, and relaxing through singing and drinking. The sharp difference is that the Western cycle starts from valuing diversity, while the Korean cycle starts from valuing commonality.

Organizational Support

The task of maintaining the conflict management norms belongs to management. There are three major activities for this purpose.

The first activity is human resource management. When recruiting new employees, companies prefer a harmony-seeking personality to a creative one. A person who is a highly qualified professional is unlikely to be recruited if he or she has a problem personality or poor human relations skills. Furthermore, through formal training and development systems the four norms are explicitly or implicitly taught and socialized.

Another supporting mechanism for conflict management is the development of senior management. The senior management is very important in the Korean management style. High performing organizations make special efforts to build and maintain a management team of excellent caliber. They recruit talent from top domestic universities or head-hunt persons with a higher educational background from foreign countries. They are usually competent to work by themselves and are able to manage outside networks with bankers or government officers.

The last organizational supporting activity is done through a budgetary system. Almost every Korean organization reserves a special budget which can be used exclusively for informal meetings. This budget is used at the discretion of managers for eating, drinking, and singing with their employees or colleagues. Depending upon the revenue size of the company, a large portion of this budget is tax-exempt.

Structural Aspect of Conflict Management Norms: Labor Relations

The four conflict management norms are also reflected in a more highly structured form of conflict management, labor relations. Korean labor relations can be described as having four key components: a company union, a labor-management council, collective bargaining guided by governmental intervention, and paternalistic caring by employers.

Company unions, mandatory for many years, are still a typical form of labor organization in Korea. They constitute a basis for a collective relationship and are an effective means of sharing context and building the emotional bonds of the ingroup. Through daily face-to-face dialogue, labor representatives and management understand each other's needs and circumstances. Because both parties are very close, their different interests are resolved while they talk about ordinary matters concerning the company and their lives. They are usually not conscious of the existence of these differences.

A labor-management council is compulsory at companies where a labor union is already organized or more than 50 employees work. It is held at least once a month, and the two parties hold more formal discussions about conflicting issues regarding, for example, working conditions and productivity. However, the discussion does not take an open and competitive form. It is rather close to smoothing. Trying to save each other's face is one of its dominant activities. As a result, the workers side particularly may become frustrated with the council.

The frustrated side brings issues into a collective bargaining process which takes a legitimate confrontation form. However, the rules of democratic and open bargaining are neither well accepted nor easily learned in Korea. Each side is very likely to lose face and the central issue becomes an emotional one.[6] Since it is very difficult to reach a solution in the collective bargaining, a forcing mechanism is instituted by law. A cooling-down period of 10 or 15 days depending on the size and type of business should be observed before going on strike, and during the cooling-down period third-party mediation comes into play. If the mediation fails to find a solution satisfying both parties, arbitration may enforce a solution. The government may order arbitration in cases of public and heavy industries, while it remains optional for most of private industry.

For severe disputes and illegal strikes in large companies, the government sometimes intervenes and this leads to a quick settlement. The effectiveness of governmental intervention is open to debate. While many

---

[6] Many labor disputes in Korea are characterized as hostile and unlawful. When they face an impasse, unions often do not wait to see the result of the formal dispute resolution process led by the Labor Committee. They readily go on strike and the employer closes the factory. This kind of behavior results from the experience of the labor movement during the Japanese occupation period in the 1930s and 40s and during the dictatorial period in the 1950s through the 1970s. (For a history of industrial relations of Korea, refer to Park 1996.)

scholars and labor leaders criticize this kind of intervention, it is widely considered as a legitimate action and may even be wanted by the parties involved.

After confrontation or forcing, the company initiates tension releasing activities to restore community feeling. The activities may include less-formal drinking meetings, a picnic to a resort, or a sports game. In any case drinking and singing can not be missed. These tension releasing activities are not mandated by law, but recognized as socially instituted.

Costs of Conflict Management Norms

It is obvious that the Korean style of conflict management has contributed to business expansion, economic growth, and the sense of community. However, its costs are considerable. Two sorts of costs can be stressed. One is the loss of creativity. While context building is less harmful, smoothing and forcing activities do not enhance an individual's creativity. The Korean style of conflict management seems good for quantitative production and quick responses, but not good for qualitative innovation and creative adaptation.

The other cost is an individual one. Contexting and tension releasing demand time and money. Even if we do not consider money, time is a serious problem. The working hours of Korean workers usually go beyond the official working hours. They spend a lot of time in informal meetings, drinking, and singing, which sacrifice time which could otherwise be devoted to family matters and personal growth. It has increasingly become a social problem.

Newly Emerging Norms

Many people say that Korea is not as it used to be, but one thing unchanged in Korea is change. One of the remarkable and influential changes in Korea is the appearance of a new breed of Korean. The new generation born in and after the 1970s do not understand the poverty that their parents experienced and have remarkably different values; more individualistic and more leisure-oriented values. The cultural legacy of collectivism has been threatened along with the increase in GNP and the emergence of the new generation.

Another change is the succession of top management. The new generation of top management, mostly founder's sons or relatives, do not have the same charismatic power as the founders had, and many of the new CEOs have had some education in western countries. More democratic leadership is now taking place in Korea.

The third change is in the social climate as a result of the change of political leadership. Since 1993, a civil government has been in power—the first time since 1961. It has triggered rapid changes in almost every aspect of society, and the military way has been challenged.

Economic and environmental changes due to globalization after the collapse of socialist ideology constitutes the fourth change. In the global market place, the rules of the game have been changed and Korean companies must dramatically increase the quality of their products and their service in general. They have already experienced decreasing cost competitiveness due to a severe challenge from recently industrialized countries such as China and South Asian countries.

As a result of these changes and imperatives, the organizational culture of Korean firms is being gradually transformed. Now is a time of transition. It is difficult to describe what kind of organizational culture Korean firms will build. However, it seems that collectivism still remains the basis with features that will be supplanted by more creative ones. The new form of Korean corporate culture may be called 'creative collectivism', collectivism which values diversity and creativity.

Newly Emerging Norms toward 'Creative Collectivism'

New norms of conflict management are now observed in Korean organizations. Confrontation or the more competitive approach is becoming more popular between equals and new forms of concrete activities in the basic norms are emerging. The change of norms can be described as follows:

1. Contexting is as important as ever, but personal contact is more and more supplemented by information technology.
2. Lateral communication is valued and the smoothing norm is gradually being supplanted by confrontation.
3. The nature of forcing is shifting from using positional power to relying on power based on expertise.
4. Tension releasing is still popular but the method used is changing. Young employees rely less on alcohol and more on sports and other leisure activities.

Therefore, the Korean conflict management cycle is changing from a cycle of contexting-smoothing-forcing-tension releasing to one of contexting-confronting-forcing-tension releasing, which reflects the emergence of 'creative collectivism'.

PRACTICAL IMPLICATIONS FOR INTERNATIONAL MANAGERS

Understand General Orientations

The Korean economy has been externally oriented since the systematic implementation of the economic development plan in the early 60s. Now it faces a fundamentally different epoch. Korea has begun to play a more active role in international business. While Korea had no overseas direct investment until 1980, since then it has increased remarkably reaching US$43.3 billion in 1995. Since 1992, it has surpassed foreign direct investment into Korea, which was a record US$41.9 billion in 1995. In other words, Koreans who have devoted their greatest efforts into export now build and operate factories in other countries. Now their workplaces are abroad. They manage foreign workers and meet with foreign customers. In addition, in the 90s, many foreign workers came into Korea. From factory workers to car designers, the number of foreign workers in Korea is rapidly increasing. This means a dramatic change in international relations and much cultural collision.

Mutual understanding and skill in conflict management between different cultures have become more and more important. However, we can easily see occasions where foreigners feel frustrated when they meet with Koreans. People from individualist countries may feel frustrated that they should meet so many people and spend so much time on personal relations to reach an agreement with Koreans. On the contrary, people from other collectivist countries may feel frustrated when Koreans do not give enough time to build emotional relations and rush to get a quick decision.

In this chapter, we are trying to help the readers understand two faces of Korean culture: one is a harmony-seeking face stemming from the long history of collectivist culture, and the other is an action-oriented dynamic face resulting from recent social climate and business changes. We call this kind of business culture 'dynamic collectivism'.

Therefore, to conduct business relations with Koreans and manage conflict with them, it is very important to keep these kinds of Koreans' basic orientations in mind. It is also helpful to understand the four basic norms reflecting dynamic collectivism.

Tactics for Business with Koreans

Basically the same four norms of conflict management: contexting, smoothing, forcing, and tension releasing are applied in the international context. However, aware of the cultural differences, Koreans probably rely less on contexting and tension releasing. In a short-term relationship they might show individualistic rather than collectivist behavior. However, when the relationship persists, Korean behavior is very likely to return to normal.

The following hints will be helpful for international managers who are seeking constructive relations with Koreans:

1. Don't neglect context building.

   Before dealing with main business issues, spend enough time in exchanging personal information to build an emotional bond. Try to find something in common with your Korean counterpart. At the initial stage including a third person whom the Korean counterpart trusts is highly recommended.

2. Negotiate with integrity with your Korean partner, but don't forget there is a high-status person who may intervene.

   When you cannot reach an agreement with them, Koreans don't like to confront you. They may instead go to their superior to get out of the impasse. Sometimes, even if you get an OK from your partners, it may not be final. Their superior can reject it.

3. If you have a serious conflict with your Korean counterpart, try to find a sufficiently high-status person who can intervene.

   Smooth decision-making is highly valued, but it is difficult to get in Korea. In a case where you have time pressure or a serious conflict, you are recommended to find a high-status person who can help you. This person should possess enough influence over your partners and be trusted by them from previous relationships.

4. Enjoy drinking and singing with your Korean partners, or at least respect such behavior.

   Tension releasing is an integral part of human relations for Koreans. If Koreans have a difficult situation with you, they want to release tension while drinking and singing. You may join them, or you can recommend a nice place. This small gesture will be appreciated.

Some Embarrassing Phenomena

Here are some specific situations which foreigners are likely to face in business relations with Koreans.

Contracts and Scheduling

De Mente's observation (1991) is not so far from reality. As he said, to Koreans contract signing means generally getting the relationship officially started. Thereafter, its contents are subject to change and negotiation. Koreans do not regard the provisions of a contract as written in stone or as the fundamental basis of a business relationship. They regard the personal relationship and the desire for mutual benefit as the foundation of any business arrangement. A contract is essentially a symbol of this relationship. By the same token, scheduling has more symbolic meaning. Koreans easily change it according to the evolving situation and the emotional mood of key persons.

The Role of the Formal Meeting

In general, formal meetings are not regarded as hot debate places. They are rather considered as places for expressing group harmony and mutual trust. Therefore, many Koreans want to resolve the differences of opinion before or after the meeting. When a person's opinion is criticized in a meeting, he feels his face is damaged. However, a higher status person uses often formal meetings to express his power and forces the participants to accept his solutions. Therefore, foreigners are recommended to use informal meetings to better understand their Korean counterparts and their situations.

Aggressiveness

Foreigners sometimes may feel embarrassed by the hasty attitude and aggressiveness of their Korean counterparts in achieving their targets. This attitude makes foreigners very puzzled because Koreans normally show harmony-seeking behavior. As already described, the dynamic nature of corporate culture and the forcing norm of conflict management induce

Koreans to act in that way. If a foreigner is to deal with this problem, he or she is recommended to meet the key, high-status person at the critical moment in the negotiations. However, bypassing the lower status person in charge from the onset of negotiations is not recommended. It violates the contexting norm.

CONCLUSION

Conflict management in Korea is not a single-shot strategy such as avoiding, obeying, compromising, competing, or integrating. It operates based upon a continuous relationship and through a cyclical process including context building, smoothing, forcing and tension releasing. This cycle is derived from dynamic collectivism, which is based upon the traditional harmony-seeking culture and other social and leadership factors. While this conflict management cycle has contributed a lot to the economic growth and social stability, it has incurred considerable costs including a lack of creativity and a threat to the quality of life.

Korea is a society of rapid change and it is now facing an increasing internal and external diversity. Korean business firms must cope with global competition and new strategic imperatives. Therefore, new organizational culture and conflict management norms are needed and these have already started to take shape. The basic collective nature is considered to remain the same while some new norms, and specific activities within the norms, are becoming more important. The new Korean conflict management cycle seems to be contexting - confronting - forcing - tension releasing. Compared with the Western, the Korean style emphasizes context rather than content. Compared with the styles of other Asian countries, it stresses the emotional aspect and the forcing mechanism.

As international relationships have been qualitatively intensified in recent years, efforts to understand other countries, particularly their cultural aspects and conflict management styles should also be strengthened. Individualists should try to understand the collectivist relationship and context building norms, while collectivists should try to understand the content-orientation and competition norms of individualists. Other Asian countries are recommended to try to understand the emotional and dynamic nature of Korean organizational culture.

Koreans have many problems in dealing with cultural diversity, since historically and geographically they do not have much experience with different cultures. This is just one of the great challenges of this globalizing economy. We expect that a more creative and diverse positive collectivist culture will be formed in Korea.

In this chapter we have tried to propose a new perspective from which we can deal with conflict management in basically collectivist countries like Korea, and to collect as much research evidence about the style of Korean conflict management as possible. However, we faced a lack of systematic research materials and therefore included lots of hypotheses and subjective propositions in this chapter. At this point, we leave further studies and discussions for the next writers who are interested in the Korean way of conflict management.

ACKNOWLEDGEMENTS

The authors appreciate Ajou University for financial support and Professor E. Han Kim, University of Michigan for providing one of authors with a research environment for a year. We also thank the editors of this book for their valuable comments.

REFERENCES

Alston, J.P. 1989. *Wa, Guanxi*, and *Inhwa*: Managerial principles in Japan, China, and Korea. *Business horizons*, March/April, 26–31.

Blake, R.R. and Mouton, J.S. 1964. *The Managerial Grid*. Houston, TX: Gulf Publishing Co.

Blake, R.R. and Mouton, J.S. 1985. *The Managerial Grid III*. Houston, TX: Gulf Publishing Co.

Chang, C.S. and Chang, N.J. 1994. *The Korean Management System: Cultural, Political, and Economic Foundations*. Westport, CT: Quoram Books.

Cho, Y.H. 1995. Corporate cultures of Korean big businesses. In Shin, Y. K. *et al.* (eds.), *Management Characteristics of Koreans Big Businesses*, Seoul, Korea: Sekyungsa, 321–77. (In Korean.)

Cho, Y.H. and Shin Y.K. 1994. Local workers' value system and expatriate managers' attitude: A case analysis of a Korean-managed company in Indonesia. A paper presented at the 2nd conference of the year 1994 of the Korean Academy of International Business, Seoul, Korea. (In Korean.)

Choi, S.C. and Choi, S.H. 1990. 'We-ness': A Korean discourse of collectivism. A paper presented at the 1st international conference on individualism and collectivism: Psychocultural perspectives from East and West, Seoul, Korea.

Chung, K.H. and Lee, H.C. 1989. National differences in managerial practices. In K.H. Chung and H.C. Lee (eds.), *Korean Managerial Dynamics*. New York, NY: Praeger, 163–80.

Cosier, R.A., Schwenk, C.R. and Dalton, D.R. 1992. Managerial decision making in Japan, the U.S., and Hong Kong. *The International Journal of Conflict Management*, **3** (2), 151–60.

De Mente, B. 1991. *Korean Etiquette and Ethics in Business*. Chicago, IL: NTC Business Books.

Deutsch, M. 1973. *The Resolution of Conflict*. New Haven, CT: Yale University Press.

Donahey, M.S. 1995. Seeking harmony - Is the Asian concept of the conciliator/arbitrator applicable in the West? *Dispute Resolution Journal*, April/June, **50**, 74–8.

Drake, L.E. 1995. Negotiation styles in intercultural communication. *The International Journal of Conflict Management*, **6** (1), 275–96.

Gudykunst, W.B., Yoon, Y.C. and Nishida, T. 1987. The influence of individualism-collectivism on perception of communication in ingroup and outgroup relationships. *Communication Monographs*, September, **54**, 295–306.

Hall, E.T. 1976. *Beyond Culture*. Garden City, NY: Doubleday Anchor Books.

Harris, P.R. and Moran, R.T. 1991. *Managing Cultural Differences*. (Third edition). Houston, TX: Gulf Publishing Co.

Hofstede, G. 1984. *Culture's Consequences: International Differences in Work-related Values*. (Abridged edition.) Newbury Park, CA: SAGE Publication.

Hofstede, G. 1991. *Cultures and Organizations: Software of the Mind*. London, England: McGraw-Hill.

Hofstede, G. and Bond, M.H. 1988. The Confucius connection: From cultural roots to economic growth. *Organizational Dynamics*, **16** (4), 5–21.

Hur, S.V. and Hur, B.S. 1988. *Culture Shock! Korea*. Singapore: Times Books International.

Kearney, R.P. 1991. *The Warrior Worker: The Challenge of the Korean Way of Working*. New York, NY: Henry Holt and Company.

Lee, H.O. and Rogan, R.G. 1991. A cross-cultural comparison of organizational conflict management behaviors. *The International Journal of Conflict Management*, **2** (3), 181–99.

Luthans, F., McCaul, H.S. and Dodd, N.G. 1985. Organizational commitment: A comparison of American, Japanese, and Korean employees. *Academy of Management Journal*, **26** (1), 368–76.

Park, H. 1996. Crossfire Ahead: Where to Go? A paper presented at the 3rd Asian Regional Congress, International Industrial Relations Association, Sept 30-Oct 4, 1996, Taipei, Taiwan.

Rahim, M.A. 1983. A measure of styles of handling interpersonal conflict. *Academy of Management Journal*, **26** (2), 368–76.

Rahim, M.A. 1986. *Managing Conflict in Organizations*. New York: Praeger Publishers.

Redding, S.G., Norman, A. and Schlander, A. 1994. The nature of individual attachment to the organization: A review of east Asian variations. In H.C. Triandis, M.D. Dunnette & L. M. Hough (eds.), *Handbook of Industrial and Organizational Psychology*, (Second edition), **4**, Palo Alto, CA: Consulting Psychologists Press, Inc. 647–88.

Ross, M.H. 1993. *The Culture of Conflict: Interpretations and Interest in Comparative Perspective*. New Haven, CT: Yale University Press.

Rousseau, D.M. 1995. *Psychological Contracts in Organizations: Understanding Written and Unwritten Agreements*. Thousand Oaks: Sage Publications.

Steers, R.M., Shin, Y.K. and Ungson, G.R. 1989. *The Chaebol: Korea's New Industrial Might*, New York, NY: Harper & Row.

Thomas, K.W. 1992. Conflict and negotiation process in organizations. In M.D. Dunnette and L.M. Hough (eds.), *Handbook of Industrial and Organizational Psychology*, (Second edition), **3**, Palo Alto, CA: Consulting Psychologists Press, Ins., 651–717.

Thomas, K.W. 1976. Conflict and conflict management. In M.D. Dunnette (ed.), *Handbook of Industrial and Organizational Psychology*. Chicago: Rand McNally, 889–935.

Ting-Toomey, S., Gao, G., Trubisky, P., Yang, Z., Kim, H.S., Lin, S.L. and Nishida, T. 1991. Culture, face maintenance, and styles of handling interpersonal conflict: A study in five countries. *The International Journal of Conflict Management*, **2** (4), 275–96.

Tjosvold, D. 1991. The Conflict-Positive Organization. Reading, MA: Addison-Wesley Publishing Co.

Triandis, H.C. 1995. *Individualism and Collectivism*. Boulder, CO: Westview Press.

Tse, D.K., Francis, J. and Walls, J. 1994. Cultural differences in conducting intra- and inter-cultural negotiations: A Sino-Canadian comparison. *Journal of International Business Studies*, third quarter, 537–55.

Yu, X. 1995. Conflict in multicultural organization: An ethnographic attempt to discover work-related cultural assumptions between Chinese and American co-workers. *The International Journal of Conflict Management*, **6** (2), 211–32.

Weisinger, J.Y. and Salipante, P.F. 1995. Toward a method of exposing hidden assumptions in multicultural conflict. *The International Journal of Conflict Management*, **6** (2), 147–70.

Weldon, E. and Jehn, K.A. 1995. Examining cross-cultural differences in conflict management behavior: A strategy for future research. *The International Journal of Conflict Management*, **6** (4), 387–403.

CHAPTER THREE

Conflict Management in Japan: Cultural Values and Efficacy

KENICHI OHBUCHI
Department of Psychology, Tohoku University, Sendai, Japan

CONFLICT MANAGEMENT IN JAPAN: THREE PERSPECTIVES

Foreigners who engage in negotiations with Japanese representatives often have a strange feeling—the negotiations are not tough, but they feel the negotiation is not progressing. To know what causes such a feeling they need to understand the psycho-social processes involved in conflict management by the Japanese.

The Japanese have a unique style of conflict management which is quite different from that of Westerners, and also from that of other Asians. In this chapter, we discuss this unique style from the following three perspectives: (1) The tactical preferences of the Japanese, that is, the behaviors displayed by the Japanese in conflict situations; (2) Japanese cultural values, that is, the motivational factors involved in the Japanese conflict management; and (3) Japanese cognitive efficacy, that is, the cognitive factors governing Japanese conflict management.

Japanese Styles of Conflict Management

Whereas Japanese industrial products are often admired, those who produce them are not so favorably appraised by foreigners. Business people often form a negative stereotype of their Japanese business contacts, describing them as self-conscious, humorless, inscrutable, devious, shy, vague, economic animals, or imitators (Deutsch 1985; Goldman 1994). The source of this stereotype is the Japanese style of conflict management. Here we concisely describe its characteristics.

In negotiations, Westerners make their demands strongly, make the differences and issues clear, and try to resolve conflict by open discussion. The Japanese style of conflict resolution is quite different. In general, the Japanese are very modest and unassertive. They patiently listen to the other party's statements or concede without vigorous discussion. They do not openly express what they privately feel or want. The Japanese generally do not like to attract attention. Such reticence may be traced historically to a closed and tight society.

Utterances by Japanese participants in conflict situations are generally vague. They frequently say, 'Yes,' but it does not necessarily mean acceptance or agreement. The word actually means 'I listened to your speech' or 'I can understand your circumstances.' Likewise, 'I will consider it,' does not have any positive meaning. While the Japanese properly interpret this utterance as an indirect rejection, foreigners frequently misunderstand it.

An underlying basis for the Japanese style of conflict management is the desire to avoid conflicts or to make conflicts covert. The Japanese do not like definite rejection or heated arguments. Social harmony is strongly valued by them and therefore overt conflicts are regarded as a threat to their social order. These collectivist values determine the way they manage conflicts. Most Japanese people see negotiations in a negative way, believing that negotiations are tricks or deceptions. Among the Japanese, a reputation as a 'good negotiator' does not connote a socially desirable character, but it is often synonymous with impudence or dishonesty. In conflicts, both parties are expected to consider the other party's concerns and to resolve conflict without bitter argument. When they feel it is difficult to resolve a conflict in such a manner, they choose to avoid it. Foreigners are puzzled or irritated by the Japanese style of conflict management and some of them come to believe that it is best to be tough in negotiations with the Japanese.

Another factor which confuses foreign negotiators is the complex decision-making systems of Japanese companies. Western negotiation teams are usually well organized, the role of each member is clearly defined, and the teams are given considerable power to make decisions. However, the case is quite different with Japanese teams. Who has the authority in Japanese teams is not clear, and the teams have little power. As a result, it generally takes a long time to negotiate with Japanese teams because negotiations are frequently broken up in order for them to go back to their companies and have conferences.

A number of empirical studies have consistently documented the Japanese passive or avoiding style of conflict management (Burgoon, Dillard, Doran, and Miller 1982; Hirokawa and Miyahara 1986; Itoi, Ohbuchi and Fukuno, 1996; Trubiskey, Ting-Toomey, and Lin 1991). Goldman (1994) listed the behavioral characteristics displayed in negotiation by the Japanese, as compared with those observed among Americans (Table 3.1). He labeled the Japanese style of negotiation *Ningensei* (relationship-oriented) and the American style 'adversarial' (self-oriented). Content-analyzing 476 episodes of interpersonal conflicts reported by Japanese and American students, Ohbuchi and Takahashi (1994) found that 73% of the American subjects decided to make conflicts overt, but, in contrast, 66% of the Japanese subjects chose to keep conflicts covert. They further found that the Americans preferred direct tactics such as assertion or persuasion, while the Japanese tended to avoid the situation or attempt indirect tactics such as hinting.

Japanese Cultural Values in Conflict Management

What produces cultural styles of conflict management? Cultural psychologists have focused on cultural values which influence both the psychological and social processes energized by conflicts and guide and regulate participants' behaviors in conflict situations (Hofstede 1980; Triandis 1995).

Social Harmony and Commitment to Groups

Japan is a collectivist culture. As compared with individualistic cultures, collectivist cultures give priority to social harmony: social relationships over personal interests or freedom (Hofstede 1980; Triandis 1995). These collectivist values may determine the Japanese tactical preferences in conflicts. Triandis (1994) regarded Japan as a tight society as well as collectivist. In a tight society, there is little variation in values and standards among the population, and transgressions against them are met with informal but harsh sanctions such as rejection, or result in a bad reputation. The most widely shared value in a collectivist culture is social order or social harmony (Haley 1991).

Table 3.1 Characteristics Displayed by the Japanese in Negotiations

	Japanese *Ningensei* Style of Communication		U.S. Adversarial Style of Communication
1.	Indirect verbal and nvc*	1.	More direct verbal and nvc
2.	Relationship communication	2.	More task communication
3.	Discourages confrontational strategies	3.	Confrontational strategies more acceptable
4.	Strategically ambiguous communication	4.	Prefers more to-the-point communication
5.	Delayed feedback	5.	More immediate feedback
6.	Patient, longer-term negotiators	6.	Shorter-term negotiators
7.	Uses fewer words	7.	Favors verbosity
8.	Distrustful of skillful verbal communicators	8.	Exalts verbal eloquence
9.	Group orientation	9.	More individualistic orientation
10.	Cautious, tentative	10.	More assertive, self-assured
11.	Complimentary communicators	11.	More publicly critical communicators
12.	Softer, heartlike logic	12.	Harder, analytic logic preferred
13.	Sympathetic, empathetic, complex use of pathos	13.	Favors logos, reason
14.	Expresses and decodes complex relational strategies and nuances	14.	Expresses and decodes complex logos, cognitive nuances
15.	Avoids decision-making in public	15.	Frequent decision-making in public
16.	Makes decisions in private venues, away from the public eye	16.	Frequent decisions in public at negotiating tables
17.	Decisions via *ringi* and *nemawashi* (complete consensus process)	17.	Decisions by majority rule and public compromise is more commonplace
18.	Uses go-betweens for decision making	18.	More extensive use of direct person-to-person, player-to-player interaction for decisions
19.	Understatement and hesitation in verbal and nvc	19.	May publicly speak in superlatives, exaggerations, nv projection
20.	Uses qualifiers, humility and is tentative, as communicator	20.	Favors fewer qualifiers, more ego-centered
21.	Receiver/listening-centered	21.	More speaker-and message-centered
22.	Inferred meanings, looks beyond words to nuances, nvc	22.	More face-value meaning, more denotative
23.	Shy, reserved communicators	23.	More publicly self-assertive
24.	Distaste for purely business transactions	24.	Prefers to 'get down to business' or 'nitty gritty'
25.	Mixes business and social communication	25.	Tends to keep business negotiating more separated from social communication
26.	Utilizes *matomari* (hints) for achieving group adjustment and saving face in negotiating	26.	More directly verbalizes management's preference at negotiating tables
27.	Practices *haragei* (belly logic) and communication	27.	Practices more linear, discursive, analytical logic; greater reverence for cognitive than for affective

* nvc = non-verbal communication

Reprinted from Goldman (1994), The centrality of '*Ningensei*' to Japanese negotiating and interpersonal relationships: Implications for U.S.—Japanese communication. *International Journal of Intercultural Relations,* **Vol. 18**, pp. 29–54. Copyright 1996, with kind permission of Elsevier Science Ltd, The Boulevard, Langford Land, Kidlington 0X5 1GB, UK.

Conflicts are caused by disagreements between individuals or groups over interests or goals. Individualists assume that every person or every group has a unique goal or interest, and therefore they tend to accept conflicts as a natural and inevitable aspect of social life. Western democracies are conceived as political systems that regulate conflicts between competing interests (Aoki 1991). In Japan, on the other hand, people dislike overt disorganization or disagreements. The Japanese may feel that overt conflicts threaten social organizations or social relationships (Lebra 1976). There are several Japanese phrases which express overt conflicts in a negative light: For example, *Koto wo aradateru* (to intensify a social conflict) and *Koto wo kamaeru* (to make a conflict overt). These popular phrases imply that the Japanese strongly value social harmony or social order.

This desire for social harmony characterizes negotiations in Japan. Table negotiations are often ritualized and agreements among participants may be pursued by informal negotiations behind the stage (*Nemawashi*). A consensus is emphasized in formal sessions even if participants have different interests. This ritualization is found in both intra- and inter-group negotiations in Japan, in areas related to organizational and political decision-making, business contracts, and labor-management negotiations (Goldman 1994; Okimoto 1990). The emphasis on social harmony or order tends to suppress individual differences in opinions, but it also prevents arbitrary actions by a majority group because the majority group must conciliate with the minority group in order to prevent differences from becoming public.

The value of social harmony or order is related to a strong commitment to their groups by Japanese individuals. Japanese people have strong family attachments, and Japanese business people identify with and show strong loyalty to their companies. Japanese companies have unique organizational structures, such as life-long employment, a seniority system, and intra-company unions. These institutional structures strengthen workers' commitment to the companies and thereby reduce intra-organizational conflicts. The Japanese style of management is called 'a family-type management' (Maruyama 1989). Employers take the role of parents and employees the role of children and each is strongly associated with the other by a life-long bond. According to Iwata (1990), a researcher of Japanese economic history, a prototype of this management style is found in the traditional merchant organization of the *Tokugawa* period in the 18th and 19th centuries, during which Japan was closed to foreigners. During the *Meiji* restoration in the late 19th century, Japan was opened to foreign trade. A Western style of management was introduced at that time, and soon Japanese industrialists encountered intense labor-management conflicts. After this difficult period, traditional personnel management procedures were revived and the current Japanese management style was developed by mixing traditional and Western styles.

The Japanese commitment to groups involves both instrumental and non-instrumental social concerns. People participate in groups to satisfy their personal needs. They receive a variety of resources from companies or communities. For example, resource incentives, such as salaries, are strong factors promoting commitment to groups. However, groups provide their members with more than resource rewards (Hogg 1992). Japanese people are strongly attracted by the social rewards given by groups, such as a positive social identity, high self-esteem, and the opportunity to contribute to society (Bowman 1984; Iwata 1990). In some groups, such as family or clubs, it is obvious that members are associated with each other by social incentives rather than resource incentives. Even in companies, where the main task is to distribute resources among members, the Japanese have non-instrumental or social concerns. Goldman (1994) stressed the concern for social 'face' shown by the Japanese in conflict management. He submits that the Japanese do not want to publicly rank participants into winners and losers. Their preference for conflict-avoidance appears to involve a motive: to protect the social identities of all the participants.

Relationship Orientations

A second collectivist value of the Japanese is a relationship orientation (Itoi *et al.* 1996; Ohbuchi and Takahashi 1994). Theories of interpersonal relationships developed in individualistic cultures, such as the social exchange theory (Thibaut and Kelley 1959) or the social resource theory (Buss 1986; Foa and Foa 1974), postulate that an individual establishes relationships with others in order to satisfy his or her personal needs. A relationship is a market for resource exchange and if the perceived costs outweigh the perceived benefits, the individual quits the relationship. The reason why individualists prefer to use direct or assertive tactics in conflicts is that they are motivated to satisfy their personal interests.

The Japanese also use relationships for resource exchange, but generally they look at the cost/benefit balance from a longer perspective than individualists. Okimoto (1990) referred to a long-term relationship built on resource exchange as an interpersonal network (*Jinmyaku*). In Japan, negotiations are ritualized, and substantial discussion is conducted in informal negotiations outside the formal sessions. These informal negotiations are carried on through interpersonal networks. Participants are more flexible in reaching agreements in informal sessions than in formal sessions. The cost/benefit balance is evaluated at both the formal and informal levels, and it is also considered in future negotiations. In Japan, informal networks are established not only among individuals but also among business or political groups.

Some American psychologists have emphasized the non-instrumental motives of relationships (Gilligan 1982; Lyons 1983), arguing that the market concept of relationships is held by men but not by women. Women, they believe, are more oriented toward other aspects of relationships, such as caring, trust, or interdependence. Ting-Toomey (1994) claimed that, like American women, collectivists give value to the relationship itself, and not only to its instrumental aspect. She argued that the instrumental concept cannot explain why collectivists often maintain relationships about which they have complaints. Collectivists are strongly committed to relationships and feel obligated to contribute to them. The low rate of divorce in Japan is regarded as evidence of this belief. Emphasizing the non-instrumental concern for relationships of the Japanese, Goldman (1994) also noted that their interpersonal behaviors are self-controlled in terms of relational values such as faith, obligation, loyalty, or caring. The self is nothing without relationships for the Japanese and self-worth depends on the values given in relationships (Markus and Kitayama 1991).

Justice and Fairness

Justice is another cultural value, which may generate cultural differences in responses to conflicts (Kidder and Muller 1991). The United States government has frequently criticized Japan because it is perceived as having a number of 'unjust' trade systems or customs, such as the strong company networks (*keiretsu*) and administrative guidance from the government. Unlike Americans, Japanese people do not see these systems and customs as unjust. Why do they disagree? They seem to rely on different principles of justice.

There may be two different types of social 'justice' implying different social justification: 'fairness' to justify the individual member's personal interests within groups, sustained by individualistic values emphasizing personal achievement and performance; and 'social order' to justify controls by groups against individual members (Easton and Dennis 1969). Leung and Bond (1984) found that collectivists prefer an equality rule when distributing resources because they believe that it reduces competition and animosity and bestows social harmony.

Whereas philosophers have long considered justice as a principle for social control, social scientists have mainly focused on 'fairness' for the protection of personal rights. Fairness coincides with individualistic values because it assumes that every individual has the right to pursue his or her own personal interests and this right must be protected in conflict situations. This emphasis on individual rights may be a major reason why fairness has been studied mainly by researchers in individualistic cultures.

Another type of justification appears to be important in collectivist cultures. Some ethnic groups of collectivist cultures believe that 'the will of God' or 'the national goals' are the supreme principles of justice. Although Japanese people are not such extreme collectivists (Hofstede 1980), they generally accept social order or social harmony as a principle of justice and sometimes feel it is more important than fairness.

Cultural Efficacy in Japanese Conflict Resolution

Concept and Research

Cultural efficacy theory explains the cultural tactical preferences from a cognitive perspective. It has been theoretically discussed by some cultural researchers (cf., Triandis 1980), and empirical findings were provided by Leung's (1987) study on procedural justice and Yamagishi's (1988) experiment on social 'loafing'. In a scenario study, Leung found that, in order to resolve conflicts, collectivists (Hong Kong Chinese) preferred bargaining and mediation more than individualists (Americans). It is important to note that the collectivists' tactical preference was apparently induced by their perception that these tactics would be more effective in reducing animosity between the participants. These results suggest that individualists and collectivists have different expectations about the instrumentality of each tactic in achieving goals. The cultural efficacy theory stresses the cultural differences in cognition of the effectiveness of tactics and in the social structure behind them.

Yamagishi (1988) examined loafing behavior among collectivists. Loafing behavior results in enjoying personal profits at the expense of other's collaborative actions. Cultural value theory predicts that collectivists who are oriented toward social harmony and group goals would be more collaborative and not demonstrate loafing. However, this prediction was not supported by Yamagishi's experiment (1988). He found instead that collectivists were collaborative only when they believed that social sanction systems against transgression were effective. They were not collaborative when they did not believe so. Based on this finding, he argued that cultural styles of behavior are not the manifestations of inner cultural values but the products of learning regarding social structures associated with reward and punishment.

Conflict Reduction Systems in Japan

Some researchers who hold the cultural efficacy perspective interpret the Japanese style of conflict management as reflecting the structural characteristics of Japanese society. For example, Tanaka and Takeuchi (1987) and Haley (1991) maintained that the low rates of civil cases in Japan are not results of Japanese' collectivist values, but results from the legal system of Japan which restricts people from using the courts for conflict resolution, because of high cost, low compensation, scarcity of lawyers, or the low standing of the plaintiff. Tanaka and Takeuchi complained that in Japan the law is monopolized by the public sector and ordinary people cannot use it as a means of conflict resolution.

Kumon (1990) argued that Japan is a network society based on traditional social structures and the Japanese preference for passive or avoidance tactics is supported by this social system. Although Japan is controlled by liberal political-economic groups, its economic system and management styles are different from those of Western countries. Japan has a number of unique economic institutions or customs regulating business activities, such as *Keiretsu* (the close networks between companies), cartels, administrative guidance by the government, etc. These customs and institutions prevent or reduce conflicts between companies or conflicts between companies and citizens, though they also tend to interfere with competitive business activities and suppress the complaints of minorities.

Japanese Business Management

The Japanese conflict reduction system can be observed in Japanese business management. Business-labor relationships have been characterized by life-long employment, seniority, organizational training, company facilities, bottom-up decision-making (*ringi*), and company unions. Most Japanese companies hire young people who have recently graduated from college and train them in the intra-organizational programs whose goals are to develop the skills and knowledge necessary for business activities and to socialize employees as members of the business organization (organizational training). This is a great investment in employee training and so, even under difficult economic conditions, Japanese companies do not fire employees but instead re-distribute them among different sections.

In Japan, an employee usually works at one company until retirement age (life-long employment). Promotion is determined mainly by his or her age (seniority). This system is based on the equality rule of resource distribution and, as a result, the life-time rewards are almost the same for all employees. This life-long equality principle may be effective in reducing intra-organizational conflicts in the following two ways. First, an individual employee is not encouraged to compete with his or her colleagues because rewards are determined based on a non-performance rule, that is, age. Second, an individual employee attempts to avoid serious conflicts and possible dismissal because benefits and promotion usually depend on the length of employment. In Japan, a job change is regarded as a detriment to personal career growth.

Most Japanese companies have facilities such as housing, insurance, pension, and medical benefits, which are referred to as the management welfare policy (Maruyama 1989). These benefits are another type of incentive for employees, and encourage them to work for a company over a long period of time and increase their loyalty to it. Company facilities are particularly useful for retaining young employees since they mitigate young employees' frustrations caused by their low levels of reward thus contributing to a reduction in conflicts between labor and management. In addition to the benefits, Japanese companies hold a number of events such as welcome/farewell parties, cherry blossom viewing parties, sports festivals, and company excursions, whose purpose is to enhance company coherence and the loyalty of employees (Uchino and Abegrain 1988).

In Japan, a company union signifies that both management and labor groups belong to the same business organization and that both parties share common goals to enlarge the total resource. In many Japanese companies, unions substantially support management, especially the personnel department. The interdependency between them mitigates organizational conflicts. Typically in Japan an average career path for employees is that they are members of the union when they are young but they move to the management side when older. This career pattern also contributes to the reduction of organizational conflicts because there are close human networks between the management and union parties.

Decision-making in Japanese companies is a 'bottom-up' procedure (*ringi*). In Japanese companies, as compared with Western companies, managers do not assume a strong leadership in decision-making processes. Instead, information and concerns are shared among all the participants and a decision is gradually made by integrating diverse opinions (Uchino and Abegrain 1988). This style of decision-making may not be understood by foreigners. For example, Western companies often complain about the Japanese style of negotiation. They say, 'Representatives of Japanese companies cannot decide by themselves. Their decision process is unclear and it usually takes a very long time.' However, within Japan bottom-up decision-making is useful in building a consensus within organizations, avoiding conflicts, making employees feel that they have participated in the decision, and thus increasing their commitment to both the decision and the company (Greenberg 1993; Tyler, Degoey, and Smith 1996).

These conflict reduction systems of Japanese companies appear to be supported by the perception of the company held by Japanese people and by the economic institutions and customs of Japanese society. Western workers perceive stockholders as the owners of a company and they view their company as divided between the workers and the management group which includes the president and other officers of the company. The employees are viewed as the means of producing benefits for the stockholders. The relationship between employers and employees is based on resource exchange.

In Japan, on the other hand, stockholders are not seen as owners of business companies, rather companies are regarded as organizations of and for employees (Iwata 1990). The separation of ownership and management took place when the Japanese plutocracy (*Zaibatsu*) was dismantled after the Pacific War, and it was promoted in every field of business in the 1960s when economic growth was rapid in Japan. As a result, the influence of stockholders over company management diminished and the management gained more power, increasing employees' commitment to and sense of responsibility for organizations.

The above discussion suggests that Japanese society, groups, and organizations have a number of systems and customs that reduce conflicts and Japanese people share common expectations that they will gain favorable results by complying with these systems and customs. Such expectations may induce the Japanese people to adopt passive or avoidance tactics in conflict situations.

MULTIPLE GOALS IN CONFLICT MANAGEMENT: AN EMPIRICAL STUDY

Participants in conflicts are motivated to maximize a number of goals. An initial issue may precipitate a conflict and generate a certain goal for a participant, but additional goals are often activated and the conflict may then involve multiple issues. A resource issue often precipitates a conflict but social motives involving justice, relationship, identities, and power-hostility are frequently involved in the conflict. In a factor analysis study (Ohbuchi and Tedeschi 1997), we distinguished two resource goals (economic resource and personal resource) and four social goals (relationship, power-hostility, fairness, and identity), as presented in Table 3.2. In another study (Fukushima and Ohbuchi 1996), we found that these goals uniquely determined tactical choice: that is, a relationship goal increased collaborative tactics but decreased assertive tactics; fairness, identity, or power-hostility goals increased assertive tactics; and an economic resource goal increased both types of tactics. Fig. 3.1 summarizes the findings regarding the antecedents and consequences of goals in conflicts.

In this section, we examine Japanese styles of conflict management in terms of multiple goals, based on a recent cross-cultural study with Japanese and American participants (Ohbuchi and Tedeschi, in press).

Hypotheses

The role of multiple goals in conflict management can be examined from three related perspectives. The first is goal orientation, that is, how strongly a participant wants to achieve a goal. Based on cultural value theory, we predicted that Japanese would more strongly want to achieve a relationship goal and less strongly want to achieve fairness and resource goals than Americans (*Hypothesis 1*).

Table 3.2 Resource and Social Goals.

Resource Goals	
Economic resource:	To protect one's economic interests.
Personal resource:	To protect one's privacy or freedom of action.
Social Goals	
Relationship:	To maintain a positive relationship with the other party.
Power-hostility:	To dominate or hurt the other party.
Fairness:	To restore fairness between the participants.
Identity:	To protect one's self-esteem or social face.

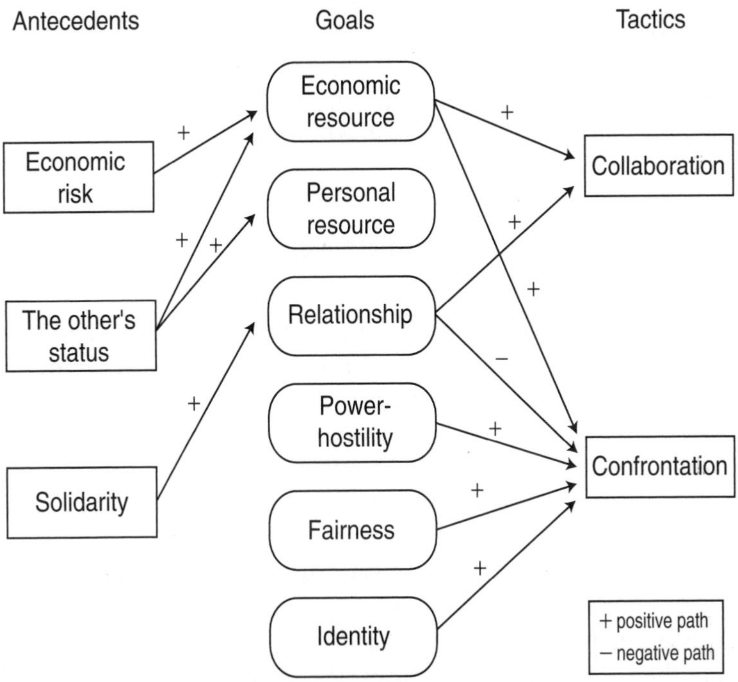

Figure 3.1 Summary of Findings Regarding Multiple Goals in Conflict Management (Fukushima and Ohbuchi 1996; Ohbuchi and Tedeschi 1997)

The second aspect of examining goals in conflicts is the association of goal attainment and outcome satisfaction. When the conflict is resolved, some goals may be fully attained but others may be only partially attained. Outcome satisfaction may depend on the extent to which the goals the participant strongly wants to achieve are attained. In other words, the participant's values in conflict resolution can be inferred from the association of perceived goal attainment and outcome satisfaction. Since we assumed that there were cultural differences in the goals that were most valued, we predicted that Japanese would feel strong satisfaction when a relationship goal was perceived as being attained, while Americans would feel strong satisfaction when justice and resource goals were perceived as being attained (*Hypothesis 2*).

The third perspective in examining goals in conflicts is the association between goal orientation and tactical choices. If the Japanese choose avoidance tactics when they want to achieve a relationship goal, do Americans also use avoidance tactics when they want to achieve a relationship goal? Or do Americans try to achieve relationship goals by the use of some other tactics? Cultural efficacy theory predicts that associations between goal orientations and tactical choice would be different for Japanese and Americans (*Hypothesis 3*).

Analysis of Interpersonal Conflicts Among Japanese and Americans

Participants were 113 male and 94 female Japanese students and 126 male and 138 female American students. Presenting them with our definition of conflict as 'overt or covert opposition or disagreement with others,' we asked the participants to recall an experience of interpersonal conflict and to rate the episode on scales measuring goal orientation, goal attainment, tactics, and outcome satisfaction. In the measurement of goal orientations, we asked the participants to indicate how strongly they wanted the outcomes described by 16 items in their attempts at conflict resolution. The items were designed to measure the six goals in Table 3.2. In the measurement of tactics, we asked the participants to indicate how strongly they engaged in the actions described by 11 items, which were designed to measure four types of tactics—conciliation, confrontation, third party intervention, and avoidance. In the measurement of goal attainment, we presented the participants with the 16 goal items again and asked them to indicate the degree to which the goals were finally attained. Finally, we asked the participants to answer how satisfied they were with the outcomes of the conflicts. In all these measurements, the participants were asked to rate each item on a 7-point scale ranging from 0 to 6.

Across all response categories, the scores of the American participants were higher than those of the Japanese. Cultural psychologists have regarded such differences as reflecting general tendencies in responding to questionnaire scales but not as reflecting actual cultural differences (Leung, Bond, Carmet, Krishman, and Liebrand 1990). In order to statistically control for such response tendencies, we computed relative scores for each participant by subtracting the mean scores from raw scores.

Tactical Choice

In an Analysis of Variances of the tactic scores treating culture, gender, and tactic types as independent variables, a significant interaction of tactics x culture [$F(3, 1350) = 29.24$, $p < .01$] indicated, consistent with past findings, that the Japanese participants preferred avoidance more and confrontation less than the American participants (Fig. 3.2). An unexpected finding that the Japanese did not use third party intervention as frequently as the Americans may indicate that the Japanese did not want to make conflicts public.

Goal Orientation

A significant interaction of goals x culture [$F(5, 2290) = 14.51$, $p < 0.01$] indicated, as *Hypothesis 1* predicted, that the Japanese participants wanted to achieve a relationship goal more strongly but a fairness goal less strongly than the American participants (Fig. 3.3). The orientation toward an economic resource goal was generally very low, though the Japanese wanted an economic goal relatively more strongly than the Americans.

Goal Attainment and Outcome Satisfaction

Table 3.3 gives the results of regression analysis treating outcome satisfaction as a dependent variable and goal attainments as independent variables. Inconsistent with *Hypothesis 2*, the Japanese and the Americans were very similar. The attainment of relationship and personal resource goals significantly contributed to outcome satisfaction in both groups. It should be noted that there were large differences between goal orientation and goal attainment among the Americans. The attainment of a fairness goal did not significantly contribute to outcome satisfaction among the Americans even though they reported a strong desire for achieving this goal. Apparently, there is something unique about a fairness goal.

Fairness is a value or standard which may be activated when a conflict potentially exists between individuals or between groups. People become

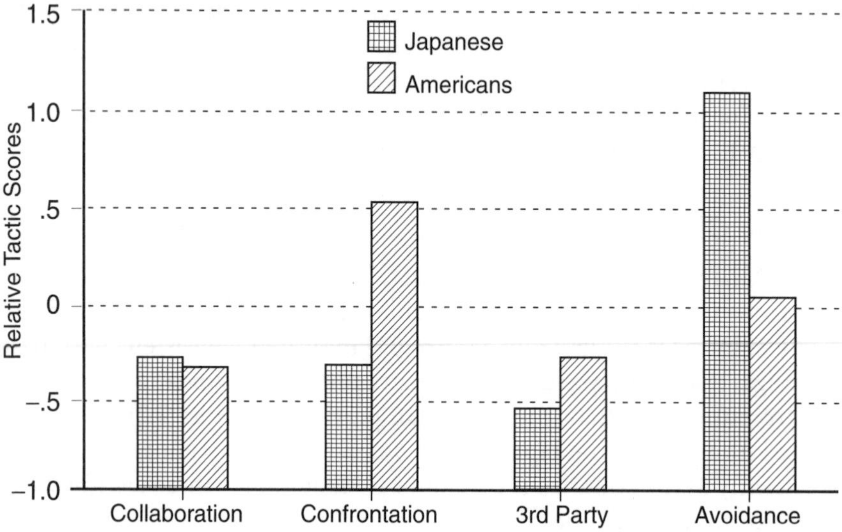

Figure 3.2 Cultural Differences in Tactical Choice

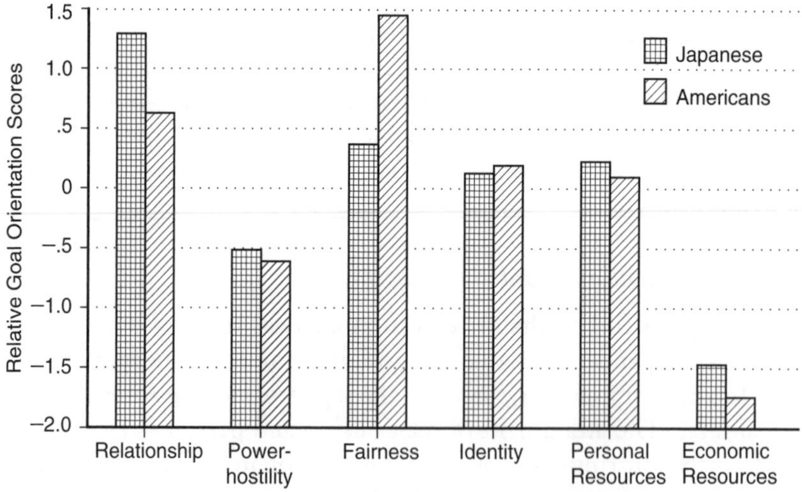

Figure 3.3 Cultural Differences in Goal Orientations

very concerned with fairness in conflict situations. Is achievement of fairness itself their final goal? Some researchers (Adams 1965; Lind and Tyler 1988) stress that fairness is a terminal value: people want to achieve fairness independently of other values. However, Thibaut and Walker

Table 3.3 Regression of Outcome Satisfaction by Goal Attainment among Americans and Japanese: βs. (Ohbuchi and Tedeschi, in press)

Goal Attainment	Satisfaction	
	Americans	Japanese
Relationship	0.48**	0.37**
Power-Hostility	0.11+	
Fairness		0.12+
Identity	0.11+	
Personal Resource	0.15*	0.25**
Economic Resource		
R^2	0.31**	0.31**

Notes: ** $p<0.01$; * $p<0.05$; + $p<0.10$.

(1975) view fairness as an instrumental value by which people attempt to achieve other terminal values. In conflict situations, participants may frequently attempt to justify their personal interests by appealing to fairness instead of protecting their interests by the use of more direct measures such as coercive power. The present results suggest, therefore, that the Japanese and the Americans did not differ in their terminal values but that the Americans were more strongly oriented toward fairness as an instrumental value. This cultural difference may result from a stronger belief by the Americans than the Japanese in the efficacy of fairness in furthering other goals. The notion that different cultural groups share common basic values is encouraging for conflict researchers, suggesting that cross-cultural conflicts could be resolved if we consider cultural values in selecting tactics.

Goals and Tactical Choice

Table 3.4 shows the results of regression analysis using each type of tactic as a dependent variable and goal orientations as independent variables. The results do not support *Hypothesis 3*. Instead, they show marked similarities between the Japanese and American participants. In both cultural groups, relationship and economic resource goals increased conciliation but a fairness goal decreased it; a power-hostility goal increased the use of confrontation; and a relationship goal increased third party intervention. Cultural differences were found regarding third party

Table 3.4 Regression of Tactics by Goal Orientation among Americans and Japanese: βs. (Ohbuchi and Tedeschi 1997)

Goals	Collaboration		Confrontation		Third Party		Avoidance	
	Americans	Japanese	Americans	Japanese	Americans	Japanese	Americans	Japanese
Relationship	0.55**	0.43**			0.19**	0.18**		
Power-Hostility			0.56**	0.21**	0.25**			
Fairness	−0.12*	−0.16*	0.10+					
Identity			−0.13*			0.17*		0.17*
Personal Resource				0.19**	0.16*		0.15*	−0.17*
Economic Resource	0.19**	0.13+		0.13+				
R^2	0.31**	0.20**	0.28**	0.15**	0.09**	0.07**	0.02**	0.04*

Notes: ** $p<0.01$; * $p<0.05$; + $p<0.10$.

intervention and avoidance, though they were not predicted. The American participants frequently used third party intervention with a power-hostility motive while the Japanese choice of avoidance was associated with an identity goal. As a result, the present results do not support the cultural efficacy theory because the effects of goals on conciliatory, confrontational, and third party tactics were common between the Japanese and American groups. This suggests that both cultural groups had similar experiences and perceptions regarding the effectiveness of a variety of tactics in conflict resolution. However, it could be argued that the present study did not provide an adequate test of cultural efficacy theory. Cultural differences were most pronounced in the use of avoidance tactics, but we failed to identify differences in the underlying motivation for their use.

IMPLICATIONS FOR NEGOTIATIONS WITH THE JAPANESE

Japanese Management: Changing or Not Changing?

There is an ample body of research or episodic evidence for the Japanese preference for a passive or avoidance style in conflict management. In this chapter, we have reasoned that this style reflects Japanese values of social harmony, social order, and relationships and is based on unique Japanese economic management systems. These social values and systems which induce people to avoid confrontations are characteristic of a closed, homogeneous, and stable society (Triandis 1994). Such values reduce conflicts within the society but sometimes restrict the rights or freedoms of minority or out-groups. Historically, the Japanese have valued social order or harmony more than personal freedom or rights.

The tight and centralized social structure of Japan has not changed for the past 500 years. The Japanese have long maintained essentially the same lifestyle, in which an individual belongs to a certain group (family and rural communities, *samurai* clans, or merchant family shops) for their entire life, identifying himself or herself with the group, and aspiring to a high rank or status within the group. This historically-reinforced group commitment has instrumentally and emotionally dominated Japanese conflict management (Nakane 1986).

The Japanese style of conflict management may not be so effective in international politics or trade. In the international economic conflicts in the 1980s, Japanese systems were criticized by foreign countries. During the domestic economic depression in the 1990s, the Japanese themselves began to question their own style of management. Both the Japanese government and companies are attempting to increase competitive factors in both public and private areas, however, such changes are limited or superficial. The traditional management style is still dominant and people are strongly motivated to avoid conflicts in Japan.

Negotiations with the Japanese

In the above sections, we emphasized that the Japanese are strongly motivated to maintain relationships with others. In a personal relationship both parties trust each other and depend on each other. Trust and mutual dependence are also characteristics of associations in business. In terms of long relationships, the Japanese make concessions in one negotiation, expecting that their interests will be more fully considered in the next negotiation. Therefore, what concerns the Japanese business person most is whether the other party is trustworthy as a partner for a long-term business relationship. In negotiations, a Japanese bargainer examines the other party in this regard. Based on these considerations, several suggestions can be offered to those who negotiate with Japanese companies or business persons.

1. Westerners begin negotiations with a high level of demands, but the Japanese favor moderate bargains. The Japanese do not like cunning or tricks because they believe that these tactics interfere with making good relationships. Contrary to most books teaching business persons how to negotiate, we encourage them to be honest in negotiations with the Japanese and to frankly talk about their goals or what they really want. The Japanese are then more likely to accept them as business partners.
2. Tough tactics such as threats also have adverse effects on negotiations with the Japanese, though they might be effective in the short-term. The Japanese may make concessions to or comply with tough negotiators in order to avoid conflicts, but they may also quit the business relationship. Westerners assert themselves or criticize the other party by referring to fairness. This is not a persuasive argument for the Japanese. Although they see fairness as an important value, they do not regard it as the supreme principle. Our cross-cultural findings suggest that fairness is just an instrumental value even for Westerners, that is, they *strategically* refer to it in conflict situations.
3. Each cultural group has its own preferred style of negotiation or conflict management. A decision on which style negotiators will adopt is strategically made. When a negotiation is deadlocked, one option is to move to more informal sessions with a small number of negotiators. The Japanese prefer this method because it enables the participants to avoid serious conflicts in the formal session, which may damage the relationship. It usually takes time and patience to continue the negotiation and to deliberately avoid serious conflicts, but through the process the negotiators can indirectly communicate to each other that they are taking care of the relationship as well as self interests. The Japanese are sensitive to these indirect messages regarding relationships and rely on this type of communication particularly in conflict resolution.

REFERENCES

Adams, J.S. 1965. Inequity in social exchange. In L. Berkowitz (ed.), *Advances in Experimental Social Psychology*, Vol. **2**, 267–99. New York: Academic Press.

Aoki, Y. 1991. Seiji shakai no antei to hendo (Stability and changes of political society). In Y. Aoki and M. Nakamichi. (eds.), *Gendai Nihon seijino shakaigaku (Sociology of Modern Japanese Politics)*, 289–312. Tokyo: Showado.

Bowman, J.S. 1984. Japanese management: Personnel policies in the public sector. *Public Personnel Management Journal*, **13**, 197–247.

Burgoon, M., Dillard, J., Doran, N. and Miller, M. 1982. Cultural and situational influences on the process of persuasive strategy selection. *International Journal of Intercultural Relations*, **6**, 85–100.

Buss, A.H. 1986. *Social Behavior and Personality*. Hillsdale, NJ: Lawrence Erlbaum Associates.

Deutsch, M.F. 1985. *Doing Business with the Japanese*. New York: Penguin Books.

Easton, D. and Dennis, J. 1969. *Children in the Political System: The Origins of Political Legitimacy*. Chicago: University of Chicago Press.

Falbo, T. and Peplau, L.A. 1980. Power strategies in intimate relationships. *Journal of Personality and Social Psychology*, **38**, 618–28.

Foa, U.G. and Foa, E.B. 1974. *Societal Structures of the Mind*. Springfield, IL: Charles C. Thomas.

Fukushima, O. and Ohbuchi, K. 1996. Antecedents and effects of multiple goals in conflict resolution. *International Journal of Conflict Management*, **7**, 191–208.

Gilligan, C. 1982. *In a Different Voice*. Cambridge, Mass: Harvard University Press.

Goldman, A. 1994. The centrality of *Ningensei* to Japanese negotiating and interpersonal relationships: Implications for U.S.—Japanese communication. *International Journal of Intercultural Relations*, **18**, 29–54.

Greenberg, J. 1993. The social side of fairness: Interpersonal and informational classes of organizational justice. In R. Cropanzano (ed.), *Justice in the Work Place: Approaching Fairness in Human Resource Management* 79–103. Hillsdale, NJ: Lawrence Erlbaum Associates.

Haley, J.O. 1991. *Authority without Power: Law and the Japanese Paradox*. New York: Oxford University Press.

Hirokawa, R. and Miyahara, A. 1986. A comparison of influence strategies utilized by managers in American and Japanese organizations. *Communication Quarterly*, **34**, 250–65.

Hofstede, G. 1980. *Culture's Consequences: International Differences in Work Related Attitudes*. Beverly Hills, CA: Sage.

Hogg, M.A. 1992. *The Social Psychology of Group Cohesiveness: From Attraction to Social Identity*. Hemel Hempstead: Harvester Wheatsheaf.

Itoi, R., Ohbuchi, K. and Fukuno, M. 1996. A cross-cultural study of preference of accounts: Relationship closeness, harm severity, and motives of account making. *Journal of Applied Social Psychology*, **26**, 913–34.

Iwata, R. 1990. Jyugyoin no ketugotai tositeno nihon kigyo: sono roots to hatten katei (Japanese companies as employees' organization: Their origins and developmental processes). In Kokusai Bunka Kaikan (ed.), *Gendai Nippon no seiji keizai*, Vol. **3**: *Nippon no bunka to shakai keizai system (Modern Japanese Politics and Economy*, Vol. **3**: *Culture and Socio-economic Systems in Japan)*, 253–88. Tokyo: Sogo Kenkyu Kaihatsu Kiko.

Kidder, L.H. and Muller, S. 1991. What is 'fair' in Japan? In H. Steemsma and R. Vermont (eds.), *Social Justice in Human relations*, Vol. **2**: *Societal and Psychological Consequences of Justice and Injustice*, 138–52. New York: Plenum.

Kumon, S. 1990. Nihon Kenkyu heno network approach (A network approach in Japan study). In Kokusai Bunka Kaikan (ed.), *Gendai Nippon no seiji keizai*, Vol. **3**: *Nippon no bunka to shakai keizai system (Modern Japanese Politics and Economy*, Vol. **3**: *Culture and Socio-economic Systems in Japan)*, 159–222. Tokyo: Sogo Kenkyu Kaihatsu Kiko.

Lebra, T.S. 1976. *Japanese Patterns of Behavior*. Honolulu: University of Hawaii Press.

Leung, K. 1987. Some determinants of reactions to procedural models for conflict resolution: A cross-national study. *Journal of Personality and Social Psychology*, **53**, 898–908.

Leung, K. and Bond, M. 1984. The impact of cultural collectivism on reward allocation. *Journal Personality and Social Psychology*, **4**, 793–804.

Leung, K., Bond, M.H., Carment, D.W., Krishnan, L. and Liebrand, W.B.G. 1990. Effects of cultural femininity on preference for methods of conflict processing: A cross-cultural study. *Journal of Experimental Psychology*, **26**, 373–88.

Lind, E.A. and Tyler, T.R. 1988. *The Social Psychology of Procedural Justice*. New York: Plenum Press.

Lyons, N.P. 1983. Two perspectives: On self, relationships, and morality. *Harvard Educational Review*, **53**, 125–45.

Markus, H.R. and Kitayama, S. 1991. Culture and the self: Implications for cognition, emotion, and motivation. *Psychological Review*, **98**, 224–53.

Maruyama, K. 1989. *Nihonteki keiei: Sono kozo to behavior (Japanese Style of Management: Its Structures and Behaviors)*. Tokyo: Nihon Hyoronsha.

Ohbuchi, K. and Takahashi, Y. 1994. Cultural styles of conflict. *Journal of Applied Social Psychology*, **24**, 1345–66.

Ohbuchi, K. and Tedeschi, J.T. 1997. Multiple goals and tactical behavior in social conflicts. *Journal of Applied Social Psychology*.

Ohbuchi, K. and Tedeschi, J.T. (in press) Cultural Values in Conflict Management: Goal Orientation, Goal Attainment, and Tactical Decision. *Journal of Cross-Cultural Psychology*.

Okimoto, D.I. 1990. Nippon no seiji kenryoku (Political power in Japan). In Kokusai Bunka Kaikan (ed.), *Gendai Nippon no seiji keizai*, Vol. **3**: *Nippon no bunka to shakai keizai system (Modern Japanese Politics and Economy*, Vol. **3**: *Culture and Socio-economic Systems in Japan)*, 69–112. Tokyo: Sogo Kenkyu Kaihatsu Kiko.

Tanaka, H. and Takeuchi, A. 1987. *Ho no jitsugen ni okeru sijin no yakuwari (Roles of Citizens in Law Enforcement)*. Tokyo: Tokyo University Press.

Thibaut, J. and Kelley, H.H. 1959. *The Social Psychology of Groups*. New York: Wiley.

Thibaut, J. and Walker, L. 1975. *Procedural Justice: A Psychological Analysis*. Hillsdale, NJ: Erlbaum.

Ting-Toomey, S. 1994. Managing conflict in intimate intercultural relationships. In D.D. Cahn (ed.), *Conflict in Personal Relationships* 47–78. Hillsdale, NJ: Lawrence Erlbaum Associates.

Triandis, H. 1980. Values, attitudes, and interpersonal behavior. In M.M. Page (ed.), *Nebraska Symposium on Motivation, 1979*, 195–259. Lincoln, NE: University of Nebraska Press.

Triandis, H. 1994. *Culture and Social Behavior*. New York: McGraw-Hill.

Triandis, H. 1995. *Individualism and Collectivism*. Boulder, CO: Westview Press.

Trubisky, P., Ting-Toomey, S. and Lin, S-L. 1991. The influence of individualism-collectivism and self-monitoring on conflict styles. *International Journal of Intercultural Relation*, **15**, 65–84.

Tyler, T., Degoey, P. and Smith, H. 1996. Understanding why the justice of group procedures matters: A test of the psychological dynamics of the group value model. *Journal of Personality and Social Psychology*, 70, 913–30.

Uchino, T. and Abegrain, J.C. 1988. *Tenki ni tatsu nihongata keiei (A Crisis in Japanese Management)*. Tokyo: Chuo Keizaisha.

Yamagishi, T. 1988. Exit from the group as an individualistic solution to the free rider problem in the United States and Japan. *Journal of Experimental Social Psychology*, **25**, 530–42.

CHAPTER FOUR

Business Negotiation with the Chinese: Evidences from China, Taiwan, and Hong Kong

ANDREW CHI-FAI CHAN
Department of Marketing, Faculty of Business Administration
Chinese University of Hong Kong

Doing business with the Chinese is by no means an easy task and we hear numerous stories of frustration. Good intentions on both sides may backfire, and negotiating with the Chinese is sometimes referred to as the hardest endeavor for foreign business people. Among the various difficulties of doing business with the Chinese, the following are typical: (1) Westerners are pursuing individual well-being while the Chinese are trying to achieve group benefits, (2) inefficient discussion processes, (3) a different negotiating style, (4) negotiators are unclear about their power, and (5) the risk-averse attitude of the Chinese.

Owing to these difficulties, good proposals that are beneficial to both parties have often been delayed or canceled. In this connection, more rigorous studies are needed to help bridge the gap between these two parties, and to help realize the objectives of the two groups.

In any successful business venture, each side has to make a contribution in the hope of adding the partner's competence to its own. However, the various concerns, competence, and contributions of both multinational corporations (MNCs) and the Chinese side are far from clear. With a few exceptions (Tse, Francis, and Walls 1994; Sheng, Chang, and

French 1994; Weldon and Jehn 1996; Leung, *et al.* 1996), we may say that there is a paucity of literature addressing this important issue. Little is known about how negotiations are made and how conflicts are being managed in China and other places (e.g., Taiwan and Hongkong) where the Chinese culture is dominant.

At times, Chinese managers dealing with MNCs are facing a dilemma. On the one hand, they are instructed to conclude deals with foreign business persons so as to obtain the benefits generated from international business activities. On the other hand, those occupying a lower job status in the hierarchy are reluctant to make key decisions which might in the future bring loss to the corporation. In a sense, the desire to do business with foreigners and the traditional Chinese authoritarian decision-making style are not entirely compatible, leading to the failure of many promising business negotiations.

Simyar and Argheyd (1986) summarize the different objectives and concerns of MNCs doing business with the Chinese. A partial list comprises: short-term profitability, local market penetration, cheap labor, cheap resources, the creation of an export base, control of managerial decisions, control of technology, maintenance of flexibility, and risk-aversion. When Chinese managers compare this listing to theirs, they find it difficult to figure out a deal which is highly acceptable to both the MNC and to their superior.

The traditional Chinese perceptions of multinationals affect the negotiation process too. First, the Chinese perceive foreign businesses as imperialist. Second, foreign businesses are in unfair competition with Chinese businesses because they exploit their Chinese workforce/business partners. Third, foreigners are unfriendly or unsympathetic to the Chinese. A foreign business person will have a difficult time in negotiations if the Chinese side brings the above-mentioned mentality to the table. In addition, long prevailing zero-sum thinking is so deeply rooted in the Chinese hierarchy that MNCs have to work harder during negotiations if they want to conclude any deals with the Chinese.

Academics and researchers working on this topic have given the following detailed description of the origin and nature of the problems faced by MNCs while they are doing business with the Chinese.

1. The Chinese philosophy and methods of negotiation will continue to differ from the Western concept.
2. The Chinese are slow to adapt to changes.

3. Managers are reluctant to make decisions—to do nothing is to do no wrong.
4. Time cost is neglected.
5. Non-productive and costly negotiation sessions are normal in business deals.
6. The Chinese are over-sensitive about giving away too much to a foreign firm.

From such a long list, we can appreciate the complications and frustrations of multinationals negotiating with the Chinese. That is why Wang (1988) notes that foreigners are having a difficult time talking business with the Chinese.

Nevertheless, the MNCs bring their distinct competencies to this Chinese connection. The Chinese need finance, technology, management know-how, and marketing skills and contacts. MNCs are in a good position to help by channeling their competence to the Chinese at a relatively low cost. Specifically, MNCs have the practical hands-on experience in business operations which is badly needed by the Chinese. This experience covers various functional areas including general management, finance, marketing, production, research and development, and transmission of this knowledge would be continuous and adapt to changes. While these areas are of paramount importance to the Chinese side, they are not costly to the multinationals. If the two parties can wholeheartedly join forces together to develop their aggregate competence, the result would be highly fruitful.

If MNCs are willing to commit themselves, and are successful in demonstrating their value to the Chinese, potential opportunities can be realized. As the Chinese are relationship oriented (the word *guanxi* is commonly used to describe this web of interpersonal relationships), the company which has developed an initial bond with them will be better protected from future competition.

From the above discussion, we can see that the potential in Chinese ventures is great, but the problems attached to them are numerous. Wang (1984, p.113) notes that tough negotiation is an integral part of Chinese trade deals. At the negotiation table, each side possesses some important monopolistic power and each side also perceives many uncertainties and issues to be discussed. Renegotiation is usually involved, as relative bargaining power varies from time to time. The situation they face is not whether they should negotiate, but whether the negotiated terms and conditions are acceptable to both parties. On the Chinese side, general policies and rules are not specific, leaving a lot of room for interpretation and clarification. Besides, the Chinese view every situation and company from a unique perspective, thus generating numerous deliberations and lengthy talks.

The cultural gap is probably the most widely discussed issue as far as negotiating with the Chinese is concerned. Foreign negotiators find it difficult to understand the Chinese language—even with interpreters, and body language often generates a lot of misunderstanding. Manners and gestures are generally misinterpreted, especially when the Chinese prefer to express their points in a subtle way.

We will now take a closer look at these cultural differences, and try to derive some managerial implications for practitioners. As the focus of this chapter is on the Chinese it should include evidence from Taiwan and Hong Kong. Unfortunately the literature and examples from these two places are very limited. The materials included below are concerned primarily with the issue in China, but they can also shed some light on behavior in the other two places. At the end of this chapter, a special section will be incorporated to discuss some observations on the negotiating behavior of people in Taiwan and Hong Kong, and it will be contrasted with the negotiating behavior of people in China.

The Chinese Cultural Difference

If we accept the tenet that cross-cultural differences do exist in international business negotiations, a natural move would be for us to investigate how two major cultures differ in their negotiation styles and what are the respective prerequisites for negotiation success. While numerous studies have been conducted in the past to shed light on issues related to international negotiations, there is a paucity of empirical studies to investigate how marketing decisions and negotiations are determined in a collectivist Chinese cultural context. Here, we hope to fill the gap and select Chinese culture as one element of an investigation into international business negotiations.

In recent years, a lot of theoretical and empirical work has been done to investigate how Chinese behavior towards Westerners differs in various social contexts. According to Hwang (1987), the assumption that social behavioral patterns and rules of exchange are universal should be challenged, as recent studies show that the Chinese society and other similar societies follow patterns that differentiate them from those of the West. In fact, the collectivism-individualism dimension as a useful way to contrast the Chinese and the Western cultures is supported by much evidence. Hofstede (1980) has empirically identified the individualism-collectivism dimension of national culture, and found that the United States attained the highest score on individualism. Taiwan, Singapore, and Hong Kong (societies with a Chinese background) are on the extreme end of the collectivism scale.

In general, collectivism suggests an emphasis on the social environment and individualism suggests an emphasis on the self. Leung gives a clear definition on individualism/collectivism using 'ingroup-outgroup differences' as a base of reference:

> *"Individualism refers to the tendency to be more concerned about the consequences of one's behavior for one's own needs, interests, and goals, whereas collectivism refers to the tendency to be more concerned about the consequences of one's behavior for in-group members and to be more willing to sacrifice personal interests for the attainment of collective interests. In individualist societies, the distinction between out-groups and in-groups is relatively unimportant, and self-sufficiency is emphasized more. In collectivist societies, behavior toward in-group members may be markedly different from behavior toward out-group members, and values such as interpersonal harmony and group solidarity are more emphasized"*
>
> (Leung 1987 p.899)

Besides collectivism, power distance is another major dimension which differentiates Chinese culture from others (Hofstede 1980). This basic issue involves how different societies solve the question of human inequality. In an organization, inequality is functional and inevitable. This inequality is often embedded in the supervisor and subordinate hierarchy. Usually, we find subordinates trying to reduce the power distance between themselves and their superiors while the management layer are trying to maintain or even enlarge it. In different societies, the level of accepted power distance will be different. Hofstede's definition of power distance is:

> *"The power distance between a boss B and a subordinate S in a hierarchy is the difference between the extent to which B can determine the behavior of S and the extent to which S can determine the behavior of B."*
>
> (Hofstede 1980 p.99)

Table 4.1 A Summary of Theoretical Works on Relationship between Collectivism and Power Distance with Social and Marketing Behavior

Study	Collectivist Antecedents		
	Outcomes	Collectivism	Power Distance
Bond and Wang (1983)	aggressive behavior	harmony conformity ambivalence equality	harmony conformity suppress aggression
Leung and Bond (1984)	reward allocation	group solidarity	social evaluation
Leung (1987)	procedural preference	harmony solidarity	animosity reduction
Hwang (1987)	social behavior	*guanxi* reciprocity	social norm *mianzi* (face)
Shenkar and Ronen (1987)	negotiation behavior	harmony attraction kinship collective indebtedness friendship	harmony control hierarchy hidden motive leadership
Yau (1988)	marketing behavior	harmony *mieutsu* (face) interrelations favor kinship	harmony *mieutsu* (face) modesty authority risk averse moderation
Tse *et al.* (1988)	international marketing decisions	harmony repayment	harmony face authority fatalism

The power distance accepted by both B and S and supported by the social environment is largely determined by culture. It deals with perceptions of the superior's style of decision-making and of subordinates' fear of arguing with superiors, and with the nature of decision-making which subordinates prefer in their managers. In Hofstede's study on collectivism and power distance, it was found that countries dominated by the Chinese culture rank higher in the collectivism scale and lower on the power distance scale. These countries include Singapore, Taiwan, and Hong Kong.

A number of authors have investigated how these two major cultural dimensions, collectivism and power distance, affect the social and marketing behavior of the Chinese. A summary of seven such studies is presented in Table 4.1. The social behavior under consideration comprises aggressive behavior (Bond and Wang 1983), reward allocation (Leung and Bond 1984), procedural preference (Leung 1987), and social behavior (Hwang 1987). These four studies can help to shed light on how a Chinese negotiator would behave under a collective cultural influence. Other authors have studied directly how collectivism and power distance have affected the marketing and negotiation behavior of the Chinese. Areas under investigation are: negotiation behavior (Shenkar and Ronen 1987), marketing implications (Yau 1988), and international marketing decisions (Tse *et al.* 1988). All these studies indicate that collectivism and power distance, two concepts that differentiate the Chinese culture from the West, are affecting the social and marketing behavior of people brought up in a Chinese cultural environment.

LESSONS FROM CASE STUDIES

To identify various important determinants of success in China trade negotiation, we can look at different successful negotiations which have been documented in various publications. By using the concepts mentioned earlier to review these cases, it is possible for us to visualize which factors seem to have significant effects on the performance of foreign negotiators in negotiations with the Chinese. When we combine the broad conclusions from empirical studies and case analysis with respect to China's trade negotiations, we can come up with more realistic and important dependent variables for MNCs' reference. Altogether nine case studies have been selected from various publications. The backgrounds of and information on these cases are drawn from the following sources. Details of the cases are included in Appendix I.

Case	*Sources*
1. Otis Elevator Company	Hendryx (1986a)
2. McDonnell Douglas	Johnson (1986) and Kraar (1986b)
3. National Products	Grow (1987a)
4. SPD Medical Technologies	Grow (1987b)

5. PepsiCo	Kraar (1986a)
6. Occidental Petroleum	Tung (1982), Langston (1984), and Langston (1985)
7. Control Data Corp. (CDC)	Depauw (1981)
8. Electronic Associates, Inc. (EAI)	Tung (1982)
9. American International Group	Tung (1982)

From the cases presented above, we were able to come up with two main observations. The issues of collectivism (to build closer ties with the Chinese) and power distance (to appeal to a superior for decisions) discussed in the previous section are vividly reflected in these cases.

Collectivism in Negotiations

First, the issue of building up friendships with the Chinese should not be underestimated. In the PepsiCo case (case 5), the major objective of the company was to develop personal and friendly relationships with the Chinese, in particular the top Chinese officials. The friendly delegation was very successful and the working and negotiation atmosphere was greatly improved by using this tactic. In the Control Data Corp. (CDC) case (case 7), the issue of friendship was constantly emphasized. To develop better linkages with the Chinese, CDC cooperated with a U.S. consulting firm, mainly because this firm had good contacts with the China Resources Company in Hong Kong and officials in China CDC also contacted Chinese officials whenever they could to familiarize the Chinese with the company and also its product. In addition, the company also established a series of technical seminars for the Chinese to build up friendships between the two parties. Eventually these actions had a good pay-off.

A long-term commitment and a cooperative attitude are also of paramount importance. In the Otis case (case 1), the company wanted to transfer more primitive products and technology to China to meet local requirements with the least technical problems and at a lower cost. On the other hand, the Chinese side hoped to gain the technical skills to produce more advanced products in China in order to substitute them for imports. They wanted to import more advanced technology and produce more advanced items from the beginning. To help close the deal, the company took a cooperative move and drew up a technology transfer schedule emphasizing both demands of the Chinese market and operational feasibility.

In the National Products case (case 3), the American team tried to be as cooperative as possible. They strove to develop a good working relationship with the Chinese engineers, and they spent a lot of time and effort to design a new production configuration scaled to the specific needs of the Fuyang plant. The U.S. selling points included: (1) hands-on training (some in the U.S.), (2) lower cost structure in the long-run, and (3) a tailor-made proposal to suit Fuyang's specific problems and requirements (unlike the Japanese offer). To establish a better relationship with the Chinese, Electronic Associates, Inc. (EAI) (case 8) also adopted a highly cooperative attitude. Mr. Sanders, V-P. of Marketing, specially made an appointment with the Director of the Bank of China in Hong Kong to foster better linkages with the PRC. The company asked the Chori Trading Company, a Japanese trading corporation (which happened to be China's old friend), to help channel EAI's literature to the proper technical agency in China. In addition, the International Marketing V-P., in conjunction with EAI's office in Japan, conducted a very successful seminar on analog and hybrid simulation with officials in China. All these cooperative moves resulted in the company receiving an invitation to Beijing for further technical discussion and negotiation. From these three cases, we can see that a strong commitment and a cooperative attitude are necessary for a foreign company to become successful in trade negotiations with China.

Power Distance in Negotiations

In order for a negotiation to be successful in the PRC, a foreign negotiator must obtain support from high-ranking executives. In this regard, a foreign manager should see to it that the needs of high-ranking decision-makers are catered to and that the key officials are involved in the negotiation. In the McDonnell Douglas case (case 2), in addition to supplying China with cheaper aircraft, the company also assisted in realizing the Chinese desire to develop a manufacturing base for commercial aircraft and eventually helped in selling the Chinese products in the international market. While a cheaper product was seemingly the major selling point, it was the company's ability to show the top Chinese management that the Americans could assist them to realize their long-term goal that actually paved the way to closing the deal.

In the PepsiCo case (case 5), the chairman of the company, Donald Kendall, led a strong delegation to China. His delegation was supported by a letter from former President Nixon (China's 'old friend'), which helped them to cut through the bureaucratic hierarchy to meet Zhao Ziyang, the then Premier of the People's Republic of China. The delegation included ten of PepsiCo's directors, and an accompanying crew of 49 people. They were backed up with information on who had the real power to make key decisions in China. In the big cities in China, the delegation was able to develop relationships with other key people in China including Liang Xiang and Ye Xuanping (top government officials in Hainan and Guangdong Province). In Beijing, U.S. Ambassador Winston Lord joined the delegation and visited Premier Zhao Ziyang. With strong involvement from the top officials, the business environment of PepsiCo was improved greatly.

For the Occidental case (case 6), we can see that a key point for the company's success was that Occidental chairman A. Hammer was able to involve key leaders such as Zhao Ziyang, Hu Yaobang, and Deng Xiaoping in the deal. The negotiation environment turned favorable when Deng confirmed the involvement of China in the venture, and that China would back up its commitment in respect to international business cooperation. Moreover, the ability of the company to meet China's high-level need—to establish its energy resources and to obtain advanced equipment and technology—was another reason for its success in the negotiation. The American International Group (AIG) people (case 9) also adopted this high-level persuasion tactic and achieved good results. A strong company delegation, including Mr. Greenberg, president and C.E.O., Mr. Manton, executive vice-president, and Mr. Freeman, regional head of the Far East operation, was able to generate a reciprocal exchange agreement from the Chinese which paved the way for further negotiation and business. Their success reflects the fact that Chinese negotiators have a due respect for power and authority, both to their own superiors and to their negotiation partners.

As most Chinese negotiators would prefer to accept orders from high-ranking officials and not take excessive risks, foreign negotiators may want, whenever possible, to help the Chinese counterpart to justify the venture before their bosses. Of course going straight to the decision-maker at the top would be useful, but in the Chinese context it is often difficult to judge who is the decision-maker or who has the final say. In the SPD Medical Technologies (SPD) case (case 4), SPD requested a contractual assurance that its proprietary formulas and manufacturing techniques would be kept confidential. SPD lawyers wanted to include provisions in the contract that would set remedial measures in motion if the conditions were violated. This hurdle was overcome when an outside agency, a municipal economic organization, was invited to assist in the drafting of the guarantees. By so doing, responsibility was shifted outward and the Chinese felt more secure.

The reluctance of the Chinese to take risks and to make prompt decisions is also indicated in case 7, the Control Data Corp. (CDC) case. In many situations, CDC tried hard to show the negotiation team that the company's technology would continue to be the state-of-the-art. The company also answered detailed queries from the Chinese with comprehensive answers and forceful arguments which helped the Chinese negotiators to face possible criticisms or enquiries from their own superiors. To minimize risk, the company included a third party at the negotiation table: the Compagnie Generale de Geophysique (CGG). CGG had sold oil exploration equipment to the Chinese for a long time and was regarded by the Chinese as their old friend. In the closing stages, much of the talk was handled by the CGG personnel. Ultimately, a contract was signed.

In the American International Group (AIG) case (case 9), we can also see that the Chinese reluctance to accept risk has strong implications for their final decision. AIG won the acceptance of the Chinese mainly because of: (1) AIG being the biggest insurance company in the world; (2) the company's long association with China; and, (3) AIG having offices full of Chinese in the Far East. All these contributed to the company's ability to minimize the perceived risk of the Chinese.

DETERMINANTS OF NEGOTIATION SUCCESS

In this section, the dimensions identified from the nine cases are combined with concepts derived from relevant works to generate the important determinants of success when a foreign negotiator is closing a business deal with Chinese negotiators. Table 4.2 presents an overview of previous studies in this area. They can help shed light on various forces affecting the success of negotiation with the Chinese. Five main determinants are identified: friendship, positive attitude, long range view, competitive tactics, and risk-averse behavior.

Table 4.2 Factors Related to Success in Trade Negotiations with China

	Positive Factors			Negative Factors	
Study	Friendship	Positive Attitude	Long-run View	Competi-tiveness	Risk
Depauw (1981)	*	*		*	*
Tung (1982)	*	*			
Pye (1982)	*	*	*	*	*
Wang (1984)		*	*	*	
Saunders and Chong (1986)	*		*	*	*
Wang (1986)		*		*	*
Tung (1986)		*	*		*
Pye (1986)	*		*	*	
Hendryx (1986b)		*			*
Brunner and You (1988)	*	*			*
Kirkbride and Tang (1990)	*		*		*
Pan, Kim, and Vanhonacker (1995)					*
Yuen (1997)			*	*	

Note: * = key factor under investigation in the study

Friendship

The issue of friendship is important in Chinese trade negotiations, and the Chinese like to deal with 'old friends'. The Chinese usually place a premium on relationship, and 'old friends' are those people who can be counted on personally and can be relied upon to recommend other trustworthy parties. Earning the term 'old friends' should be a trader's goal in the negotiation exercise. Basically, the Chinese distrust total strangers and will try to avoid them. However, they may welcome strangers whom they meet through relatives, good friends, or colleagues. They are interested in establishing *guanxi*, a term meaning relationship and suggesting also mutual benefit.

In this regard, companies should persist in their efforts to develop friendships with their Chinese partners, no matter how difficult the situation may be. The Chinese will favor old friends who have stood by them, and they will substantially benefit their old friends when a favorable situation arises. Chinese people are very appreciative of those who are loyal and have supported them in hard times, and will duly reward them when the opportunity arises. Long-term relationships or friendships are preferred by the Chinese.

Friendship in the Chinese context includes an expectation of what friends should be willing to do for each other, and this goes well beyond American notions of friendliness. The constantly repeated theme of Chinese negotiators' friendship is considered a major element in shaping the atmosphere surrounding negotiations. The Chinese seem to have a compelling need to dwell on the subject of friendship, and reciprocity is a norm for doing Chinese business. Sometimes, the Chinese will consider the other party unfriendly if it does not give them special treatment.

The personal and friendly approach is stressed by many successful businessmen negotiating with the Chinese. For the Westerner, business and personal relationships are often kept strictly apart, but this is generally not true for the Chinese for whom people, loyalty, and trust have a high priority. Courtesy and manners should be given the greatest attention at all times and businessmen should never underestimate any member in a negotiation team.

When making deals with the Chinese, special attention must be paid to the Chinese notion of friendship (Pye 1986). He suggests that a foreigner should not over-emphasize, define, or seek unduly to constrain the Chinese partner with a formal contract. To the Chinese mind, a deal is shaped much more through human relationships established through the negotiations and actual conduct of the business than through the written word. One should understand that the Chinese place great value on loyalty and the contract is not as important as relationships. As a matter of fact, the Chinese can make heavy demands on friends, and they do not place many limits on how they can use friendships to their advantage. Discussions about the contract may be reopened after contract signing, because the Chinese might consider that the two parties are now old friends who can bring matters up anytime.

Relating to the dynamics and consequences of 'face' to the Chinese, it is suggested that foreign negotiators should not cause the Chinese to lose face, but instead endeavor to give face whenever appropriate. Face is closely tied to friendship. If a negotiator is effective in developing a bond of friendship by 'giving face', the Chinese will reciprocate by doing the same. A sense of *guanxi* may evolve and this bonding implies that 'we all have face'. Throughout the meeting, the Chinese group will emphasize the importance of mutual respect, cooperation, and an enduring and deep friendship. Usually, gifts will be exchanged as a gesture of status, respect, and to 'give face' to the recipient, which will help solidify friendship and business relations.

However, the building of friendships with the Chinese may lead to negative impacts too. According to the above discussion, the Chinese will reward persons who have supported them, give special treatment to friends, and make significant sacrifices for good friends. The other side of the coin is that the Chinese will demand all these if a MNC negotiator is qualified as an old friend of the Chinese. In this circumstance, the Chinese may make 'unreasonable' demands on the western negotiator. Being a 'friend' of the Chinese brings both privileges and responsibilities.

The situation is further complicated if an ethnic Chinese is present in the MNC negotiation team. While there are positive impacts if an ethnic Chinese is sitting at the negotiation table, negative impacts are introduced too (Wang 1986, Lee 1989, Lee 1990). One key question being asked by most MNCs in assigning ethnic Chinese to a trade talk in China is: will split-loyalty affect the ethnic Chinese negotiator? One speculation is that if *friendship* would imply excessive demands from the Chinese side, an *ethnic Chinese* would face the same pressure from the Chinese side, especially in behind-the-scenes discussion (Lee and Lo 1988). If the ethnic Chinese has already developed a good friendship with the Chinese side, the role conflict of that boundary person would be even greater—the Chinese can make heavy demands on good friends, and an ethnic Chinese is expected to be patriotic and give special favors to his or her motherland. Put differently, friendship between MNC ethnic Chinese and the Chinese side would have its pros and cons. It is the MNC's duty to determine whether ethnic Chinese should be employed and how they should be deployed under such circumstances.

Positive Attitude

Besides friendship, it is also important for a negotiator to adopt a cooperative attitude to foster a coordinative relationship with the Chinese counterpart. A negotiator should try to demonstrate a positive attitude which can help him in earning genuine respect from the Chinese. In establishing relationships with the Chinese, a lengthy period is necessary in most instances. This sometimes reflects the Chinese emphasis on getting to know each other and their real concern to test a business partner's friendliness and sincerity. Whenever possible, a negotiator should try to understand the value to the Chinese of achieving a more favorable convergence of interests. In this connection, Depauw (1981) has suggested the use of a Chinese 'old friend' to act as middleman in the negotiation process. In all events, gestures of cooperation and good will are beneficial in the business negotiation.

To build up a cooperative attitude, one should try to understand the needs of the Chinese as far as technical knowledge, economic strength, self-reliance and social construction are concerned. A negotiator with a positive attitude will be more successful, as the Chinese really mean it when they say that business should be operated under the principle of 'equality and mutual benefit'.

Generally, the Chinese would expect that senior executives would visit them—that is, go to the place where the Chinese side is located—as an indicator of a good attitude. 'Face' is gained if the president or other high official can initiate the negotiating process. If this high executive can also establish relationships with the leaders in the local political hierarchy, such as the mayor or trade minister, greater legitimacy can be established. This type of cooperative attitude will symbolize possession of 'face' and a smooth business relationship can be fostered.

Generally, the Chinese view is that all successful negotiations require a high degree of mutual trust and respect. Usually, the Chinese are not only interested in buying advanced technology for the sake of production. They also like to use the acquisition as a way of obtaining formal training for their engineers. The Chinese are looking for self-reliance, and they want their engineers to be able to use the latest technologies with minimum instructions from the foreign partner. Basically, a positive and cooperative attitude will improve the outcome of a business negotiation.

On the issue of cooperation, Wang (1984) stresses that a foreign negotiator should be able to put himself in the shoes of the Chinese and understand what the Chinese are faced with. It is to the foreign parties' advantage to find a way through the bureaucratic layers and official guidelines. For example, incentives such as free technical assistance are valued highly by the Chinese. In most cases, making use of ethnic Chinese personnel can help narrow the cultural gap. Multinationals with a positive attitude will perform better in their negotiation activities.

In order to demonstrate a positive attitude, businessmen doing business with China should try to understand the real needs of the Chinese. Firms should be concerned with issues considered by the Chinese in their long-term plans. The negotiation team should be able to answer any technical questions raised by the engineers and technical people on the Chinese side. If possible, the team should approach both the trade corporations and the end-users in China. Second, the team should try to eliminate the negative effects caused by the language barrier. They should understand what the Chinese are capable of understanding. Important documents should be prepared in both languages and ample copies should be made available to all the relevant decision-makers. The team may also use American-Chinese to serve as channels for communication and to interpret the real meaning of the hidden language. Third, a genuine willingness to help and a frank attitude can minimize the negotiator's worry that they may be caught by hidden implications. All these will help in building up a good business relationship with the Chinese.

To obtain a successful joint venture, managers must be able to locate the origins of problems and be able to lobby the local bureaucracy in order to strengthen the business relationship between them. Rigorous and properly directed efforts of the foreign partner are required in order to generate more cooperation on the Chinese side, and to make the bureaucracy more receptive to the value generated by the MNC.

Long Range View

Researchers usually criticize the Americans' short-term view and myopic calculation of the *quid pro quo* when they are doing business with the Chinese. The Chinese have a longer range view of things and are in less of a hurry. They have a different definition of timeliness and insist that 'investment' in a relationship cannot be hurried.

As far as the time horizon is concerned, it is suggested that a MNC should develop business even if there is no immediate profit at all. If steps are not taken in advance, and friendships are not developed to a certain extent, the Chinese market may become too crowded for the MNCs to attempt entry at a later stage of China's development. In addition, the multinational should be careful not to project an image of deception or of being too clever. The Chinese favor the gradual building up of relationships and consider some expedient measures as deceitful. A reputation of dishonesty is extremely harmful in Chinese business negotiations, as information will soon spread among officials and a clean reputation cannot be established overnight.

On the issue of patience, it was suggested that we should not undervalue the importance of preliminary discussions and talks with subordinates. While big sales are usually made in the headquarters, contacts and negotiations at other places such as the user sections are prerequisites. In some cases it may take months or even years for progress to be made; but if one wants to do business with the Chinese, patience and a long-range view are necessary.

In general, short stays and a limited commitment in the Chinese venture will not result in high performance because the expatriate barely has the time to adjust to the Chinese cultural and business system. Furthermore, the building of a constructive business relationship takes time. A longer-range involvement is therefore recommended if a foreign firm wants to establish something substantial in China.

Hence, businessmen should be patient in the actual negotiations and in designing an overall strategy. Impatience will make a businessman vulnerable to manipulation and will produce premature agreements that can later lead to misunderstanding and conflicts.

Competitive Tactics

Chinese competitive tactics are considered to be critical factors which will influence the outcome of a business negotiation in China. A businessman closing deals with the Chinese must place great emphasis on this issue in order to negotiate forcefully in China. Basically, the Chinese are tough negotiators and they like to rely on competition to ask for greater concessions.

Sometimes, the Chinese negotiator will purposely stimulate other competitors to enter the scene by publicizing the business negotiation, hence strengthening the bargaining power of the Chinese side. The Chinese believe that their bargaining position can be improved by keeping their partners slightly uncomfortable. By encouraging passive trading partners to become more active, the current partners will serve the Chinese need better and will not take their successes for granted. To achieve this, the Chinese like to play the host's role which allows them to be able to play off competitors against each other. Pye (1982) reported that in certain cases, competitors were presenting their seminars at the same time on different floors of the same hotel. The Chinese went from one floor to the other, commenting to each rival about the selling points of the others. In such a situation, foreign companies become especially vulnerable. Generally, competitiveness, either natural or deliberately induced by the Chinese, will affect the success of a foreign businessman negotiating with the Chinese.

In addition to the competition coming from other businessmen, Chinese corporations negotiating foreign deals have the backing of the entire state. Internal competition among themselves is kept to a minimum. This sort of centralized endeavor gives the Chinese negotiators an upper hand when they are dealing with MNCs. Collusion among transnationals is rare and they generally compete with one another for the contract from China.

Though the Chinese generally prefer a slower pace in the negotiation process, they are by no means weak negotiators. In some cases, they will quite ruthlessly play off one company against another. The leaking of a firm's proposal to competitive companies is not uncommon (Saunders and Chong 1986).

It is also noted that the Chinese negotiators will play their cards 'close to the chest' while at the same time insisting that visitors show their hands. It is a common strategy for the Chinese to reveal information about competitors as a way of trying to pry out secrets.

The Chinese are also good at increasing their bargaining power by using friendship as a weapon. In trade talks, it is common for the Chinese to demand extra favors or treatments from MNC negotiators—in exchange for long-term friendship with the Chinese. If the negotiator is an ethnic Chinese, the Chinese side may also appeal to the negotiator's patriotism, both in front of and behind the negotiation table, to get the biggest advantage they can in the trade deal. In this regard, though the use of ethnic Chinese in China business negotiator may have its advantages, MNCs should pay special care in order not to be hurt by this double-edged sword.

Risk-averse Behavior

When negotiating with the Chinese, a businessman may find himself facing a group of risk-averse persons. The Chinese tend to negotiate in very literal terms, as the complex Chinese bureaucratic structure demands this. Terms that are taken for granted in the U.S. are given very careful and detailed treatment in China. This risk-averse behavior makes negotiations lengthy, difficult, and demanding. Before a decision is made to purchase a product, Chinese buyers will try to learn as much as possible about the product and the technology related to it. This will inhibit the efficient progress of a business negotiation.

Chinese negotiators take the issue of risk very seriously. They know that their careers can be jeopardized, and they can be punished, if the negotiation results are criticized by others. Hence, they try to back away from responsibility and this inevitably delays or even hampers the negotiation process. The situation becomes even worse when the negotiating team reports to another group of officials who have similar concerns for their own safety. In the Chinese context, the critical act in a bureaucratic process is to avoid responsibility. More often than not, commands and decisions are diffused and not precise at all. No one person can clearly cut through the problems and procedures and produce an effective decision. The rules of the game are to leave nobody vulnerable to criticism. Moreover, the layers of committees in the Chinese hierarchy will allow no one to definitely say yes or no.

In order to play it safe, the Chinese move at a slow pace. Cautious and suspicious, especially when they are dealing with unfamiliar foreign negotiators, they are strongly inclined to keep their objectives and positions secret throughout the whole negotiation process. Nonetheless, they like to insist that the other party reveals its interests first.

The Chinese concern for safety is further manifested in their negotiation behavior. The Chinese want to deal with the 'number one' or the 'best', regardless of cost. Chinese culture is hierarchical, and one should care for whoever is at the top. When the idea of 'familiarity' conflicts with the idea of 'dealing with the best', the latter usually wins out. The Chinese welcome friendly businessmen but will prefer doing business with enterprises that have been classified as among the best. In the Chinese system, clear requirements and specifications are lacking, so that negotiators must report on the business situation to their superiors and then learn whether they find it of value. Though Chinese enterprises are now allowed to negotiate separately, Chinese negotiators still think that it is inappropriate for them not to consult with their supervisors and other parties concerned. To them, autonomy means vulnerability.

Following this argument, it is recommended that negotiators never show impatience. Patience is the watchword in Chinese trade negotiation as the Chinese feel that patience and time-consuming talks can help one know one's counterpart better. This will avoid negative comments from superiors and minimize the possibility of punishment.

In addition, the Chinese prefer to talk business with someone who has the reputation of putting all his cards on the table. When they have even a slight suspicion about the hidden implications of a deal, they will hold back from making their decisions. Hence, even when a negotiator is asked to take charge of the whole deal, he may still want to get the 'green light' from his superior from time to time.

A major problem in negotiation with the Chinese is that it is often difficult for a foreign businessman to figure out who is in charge and who is supposed to make the decision. To avoid criticism and responsibility, several different departments will devise plans on their own, and then gradually reach a consensus with the other departments. Generally, ideas are submitted to different groups for review, hoping for a consensus. A single decision may require agreement among the heads of several departments within the enterprise. If the decision requires higher approval, a consensus among several bureau heads or other high officials may be necessary.

This situation is further aggravated by the fact that different departments in a Chinese company may have more affiliations or ties with their counterparts in the planning and government bureaucracies than they have to other departments in their own organization. It is common to find a series of local functional bureaus overseeing various functions within a company. The department heads report not only to the general manager of the plant but also to the respective municipal functional bureaus, and each local bureau reports to its corresponding ministry. This sort of reporting system usually affects the effectiveness and efficiency of business negotiations in China.

To summarize, we can see that the first four issues mentioned above (friendship, positive attitude, long-range view, and competitive tactics) are related to collectivism while the fifth one (risk-averse behavior) is related to power distance. If a long-run friendship develops between the foreign negotiator and the Chinese, the collective value will prevail which is greatly beneficial to the foreign negotiator. When the Chinese regard a person as an insider, they may be willing to sacrifice part of their personal interest in exchange for collective interest. This sort of advantage is usually attached more to the person than to the terms of the deal (Shenkar and Ronen 1987). Inexperienced businessmen doing business in China will be puzzled about why their sales pitch fails even if their terms are more competitive than their competitors.

Conversely, if the Chinese treat a foreigner as an outsider, the Chinese can be very competitive. Sometimes, the Chinese will encourage more competitors to join so as to gain more bargaining power. Tough tactics will be used which will lower the profit margin of a foreign company. This factor interacts with the accepted power distance of the Chinese to further aggravate the situation. They are unlikely to challenge their superior to change to a new way of doing business. Lines of authority are vague and nobody is absolutely certain as to who has the real decision-making power. The more the negotiator understands about the power structure of the Chinese hierarchy, the better he is able to jump over the bureaucratic hurdles and reach the closing stage of the negotiation exercise (Warrington and McCall 1983; Shenkar and Ronen 1987).

In relation to the boundary role position of ethnic Chinese in a MNC, it is argued that the ethnic Chinese can help generate a more efficient and satisfactory negotiation environment than a western negotiator. Nevertheless, they are subject to negative impacts including (1) a second-class image and (2) the Chinese side will take advantage of them. In addition, split-loyalty may be another concern that hinders the ethnic Chinese from making the most appropriate decision for the venture. To realize the benefits generated from employing ethnic Chinese in trade talks in China, the specific pros and cons of them should be carefully studied by MNCs.

SUGGESTIONS TO NEGOTIATORS

Overall Implications

Looking at the case studies and relevant Chinese negotiation studies, several inferences can be made. Nearly all studies indicate that foreign negotiators should try to understand the Chinese culture and to develop interaction, *guanxi*, and long-term relationships with the Chinese. In many cases, the decision to cooperate is not made at the negotiating table; agreements and acceptance are established in informal gatherings or even social encounters. An ethnic Chinese executive from the home country would be helpful to further build up the atmosphere of kinship. In all events, a strong commitment and a genuine willingness to work with the Chinese towards a collective goal is mandatory to establish a successful deal. When strong ties are established and the Chinese officials accept a person as an in-group member, discussions will be more open and hurdles will more easily be eliminated. To build up close bonding, one common method is to give 'face' or deliver some favors to the

Chinese negotiator. Though it is difficult to build up a friendship with the Chinese, once built it will last for a long time. This friendship is particularly useful to a foreign negotiator as the Chinese will try to compensate an 'old' friend who knows how to give 'face' and who has helped the Chinese in their difficult times. However, if a person is not classified by the Chinese as their friend, the Chinese can be extremely tough and competitive and being 'in-group' or 'out-group' makes a lot of difference (Leung 1987).

These studies also indicate that the Chinese negotiators would prefer to follow instructions from their superiors and are reluctant to accept risk. Individual decisions are de-emphasized and nobody wants to 'rock the boat'. Rules and guidelines should be observed and the party policies should always take a dominant position. Within such a system, only executives in a very high position can actually interpret the rules and make concrete decisions. To minimize risk, the Chinese rely heavily on time-consuming group interaction, deliberation, and consensus. A simple decision may have to go through numerous groups and committees making the negotiation very inefficient. In Chinese negotiations, the rule of the game is to think long-term and help every individual concerned to justify his case in front of his superiors and other influential bodies. Foreign negotiators who are impatient and who are unable to help the Chinese minimize their risk exposure in the hierarchy seldom become successful in the Chinese business culture.

Another issue closely related to obtaining support from high officials in China is that the venture must be able to benefit all the various parties concerned. Prompt approval will be given when the venture fits the group priorities. Moreover, the goodwill and reputation of the foreign company will be an asset when its negotiators call on Chinese officials. By negotiating with the market leader in the industry, the Chinese negotiators can evade responsibility by claiming that they are now dealing with the biggest company, one which offers state-of-the-art technology.

Practical Guidelines

The following are some practical guidelines for MNCs while negotiating with the Chinese. It is suggested that the precise role of the MNC and its value to the Chinese should be explained at the outset of negotiations. The better both sides understand one another, the greater will be the probability of closing a good deal. Following the principle of mutual benefit and the adoption of a positive-sum game philosophy, differences between the objectives of the Chinese and the demands of profit-seeking multinationals could be reconciled (Wang 1988). Mun (1988, 1989) has made several suggestions for both the multinationals and the Chinese negotiators: (1) appropriate specification of terms in a contract, (2) choice of a good partner, (3) a cooperative attitude towards the other's goals, motivations, and expectations, and (4) a win-win mentality.

In overcoming hurdles in negotiations with the Chinese, other guidelines are suggested. First, presentation of important documents in both languages (with many copies) can give the relevant decision-makers an opportunity to fully appreciate the possible benefits that could be generated by the venture. Second, multinationals should take the initiative to approach and understand the concerns of the Chinese, and try to present to them, in the most simple and direct way, the benefits the venture would bring. Third, high-level foreign executives should try to visit the Chinese corporations, as the Chinese are hierarchy-minded. Fourth, in significant business negotiations all relevant Chinese parties should be catered to, as both the high-level decision-makers and the lower-level users are important groups. Fifth, the inclusion of Chinese personnel on the MNC side is usually suggested. Finally, MNCs can utilize trade linkages (to people, institutions, or government bodies) to meet the competing needs and concerns, thus facilitating a more effective and efficient business outcome.

The recruitment and training of appropriate staff for the negotiation team is an important element in an MNC's agenda. Many Chinese negotiation experts agree that it is important to train to reduce the cultural distance and select the right people for the foreign negotiation team. Hence, many negotiation experts recommend the inclusion of Chinese in the foreign team. As they are familiar with the Chinese culture and the 'silent language' used, they will be in a better position to make suggestions regarding the presentation of certain point of views that involve cultural differences.

Chinese executives in an MNC can make significant behind-the-scenes contributions in trade negotiations with China, as the Chinese side would prefer to approach these 'bridges' (between cultures) if they have queries or want to solve any issues. As we know, the Chinese have the habit of making the real decision before the formal meeting; this behavior increases the value of having Chinese personnel on the foreign team.

CONFLICT MANAGEMENT IN JOINT VENTURES

The previous sections emphasize closing deals with the Chinese. Nevertheless, MNCs should also consider future day-to-day cooperation with the Chinese after signing of the contract (Leung, *et al.* 1996; Ding 1997). Once the contract is signed, many foreigners might think that that is the end of the business transaction. The Chinese, however, probably think that it is the beginning of a new business relationship. To the Chinese, a good relationship is hard to build and also hard to break. The MNCs should therefore capitalize on any old relationships and further deepen them, as the Chinese constantly re-define the relationship between the two parties to develop new ways to cooperate in the future.

While it would be difficult for newcomers to break the relationship, a foreign businessman should never be too complacent about a working relationship with the Chinese, even if a written agreement has been signed. Once the Chinese label a person as an in-group member, the Chinese will treat him or her as an 'old friend', but they also expect an 'old friend' to behave as an 'old friend'. The aforementioned factors for success in business deals, including friendliness, a positive attitude, a long-run view, risk-avoidance, the face dynamic, and favor-giving will continue to apply in the day-to-day management of the joint venture. In fact, the MNC should consider each day a new day and an opportunity to re-define the working relationship with the Chinese, with the contract acting as a rough guideline to the scope of the venture. That is, the MNC should adopt the concept of relationship marketing, but not the traditional transactional marketing concept, when they deal with the Chinese in the course of implementing the joint venture plan (Kirkbride and Tang 1990). As suggested by the relationship marketing concept, a foreign businessman has to constantly appraise his present relationship with the Chinese, estimate the bargaining power of both sides, estimate the value of the existence of the joint venture, determine how the relationship could continue, and, most importantly, try to develop true bonding between the two parties. A successful foreigner should be able to make the Chinese partner happy and comfortable, and should not create any trouble that would hamper a good working relationship.

Any relationship building endeavor should not be confined to the top Chinese executives. The Chinese are very relationship conscious: they constantly appraise whether the foreign partners have good relationships with their colleagues and subordinates. The balance theory in psychology applies beautifully in Chinese business management. Nevertheless, one note of caution is that relationships should be built within some acceptable limits. The foreign businessman should never try to win too much acceptance from the significant others, as this would lead to suspicion and may spoil the relationship. In the eyes of the Chinese, an excessive degree of friendliness with significant others will do more harm than good, especially when the business deal is closed and the foreign partner is considered to be an insider. Once considered as an in-group member, a foreign partner has to re-define his role and has to adapt to a new set of rules.

In managing a joint venture, a good principle is to think of terms in the contract as guidelines, and recognise that the real venture relies on the daily re-definition of the working relationship. This working relationship includes bonding with various segments, and whether the venture can be carried out smoothly depends on the aggregated effect of these bondings. As mentioned earlier, the Chinese are strong negotiators, and they will from time to time bring competitors into the play. The foreign businessman should continuously justify to the Chinese side that their business relationship is the optimal one and there is no need for the Chinese side to consider new partners. The best strategy is to demonstrate to the Chinese executive that the two partners are on the same wavelength, and the well-being of both sides rests on the shoulders of both parties.

Another good strategy in managing a joint venture is to develop new joint ventures (of course, better joint ventures) with the Chinese. The MNC should be able to lead the game by constantly reviewing the business environment, the changing competencies of various parties, and to develop its value to the venture. It should always try to develop win-win situations whereby the Chinese executives not only benefit, but are also considered by their peers to be doing a good job. When the Chinese are working with you on new ventures, existing ones are better protected. Of course, the MNC should carefully handle the existing joint ventures as their failure will affect the face mechanism and damage the good relationship with the Chinese side.

DIFFERENCES BETWEEN TAIWAN AND HONG KONG

As suggested by Pan (1996) and Hung (1997), there is a need for researchers and businessmen to adopt new paradigms and research tools to cope with the great differences in the Asia Pacific region in general, and in countries with a dominant Chinese culture (namely China, Taiwan, and Hong Kong) in particular. Nevertheless, literature and academic works on Taiwan and Hong Kong are very limited. In the following, some observations on the similarities and differences of the behavior in these places are described, and some implications are noted to guide researchers and conflict management practitioners.

In general, we are able to find many similarities among Chinese in these three places. The concepts of collectivism, power distance, risk-aversion, face, *guanxi*, etc. can easily be found in many social settings and business occasions. Naturally, because of historical reasons, the norms of social behavior in Taiwan and Hong Kong deviate somewhat from those in China. In fact, the norm in China nowadays also differs from the traditional Chinese doctrines, as it is affected by both political and ideological factors. Broadly speaking, the negotiation behavior in Taiwan and Hong Kong is shaped by two major forces: traditional Chinese culture and a western philosophy of business management.

Businessmen in Taiwan and Hong Kong are group conscious in the sense that they treat in-group members better than out-group members. Being affected by the traditional culture, they are also order or power conscious. Everybody in the management ladder has his or her unique position, and a person is expected to behave and speak according to that specific position. The issue of *guanxi* or relationship is important, and the negotiator will act, respond, and give concessions according to the *guanxi* between the two parties. Of course, the effect of face should not be underestimated. Though it may not be strong enough to close a big business, it can hamper the good relationship between the parties and create hurdles in negotiations and conflict resolution cases (Dai 1993).

Nevertheless, as managers in Taiwan and Hong Kong are also influenced by the western management philosophy (including American and British), they are also assertive, innovative, and flexible in meeting challenges (Pan, Kim and Vanhonacker 1995). The ownership and reward system also affects the way negotiators behave. In China, a majority of the decisions are made for the state, the province, and other public institutions. The line of authority is very unclear and Chinese executives tend to adopt risk-avoidance strategies, especially when the foreign party is not recognized as an 'old friend', or when the executive is not at the top of the management ladder. On the other hand, executives in Taiwan and Hong Kong are generally entrepreneurs or are working for risk-taking profit-making business enterprises. The management norm will reward risk-taking but profitable ventures. Hence, it is quite common for us to see many big business talks being closed in a very short period of time. Negotiators from Taiwan and Hong Kong are both flexible and efficient, as they have greater power and autonomy to negotiate deals. In China, face will be lost if a person takes too big a risk and makes an error. In Taiwan and Hong Kong, face will be lost if a person takes too few risks and misses a golden opportunity. Hence, we can see that the deep-rooted traditional Chinese cultural norms and the modernized western management philosophy are both important determinants in business negotiations and long-term international cooperation.

Owing to their unique characteristics, the Chinese in Hong Kong and Taiwan can work effectively and efficiently with both the Chinese in China and businessmen from western countries. They are able to adapt to various bargaining situations and change their strategies accordingly. In addition, they could serve as an excellent 'bridge' or middleman between China and the rest of the world as they are familiar both with the cultural values and bureaucratic practices in China and with the mentality and decision-making rules of Westerners. They are in a very good position to detect areas for cooperation and so generate many workable alternatives, and to clear the hurdles in negotiations. Acting as a 'lubricant', businessmen from Taiwan and Hong Kong can add value to a coalition (Mun and Chan 1986; Pan and Tse 1996).

If multinationals can clearly understand the specific differences and similarities in the negotiation behavior of the Chinese, they can better design their investment strategies to grasp opportunities and meet challenges in this part of the world. At the end of the day, all parties would benefit.

REFERENCES AND BIBLIOGRAPHY

Bond, M.H. and Wang, S.H. 1983. 'China: Aggressive Behavior and the Problem of Maintaining Order and Harmony' in A.P. Goldstein and M.H. Segall (eds.), *Aggression in Global Perspective*, N.Y.: Pergamon Press, 58–74.

Brunner, J.A. and You, W. 1988. 'Chinese Negotiation and the Concept of Face', *Journal of International Consumer Marketing*, **1**, 27–43.

Dai, Z.Y. 1993. *Negotiation*, Taiwan, ROC: Growth International Cultural Enterprises. (In Chinese.)

DePauw, J.W. 1981. *US-Chinese Trade Negotiation*, N.Y.: Praeger Publishers.

Ding, Daniel Z. 1997. 'Control, Conflicts and Performance - A Case of U.S.-Chinese Joint Ventures', *Marketing Department Working Paper Series* **No. MKT97-03-0**, City University of Hong Kong.

Grow, R.F. 1987a. 'How Factories Choose Technology', *The China Business Review*, May-June, 35–9.

Grow, R.F. 1987b. 'A Pharmaceutical Deal', *The China Business Review*, November-December, 40–3.

Hendryx, S.R. 1986a. 'Implementation of a Technology Transfer Joint Venture in the People's Republic of China: A Management Perspective,' *Columbia Journal of World Business*, Spring, 57–66.

Hendryx, S.R. 1986b. 'The China Trade: Making the Deal Work', *Harvard Business Review*, July-August, **75**, 81–4.

Hofstede, G. 1980. *Culture's Consequences: International Differences in Work-Related Values*, Beverly Hills, CA: Sage Publications.

Hung, C. 1997. 'Using the Third Eye to Look at China: Exploring Strategies for Foreign and Hong Kong Businessmen in China Investment', *The Hong Kong Economic Journal*, May, 32–4. (In Chinese.)

Hwang, K.K. 1987. 'Face and Favor: The Chinese Power Game', *American Journal of Sociology*, January, **92**, 944–74.

Johnson, M. 1986. 'The Saga of Starting up a New Industry in China', *International Management*, March, 47–8.

Kirkbride, P.S. and Tang, Sara F.Y. 1990. 'Negotiation: Lessons from Behind the Bamboo Curtain', *Journal of General Management*, **16** (1), 1–13.

Kraar, L. 1986a. 'Pepsi's Pitch to Quench Chinese Thirsts', *Fortune*, March 17, 54–8.

Kraar, L. 1986b. 'How One Man Landed China's $1 Billion Order', *Fortune*, August 18, 34–7.

Langston, N. 1984. 'Hammer Cracks Coal', *Far Eastern Economic Review*, September 6, 114–5.

Langston, N. 1985. 'Open Pit-Close Deal', *Far Eastern Economic Review*, July 11, 66–7.

Lee, K.H. 1989. 'Culture and Marketing Negotiation: The Case of Hong Kong Chinese Executives in US-China Trade', in E. Kaynak and

K.H. Lee (eds.), *Global Business: Asia-Pacific Dimensions*, N.Y.: Routledge, 318–32.

Lee, K.H. 1990. 'The Function of MNC Chinese Managers in China Trade Deals: Influence of Cultural Background on Marketing Negotiations', in N.T. Wang and W. Teng (eds.), *Transnational Corporation and China's Open Door Policy*, Tianjin, PRC: Nan Kai University Press. (In Chinese.)

Lee, K.H. and Lo, T.W.C. 1988. 'American Businesspeople's Perception of Marketing and Negotiating in the People's Republic of China', *International Marketing Review*, Summer, 41–51.

Leung, K. 1987. 'Some Determinants of Reactions to Procedural Models for Conflict Resolution: A Cross-National Study', *Journal of Personality and Social Psychology*, **53** (5), 898–908.

Leung, K. and Bond, M.H. 1984. 'The Impact of Cultural Collectivism on Reward Allocation', *Journal of Personality and Social Psychology*, **47** (4), 793–804.

Leung, K., Smith, P.B., Wang, Z. and Sun, H. 1996. 'Job Satisfaction in Joint Venture Hotels in China: An Organizational Justice Analysis', *Journal of International Business Studies*, **27** (5), 947–62.

Mun, K.C. 1988. 'The Vitality of Chinese Enterprise: A Systematic Analysis', in S.L. Zhou and K.C. Mun (eds.), *Management, Mechanism of Enterprises*, Beijing, PRC: Economic Management Publishing, 131–10. (In Chinese.)

Mun, K.C. 1989. 'The Guilin Garden Hotel: A Case Demonstrating Conflict in a Contractual Joint Venture in China', in F.C. Qiu (ed.), *Proceedings of the Meeting of the SEA Region Academy of International Business*, Nanjing, China: 233–45.

Mun, K.C. and Chan, T.S. 1986. 'The Role of Hong Kong in US-China Trade', *Columbia Journal of World Business*, Spring, 67–73.

Pan, Y. 1996. 'Influences of Foreign Equity Ownership Level in Joint Ventures in China', *Journal of International Business Studies*, **27** (1), 1–26.

Pan, Y. and Tse, David K. 1996. 'Cooperative Strategies between Foreign Firms in an Overseas Country', *Journal of International Business Studies*, **27** (5), 929–46.

Pan, Y., Donghoon Kim, Vanhonacker, D. and Wilfried, R. 1995. 'The Need for Cognition: A Comparative Study of American and Chinese Business Executives', *Journal of International Consumer Marketing*, **7** (3), 95–106.

Pye, L. 1982. *Chinese Commercial Negotiation Style*, Cambridge, MA: Oelgeschlager, Gunn & Hain, Publishers, Inc.

Pye, L. 1986. 'The China Trade: Making the Deal', *Harvard Business Review*, July-August, **74**, 76–80.

Saunders, J. and Ton, H.C. 1986. 'Trade with China and Japan', *Management Decision*, **14** (3), 7–12.

Sheng, P., Chang, L. and French, W.A. 1994. 'Business's Environmental Responsibility in Taiwan - Moral, Legal or Negotiation', *Journal of Business Ethics*, **13**, 887–97.

Shenkar, O. and Ronen, S. 1987. 'The Cultural Context of Negotiations: The Implications of Chinese Interpersonal Norms', *The Journal of Applied Behavioral Science*, **23** (2), 263–75.

Simyar, F. and Argheyd, K. 1986. 'China: Crossroad to Fame or Failure?', *Business Quarterly*, November, 30–8.

Tse, David, K., Francis, J. and Walls, J. 1994. 'Cultural Differences in Conducting Intra- and Inter-Cultural Negotiations: A Sino-Canadian Comparison', *Journal of International Business Studies*, **25** (3), 537–55.

Tse, David, K., Lee, K.H., Vertinsky, I. and Wehrung, D.A. 1988. 'Does Culture Matter? A Cross-Cultural Study of Executives' Choice, Decisiveness, and Risk Adjustment in International Marketing', *Journal of Marketing*, October, **52**, 81–95.

Tung, Rosalie, L. 1982. *U.S.-China Trade Negotiations*, N.Y.: Pergamon Press.

Tung, Rosalie, L. 1986. 'Corporate Executives and Their Families in China: The Need for Cross-Cultural Understanding in Business', *Columbia Journal of World Business*, Spring, 21–5.

Wang, N.T. 1984. *China's Modernization and Transnational Corporation*, Lexington, MA: Lexington Books.

Wang, N.T. 1986. 'United States and China: Business Beyond Trade-An Overview', *Columbia Journal of World Business*, Spring, 3–11.

Wang, N.T. 1988. 'China's Learning Curve in Its Relations with Transnational Corporations', in W. Teng and N.T. Wang (eds.), *Transnational Corporations and China's Open Door Policy*, Lexington, MA: Lexington Books, 251–66.

Warrington, M.B. and McCall, J.B. 1983. 'Negotiating a Foot into the Chinese Door', *Management Decisions*, **21** (2), 3–13.

Weldon, E. and Jehn, K.A. 1996. 'Conflict Management in US-Chinese Joint Ventures', in J. Child and Y. Lu (eds.), *Management Issues in China: Volume II*, N.Y.: Routledge, 89–105.

Yau, O.H.M. 1988. 'Chinese Cultural Values: Their Dimensions and Marketing Implications', *European Journal of Marketing*, **22** (5), 44–57.

Yuen, C.S. 1997. 'The Conflict between Mickey Mouse and China', *The Hong Kong Economic Journal*, January, 24–6. (In Chinese.)

APPENDIX I

CASE DESCRIPTIONS

Case One: Otis Elevator Company

Otis is a 130-year-old multi-billion dollar company which has operations in more than 100 countries. It has a long history of operation in China, with establishments well before 1949 and even before World War II. It was among the first pioneers to do business there once China started to open its doors in 1979. In 1982, Otis and the Tianjin Elevator Company formed a marketing joint venture to market Otis equipment in China.

After this initial friendship-building cooperation, a new plan was proposed between Otis and the Tianjin Elevator Company: to establish another full-scale manufacturing and service joint venture. In this business venture, Otis and the PRC had different concerns. Like many global organizations, Otis has a policy of global configuration and coordination of manufacturing activities, seeking the advantages of economies of scale and balancing these against a concern for local requirements and currency considerations. Its primary objective in China is to participate in the China market. The need for manufacturing in China to serve regional or global requirement is not its major motive for doing business in China.

On the contrary, China's basic purpose for forming an international joint venture with Otis is to acquire advanced technology, foreign exchange, and management expertise. Hence, China would definitely favor manufacturing inside China, in order to foster its own industry and to earn extra foreign exchange.

During the negotiations, three major hurdles were encountered. Nevertheless, both the U.S. and Chinese parties tried their very best to be flexible, and to be as cooperative as possible, to make the business deal a reality. First, the Chinese hoped to gain the ability to produce the more-advanced products in China in order to substitute for imports and hence save precious Chinese foreign exchange. They wanted to import more-advanced techniques and produce more-advanced items immediately. As far as Otis was concerned, they wanted to initially transfer their more primitive products and technology to China since these could still meet the needs of the massive market. By so doing, the local requirements would be met with fewer technical problems and at a lower cost. More complex and advanced products could be transferred as the Chinese gained more experience in the technology. After negotiation, the Chinese bought Otis' conservative but flexible plan. They drew up a technology transfer schedule which emphasized the demands of the Chinese market and operational feasibility but did not import the latest technology in the initial period.

Second, unlike many joint ventures in China, the idea of true shared management was introduced in the agreement. The contract specified that the assent of Otis, the minor partner, would be necessary for major decisions of the management board including: the appointment of key management personnel, new product development, export sales, and potential ventures with new partners. This reflected the great cooperative attitude of the Chinese in the business venture.

Third, the two negotiating partners faced the most difficult issue, profit remittance and foreign exchange. The Chinese view joint ventures as sources of foreign exchange. The Chinese renminbi (RMB) is a nonconvertible currency and the Chinese government seldom converts foreign businessmen's earnings into foreign exchange. The Chinese pressed for Otis to agree on a stipulated level of exports from China, to help generate foreign exchange for China. However, Otis already had sufficient manufacturing capacity in the region, and it would have been less than economically advisable to accept exports from China. Otis tried hard to avoid agreeing in the contract to purchase a fixed amount from the joint venture. The two sides came to a compromise after much negotiation. The Chinese government did not have to guarantee conversion of RMB earnings and Otis was not required to buy a fixed amount of products. Otis' purchase obligation was allowed to be based on quality, delivery, competitiveness, and market factors. The joint venture was required basically to balance its own foreign exchange. No restrictions were set on remitting earned profits as long as the joint venture could generate the foreign exchange needed to do so.

With the help of China International Economic Consultants (CIEC), a subsidiary of the China International Trust and Investment Corporation (CITIC), which provided numerous suggestions to the two parties, a formal joint venture contract was signed in July 1984. Terms of the contract are for a period of thirty years and are renewable by mutual agreement. In the joint venture, 2,400 employees, four factories, a research center, a corporate headquarters, and a nationwide network of marketing and services affiliates are involved.

Case Two: McDonnell Douglas

McDonnell Douglas first negotiated a co-production deal with China on 125 medium-range MD-82 aircraft in 1979. The contract was then considered to be among the largest commercial contracts the Chinese had negotiated with Westerners. In the course of negotiations, numerous hurdles were encountered. Nevertheless, through the cooperative attitude of the two parties, a substantial contract was closed. Key to winning the contract was the ability of McDonnell Douglas to offer extensive management training to local people up to the level required for performing complicated manufacturing duties. The company tried to establish closer relationships with the Chinese in every possible way. First, it sold outright two MD-80s to China for its routes from Beijing to Shanghai, Hong Kong and Tokyo. In addition, Mr. Gareth Chang, president of McDonnell Douglas China, and whose father was an acquaintance of Deng Xiaoping, lectured widely in China at that time on management and the function of private enterprise in the capitalist world to gain publicity for the company. Before the signing of the contract, some 300 Chinese engineers were sent to the Douglas manufacturing complex in Long Beach to ensure a comprehensive understanding of the complicated technical problems surrounding the venture. Translation of the final contract was a hurdle too. Mandarin lacks many of the technical and legal terms needed in the agreement. Moreover, qualified technical people were missing due to the Cultural Revolution. To ensure accuracy, a Chinese translation was translated back into English. Significant changes had been made on 100 pages of the 500-page document.

The Chinese showed their positive attitude towards the joint venture too. The Chinese wanted to complete the deal as they wanted to establish a manufacturing base for commercial aircraft at a later date. Besides the issue of buying cheaper aircraft, the Chinese wanted to get a partner to help sell their products on the international market eventually. As the venture was new to the Chinese, methods had to be created by both parties for arbitration of potential disputes, handling of liability insurance on aircraft built at the plant, obtaining airworthiness certification, and meeting tax obligations. The Beijing legal authorities were involved to accept submissions from the venture. In effect, Chinese tax law was changed along with the development of the joint venture. Innovative ideas and tactics were constantly introduced when the two parties meshed their motives together.

A long-term perspective is considered as a key when one is doing business in China, and McDonnell Douglas has capitalized on this view. While many people would consider short-run profit as highly attractive, the company deems it far more important for them to pave the way for future business. China is attractive to the company because of its great potential. In order to gain a presence in China, the management heavily emphasized McDonnell Douglas' corporate flexibility and persistence and this helped them beat competition for the co-production contract.

According to Gareth Chang, McDonnell Douglas took the first step towards business in China in 1975, proposing a technology transfer contract to produce DC-9. A response came, expressing interest, after three years. A task force was then set up to handle the negotiations. Three delegations of Chinese engineers fluent in English were sent to Long Beach before the end of 1978. However, the negotiations were postponed due to the downward adjustment of the 'Four Modernization' program in late 1979. At this point, Chang arranged the meeting between Deng Xiaoping and Sandy McDonnell, chairman of the company, to reaffirm the steady progress of the negotiations. After that, the company took every opportunity to establish relationships with the Chinese including the sale of smaller aircrafts and public relations work in China. After a series of negotiations, a deal was closed which called for 25 medium-range MD-82 aircrafts and an option for another 15. It was potentially worth US$1 billion, which was the largest ever commercial contract with foreigners.

Case Three: National Products

The Fuyang Parts Plant is located on the outskirts of Shenyang, capital of the Liaoning province. It was established in 1940 as a supplier of small parts for tracks. By the early 1980s most of its equipment was old and obsolete. Many of the plant's customers complained about the quality and cost of products and the delivery problems of the Fuyang Parts Plant. The management set out to find new die-casting technologies to improve the entire production process.

In 1983, Mr. Xiu, the plant manager, set up a central study group to rethink the plant's production capabilities. The plant wanted to introduce a more advanced die-casting system to stay competitive with the

South China factories. As with other technology transfer ventures, the plant wanted to obtain manufacturing expertise, management strategies, and scientific formulae from their foreign partner. When manager Xiu learned that his old friend in the municipal government would visit Japan and the States as part of a Shenyang delegation, he took the initiative and asked his friend for help. He briefed his friend on the factory's requirements and prepared an overview of what the plant was seeking.

National Products, an American supplier of heating furnaces for small and medium-sized industrial firms, decided to follow up the request when they learned of the Fuyang project. In fact, the company had been seeking a point of entry into the Chinese market for some time. As neither the U.S. Department of Commerce nor its Hong Kong agent could tell them more about the Fuyang project, two teams were sent to the Fuyang plant to explore this opportunity for new business. The teams proposed upgrading the Fuyang Parts Plant in stages. The first phase would involve replacing the heating furnace, incorporating stands for new types of dies, and installing a larger cooling system. The second phase would involve adding an electric plating system and several presses to handle different aspects of the metal forming process. Components would come from three different U.S. firms. The proposal also involved training Fuyang employees in the United States. The price of the project was estimated at slightly over US$8 million.

In the course of negotiations, National Products adopted a highly cooperative strategy to come up with a plan that best met the needs of the Chinese. They spent most of their time and effort designing a new production configuration scaled specifically to the needs of the Fuyang plant. A seven-man team was sent to Shenyang and met regularly with Xiu during the negotiation period. Their discussions covered basic considerations like: delivery, training, warranty, service, and financial details. As it was National Product's first negotiation in China, the company had difficulty with both the Chinese procedure and pacing. Tension and friction were common, and the negotiation game was not the same as in the U.S. For example, every change in the Fuyang and American positions had to be re-negotiated and approved by numerous Chinese groups and bureaus. To overcome these hurdles, the American team tried to be as flexible as possible. In addition, the technical people successfully established a good working relationship with the Chinese engineers. This helped the Americans a lot in the final closing of the negotiation.

Meanwhile, the Japanese had exerted great competitive pressure on National Products. While Xiu was asking assistance from his friend to solicit contacts in the States, several Liaoning provincial officials were putting together their own economic plan with the Japanese Mitsubishi Group. The Group had long followed developments in China's steel industry, especially at Shenyang's Anshan Iron and Steel Complex, built by the Japanese in the 1930s. They had visited most of the Anshan-related plants in the vicinity, including Xiu's plant. Instead of working with the user, the Group had chosen to work with provincial and central government officials to upgrade the province's production capacity. The Japanese had a very attractive pricing strategy. The price of the Mitsubishi proposal was about half that of the American proposal. It was only made possible if the Group could sell, as a package, several dozen furnaces to a number of factories in northern China. Actually, the Group had devoted much energy to forming a consortium of potential buyers having the same general needs and then trying to tie them up in a huge project.

This competitive move affected the American business. The Fuyang plant is part of a complex network of suppliers in Shenyang. The plant receives energy, water, alloys, and other inputs from upstream suppliers and the finished products are sold to downstream customers near the region. Mitsubishi had been very successful in cultivating a reputation of quality and reliability in the region. As far as Fuyang's suppliers and customers were concerned, there was a good perception tilt towards the Japanese proposal.

Nevertheless, the Japanese faced two major objections. First, there were concerns about China's growing trade deficit with Japan. Second, and more importantly, as the Japanese were designing a general package for various plants having specific needs, they could not handle some specific but important questions raised by Xiu. As risk was a major criterion adopted by the Fuyang plant, the Japanese concept was eventually declined.

The American proposal was not without pitfalls. The price of the project was higher, and the Fuyang people had to overcome resistance from suppliers, customers, and other provincial officers. In this connection, National Products tried their best and supplied Xiu with various selling points: (1) hands-on training (some in the United States), (2) a less costly structure in the long-run, and (3) a proposal tailored to Fuyang's specific problems and requirements.

As the American proposal was viewed as 'safer', the contract was granted to National Products in 1985. The contract called for a four-year phased development project beginning with the replacement of the heating furnace and including the eventual rehabilitation of the whole Fuyang plant.

Case Four: SPD Medical Technologies

SPD Medical Technologies began its export business to China's Ministry of Public Health (MOPH) in early 1982. Its vitamin supplement product quickly made a name for itself. In 1984 SPD received the news that their contract would not be renewed. It took more than four months for the company to discover that the agencies under MOPH no longer had the funds or authority to buy health care products. Administrative and financial responsibility had been shifted to provincial, municipal, and county-level organizations.

SPD did not give up. In early 1985 it began a rigorous investigation to determine which Chinese organization had the authority to buy vitamin supplements. During one of the visits, the SPD salespeople called on a local pharmaceutical manufacturer in Liaoning Province. The organization, known as China Pharmaceutical, was headed by Mr. Bu, who took up his appointment in 1983. He faced many difficult problems at the outset including the lack of authority and autonomy to run his business. But in 1985, many of the rules governing enterprise operations were changed, and managers began to have far more authority and flexibility to negotiate with foreign businessmen.

When Mr. Bu met the SPD team in 1985, he was very interested in the company's products, especially the methods used by SPD to manufacture over-the-counter remedies and hospital drugs. He was also interested in purchasing equipment and licensing several procedures for his own facility. They met several times during the 1985 visit. The SPD people wanted a direct sales agreement but Mr. Bu was more positive and ambitious. He wanted to develop a joint venture between China Pharmaceutical and SPD to manufacture the pharmaceutical products in China. Mr. Bu needed four kinds of transfer: packaging technology, temperature control equipment for antibiotic preparation, licenses to produce certain SPD drugs, and management expertise. They reached a general agreement about these four areas rather quickly, and then they proceeded to establish guiding principles for operating the joint venture.

In the course of negotiating the final contract, three major stumbling blocks were found. SPD wanted to include a technology development fee to help recover some of the firm's past development cost. To the Chinese, this fee was a double payment for the same goods. More importantly, the Chinese superiors and reviewers would question this payment for 'soft product'. To the Chinese, the enterprise would only purchase hard goods—machines, formulas, management know-how—not research. In order to play safe, Mr. Bu consulted two officials in different provincial agencies and the Chinese finally proposed a lower figure which was acceptable to SPD.

The second hurdle was that SPD requested contractual assurance that its formulas and manufacturing processes would be kept confidential, would only be applied within the joint venture operation, and that they would be used in the manner stipulated in the agreement. To protect the proprietary information, SPD lawyers also wanted to include some provisions that would set specific remedial measures in motion if some of the conditions were violated. The Chinese considered this issue with care and Mr. Bu finally turned to an outside agency, a municipal economic organization for help in drafting these guarantees. In this context, the Chinese had made a big cooperative gesture.

Convincing potential customers and other outside powers was the third, and supposedly, the biggest hurdle the joint venture had to overcome. Hospitals were Mr. Bu's major target. He planned to gain access to the regional hospital associations to generate steady sales and cash flows. By so doing, the expenditure for the new production facilities could be more quickly written off. Though the hospital associations had considerable autonomy to select their supplier, they were also tied to the State Pharmaceutical Administration (SPA), which advised the association from time to time. At that time, the SPA was negotiating with a large Japanese firm on a general plan to develop several large-scale drug production and packaging projects, and the SPA worried that the SPD arrangement might affect this master plan. Hence, the SPA official counseled the hospital associations to be careful in signing agreements with China Pharmaceutical. Once the SPA had declared its basic objections to the joint ventures, several other agencies made further inquiries. Moreover, the China National Packaging Corporation wanted to know what materials would be used in packaging the new drugs and whether they met national guidelines. In addition, the China

National Chemical Import-Export Corporation requested a list of all materials the joint venture planned to use in their processes and whether these chemicals were on the approved list. In these regards, Mr. Bu and his Liaoning patron stood firm. They answered all queries and insisted that China Pharmaceutical was well within its authority to close deals with SPD.

Despite these bureaucratic stumbling blocks, the two firms finally signed a formal agreement in late 1986. SPD would provide equipment over a three-year period and would oversee management and training for five years. China Pharmaceutical would assign 40 percent of its existing facility to the new venture, provide expert labor, and be responsible for all on-site costing. The contract also included provisions to protect SPD's proprietary information, trademarks, and brandnames. SPD also agreed to train Chinese engineers in production techniques, quality control, and basic research. As is common in other joint ventures, SPD would also sponsor Chinese engineers to visit the States each year to receive training.

Case Five: PepsiCo

Coca Cola made its first and exclusive deal with a Chinese central government trading company in 1978. In 1979, when Deng Xiaoping began to give local and provincial agencies more autonomy, PepsiCo grabbed the chance to enter the Chinese regional markets. It built two bottling plants in Zhenghen and Guangzhou, with about the same production capacity as Coca Cola's four plants in China.

To pitch for further business and to build up a strong friendship with officials in China, PepsiCo chairman, Donald Kendall, formed a strong delegation to China in January 1986. Armed with a letter of introduction from former President Nixon (China's old friend), the PepsiCo directors were able to meet Premier Zhao Ziyang in Beijing. The delegation to China included PepsiCo's three internal directors, seven external directors, and an accompanying crew of 49. The tour in China mostly consisted of working lunches and dinners. In each city the directors were assigned particular Chinese officials. They were equipped with thick briefing books which described who had the power to negotiate and make decisions. In the course of dealing with the Chinese, the major objective was to develop personal and friendly relationships, which would definitely help cut through the thick bureaucratic layers. Before the arrival of the directors, advance teams were sent to nail down last-minute arrangements. One hundred and thirty cases of Pepsi-Cola and gifts of leather briefcases and wallets for Chinese officials were used as 'door-openers'.

In Shenzhen, the local Communist party secretary, Liang Xiang, praised the PepsiCo bottling plant for generating export earnings for the special economic zone. In Guangzhou, Guangdong Province governor Ye Xuanping, who was mayor of Guangzhou when PepsiCo agreed to build the plant there, greeted the directors in his office.

In Shanghai, PepsiCo hosted Shanghai's former mayor, plus other municipal and party officials. In Fudan University, widely regarded as the Harvard of China, Kendall announced that PepsiCo would sponsor two Chinese students to attend Northwestern University, where they would be known as PepsiCo Fellows. He also endorsed a letter of intent to build a Shanghai bottling operation.

In Beijing, the PepsiCo delegation joined U.S. Ambassador Winston Lord and paid a visit to premier Zhao Ziyang. Kendall handed Zhao the Nixon letter, and conveyed regards from Vice President Bush, another old friend of China. The premier assured them of China's open door policy and further proposed an international cooperation in the food industry.

The friendship delegation was so successful that Robert Briggs, Pepsi's point man for China, summed up his view: "These eight days moved our effort ahead by at least one and one half years."

Case Six: Occidental Petroleum Corporation

In the beginning of the 1980s, the Chinese planned to further establish their energy resources and sought assistance from U.S. companies to supply to them with equipment and technology. Occidental Petroleum Corporation was one of the American firms that had entered into collaborative arrangements with the Chinese on the exploration of Chinese energy resources. Even though the company was not among the first to enter the Chinese market it had developed good relationships with the Chinese. In 1979 the company received approval from the Chinese to take part in an examination of the energy potential of China.

According to Richard Chen, Occident's director of business development in China, long-run profitability was the major reason behind the company's decision to engage in the deal with China. Basically, it was the company which took the initiative to contact the respective ministries and corporations in China. After opportunities were spotted, the company went ahead to initiate contacts with the Chinese. Based on such initial contacts, further field visits and negotiations were organized. Where appropriate, the company was ready to follow up and make proposals. A Business Development Department was set up in the Beijing office whose job was focused on activities in China. This office helped accelerate sorting out the preliminary set-up before the talks and facilitate the efficient running of the negotiation. To assist in bridging culture differences between the two negotiating teams, the company was staffed by Chinese-Americans. Though this might not help on the basic closing of a deal, in the initial stages it should help the teams to get acquainted with each other, to understand each other, and to move faster to the core of the negotiation. In any event, the company tried to be as cooperative as possible so as to create a good impression for the Chinese, one which would be highly valuable in the closing of a deal.

Occidental's past experience with Russia was also a major advantage. The Chinese felt that a corporation which had long experience in dealing with a socialist country like Russia would be in a better position to understand China and to avoid doing things not acceptable to the web-like bureaucratic hierarchy of the country. In the Chinese context, risk is not preferred and officials would try their best to deflect it or avoid it altogether. According to Chen, if the Chinese sensed that something was out of order, they would ask for a postponement, even if everything was ready as far as the American company was concerned. That sort of delay was frustrating, especially when the American delegation considered that everything was well organized and a lot of energy and effort had already been spent.

The situation was further complicated as the risk-averse Chinese were called on by many other foreign corporations who were also interested in dealing with China. The Chinese were confused as many corporations were pitching simultaneously, and presenting various conflicting pictures. It took the Chinese a long time to sort out who were good partners, and who were just mediocre businessmen.

In 1982, Occidental and the China National Coal Development Corp. (CNCDC) finally agreed to proceed with a feasibility study on the development of a coal mine site 500 km west of Beijing with proven reserves of 1.4 billion tons and an expected annual capacity of 15 million tons a year at full production. In 1984, the two sides were deadlocked over issues including salaries and guarantees from the Chinese to make up the difference in foreign-exchange earnings generated by the coal designated for export should they fall below the expected revenue level.

By early 1984, rumors that the deal was on the verge of collapse were so strong that Occidental chairman Armand Hammer had to write to China's top leaders, Deng Xiaoping, Hu Yaobang, and Zhao Ziyang promising that the project would definitely proceed. The Chinese had indicated their commitment too. In April 1984, Deng was reported by Xinhua Newsagency as having told Hammer that 'cooperation with China involves very little risk because China is not a country lacking ability to pay. On the contrary, China has a large potential which has not yet been brought out.'

With strong commitment on both sides, Occidental and China finally signed their joint venture contract to develop one of the world's largest coal mines, the giant Antaibao No. 1 open-cut pit in the Ping Shuo coal mine in Shanxi province. The company took five years of negotiation to yield a firm deal—an investment cost of US$650 million.

The two major stumbling blocks which held up the final agreement for more than one year were finally resolved. The China National Coal Import-Export Corporation signed an agency contract with Island Creek of China Coal (ICCC), a 50–50 partnership between Occidental and the Bank of China Trust and Consultancy Company, to sell its coal abroad. The contract stipulated that if they failed to sell all the coal the Chinese Corporation would pay Occidental a minimum price based on the average coal price of selected coal-producing countries.

On the salary issue, Chinese laborers would be paid US$7 an hour, or half of the U.S. miners' wage. The wages would actually be paid to a labor organization, which would keep well over half of the earnings. As the money would be turned over to the state to help support the Chinese infrastructure costs, Occidental was actually contributing to China's infrastructure construction.

Case Seven: Control Data Corporation

Since 1971, Control Data Corporation (CDC) of Minneapolis, Minnesota has been actively interested in marketing computers to China. In 1978, CDC had mainframe computer sales that constituted about 6% of the total world mainframe computer market. China has relied heavily on imports of computers since 1964. During the period 1964 to 1975 about 16 different types of computers were sold to China. Ten of these were basically parts of seismic or geographical exploration systems, the types marketed by CDC. The company became interested in the Chinese market about the time when U.S. and China renewed cordial relations in 1971. The initial CDC contact was a proposal to the Chinese Ministry of Science and Technology.

The initial proposal submitted was both comprehensive and detailed to allow the Chinese to evaluate it commercially. Full information about CDC, its activities and its entire range of products were included. The proposal also indicated the firm's willingness to provide additional details, answer further queries, and arrange follow-up gatherings.

At the time CDC was exploring opportunities in the PRC, China had a great demand for computers with specific applications, particularly in petroleum exploration. In 1979, China ranked about tenth in the world as an oil producer. Its search for oil had accumulated a great deal of seismic data. In this regard, CDC had exactly the type of product to meet China's processing need. The great Chinese need for large mainframe computers eventually induced CDC's huge marketing efforts beginning in the 1970s.

CDC's initial business objectives could be summarized as: to assess China as a potential market for the future, to determine the political climate for business, and to get China acquainted with the company. The company's strategy eventually developed into a twofold one: pursuing immediate prospects and improving future relationships with the Chinese corporation. The first part would mean aiming for immediate revenue and the second part would mean aiming for future sales, technical sales, and joint ventures. Besides short-run profits, CDC was clearly making a commitment to the future. They stressed the importance of maintaining an image of having interest in building a long-term relationship with China.

The issue of friendship was emphasized in difficult phases of the negotiations. In order to develop a linkage with China, CDC entered into an agreement in October 1971 with a Washington-based consulting firm which had good contacts with the China Resources Company in Hong Kong as well as with many Chinese officials in China, for the purpose of strengthening the company's position in dealing with officials in China. In fact, one of the key persons in the consulting firm was a former acquaintance of Premier Chou Enlai, and thus in a very favorable position.

The company also developed various strategies to help the Chinese get to know CDC. In April 1972, CDC sent a letter to the China National Machinery Import and Export Corporation introducing CDC and its personnel. In their reply the Chinese indicated that they had already received CDC brochures and other materials forwarded to them by China Resources. They also indicated their interest in CDC's products and asked for a price list. The CDC then informed the Chinese about the pricing of software and other pertinent materials to allow the Chinese to configure their specific system.

Other CDC contacts included a meeting with Chinese officials in Bucharest, Rumania and the exchange of business views with China Resources officials over dinner in Hong Kong. The basic motive of these contacts was to familiarize Chinese officials and end-users with CDC personnel and computers. When a group of Chinese computer engineers visited America in 1973, CDC had the chance to meet face-to-face with Chinese decision-makers. The visit was considered a pleasant encounter, and in a follow-up letter in 1974, CDC went on to suggest the establishment of a series of seminars on computer facilities at a location to be designated by the Chinese. As before, the main purpose of these seminars was to establish a friendship with the Chinese and generate an opportunity for both parties to get to know each other better. In late 1973, emphasis had been placed on the establishment of closer contact on a direct basis and CDC started to use terminology such as 'old friends' in its sales letters.

CDC had also taken every opportunity to minimize the perceived risk to the Chinese since risk is not preferred in the Chinese culture. In many cases, CDC tried very hard to convince the Chinese that the company's technology would continue to be state-of-the-art. During the negotiations, the Chinese asked very detailed questions about the CDC computer involved in the transaction. To each and every question, a detailed and comprehensive answer was supplied to help the Chinese negotiators to face any queries or criticisms from their superior. Despite China's great need for the computer system, the Chinese preferred safety and a contract was not agreed. To further minimize the risk, CDC added a third partner in the sale: Compagnie Generale de Geophysique (CGG). The basic asset of CGG was that the company had been selling oil exploration equipment to the Chinese for over ten years and had earned their respect. The CGG people were considered old friends of the Chinese and hence, the CGG personnel was assigned to do much of the negotiating, particularly in the final closing talks.

On August 14, 1974, a contract was finally signed between the China National Technical Import Corporation (Techimport) and CDC for the delivery of two Cyber 172 systems to the Chinese National Oil and Gas Exploration and Development Corporation. The total value of the contract was approximately US$6.8 million. That turnkey package for the large national seismic data processing center located in the Beijing area was then the largest contract signed by Techimport and a single computer manufacturer.

Case Eight: Electronic Associates, Inc.

Electronic Associates, Inc. (EAI) is a developer and manufacturer of computer systems used in dedicated and general-purpose simulation applications for training and advanced research and development studies. Although EAI is considered a small company—under US$450 million in total sales per annum—it has over the past decades aggressively pursued the marketing of its products in the States and other parts of the world.

At the Canton Fair in 1972, an aggressive EAI salesman discussed the establishment of an intercity network of CRTs for the exchange of digital information with the Chinese. They found the idea extremely interesting and were enthusiastic about a commercial deal. Over the years EAI's Marketing Department continued to mail pertinent materials to various departments in China. They also publicized in the public media from time to time that China would be a promising candidate for purchasing EAI equipment. Besides governmental organizations, EAI also investigated whether technical universities and research centers in China would be interested in the company's product. Over a period of six years, no word was ever received with respect to the sales letters, nor in fact was there any indication that the literature was being read by potential buyers in China.

During the summer of 1977, Mr. Sanders, EAI's vice-president of Marketing, made a tour to the Association of Southeast Asian Nations (ASEAN) offices. Having heard that the Bank of China in Hong Kong had served usefully as a gateway to the Chinese market, he made an appointment with the director of the Bank. He was courteously entertained, and was allowed to make a presentation of the company's products. After receiving the brochures and product catalogs, the Chinese assured Mr. Sanders that the material would be sent to the right authority in Beijing for a decision.

EAI had also relied on a third party to help develop additional contacts with China. The Chori Trading Company, a Japanese trading corporation which had good relationships with the Chinese, was asked to channel some of EAI's literature to the proper technical agency for the company. Nevertheless, this also produced no immediate effect.

In the meantime, the International Marketing vice-president in conjunction with EAI's office in Japan proposed a technical seminar in China. They were able to conduct, at last, a very successful seminar on analog and hybrid simulation for Chinese officials in Beijing. All the above moves resulted in EAI's receiving an invitation in June 1977 from the Chinese to visit Beijing for further technical discussion on EAI's products.

A group of three from EAI was dispatched to Beijing in September 1977 including the vice-president of International Marketing, the general manager of the Tokyo office, and a sales engineer who had a modest command of the Chinese language. Naturally, the Japanese middleman was also included as the Japanese were, at that time, well received by the Chinese officials.

The delegation was hosted by a deputy dignitary of China and the discussions were attended by several scientists from the University of Harbin. The EAI group was intensively interviewed over a period of two weeks, and was asked to make presentations of the characteristics and functions of different EAI products. Its most advanced and largest analogy hybrid complex (known as Series 700) was the core subject for discussion.

In the course of their discussions, EAI found that some young people were very open and were eager to acquire as much scientific knowledge as possible. They very much wanted the new computer and the technology coming with the end project. However, some members of the Chinese group were still reluctant to open up. Though the Chinese had not treated the EAI people as enemies, they were obviously still on guard in terms of how much they wanted the Americans to know about what their real business undertakings were. There were still others who were overtly politically oriented, and some questions were not addressed to business *per se*.

In the negotiations, a lot of consideration was given to the determination of a right configuration. The Chinese were very thorough and a lot of investigations were undertaken, even for very small details in technical matters. In this connection, the EAI group maintained a persistent stance and tried to be as patient as possible since patience was a successful technique when negotiating with the Chinese.

According to Sanders, following the timetable set by the Chinese and not appearing to be impatient at the slow progress was a major technique they had learnt in the business talks with the Chinese. The company had constantly indicated that they had commitment in the deals, they were not there for hurried business, and that they were taking a long-range perspective in the China business.

At the end of a long period of extensive technical presentations, the Chinese were eventually convinced about the advantages of the EAI product and simply declared their intention to issue a purchase contract—a configuration of equipment which represented the top of the line in the series 700. An order in the amount of US$4.47 million was announced. Price discussions were minimal until the final purchase order was drawn up and only a small discount to show EAI's good intentions was requested.

Case Nine: American International Group, Inc.

The American International Group (AIG) is the largest U.S. insurance company operating in the world. The People's Insurance Company of China (PICC) is a state-owned insurance company that is entitled to underwrite insurance within China. After the signing of the Shanghai Communique in 1972, AIG wrote to PICC to explore business opportunities between the two companies. Periodic contracts were also made through an affiliate of the PICC based in Hong Kong, the Ming An Insurance Company. The AIG was motivated to begin negotiations because they wanted to remain a leader in the world's insurance business and they were of the opinion that the venture would be profitable for the Group.

In Spring 1975, the AIG submitted a formal proposal to the PICC and expressed their desire to develop commercial relations with them. Copies of the proposal were given to representatives of the PICC at the Spring 1975 Canton Trade Fair. The aim of this move was to solicit an invitation for AIG senior management to visit Beijing. Five months elapsed before the AIG received the formal invitation from the Chinese. A delegation from the AIG was sent to Beijing in November 1975. The Group was represented by Mr. Greenberg, president and chief executive officer, Mr. Manton, executive vice-president, and Mr. Freeman, regional manager for Far East Operations. As a result of the visit, a ceremonial reciprocal exchange agreement was signed. The agreement served as a mechanism for continuing discussion, and enabled each party to get to know their counterpart better. This agreement also provided for a small amount of business and for some informal technical cooperation.

In negotiations, the AIG found that the Chinese were very cooperative and friendly. They were profit-minded and were anxious to do business with other countries. The image of being the biggest international insurance company helped AIG a lot. The PICC would be able to participate in markets to which they did not have access. In the period of the negotiations, China wanted to expand their service industry to earn more foreign exchange. By joining forces with AIG, the Chinese would not have to invest a lot in setting up facilities and contacts. As the two parties had similar interests, both parties were frank and open and the negotiations were carried out smoothly.

Though both parties were cooperative, the Americans faced a common hurdle in Chinese trade negotiation: competition. During the negotiation period, the people from PICC spent a week in New York. When the Chinese arrived in the States, they said they would like to visit other insurance companies too. Actually, the PICC people had made complimentary visits to every major competitor of AIG, and even to brokers that were not related to AIG.

To minimize this competitive pressure and to build up stronger friendships, the Americans tried to be as helpful as possible. Shortly after the conclusion of the reciprocal agreement with PICC, the Group provided assistance when a Chinese-flag vessel was approaching the Panama Canal. There is a statute requiring vessels in waters under U.S. jurisdiction to give evidence of financial security sufficient to remove any oil pollution caused by the vessel. As the Chinese vessel approached the Canal, they cabled AIG for help and they arranged for the issuing of a bond to support the Chinese. This incident greatly strengthened the friendship between the two parties.

As the Chinese are risk-averse, the company's long association with China was valuable in the negotiations. AIG was the first to contact the Chinese after the signing of the Shanghai Communique in 1972 and the Chinese were well acquainted with the company. They knew that the company had offices full of Chinese out in the Far East. They had cooperated for many years through their subsidiaries in Hong Kong and

Singapore. The Chinese felt that AIG would understand them best, and the two partners were closer than the others.

In 1980, a letter of intent was signed which covered a 50–50 joint venture between AIG and PICC. The joint venture would be known as the China-American Insurance Company, with authorized capital of US$25 million, with US$5 million paid up. Each partner would initially contribute US$2.5 million. The operation would operate worldwide, using the AIG global network of offices in 130 countries. It would insure different aspects of the trade between China and various other countries.

Singapore. The Chinese felt that AIG would understand them better, and the two partners were closer than they thought.

In 1995, a letter of intent was signed which created a 50-50 joint venture between AIG and PICC. The joint venture would be known as the China America Insurance Company, with authorized capital of US$25 million, with US$5 million paid up. Each partner would initially contribute US$2.5 million. The operation was to operate worldwide using the AIG global network of offices in 130 countries. It would insure different aspects of the trade between China and various other countries.

C H A P T E R   F I V E

Social-Cultural Context of Perceptions and Approaches to Conflict: The Case of Singapore

EDITH YUEN CHI-CHING
Faculty of Business Administration, National University of Singapore

Culture, with its systems of knowledge, language, beliefs and values bestows upon each person a patrimony of concepts which become part of the individual (Arieti 1970). Through these concepts, culture has a significant influence on how an individual defines the meaning of his life; how he perceives and interprets his experiences and life situations; and what kind of solutions he finds practical and desirable to solve his problems. Culture can lead a person to narrow or broaden his perceptions of an event, focus or diffuse his senses, or discard certain information as irrelevant.

The relationship between culture and social structure is complex. Not only is social structure influenced by culture, it reflects cultural characteristics. In turn, structure reinforces culture. In human history, social and political elites have not infrequently used their power and influence to shape values and create ideologies which are then assimilated through socialization without much objective scrutiny or reflection by members of the society. Values and ideologies are also institutionalized, a process which not only reinforces their legitimacy, but ensures their continuity over time.

Social systems invariably involve differences, inequality and divisions. Conflicts are thus inevitable. As conflict threatens the stability of a system, all societies have values, beliefs, ideologies and institutionalized means to interpret differences, to define relationships, to justify inequality, and to deal with conflicts. An examination of conflict in social-cultural contexts can therefore enhance our understanding of national differences in perceptions of, and approaches to, conflict.

In preparing the present chapter on Singapore, the author came across a number of problems which ultimately affected the structure and presentation of the chapter. Singapore has a relatively short history as a nation. Before it became a city-state in 1965, Singapore was little more than a rat and mosquito infested entrepôt for the Malay hinterland. It had a transient, migrant population comprising merchants, coolies and colonial administrators. Hence, the first issue that the author had to deal with was 'Is there a Singaporean identity/culture?' Secondly, in the three decades since 1965, the society has gone through rapid economic and social changes. While a lot has been written about Singapore's economic policies and development, there are few academic studies on social values and culture, not to mention the cognitive aspect of conflict. Hence, the author had to construct a 'Singaporean' conflict frame based on an analysis of the society, its past developments, and emergent social trends. To provide some referents for subsequent analysis, the author decided to begin the chapter with an examination of empirical findings on conflict management styles and conflict behavior in Singapore.

The Conflict Management Styles of Singaporeans

A literature search yielded five studies, four published and one unpublished, that touch on the conflict management style/behavior of Singaporeans. Although the sample size of some of the studies was small and the methods used were not consistent, the studies nonetheless provide a picture of the style preferences of Singaporeans in handling conflicts.

McKenna (1995) administered the Thomas-Kilmann Conflict Mode Instrument (Thomas and Kilmann 1974) to 60 employees (22 expatriates mainly from the U.S. and Canada, and 38 Singaporeans, all of Chinese descent) working in a U.S. company in the computing and telecommunications industry in Singapore. He found substantial differences between the conflict management style of local (Singaporean) managers and that of expatriate managers. Local managers were low in competing (only 3% of the managers had competing as their dominant mode) and collaborating

(10%), but high on avoiding (40%) and accommodating (30%). In comparison, expatriate managers were high on competing (30%) and collaborating (30%), but low on accommodating (3%) and avoiding (10%).

The results of an unpublished survey by Yeo (1995) by and large supported the findings of McKenna (1995). The Thomas-Kilmann Conflict Mode Instrument was administered to 39 local managers in middle management and the scores were, in descending order of preference, avoiding (7.47), compromising (7.22), accommodating (6.02), collaborating (5.87), and competing (3.42). There was no difference between the sexes in the ranking of the five conflict handling modes.

Kau and Yang (1991), in a survey on the values and lifestyles of young Singaporeans (n=2130; with the age of respondents ranging from 15–40), found that Singaporeans preferred compromising to confronting. In response to the statement 'I would rather fight than compromise', 35.7% of the respondents disagreed while 23.3% agreed. (Avoiding, collaborating and compromising were not indicated as alternatives.)

Different findings were however reported by Lim (1994) who administered the Rahim Organizational Conflict Inventories (Rahim, 1983) to 156 MBA students at a local university. Although 'competing' (mean = 2.83) was again rated the least preferred mode, 'avoiding' was rated the second lowest with a mean score of 3.11. Contrary to the findings of the other studies, the most preferred mode was collaborating (3.66), followed by compromising (3.34) and accommodating (3.23). Lim however cautioned that 'It is...pertinent to consider the characteristics of the sample used in this study before generalizing the results.' The study used a sample of MBA students who were relatively young (26–35 years) and more educated. Differences in findings could also be due to the use of a different instrument.

While it is convenient to dismiss the findings of Lim (1994) as an aberration, the findings of an earlier study also suggest the need for caution. In an administration of the Thomas-Kilmann Conflict Mode Instrument to managers of Chinese origin in Singapore, Chew and Lim (1991) found that the conflict management mode of Singaporean managers were, in order of preference, compromising, collaborating, avoiding, competing, and accommodation. The style preference of the respondents in this study was closer to that reported by Lim (1994) than to those by McKenna (1995) and Yeo (1995).

The findings of these studies can only be treated as indicative as the studies differed in both sample characteristics and the contexts of questionnaire administration. McKenna's study was administered in an MNC to expatriate and local managers whose relationships were not detailed in the article, but could have involved status differences. Lim's study was administered in the context of subordinates' behavior towards their superiors. Yeo's survey involved a number of middle managers from different organizations attending an executive training program. While Kau and Yang's survey involved a large random sample of the general population, the project was not specifically designed to study conflict management styles and the authors did not use an established instrument of conflict management.

While one can criticize the methodology of these studies, cumulative findings from the studies did allow a couple of conclusions to be drawn about the conflict management style of Singaporean managers:

1. There is considerable variation in the findings of the different studies which could be due to differences in sample characteristics. If this was indeed the reason, then the findings suggest considerable diversity in the population.
2. In spite of the variations in ranking, Singaporean managers are generally low in competing and high in avoiding and compromising.

If one compares the conflict management styles of Singaporean managers with those of Hong Kong managers as reported by Kirkbride, Tang and Westwood (1991), certain similarities can be observed.

Table 5.1 Summary of Studies on the Conflict Management Styles of Singaporean and Hong Kong Managers

	Singapore				Hong Kong
	Chew & Lim (T-K)	Lim (Rahim)	McKenna (T-K)	Yeo (T-K)	Kirkbride, etc.
Competing	4	5	5	5	5
Collaborating	2	1	4	4	3 (equal)
Compromising	1	2	3	2	1
Avoiding	3	4	1	1	2
Accommodating	5	3	2	3	3 (equal)

Note: T-K = Thomas-Kilmann Conflict Mode Instrument
Rahim = Rahim Organizational Conflict inventories

Both Singaporean and Hong Kong managers were low in competing and high in avoiding and compromising. Can the similarities be due to Singapore and Hong Kong sharing the same cultural heritage?

Is there a Distinct Singaporean Identity/Culture?

In studies on the culture of overseas Chinese communities like Singapore, Hong Kong, and Taiwan, the conventional approach was to consider them as extensions of the traditional Chinese social and cultural heritage. This approach has been given much credibility by the works of Redding (1990) and Bond (1986) in their thesis of neo-Confucianism. However, Clammer objected to any argument that a Singaporean Chinese society might be seen as a kind of social extension of China. He was strongly of the view that a Singapore culture did exist. 'A culture organizes, integrates and maintains a system of values and pattern of characteristic behavior, and in this sense a distinctive, although still fluid Singapore culture already exists (as can also be seen by contrast: Singapore is a quite different society from Hong Kong, and is very different indeed from its close neighbors Malaysia and Indonesia)' (Clammer, 1985). Clammer's view was shared by De Glopper (1991) who noted that a Singapore identity/culture is evolving, or is perhaps consciously being built by government policies and public education.

One way in which Singapore differs from Hong Kong is its geographic situation. While Hong Kong is predominantly Chinese in a region dominated by the Chinese, Singapore's majority Chinese exist in a region of predominantly Malays. Before Singapore became an independent state with its own identity, descendants of Chinese migrants were already assimilating and becoming 'de-Sinified', resulting in the emergence of the culture of the English- and Malay-speaking Baba or Peranakan Chinese. Another way in which the two societies differ is language: English is the official language of the Republic of Singapore and although the use of Mandarin has been promoted in recent years, the use of Chinese dialects has all along been discouraged. In Hong Kong, Cantonese and other Chinese dialects are widely used in daily life. Thirdly, the emergence of a Singaporean society/culture is, to a large extent, due to the decades of nation-building efforts by a government which has sought to integrate social, economic, political and cultural developments into a mutually reinforcing system.

In order to place Singaporean society and culture in context, the following section provides some background information about the economic, political and social developments of the Republic over the past three to four decades.

Political, Economic and Social Development of Singapore

Chinese migration to Singapore took place mainly between the mid-18th century and the 1930s. Due to its distance from mainland China, its hot climate and tropical diseases, Singapore and Malaysia attracted mainly the poor and the uneducated from the coastal provinces of China who had turned to the Nanyang (Southern Seas) either to escape from famine and war or to seek opportunities which they could not find in their homeland. Early migrants worked mainly in manual jobs (as plantation workers, coolies, etc.). However, the abundant natural resources and agricultural products of Southeast Asia provided the migrants with opportunities for social mobility. Attracted by the rich resources of the region, western colonial investors soon set up large-scale enterprises (Wu and Wu 1980) which in turn created a demand for intermediaries between the native producers and the consumers. Consequently, many Indian and Chinese merchants emerged to fill the gap. Migrant merchants who had saved sufficient capital would set up their own businesses and some even acquired their own plantation. Subsequent migration tended to be family-related as many new migrants came to work for their kin.

Migrants of this era went through much hardship. Many risked their life in unseaworthy vessels to travel from their homeland, while the weaker ones succumbed to malaria and other tropical diseases rampant in the hot, swampy environment. Being poorly educated and exposed to the vicissitudes of life, many of the overseas Chinese were superstitious. Cults rather than Confucianism permeated their culture while clans, triads, trade associations/unions formed the rudimentary social structure. Singaporeans of this generation were entrepreneurs. They learned from their life experiences and possessed strong survival instincts as well as survival skills. As intermediaries and traders, many were shrewd businessmen and negotiators.

With the separation of Singapore from the Federation of Malaysia in 1965, the government, led by the People's Action Party (PAP) quickly embarked on a program of industrialization to solve the problems caused by high unemployment and high birth rates. Besides infrastructure development and the development of the manufacturing sector, the government also introduced basic medical care, embarked on public housing projects, and put together an education system. With these rapid economic and social developments came the emergence of a new generation of Singaporeans who, in terms of upbringing, experiences and values, are considerably different from earlier generations. Indeed, the decline of traditional values has become so apparent in recent years that the government decided to take concrete measures to reinforce such traditional Asian values as hard work, filial piety, collectivism and community. In a 1988 speech proposing the National Ideology, the then deputy prime minister, Goh Chok Tong, stressed certain desirable core values: community over self, upholding the family as the basic building block of society; community support for the individual, and racial and religious harmony.

In the context of past developments, I shall proceed to examine aspects of the socio-cultural environment which could have affected young Singaporeans' cognition of conflict and their conflict management styles. By 'young Singaporeans', I refer to those below 40 years of age who were socialized under an independent Singapore state.

The Social Context of the Singaporean Conflict Frame

1. Starting from the macro-perspective I shall examine the political and social systems of the nation-state. Since its independence in 1965, Singapore has been under the rule of one political party, the People's Action Party (PAP), which has remained the only viable political party in the nation-state. The PAP's uninterrupted rule of 33 years has been characterized by a unique blend of western efficiency and oriental paternalism. It advocated strict, clear-cut and no-nonsense policies/rules which were not only wide-ranging in scope, but penetrated most aspects of the life of its citizens. Not only were there policies on economic and national development, the government also introduced policies which have implications on many aspects of the citizen's life (from education, family size, car ownership, house ownership, medical care, and drugs, to hair-length, smoking, littering, spitting, and chewing gum). Using a plethora of incentives (monetary as well as non-monetary), fines, and public education, most of the policies have been successfully implemented, resulting in a society that is clean, orderly, efficient,

and well synchronized. The negative side, as noted by a sociologist, is the 'hegemony of the State: its ubiquitousness and intervention at every level of life'. (Clammer 1985, p.160).

The high level of control was accompanied by a fair measure of oriental paternalism. The government made it a policy to place some of the brightest people in the nation in key government positions. In 1994 when the economy was booming and private sector demand for managerial manpower was great, the government decided to raise ministerial pay to an unprecedented level in order to entice the best talent to join the public service (Kwok 1995). Although the decision was controversial and unpopular among the electorate, the government pressed ahead with it. With a pool of highly-qualified policy makers and administrators, public policies were often carefully thought through before being presented to the public as the 'best solution'. Being a small nation, the government has been effective in explaining policy matters to the people and communicating to them that even though some of the measures might appear harsh, the government is a responsible economic manager and has the long-term well-being of the nation in mind.

In Singapore, paternalism is manifest in the behavior of public-office holders. For example, the PAP expects its elected members of Parliament (many of them are senior managers in the public or private sector) to visit their constituencies regularly and to hold regular feedback sessions. As for the citizens, it is sometimes noted that Singaporeans are a complaining lot. Commenting on local habits, Dhaliwal (1994) wrote, 'They complain about almost everything.... Not only do they grouse, they compare...with others what they get.' However, taking everything into consideration, it must be noted that Singaporeans do 'listen' to their government and are law-abiding. Their behavior resembles that of a subordinate who knows that he/she should obey, but nonetheless complains because he/she perceives that there is little freedom to choose or to make his/her own decisions. Commenting on the trend of teenagers who sought to express their individuality and freedom in the way they dress, Chua and Tan (1995) noted that 'freedom and difference are perceived by the teenagers to be grossly lacking in Singapore'.

In comparison to western societies at a similar level of economic development, Singapore lacks the pluralism that is often characteristic of industrialized societies. The lack of interest groups, political parties, and groups advocating alternative perspectives means that Singaporeans are generally not personally involved in a multitude of viewpoints or perspectives. Living in a planned society, Singaporeans tend to be passive. Passivity is sometimes extended to the work place and school as these organizations tend to be well-planned and have clearly specified goals, procedures and guidelines. In this context, it is not surprising that foreign managers in Singapore often complain about local managers' lack of initiative. The matter was recently taken up by the Prime Minister, Goh Chok Tong, in a Teachers' Day Rally speech, '... employers now felt that school-leavers and graduates here were hard-working but required too much 'hand-holding' and had difficulty working independently. They were also low on initiative and in persuading others to accept new ideas.' (*Sunday Times*, September 29, 1996).

In relation to conflict management and negotiation, the development of a collaborative, integrative solution to a conflict situation requires initiative, innovation and creativity. It involves a willingness to go outside the established ways of doing things. The ability to do so also involves a broad mind-set, one which can see the whole picture instead of focusing on details. The observation that Singaporean graduates are poor at persuading others to accept new ideas is of particular relevance to conflict management and negotiation since successful negotiation invariably entails persuading others to change their views/positions.

However, a word of caution is needed in relation to Singaporeans' lack of initiative. Firstly, this lack of initiative could well be confined to politics and dealings with bureaucratic organizations. These can be overly planned and administered so that individuals acquire the habit of passively accepting goals and directions and simply executing them efficiently. As shown in a subsequent section in this chapter, Singaporeans can show considerable initiative in private matters, especially when it comes to ensuring that they do not lose out to others. Secondly, passivity and the lack of initiative at work should not be confused with a general lack of confidence. Singaporeans are confident. As Willmott (1989) noted, the economic success of Singapore has brought to its people a substantial injection of self-esteem and national pride.

2. Another set of factors relates to the local education system which places heavy emphasis on examinations. At various stages in primary and secondary schools, students have to go through nation-wide examinations for screening and placement purposes. As schools are ranked by the examination results of their students, they compete fiercely, resulting in a strong examination orientation as well as the practice of 'spoon-feeding' the students to prepare them for examinations.

In comparison with the American education system which emphasizes active experimentation, students in the local education system learn mainly by abstract conceptualization. In a study on the learning style of Singaporean students, Yuen and Lim (1994) administered Kolb's Learning Style Inventory to 1032 final-year university students and compared their scores to those reported in Ruble's (1990) study which used American undergraduates as the sample. It was found that Americans students scored considerably higher in active experimentation (34.1 versus 29.5 for the local undergraduates) while Singaporean students scored higher in abstract conceptualization (34.6 for the local students versus 30.3 for their American counterparts). Using the American norm provided by Kolb and Fry (1975), students in all the seven academic disciplines included in the local sample belonged to the category of 'assimilator'. According to Kolb and Fry, 'assimilators' are good at inductive reasoning. They create theoretical models by assimilating disparate observations into an integrated explanation. If a logical and precise theory does not seem to be consistent with the facts, the assimilator is likely to disregard or reexamine the facts rather than the theory. At work, assimilators are at ease with principles and rules and 'find those activities requiring some conformity to directions or rules helpful'. As students, 'they...prefer assigned readings, examinations, and being given a task' (Kolb and Fry 1975). If young Singaporeans, due to their training and education, are prone to approach problems and conflict situations with theoretical models in mind and try to solve problems by applying theoretical models to situations, they are likely to be inflexible.

The learning style of Singaporean students is further reinforced by their up-bringing. Unlike their forefathers, young Singaporeans are brought up in a safe, orderly and affluent society. They are well-protected and do not have to go through the hardship experienced by their forefathers. As a result, they are relatively 'unexposed', and compared to youngsters in Hong Kong, are not as 'street-smart'. This lack of experience/exposure may be one of the factors contributing to the Singaporean graduates' lack of persuasiveness, noted earlier.

3. Another factor which may have affected the conflict frame of Singaporeans is the early and heavy emphasis on specialization. Students in Singapore are streamed into Science, Commerce, Humanities, and Technical education as early as Secondary 3 (Grade 9). Although students also have the choice of a mixed stream, this alternative is not very popular. General education is also not emphasized in tertiary education. As a result, while Singaporean graduates are good technical managers, they tend to have a rather narrow knowledge base. Many of Singapore's successful industries/businesses, (for example, communication networks, airline, port facilities and cargo trans-shipment, banking and financial services), can be attributed to the technical expertise of Singaporean managers.

   This strong technical orientation and 'narrow' education have implications for the conflict frame of Singaporean managers who are trained to analyze problems from the perspective of their specialization. Hence, they may not be good at appreciating a problem from different perspectives.

4. **Instrumental pragmatism**

   Post-independence Singapore has often been described as an economic miracle. Lester Thurow, in his preface to Schein's book, *Strategic pragmatism, the culture of Singapore's Economic Development Board*, claimed that no society has developed faster (than Singapore) (Schein 1996). The value behind the economic success of the city-state is best described as 'instrumental pragmatism'. The term refers to an approach to problems and situations in which the expedient and efficient attainment of material value is emphasized. There are three elements to Singaporean instrumental pragmatism: economic development as an ideology, material value orientation, and strong goal orientation.

   a) Ideology of economic development

   Economic development is an ideology which the government has promoted partly as it legitimizes the PAP as the architect of the economic 'miracle'. In as far as there is no qualitative end-state towards which the nation is striving, economic development is an ideology, a terminal value. It is an ideology of incessantly striving for excellence, for a higher and higher standard of living. As Clammer (1985) described it, Singapore is a 'problem state'. There is a 'permanent sense of crisis' and 'today's solution often becomes tomorrow's problem.' A good example is Singapore's Changi International Airport which has for many years been rated amongst the best in the world. In the early 1990s, the second Changi terminal was opened to increase the airport's capacity to handle anticipated passenger traffic into the next century. A few months after the second terminal opened, it was announced that planning for a third terminal had already started.

b) Material value orientation and pragmatism

With economic development as the terminal value, material value orientation and pragmatism are the instrumental values. Singapore is a society in which things of economic value or those which will help generate material value are given priority over those with little or no material value. It is a society in which science and technology are held in high regard whereas the arts, humanities and the social sciences are given attention only as far as they aid in the attainment of economic development. Clammer (1985) felt that pragmatism could have accounted for the paucity of research on culture and society, presumably because they are seen as being marginal to the 'real' issues of economic and technological development. In this context, he lamented an excess of pragmatic thinking in Singapore.

c) Strong goal orientation

Singapore as a society is single-minded about goal attainment. From the government down, targets are constantly set and employees and civil servants are exhorted to achieve tangible objectives. In the mid-sixties, the government set the targets of eliminating unemployment, controlling the birth rate, developing the nation's infrastructure, and providing basic medical care and housing for its people. By 1979, all the objectives had been achieved. The government then set the next objective: moving into high-skilled, high-technology and higher value-added industries. To achieve this objective, it relentlessly pushed up national wages to drive low-skilled, labor-intensive industries to relocate to other countries. It adopted aggressive measures to attract high-technology firms to invest in Singapore, and focused on the training and development of its workforce. By the early 1990s the Republic was well on track to achieve its long-cherished objective of attaining developed nation status.

Under the materialistic culture of the society, Singapore managers are rational, pragmatic, and goal-oriented. As negotiators, they focus on tangible outcomes. Unlike the Japanese, Singaporeans may not appreciate the need to spend hours socializing and building rapport. They are also likely to be impatient with differences and may perceive differences as impediments/barriers to goal attainment.

5. Related to Singaporeans' materialism is a Singaporean characteristic known as *kiasu*. Soh (1994) referred to *kiasu* as the infamous Singlish (Singapore English) phrase meaning 'afraid to lose, be left out or be without'. Singaporeans use the word in a self-deprecating way to describe a funny, yet undesirable aspect of the Singapore mentality. The term is so popular that *kiasu* cartoon characters appear regularly in newspapers, and there is even a series of comic books entitled, *Mr Kiasu, Everything also Scared Lose.* The following description of the comic character, 'Mr Kiasu', will help illustrate this Singaporean mentality:

"'Everything Also Scared Lose' - A very accurate description of Mr Kiasu who is so afraid of losing that he will do anything humanly possible to stay ahead of the competition. It doesn't matter what others think of him. As far as Mr Kiasu is concerned, it is a kiasu universe out there and only the kiasuest will survive."

Yu, Lau, and Suresh 1994.

This 'afraid to lose' mentality manifests itself in all types of social situations:

In restaurants...

"The kiasu Singaporeans will hoard or pile their plates up with food during a buffet, but leave it ultimately uneaten"

Soh 1994.

As a traveler...

"A Singaporean travelling in a tour group packed the pillow case provided by the hotel 'just in case' the next hotel does not provide clean pillow cases"

Dhaliwal 1994.

On the campus...

"Bulky files, containing all the study material and notes industriously highlighted with luminous markers; textbooks with almost every line judiciously underlined—just to make sure no important point gets missed out."

Chia *et al.* 1985.

The above, being excerpts from the popular literature, might have exaggerated the situation. However, the following incident (a news headline in a December, 1995 issue of a local newspaper) was used by the government to remonstrate with Singaporeans for being 'ungracious'. A cooperative society organized a collection of used primary school textbooks for distribution to needy students. The distribution, administered by student volunteers, was held at a public housing estate. A scuffle broke out as members of the crowd tried to get ahead in the queue to get the freebies. It was observed that some of the people who joined in the scuffle were actually quite well-off. Some even arrived in expensive cars. The *kiasu* mentality can be linked to two conflict-related behavioral traits. Firstly, Singaporeans are constantly comparing themselves with others to see how well they are faring. Thus, in negotiations, Singaporeans will always be comparing alternatives. Secondly, Singaporean managers are so *kiasu* that they cannot leave matters to chance or to others. Singaporean managers/students typically score very low in delegation in leadership instruments and when asked for an explanation, will say that they want to attend to the problem personally. In negotiations, Singaporean managers always plan for future contingencies and seek assurance—a behavior which may be interpreted by the other party as suspicious and lacking in trust. In reality, these are reflections of the insecurity and the *kiasu* mentality of Singaporeans and imply little about the trustworthiness of the other party.

6. Power distance

In Hofstede's cross-cultural study on work-related values, Singaporean managers scored high in power distance (Hofstede 1980). In many Asian societies, industrialization and westernization have weakened the traditional Asian value of respect for authority. In Singapore, while westernization has no doubt weakened young people's respect for authority, the value is still very much upheld in schools, at work, in the family and in society in general. In a survey of 2130 young adults in Singapore (39% in the 15–20 age category; 40% in the 21–30 category, and the remaining 21% in the 31–40 category), Kau and Yang (1991) found that 'As many as 87% of the Singaporeans surveyed agreed (from strongly to mildly) that it was important to respect authority in our society, ... only a very small 3% of them disagreed.' According to the authors, respect for authority was considered essential to the building of a disciplined society in which development, both social and political, can be enhanced.

Regarding the authority of elders in the family, the same study reported that 'Only 4% of the respondents felt that they did not have to listen to the advice of elders as compared to 42% who still believed in the importance of listening to the advice of the senior members of their families.' (Kau and Yang 1991 p.24.) However, when it came to filial piety, only 36% agreed with the statement that filial piety was still very much alive in Singapore. On the other hand, only 8% disagreed with the statement. The rest held a moderate opinion on this matter. Malays and Indians were found to be more tradition-bound in their values than the Chinese.

Singaporeans' respect for authority and high power distance are consistent with our earlier analysis of the macro socio-political environment of the nation-state, and with the government's emphasis on traditional family values. In relation to conflict, Singaporeans' acceptance of authority suggests that they are unlikely to openly challenge or speak up against decisions made by people in authority, even if they do not agree with the decisions. The findings of Lim (1994) cited in an earlier section can perhaps be explained in the context of power distance. Lim's study was designed to explore the conflict management behavior of subordinates. It is not surprising that the reported conflict management styles, in order of preference were: collaborating, compromising, accommodating, avoiding, and competing. After all, subordinates in a high power distance culture would not compete with their superiors. Neither would it be appropriate to adopt an avoidance strategy. Thus, in relation to a superior in the hierarchy, the appropriate modes of response were collaborating, compromising, and accommodating.

7. Multi-racial society

Singapore is a multi-racial society with three main racial groups: Chinese (75%), Malay (15%) and Indian (7%). The official statistics however mask a society which is considerably more diverse, as each racial category comprises many subgroups based on language, dialect, class, caste, and place of origin. While race is always an issue in a multi-racial society, in Singapore, it is a particularly thorny one due to the size of Singapore and its location among much larger, Malay dominated countries. Singapore's Malay minority shares an ethnic, cultural, and religious affinity with Malay Muslims in Malaysia and Indonesia.

Singapore's racial policy emphasizes multi-racialism rather than the ideology of the melting pot. The different ethnic groups are to retain distinct languages, religions, and customs, but participate in common institutions on an equal basis. Singapore's racial policy reflects the discretion and caution of the government. Had the government tried to assimilate the Malay minority by changing their cultural or religious identity, its Muslim-dominated neighbors might have perceived it as an attempt to 'de-Muslim' the Malays in Singapore. Given the sensitivity of racial and religious issues in Singapore, the government was determined to break up ethnically exclusive communities. The large-scale resettlement of the population from 'atap huts' to public housing estates provided the government with an opportunity to disperse the ethnic groups. Efforts were also made to foster a sense of community in the housing estate complexes. However, in spite of the efforts to mix the ethnic groups, few tenants regard their apartment blocks as communities in any meaningful sense. Residents' primary social ties are with relatives, old classmates, fellow-workers and others of the same ethnic group. In schools, students take English as the common language, but they also learn their mother-tongue. Housing estates are generally peaceful and orderly, and the relations between residents are marked by civility and mutual tolerance. (De Glopper 1991.)

The racial policy of Singapore requires the ethnic groups to retain their cultural heritage and to participate in social institutions without barrier. The apparently contradictory elements of the multi-racial policy have considerable impact on the way Singaporeans approach and handle conflict. The ethnic groups differ considerably in their social habits, cultures, values, and religious beliefs. Yet they are required to live, eat, shop, study, work in close proximity, and to use the same public facilities. To achieve racial harmony, a large dose of mutual respect, tolerance and restraint is required. Ultimately, the policy requires that Singaporeans do not confront openly but avoid situations which are prone to conflict, and gloss or smooth over contentious issues. Indeed, in the 'national ideology' formulated by the government, one of the core values was 'resolving issues through the search for consensus rather than contention, and promoting racial and religious tolerance'.

8. Face and avoidance of unpleasant situations

While 'face' and 'shame' are universal human characteristics, they have been observed to be more salient for oriental peoples. The importance of 'face' in social and business interactions in East Asia has often been noted (Redding and Ng 1982; Lindsay and Dempsey 1985; Wilson 1970; De Mente 1975) and Singaporeans are no exceptions. As the concept is likely to be discussed in other chapters in this volume, it will not be dealt with in detail here. Suffice it to say that in conflict situations, Asian concern for 'face' has often resulted in issues not being brought into the open for fear of 'losing face' or causing 'a loss of face' to the other party. Concern for 'face' has also resulted in the common use of intermediaries for fear that if a proposal is rejected, either or both parties may feel embarrassed or suffer a 'loss of face'.

Related to the concepts of 'face', 'loss of face' or 'shame' is the inability of many Asians to cope with embarrassment. Asians generally find it difficult to laugh off or shrug off an embarrassing situation. Hence, in order to avoid embarrassment, a person may choose to avoid a potentially embarrassing situation altogether, to use an intermediary, or to resort to subtle hints to get a message across.

The Singaporean Conflict Frame

Before discussing the Singaporean conflict frame, it should be noted that there is considerable variation among Singaporeans, especially along the age and race dimensions, in the way they perceive and handle conflict. Specifically, those in their mid-forties or older have been socialized and educated quite differently from the younger generations and may react differently. However, since the present paper focuses on developments after Singapore became a nation, the present discussion is confined to the conflict frame of younger Singaporeans.

The Singaporean managers we have depicted are rational and capable. They are confident as past collective success has given them a new self-esteem. Being brought up in an urban setting where MNCs abound and where people of different races, cultures, and religions mix and interact, they are tolerant of differences, and are racially and culturally sensitive. Relative to other managers in the region, they are well-trained, efficient, and task-oriented. In negotiations with Singaporean managers, while impression management and rapport building are important at the initial contact stage, it is unnecessary to spend too much time on relationship building (unlike dealing with Japanese managers). As with the Chinese and other orientals, *guanxi* (interpersonal connections) is important, but such relationships are more likely to be developed over time as each successful transaction adds to the mutual trust within the long-term relationship.

With their strong task orientation and materialist values, Singaporean managers are likely to focus on tangible outcomes and issues of economic relevance in negotiations. They are less likely to be interested in issues that are not instrumental or pragmatic in nature (for example aesthetic, cultural, or humanitarian issues). This does not mean that Singaporean managers are unethical. They are law-abiding and decent people, but in their value system, such issues just have low priority.

Singaporeans are afraid to lose out to others. The *kiasu* mentality reflects a strong concern for one's own interests. In a conflict management model, this mentality would place them towards the competing and avoiding end of the 'concern for self/others' interests' continuum. However, in spite of Singaporeans' concern for their own interests, they are rational and reasonable, and can appreciate others' concerns too. Thus, they are not aggressive in the sense that they would totally disregard the other persons' interests. Here, one can see the influence of a racial policy which requires different ethnic groups to retain their cultural heritage and to participate in social institutions without barrier. The fact that differences are tolerated and respected helps explain why Singaporeans consistently scored low in competing in spite of their *kiasu* mentality, and why compromising was the most preferred mode of conflict management across the four studies mentioned. (Using the crude method of adding the rankings of each style for the four studies, compromising scored the lowest—one point below avoiding, making it the most preferred mode of conflict management.) It is also important to note that while Singaporeans scored low in competing, they were not particularly prepared to accommodate their own interests either. (Accommodating is the second last in terms of style preference.)

The *kiasu* mentality however does mean that Singaporeans are likely to perceive a conflict situation with a fixed-pie/zero-sum mentality and adopt an initial defensive posture. In a discussion with a local HR manager on the conflict management styles of Singaporean managers, the manager compared local graduates with their overseas-educated counterparts and noted, 'The locally-educated managers tend to have a fixed-pie, win-lose mentality. They may know all the theories about collaboration and the win-win approach, but they are so afraid of losing out that they end up being defensive.' With their defensiveness, Singaporeans tend to be cautious in negotiations. Until they are sure of the ground, they are not likely to be open with their positions and will allow themselves sufficient room for bargaining in their opening positions. Cautiousness may also be reflected in the Singaporean's need for assurance—assurance that the other party will deliver their part of the deal on time and as agreed. This may at times be interpreted as a sign of lack of trust.

The *kiasu* mentality also leads to other behavioral traits. In matters that are important to them, Singaporeans will make every attempt to ensure that they do not lose out to others. In the education of their children, they will join the right society, church or association, do voluntary services for schools years before their children reach the schooling age, pull whatever strings they have, or wait in long queues in order to register their children in a good primary school. Once in it, those who can afford it often engage a small team of private tutors to ensure that their children stay ahead. Parents themselves tutor their children and monitor their progress. (Even ministers talk proudly to newspapers about how they personally tutor their primary school children to help them pass examinations with flying colors.) In any important matters that involve queuing, Singaporeans will do that extra bit to ensure that they do not lose out. If others may start queuing the night before, they will do so two nights before....

In business dealings, the way to ensure that one does not lose out is to plan for contingencies and to have options ready should things turn out to be different from what one expects. The *kiasu* Singaporean manager is unlikely to leave himself/herself in a vulnerable position. When a negotiation gets tough and open confrontation seems inevitable, or when it becomes apparent that differences cannot be resolved, the Singaporean is likely to opt out quietly. "They will say, 'I'll get back to you later', but of course, they never will", said an experienced business consultant, "They will just go for another alternative, to another supplier..."

The tendency to avoid confrontation and aggressive behavior (which may cause embarrassment), is related to Singaporeans' concern for 'face'. The more threatening/aggressive a local manager perceives the other party to be, the more likely it is that he or she will take the quiet way out. Commenting on the behavior of engineers working in a large electronics manufacturing firm, the personnel director of the company had this to say, "They don't complain. If they are unhappy with the company, they don't talk about it. But one day, out of the blue, they will hand in their resignation. And when you ask around, you find out that all along, they have been unhappy about this policy and that." Some expatriates may find this practice of quietly opting out frustrating. However, for the local managers, it is a way of avoiding unpleasant situations.

While young Singaporeans are generally well-versed in the desirability of integrative problem solving and the win-win approach, collaboration did not rank high as a preferred conflict management style in the four studies mentioned. This may be attributed to the fact that the socialization, education, and training of Singaporeans do not predispose them to this particular conflict management mode. Collaboration requires a person to take the initiative to break a deadlock and to put aside his or her defensiveness. It requires the ability to get out of established ways of thinking to come up with new ideas or alternatives. Collaboration also involves the ability to think across boundaries in order to come up with integrative solutions. As noted in our discussion, the overly-regulated system, the lack of pluralism in society, the highly pressurized examination-oriented education system, the lack of active experimentation in learning, and early specialization are not conducive to the qualities required for collaboration.

In response to employers' concerns, the government is actively examining the education system and the quality of learning. Another development which may change the situation is the regionalization drive of the government. Initiated in the early 1990s, regionalization results in many managers having to travel regionally on business and to take up overseas postings in countries like China, Vietnam, Hong Kong, Indonesia and the Philippines. This will definitely broaden the horizons of the local managers and, with more experience, Singaporeans will find it easier to persuade others to accept new ideas.

Finally, caution must be exercised when one talks about national traits (although Singapore is very small). Conflict management styles are likely to vary across races, age groups, organizational settings, and may differ depending on the status of the party(ies) involved. This point was clearly shown in Lim's (1994) study in which subordinates in a high power distance culture practiced different styles towards their superiors.

REFERENCES

Arieti, S. 1970. The role of cognition in the development of inner reality. In J. Hellmuth (ed.), *Cognitive Studies*, **1**, New York: Brunner/Mazel.

Bond, M.H. 1986. *The Psychology of the Chinese People*. Hong Kong: Oxford University Press.

Chew, I. and Lim, C. 1991. Is compromising the most preferred conflict resolution mode among the Chinese businessmen? Paper presented at 3rd International Eastern Academy of Management Conference, France.

Chia, C., Seet, K.K. and Wong, P.M. 1985. *Made in Singapore*. Singapore: Time Books International.

Chua, B.H. and Kuo, Eddie C.Y. 1991. The making of a new Nation: cultural construction and national identity in Singapore. Working papers, **no. 104**, Department of Sociology, National University of Singapore.

Chua, B.H. and Tan, J.E. 1995. Singapore: new configuration of a socially stratified culture. Working papers, **no. 127**, Department of Sociology, National University of Singapore.

Chua, B.H. 1995. Culture, multi-racialism and national identity in Singapore. Working papers, **no. 125**, Department of Sociology, National University of Singapore.

Clammer, J. 1985. *Singapore: Ideology, Society, Culture*. Singapore: Chopmen Publishers.

Clammer, J. 1993. Deconstructing values: the establishment of a national ideology and its implications for Singapore's political future. In G. Rodin (ed.), *Singapore Changes Guard: Social, Political and Economic Directions in the 1990s*. New York: St. Martin's Press. 34–51.

De Glopper, D.R. 1991. The society and its environment. In LePoer B.L. (ed.), *Singapore, a Country Study*. Federal Research Division, Library of Congress. 65–117.

De Mente, B. 1975. *Japanese Manners and Ethics in Business*. Tokyo: Simpson-Doyle & Co.

Dhaliwal, R. 1994. *The Kiasu Traveller - True Stories of the Ugly Singaporean Overseas*. Singapore: Brit Aspen Publishing.

Freedman, M. 1969. Why China? *Proceedings of the Royal Anthropological Institute of Great Britain*. London.

Hofstede, G. 1980. *Culture's Consequences: International Differences in Work-related Values*. Beverly Hills, CA: Sage Publications.

Kau, A.K. and Yang, C. 1991. *Values and Lifestyles of Singaporeans: A Marketing Perspective*. Singapore: Singapore University Press.

Kirkbride, P.S., Tang, S.F.Y. and Westwood, R.I. 1991. Chinese conflict preferences and negotiating behavior: cultural and psychological influences, *Organization Studies*, **12**.

Kolb, D.A. and Fry, R. 1975. Towards an applied theory of experiential learning. In C.L. Cooper (ed.), *Theories of Group Process*, London: Wiley, 33–58.

Kwok, K. W. 1995. Singapore: consolidating the new political economy. In *Southeast Asian Affairs*. Singapore: Institute of Southeast Asian Studies.

Lim, J.C. 1994. *Conflict Management Behavior of Subordinates in Singapore*. Academic Exercise, Faculty of Business Administration, National University of Singapore.

Lindsay, G.P. and Dempsey, B.L. 1985. Experience in training Chinese business people to use U.S. management techniques, *Journal of Applied Behavioral Science*, **21** (1).

McKenna, S. 1995. The business impact of management attitudes towards dealing with conflict: a cross-cultural assessment. *Journal of Managerial Psychology*, 10 (7), 22–7.

Purushotam, N. 1995. Disciplining differences; 'Race in Singapore'. Working papers, **no. 126**, Department of Sociology, National University of Singapore.

Rahim, M.A. 1983. *Rahim Organizational Conflict Inventories*. Palo Alto, CA: Consulting Psychologist Press.

Redding, S.G. and Ng, M. 1982. The role of face in the organizational perceptions of Chinese managers. *Organization Studies*, **3** (3), 201–9.

Redding, S.G. 1990. *The Spirit of Chinese Capitalism*. Berlin/New York, NY: Walter de Gruyter.

Ruble, T.L. 1990. A psychometric analysis of Kolb's Revised Learning-Style Inventory, *Proceedings of the 17th Annual Conference of ABSEL*, **17**, 147–9.

Schein, E.H. 1996. *Strategic Pragmatism: The Culture of Singapore's Economic Development Board*. Cambridge, Mass.: MIT Press.

Soh, P. 1994. *Ah Soh's Collection of Singapore Catchphrases*. Singapore: EPB Publishers.

Straits Times, Singapore, Singapore Press Holdings, various issues.

Sunday Times, Singapore, Singapore Press Holdings, 11 August, 1996; 8 September, 1996; 29 September, 1996.

Thomas, K.W. and Kilmann, R.H. 1974. *Thomas-Kilmann Conflict Mode Instrument*. Tuxedo, NY: Xicom. Inc.

Willmott, W. 1989. The emergence of nationalism. In Sandu, and Wheatley (eds.), *Management of Success*. Singapore: Institute of Southeast Asian Studies.

Wilson, R.W. 1970. *Learning to be Chinese*, Cambridge, Mass.: MIT Press.

Wu, Y.-L. and Wu C-H. 1980. *Economic Development in Southeast Asia: The Chinese Dimension*. Hoover Institute Press, Calif.: Stanford University Press.

Yeo, K.C. Unpublished findings of survey conducted in 1995. Data computed and compiled, but not written up.

Yu, C., Lau, J. and Suresh, J. 1994. *Mr Kiasu - Everything also Scared Lose*. Singapore: Comix Factory.

Yuen, C.C. and Lee, S.N. 1994. Learning styles and their implications for cross-cultural management in Singapore, *Journal of Social Psychology*, **134** (5), 593–600.

CHAPTER SIX

Managing Conflict in Malaysia: Cultural and Economic Influences

NORMA MANSOR
Faculty of Economics and Administration,
University of Malaya, Kuala Lumpur, Malaysia

INTRODUCTION

Conflict happens when two incompatible actions or behaviours occur (Deutsch 1973). Organizations have to deal with conflict all the time. It ranges from work issues of responsibility, power, authority, and ethics to interpersonal matters like misunderstandings, difference of opinion and poor communication between two persons that, if allowed to degenerate into anger or hostility, would adversely affect the company's performance. As businesses become more competitive they generate more conflicts, and managers cannot get off the hook by rationalizing, 'I thought the rules were clear' and '... this case has nothing to do with me'. Those words may sound good and logical at the time, but at the end of the month productivity may fall short of expectations. Action or behavior, argued Schein (1985), is a manifestation of values and underlying assumptions. Therefore, it is important for managers to understand what is valued by the person/s being managed. Deutsch (1973), who has written widely on conflict, said conflict is determined by what is valued by the conflicting parties.

The objective of this paper is to highlight some of the dynamics of conflict management in Malaysia. However, to understand some of the factors that could contribute to conflict in Malaysia, it is necessary to understand the basic values underlying employees' behavior in Malaysian organizations.

This chapter will therefore examine some Malaysian core values, particularly Malay values, and the economic and social changes that could have influenced these values. Also, some reminders will be given on ways of handling problems and avoiding barriers to effective conflict management.

Consider the following two stories.

Story 1

The Faculty of Sociology recently had a new administrator, Mr. Sabri. He was relatively young and reputed to be a very dynamic and efficient officer. On the Monday morning of the second week of his appointment he stormed into the record's office of the faculty and, appearing visibly upset, scolded Ms. Ho the office supervisor for improper filing of students' records. He said he had had problems in retrieving a student's file.

Ms. Ho the senior supervisor had been with the record's office for the past 21 years and had held the supervisor's post for a decade. She did not react to the administrator. However, two weeks later she went to the Dean and applied for 20 days leave, the balance of her annual leave, and indicated her intention to resign.

Story 2

Company ADAM, a property company, wanted to sell a 20,000 sq. ft. piece of land. Mr. Lim, one of the executive officers, said that his friend, Mr. Ram offered RM500,000 for the land and that he had given Mr. Ram his word that he was going to sell it to him. Mr. Wan, another company employee, argued that the land was worth more than RM500,000.

The cases above are common in a business setting. However, the first story illustrates a common trait among Malaysians: that a subordinate would not confront her boss, even when she was not pleased with his behavior. A disagreement is not easily expressed in public. However, her non-reaction does not mean that the supervisor's behavior is acceptable. The consequence is uncooperative behavior followed by a resignation.

The second story is about a difference of opinion that could lead to a conflict situation. Another important factor in Malaysian business is the consideration given to friends and relations. Friendship ties that are long established are built on trust and loyalty. Many business deals are built on trust. However, despite being relationship-oriented Malaysians are also rational businessmen.

In Malaysia many more sensitivities are added to an issue. These sensitivities can be traced back to hierarchy, relationship, religion and 'how' conflict is handled. A senior versus a junior employee; a problem involving two good friends; a muslim who will not drink alcohol; and direct comments in public would be among the issues to be avoided in Malaysia.

An underlying premise of this chapter is that when conflicts within organizations are handled in a co-operative context, there are beneficial outcomes like increased work effort, acceptance of agreement and better relationships (Chia, 1984).

A literature search showed no published or unpublished work that deals specifically with conflict management or conflict behavior in the Malaysian context. Also, no work has been done on the changing value system among Malaysians. There were, however, articles written on local Malaysian culture and the Malaysian value system. The work of Dahlan (1991), *Local Values in Intercultural Management*; Mano Maniam (1986), *The Influence of Culture in Management in Malaysia*; and Hamzah Sendut and Gregory Thong (1989), *Managing the Plural Society* are observations and reflections on the core values of Malaysians. Although the articles are qualitative writings and no survey was conducted as such, the articles nonetheless provide information on the beliefs and values among Malaysians.

There were five scientific studies conducted on the work value system among Malaysians. These studies are by Scott (1968), Rashid (1977), Huat (1988), The Malaysian Institute of Management (1990–1992) and Sabri Tajuddin (1995). In the absence of works on conflict management, these works on Malaysian work values will be highlighted. Scott conducted in-depth interviews on political beliefs with 17 Malaysian civil servants in Kuala Lumpur. By adopting Florence and Kluckkohn he found that these civil servants were traditional-oriented, fatalistic individuals who see life as a struggle for a share in a 'constant pie' (Scott 1968).

Rashid (1977) administered the Graves' framework of 'Level of Psychological Existence' in a study of the work-related value system of managers of the three main ethnic groups in Malaysia namely, Malays, Chinese, Indians. Forty-eight items were used to measure six value systems: the tribalistic, the egocentric, the materialistic, the conformist, the socio-centric, and the existential, against the perceived importance of company loyalty, the boss, money, profits, work, job freedom, role of big companies, and company rules. Tribalistic values are held by people who respect and adhere to tradition. An egocentric person views things in relation to himself, divorced from the constraints of the society.

Manipulative people are associated with materialism and objectivity. A conformist has a high regard for authority and rules. Socio-centric people prefer to be with other people since they have a greater need for affiliation. Existential people like to work on their own and prefer challenging jobs. Rashid's findings showed that Malay managers were more egocentric than Chinese managers, especially in their opinion on the value of money. Chinese managers were more conformist than Malay managers, particularly with regard to company loyalty and company rules. Chinese managers were more materialistic than their Malay counter parts in terms of profits, job freedom and working for a big company, but Malay managers were more materialistic than Chinese managers, especially in their choice of preferred superiors and on profits. Malay managers were also more socio-centric than Chinese managers in relation to preferred superiors and corporate profits. Malay managers were more existential than Chinese managers *vis-a-vis* company loyalty and preferred type of superior. However, Rashid concluded that successful managers from both groups share common value systems.

The result of an unpublished study by Huat (1988) showed that Malaysian managers had pragmatic, moralistic, aesthetic and mixed value systems. Pragmatic in this case refers to people whose actions are dictated more by practical consequences than other considerations. Moralistic people conform to certain standards expected by society. Aesthetic people are more inclined to regard the artistic aspects of life as very important. Using England's Personal Values Questionnaire (PVQ), Huat studied the personal value systems of 106 Malaysian managers in small manufacturing firms. A total of 34 items were used to measure three personal value systems—the pragmatic, the moralistic and the aesthetic.

A team (which included the author) from the Malaysian Institute of Management (MIM) carried out a study on Malaysian values in 1990–1992. Employing England's PVQ framework, it surveyed 1678 Malaysian managers on managerial values. Sixty-six items were used to measure 66 managerial values classified in two different categories, the strongest values (top ranking according to mean) and the weakest values (lowest ranking according to mean). Table 6.1 shows the ten strongest and the ten weakest managerial values. Goal clarification, cooperation and decisiveness are top ranked values whereas authoritativeness, honesty in business and nepotism are the weakest values.

Table 6.1 The Ten Strongest and Weakest Managerial Values

	Strongest Values	Weakest Values
1	Goal Clarification	Authoritativeness
2	Cooperation	Honesty in Business
3	Decisiveness	Nepotism
4	Commitment	Aggressiveness
5	Achievement	Female Non-assertion
6	Accountability	Competitiveness
7	Mentoring	Equality of the Sexes
8	Meritocracy	Religion
9	Creativity	Loyalty
10	Deadlines	Consultation

Source: MIM, Summary Report, 1992

Table 6.2 Comparison of the Ten Strongest Managerial Values by Ethnic Group

National Survey: Strongest Values	National Ranking	Malays	Chinese	Indians
Goal Clarification	1	1	4	2
Cooperation	2	2	3	3
Decisiveness	3	3	2	1
Commitment	4	5	5	4
Achievement	5	4	6	5
Accountability	6	6	7	9
Mentoring	7	7	9	8
Meritocracy	8	9	8	6
Creativity	9	8	10	7
Deadlines	10	10	1	10

Source: MIM, Summary Report, 1992

The comparison by ethnic groups are given in Table 6.2. The strongest values were: goal clarification for the Malays, deadlines for the Chinese, and decisiveness for the Indians.

Another unpublished work on Malaysian values is by Sabri Tajuddin (1995). Sabri was inspired by Rashid's 1977 study. He adopted the Values for Working Questionnaire (VWQ) and surveyed 168 engineers on the value systems of different ethnic groups. The second part of the study examined whether the value systems affect organizational, performance, and work competence. The findings confirmed the earlier study by

Rashid. Malaysian engineers of different ethnic groups do not differ in their value systems. The study indicated that they view company loyalty, the boss, money, company profit, work, job freedom, roles of big companies and company rules in the same manner.

However, in terms of ranking the values of the engineers, the following order was observed. As far as company loyalty is concerned, the engineers, especially Malay and Indian engineers, prefer to work on their own and enjoy a job that is challenging (existential). In terms of preferred superiors, Malays, Chinese and Indians expressed emphasis on the existential value system. This is indicated by their high score on the existential value system scale. With regard to money they prefer the conformist value system. As far as work is concerned, Malay and Indian engineers are inclined to the materialistic value system, i.e., they measure their success in terms of materialistic gains and prefer to work on their own without much interference from the boss. In terms of job freedom, Sabri found that engineers gave more emphasis to the conformist value system.

Although these studies used relatively small samples and were limited to certain professions several conclusions could be drawn:

(i) It is generally accepted that there is not much difference as far as work values are concerned among Malaysians of different ethnic groups.

(ii) An earlier study by Huat (1968) found that civil servants were more traditional and fatalistic in outlook.

(iii) Later studies by Rashid (1977) and Sabri (1995) found that engineers in the private sector were more egocentric, materialistic and existentialist.

All these findings did not altogether reject the fact that Malaysian engineers could be tribalistic or traditionalist and conformist in some aspects of their work. Over the years, undoubtedly work values have changed, especially among Malaysian professionals.

WHO ARE THE MALAYS AND WHAT ARE THE MALAY VALUES?

Malay is a term describing the indigenous people of the Malay Archipelago, a group of islands which now form part of Indonesia, the Philippines, Singapore, Brunei, and Malaysia. There are various groups among the Malay such as the Minangkabau, Achinese, Javanese, Bugis,

Banjarese and Malays in different parts of the Archipelago. In the Malaysian constitution, a Malay is defined as a person, born of Malay parents, and residing in Malaysia, whereas citizens who are Malays, Chinese, Indians and members of other ethnic groups in Malaysia are called Malaysians.

The Malays and other indigenous peoples of Sabah and Sarawak, are considered '*bumiputra*'. They were generally farmers, but included a small number engaged in fishing and they lived in rural areas. The colonial administration reinforced the occupational pattern and thus the *bumiputras* were not included in the mainstream of development. The early independence administration continued the same *laissez-faire* system until the 1970s when a serious effort was made by the government to develop a new generation of Malays and other indigenous groups equipped with skills and with knowledge of economics and trade.

Essential Values in the Malaysian Society

The Malays are described as 'humble, self -effacing ... and above all, he is polite and courteous'. In fact, the British are reported to have seen many of the same refinements in Malay culture that they valued in their own and considered Malays 'nature's gentlemen' (Funston 1980). These characteristics could mean that he is seldom fully frank, will generally not call a spade a spade. Open criticism is not a natural response; aggression is normally sublimated (Rao 1977). As a result, this indirectness could cause misunderstanding and give rise to conflicts. The behavioral traits of being hospitable, accommodating, forgiving, peace loving and charitable had been misread as inability to be aggressive or decisive, undermining his diligence and his capacity for work (Maniam 1986).

The Malays live in *kampung* (villages) where the *adat* or the norms are important. It is of utmost importance to uphold the good name of the *kampung*. This community-oriented feeling is similar to the concept of collectivism adopted by Hofstede in his study on the influence of national culture on management. In contrast with a society that values individualism, to the Malays rules and traditions upheld by the community are more important than an individual's rights and freedom. Whereas in the individualistic society, one's independence and identity is asserted, in the Malay community the harmony of the community supercedes any individual's interest. As a Malay proverb says '*Biar mati anak jangan mati adat*'. It means 'It is alright to lose one's child but not to lose one's customs and traditions'. A strong and cohesive community has a very strong hierarchical order and the elders are highly respected. It is an obligation for children to respect their parents and the elderly. An extension of this is reflected at the village level whereby the headman and religious *guru* is paramount. Conflict is generally avoided and even suppressed. The rule is that the younger member must accommodate the needs of the elder. Similarly, when a conflict situation arises between an ordinary member of the community and a highly respected person in the community the latter has the upper hand. People try to conform to the norms that guide day-to-day behavior. Norms are the unspoken rules inherent in behaviors and practises. For Malays a number of these unstated understandings are contained in the *peribahasa* (proverbs) and *perumpamaan* (metaphors). To avoid conflict, a decision or crisis is usually reached through consensus led by the village head. Although some of these values are changing, particularly for the urban and more industrialized people, they are still widely upheld.

Malays were governed by a sultanate system, characterised by patronage and feudalistic tradition. The Sultan had absolute power and he appointed people to rule and collect taxes on his behalf. The ruling hierarchy started with the Four Major Chiefs (*Orang Besar Berempat*), each heading one of the four major regions. This was followed by the Eight Major Chiefs, Sixteen Minor Chiefs, and finally, the lowest recognised member of the ruling class was the village head. The Sultan was associated with mystic powers by his subjects and so commanded respect and undivided loyalty from his people. The ruler was also the guardian and protector of the ruled, taking care of their welfare. The Sultan was thus perceived to be benevolent. In modern-day Malay society, despite the eroding status of the Sultans, it is evident that the value of tolerating authoritarianism, especially when it is accompanied by benevolence, is still prevalent.

On the other hand, loyalty is mandatory of the ruled. Unquestioning loyalty runs high even in the modern Malay community although not necessarily to the Sultans. Often it is to political leaders or respectable members of the community. Deference to authority is considered an important element that holds together the fabric of the social order. The legendary figure called Hang Tuah is believed to have sacrificed his best friend to uphold his loyalty to the Sultan. The concept *durhaka* is associated with 'disloyalty or disobey' and the punishment is death. One is considered disloyal not only for disobeying formal orders but also when the Sultan's wishes or perceived needs are not acceded to.

Despite the colonial administration, the Malay Sultanate structure is still maintained. According to the hierarchical structure of Malay society, the Sultan is highest placed, followed by Major Chiefs and then village headmen who were appointees of the Sultan. This concept of reverence is translated in contemporary Malaysian society into titles conferred on distinguished persons by the King and Sultans (heads of states). Historically, this was done to honor civil servants who had provided good service to the public; today, these titles are also awarded to politicians and businessmen who have made contributions to society. The titles are '*Tan Sri, Tun, Datuk Seri, Datok, Datin Paduka* (female only)'.

Another common trait among Malays is the *tidak apa* attitude. *Tidak apa* is a Malay phrase that can be translated as 'it's alright', 'never mind' or 'don't worry'. This *tidak apa* attitude describes the easy-going Malays well. The phrase is often uttered in everyday conversation. For example, a crane falls on some houses, and someone still could say *tidak apa*. This attitude makes Malays sometimes lax about safety and security. On the other hand, Malays are forgiving, especially when the other party apologises. Because of this *tidak apa* attitude, Malays are usually better at handling ambigious situations.

Budi describes a good deed performed. The receiver of the kind gesture is 'indebted for life' to the doer. Although 'for life' is a bit of an exaggeration a person who is the recipient of the *budi* would go out of his way to help a person who had helped him out earlier. Or, at the very least, not do anything that would offend a person who had *berbudi*. On the contrary a person is considered *tidak mengenang budi* when he forgets a person who has helped him *berbudi*. As an example, among fishermen when the catch is not good he will go to a middleman 'A' to get his daily supplies, on credit. When the catch is good he will sell to the middleman 'A', even when middleman 'A' buys at a lower price. Similarly, a friend who helped close a deal would always be remembered and would probably be given the same support when required. Story 2 about Mr. Lim and Mr. Ram described earlier could be motivated by this value.

Islam is the official religion and although there is freedom to practise any religion, Islam is a religion of the Malays and several other indigenous groups. The adherence to Islam is relatively moderate although Muslims in Malaysia are pious. In their everyday lives, the five times a day prayers are generally performed and many work places provide a prayer room. Two of the prayers fall during working hours, and can be performed during the lunch and tea breaks. Friday prayers, which affect only Muslim males, are performed at mosques or any place with a minimum of 40 persons. A Muslim man should not miss Friday prayers three times consecutively. Fasting (abstaining from food and drink) during the day in the month of Ramadhan is another obligation of the Muslim population. Non-Muslims are of course free to eat and drink during this time. The Muslim diet excludes pork and ham. It would therefore be insensitive to serve pork to a Muslim.

Muslims in Malaysia are, however, a pragmatic group unlike the Muslims in the middle-east or Pakistan. Malaysian Muslims manage to practise Islam and yet be liberal and competitive in business and trade. Instead of following the middle-eastern model of Islam and emphasizing Islamic jurisprudence, Muslims in Malaysia created their own economic system including Islamic banking and insurance and established Islamic foundations such as the *Lembaga Tabung Haji*. These systems are as competitive as other banks, investment bodies, and insurance companies in Malaysia.

It is important to mention that the Chinese who came to Malaysia in large numbers in the last century have developed their values and social structure within the wider Malaysian society of which they are a part. They value hard work and their practical approach to life makes them very successful in business. They also brought with them their cultural heritage and traditions. Wealth is important as it gives high social status. A close-knit family is also very important to the Chinese. Filial piety is shown by helping to operate the family business in return for only board and lodging. When the business thrives, family members are rewarded. The family unit is expanded to the community level in the form of the clan. In return for clan support the member has to pledge his or her undivided loyalty. Modern Malaysian Chinese enterprises retain ownership and control within the same family and clan wherever possible.

Respect for one's elders is evident among the contemporary Chinese especially on the paternal side of the family. The family unit revolves around the oldest member of the family alive, whether grandfather, grandmother, or father.

Elements from the long tradition of the Indians have long been part of the Malay culture due to historical factors such as trade and religion. There was Hinduism in Malaysia before Islam. Authority and a hierarchy which reflects a person's status in the government and professional services play an important role in the lives of Indians.

The concept of 'face' is important to almost all Malaysians irrespective of ethnic groups (Asma ed. 1995). The Chinese call it 'face', the Malays *maruah* and *air muka*. Face means more than a literal English translation of the word i.e., 'the front part of a person's head'. In Malaysian culture it is associated with dignity: the ultimate measure of a person. Dignity is associated both with how a person regards himself and how he is regarded by others. Others can be his family, friends, work mates or society in general.

A Malaysian strives to exhibit traits such as honesty, generosity, respect, sincerity, righteousness, love, and caring (Mansor 1992). A Malaysian expects these qualities to be valued by the person interacting with him. This reciprocity is an act of respect for the other person. It would be unacceptable not to show such respect to another because that would be tantamount to 'losing face'. 'Loss of face' is worse than physical maltreatment and is near impossible to redeem.

Take the first story at the beginning of this chapter. The administrator was so direct in his approach, pointing out errors in front of the supervisor's subordinates. The implication as perceived by the supervisor was that she was not capable of doing her job. The supervisor did not react openly to the boss despite her loss of face since that would be perceived as confrontational, but she became less co-operative and eventually left the organization.

In the last two decades Malaysia has undergone rapid economic changes followed by changes in the social structure. Such rapid change raises several important questions. What impact have these economic changes had on Malaysians, particularly on their mind-set, attitudes and values? Is it possible that despite all the changes around them their cognitive processes remain unchanged? Or is 20 years too short a period to witness any real change in people's perception? The traditional values mentioned above could impede progress and development but in Malaysia this does not seem to be the case. In an attempt to answer the above questions and concerns we have to look at the dynamics of the economic and social changes in the last two decades.

Economic and Social Changes

Covering an area of 330,000 square kilometers, Malaysia has a population of almost 20 million people. The people are of diverse ethnic backgrounds; Malays and other indigenous groups (61.7%), Chinese (27.2%), Indian

(7.7%) and Others (3.4%). Despite the diverse nature of the Malaysian population, the concoction of ethnic groups has co-existed through a history of western and eastern imperialism. The British ruled Malaya (the former name of Malaysia) in the late 19th century and during World War II the Japanese were in Malaya for a brief period. The religious beliefs include Islam, Hinduism, Buddhism, and Christianity. This diversity is reflected in the educational system. At the primary level children may be educated (a matter of choice) at any one of the National, Chinese, Tamil or (until mid-1970) English-medium schools. Students in tertiary education attend local and foreign institutions in equal numbers.

Economic progress in the last 10 years has been remarkable averaging 6.7% growth in 1986–89 and 8.4% in 1990–95. Over the period 1970–90, the Malaysian economy has been growing at an average rate of 6.7% per annum. The leading sector is manufacturing, growing at the rate of 11.6% per annum in 1971–75, 13.5% in 1976–80, 4.9% in 1981–85, 13.7% in 1986–90 and 12.5% in 1995.

This transformation of the economic structure started about three decades ago. Historically, the Malaysian economy had been dependent on exports of tin and rubber. During the independence years of the 1950s, those two primary commodities comprised 46% of the country's gross domestic product (GDP). The Malaysians were mainly farmers, planting *padi* (rice) once a year and rubber tapping, and 70% of the population lived in rural areas. However, in response to both internal and external factors, the government began a series of economic reforms. In the 1950s, government policies were aimed at promoting growth, adopting a *laissez-faire* approach. There were a few industries, mainly concentrating on manufacturing limited ranges of processed foods for domestic consumption and the business was small-scale. These industries were faced with the problem of a large capital investment and a small market. Business was localized and there was no marketing and distribution network. Very few manufactured products were exported and the manufacturing sector's contribution was only about 13% of GDP. Participation in this sector was predominantly by Chinese Malaysians, the Malays and Indians remaining in the agricultural sector. Export business was largely limited to raw materials, trade in which was dominated by the colonial capital, and had nothing to do with local businesses.

However, the racial riots that broke out in 1969 reflected the Malays' discontentment about their lack of economic advancement, a lack which was very much tied to the ownership of capital. The Malays owned only 1.5% of the total shares issued by limited companies, the Chinese owned 22.8%, the Indians 0.9% and foreigners owned 62.1% (Second Malaysia Plan 1971–75). The segregation was clear: the Chinese controlled business and manufacturing activities; agricultural activities were dominated by Malays. Following the riots, the government implemented the New Economic Policy (NEP) 1970–1990. The policy aimed to reduce and eventually eradicate poverty by revising income levels and increasing employment and business opportunities among all Malaysians, irrespective of race; and by restructuring Malaysian society to correct economic imbalances. The objective was to eliminate the identification of particular races with particular economic functions and especially the identification of economic backwardness and race. The NEP was also a social engineering program to provide support for Malays and other indigenous groups and enable them to participate in business activities. The policy has resulted in an overall rapid expansion of business and commercial activities at the same time as the economy was purposefully directed towards export-led growth. New business ventures, especially manufacturing, were also promoted and the production base was diversified to include more productive, higher value-added processes.

To overcome the problems of lack of capital and modern technology the government introduced policies to attract foreign companies particularly those in export-oriented industries. These policies include the Pioneer Industry Incentive (PII) which grants tax holidays of between two to five years to firms depending on the value of their fixed capital investment. Additional tax relief of one year each is granted if firms are established in a development area and numerous fiscal incentives, including special incentives to export-oriented industries, are offered to firms locating in free trade zones. From the 1970s onwards many foreign multinationals came to Malaysia because of the low cost of labor which was relatively highly educated and the country's improved infrastructure. During the 1980s Foreign Direct Investment in Malaysia constituted about 60% of the total approved investment. These foreign companies employed Malaysians to work at various levels.

The process of transforming the economy can be described as a shift over the last 25 years from producing mainly agricultural products to a more industrialized and modern economy.

Table 6.3 shows the decline of the agricultural sector from 44.3% in 1970 to 20.5% in 1995 with a corresponding increase in the secondary sector. The tertiary or services sector is growing at a slower pace but the

Table 6.3 Malaysia: Percentage Contribution of the Primary, Secondary and Tertiary Sectors to GDP, 1970–2000

	1970	1980	1990	1995	2000
Primary *	44.3	33.9	28.1	20.5	15.5
Secondary **	18.3	24.9	30.0	36.5	40.6
Tertiary	37.4	41.2	41.9	43.0	43.9

Notes: * Includes agriculture and mining
** Includes manufacturing and construction
Source: Malaysia 1991: **72**; Malaysia 1996: **52** extracted from Abdul Rahman Embong (1996)

government is pushing hard to further enhance the financial, education and information technology sectors and they are expected to contribute 43.9% to GDP by end of the century.

The transformation of the economy has changed the employment structure. The agricultural sector which employed 53.5% of the workforce in 1970 declined to 27.8% in 1990. (Malaysia 1991: 116–117). In contrast, the manufacturing sector increased from 8.7% in 1970 to 19.5% in 1990, recording an annual growth rate of 10.3%. Employment in the non-government service sector also increased, from 20.5% in 1970 to 35.8% in 1994. These proportions will change further with future changes in the economic structure. The manufacturing sector is expected to employ 23.9% of the workforce by the year 2000.

The rigorous development efforts in the past three decades were followed by rapid urbanization. In the 1970s about 26.7% of the population lived in urban areas. The rapid expansion of the secondary sector, especially manufacturing, which occurred in the big cities such as Kuala Lumpur, Penang and Johore Bahru contributed to a large rural-urban migration. By 1991 the urban population had increased to 50.7% of the total population (Malaysia 1995) and by 1995 it was 54.7%.

Education has been an important part of Malaysia's economic development. Following the New Economic Policy (NEP), since 1970 the government has increased its efforts to develop its human resources. The budget for public education has been the third largest item in all development plans since the 1970s, from the Second Malaysia Five Year Plan to the current Seventh Five-Year Development Plan. Although in the 1970s education was conceived as part of the overall socio-economic development of the country in the 1980s and 90s it was felt to be vital in order to fulfil the industrial and commercial aspirations of the country.

In the third quarter of the 1980s, when foreign companies came in large numbers to operate their businesses in Malaysia, there was an increasing demand for skilled and competent workers. This increased demand coupled with limited places at local tertiary institutions led many students to go overseas to pursue their education. Altogether it was estimated that, at any one time, 70,000 students were studying abroad (The Star, April 3 1994). These students included government and privately sponsored candidates. They were mainly in universities in the U.S., U.K. Australia and Canada. The majority of them returned to Malaysia and formed professional, managerial and executive groups.

A large number of Malaysians have thus been exposed to the western mindset, which includes theories and concepts (especially in the social sciences) which originated in the west. In addition, the interactions that these Malaysian students had during their early adult years (between the ages of 17 to 30 years) will have influenced their behaviors and values. Consequently, many Malaysians may have adopted western attitudes and assumptions. Recently many more private colleges have been set up as result of a more liberal approach to education. Under the 'twinning' programmes, new arrangements with foreign universities have been established. The free flow of professors mainly from the West could presumably see the introduction of theories originating from the West that may have an impact on the values of graduates studying in Malaysia.

Implications for Conflict Management

In spite of the rapid economic growth and social changes, Malaysians by and large (irrespective of ethnic groups) are guided by traditional values (Sabri 1995). Probably it is still too early to witness any real change as far as attitudes and values are concerned. The transformation of the economy and the change in the employment structure as described earlier happened in a span of 20 years and the process of urbanization is equally recent. Evidently, Malaysian workers in general but Malays in particular prefer to maintain harmonious relationships. An open and direct confrontation may be more transparent but the outcome could be disastrous. The persons in conflict could possibly withdraw and the negative reaction be reflected in an uncooperative manner. As in the first story, involving the supervisor, it is wise to point out errors in private.

Given the importance of collectivism and 'face' among Malaysians, conflict should be handled in a non-confrontational way. A more compromising approach could be beneficial to the group. Malaysians are more cooperative when they are convinced they are in a win-win situation. Top management therefore has to impress upon company employees that they are members of a group and group members should help each other since the company suffers if one employee does not perform well. If an employee is weak he needs support from other team members: cooperation is vital for the sake of company's survival. This approach might go against managerial efficiency theories taught in management schools, but in Malaysia to act differently would further complicate the matter. A more direct method could be perceived as a personal attack as often task and personal issues get entangled. The NEP that was mentioned earlier is clearly an affirmative action. A substantial amount of public revenue is allocated for the advancement of education and business of the *bumiputra* group. Apparently the policy is acceptable to the other ethnic groups because they are convinced that the end result, a better distribution of wealth, is for the good of everybody.

Seniority is one of the cardinal principles of Confucianism and it is equally valued by the Malays and Indians as well as the Chinese. It also remains important at the workplace. Although meritocracy is gaining importance, the traditional concept whereby authority is closely associated with seniority is still very much in a Malaysian's mind and subordinates tend to accept second place when dealing with someone senior. Therefore, when faced with conflict in the Malaysian context it is always useful to find out which party is more senior.

In some conflict situations a senior, especially an elderly person, can act as a 'third party'. When two partners cannot agree on an issue or reach a deadlock in discussions, sometimes a neutral senior will mediate or at least clarify some key points.

Seniority in position carries the same weight as seniority due to age. When resolving a conflict, knowing the seniority levels of the different parties involved is useful. One is expected to be very cautious when dealing with the situation—polite behavior is usually appreciated. The same is true when dealing with titled gentlemen and ladies.

The inherited traditional values of respect and loyalty to the Sultan are translated into deference to authority in everyday Malaysian life. As is often said, 'he is the boss and the boss is always right'. This is confirmed by Hofstede's (1983) study which shows that Malaysia falls into the category that has a large power distance. Although a manager may be perceived as being authoritarian when he intervenes in a conflict or makes a decision on a vital issue, Malaysians expect that of a manager.

The conflict need not necessarily be over a major issue but it is easily resolved when 'the boss' intervenes.

Malaysians are generally religious, as mentioned in the preceding section and all parties should be aware of the implications of this. When two parties are in conflict, the issue might have little to do with religion but it may, as illustrated by the following example. When a deadline is to be met, a conflict may arise when a Muslim man is asked to skip his Friday prayers to meet the deadline. It would cause less conflict if he was asked to stay late in the evening.

Although traditional values are still important to Malaysians, the advent of western education and the demands of industrial work also have an impact on Malaysian mind-set. This is true especially among middle-level employees. Middle-level managers of all ethnic groups share some common attitudes about work. This could be due to education. Both the studies conducted by Rashid (1977) and Sabri (1995) confirmed the emergence of this phenomenon. The influence of foreign education is apparent on a large number of them, since even those who graduated from local universities were taught western management practices which are essentially based on a somewhat different value system. However, it is inaccurate to assume that they have abandoned traditional values. It is not a question of one or the other—in most cases there is a coexistence of traditional and western values.

As mentioned earlier, since the 1970s people have migrated from rural areas to big towns in search of industrial jobs. The majority of these employees occupy the lower levels of organizations, but some of them educate themselves and are promoted to supervisory positions. Generally however, these employees stick together and very much adhere to traditional values. Managers must be sensitive to this fact as what works among foreign-educated, middle-level Malaysian executives will not necessarily generate the same results from the production line workers.

To avoid any misinterpretation of events a manager should listen to more than one source. Interacting with employees also gives a manager access to the 'grapevine'. In Malaysia, where confrontation and direct feedback is usually avoided, the 'grapevine' is a good start for information gathering, It would be dangerous to rely solely on the formal channels for information. Sometimes what is reported is not the whole truth.

Another pertinent point in an indirect society is the fact that people generally are more observant. It is hard for employees to trust a leader who does not practise what he preaches so it is important not only to act consistently, but also to be seen to be consistent. Otherwise that trust is broken. Malaysians sometimes have problems in distinguishing between the private life and the business life of a manager. What a manager does in his private life often gets associated with his professional life.

Concluding Note

Managers could benefit from an amicable style of conflict management. It is important in a country like Malaysia to be aware of the different dynamics affecting people's behavior. This implies understanding one's employees. A good relationship with employees goes a long way in the Malaysian environment and could be achieved by frequent interaction with both subordinates and co-workers. Focusing only on tasks could prove a less successful strategy in the long-run. The context or the environment surrounding the task is equally important.

Malaysians are essentially adaptable to change and their surroundings. It is due to their pragmatism that the country has managed to attain its present level of economic success and prosperity. They have adopted efficient work attitudes and striven for success. However, the majority of Malaysians have maintained some traditional and religious values.

REFERENCES

Abdullah, A. (ed.), 1993. *Understanding the Malaysian Workforce - Guidelines for Managers*, Kuala Lumpur, Malaysian Institute of Management.

Chia, L.C. 1984. *Constructive Conflict Management Between Superiors and Subordinates in Companies in Singapore*, Ph.D. Thesis, Kuala Lumpur, Universiti Malaya.

Dahlan, H.M. 1991. 'Local Values in Intercultural Management', *Malaysian Institute of Management Journal*. April.

Deutsch, M. 1972. *Productive and Destructive Conflict: The Management of Change and Conflict*, (eds.), Thomas, Ng John and Dennis, Warren G., London: Penguin Books.

Deutsch, M. 1973. *The Resolution of Conflict: Constructive and Destructive Processes*, New Haven and London: Yale University Press.

Embong, A.R. 1996. 'Social Transformation, the State and the Middle Classes in Post-Independence Malaysia', Mediating Identities in a Changing Malaysia, (ed.), Ibrahim, Z., Special issue - *Southeast Asian Studies*, **34** No. 3, Center for Southeast Asian Studies, Kyoto University, Japan.

Funston, J. 1980. *Malay Politics in Malaysia, A Study of UMNO and PAS*, Singapore: Heinemann Educational Books (Asia) Ltd.

Hofstede, G. and Bond, M.H. 1988. 'The Confucius Connection: from Cultural Roots to Economic Growth', *Organization Dynamics*, **16** (4), 5–12.

Hofstede, G. 1983. 'The Cultural Relativity of Organizational Practices and Theories', *Journal of International Business Studies*.

Huat, K.H. 1988. An Empirical Study on Managerial Values in Small and Medium-Sized Firms in the Manufacturing Industry, Unpublished MBA Dissertation, Kuala Lumpur: University of Malaya.

Malaysia, 1971. *Rancangan Malaysia Kedua, 1971–1975 (Second Malaysia Plan, 1971–1975)*, Kuala Lumpur, Jabatan Cetak Kerajaan.

Malaysia, 1991. *Second Outline Perspective Plan, 1991–2000*, Kuala Lumpur: Percetakan National Malaysia Berhad.

Malaysia, 1996. *Seventh Malaysia Plan, 1996–2000*, Kuala Lumpur: Percetakan National Malaysia Berhad.

Malaysia, 1996. *Monthly Statistical Bulletin*, Kuala Lumpur: Department of Statistics, July.

Malaysian Institute of Management 1992. Summary report of Intercultural Management Project, (Unpublished) Kuala Lumpur.

Maniam, M. 1986. The Influence of Culture in Management in Malaysia, *Malaysian Management Review*, **21** (3), Malaysian Institute of Management.

Mansor, N. and Larsen, P.D. 1992. Corporate Cultures and the Complexities of National Cultures: The Eastern Value System, *Pakistan Journal of Administration*: **XXIX** No. 1.

Mansor, N. 1993. Building a Multicultural Team in Abdullah, A. (ed.), *Understanding the Malaysian Workforce – Guidelines for Managers*, Kuala Lumpur: Malaysian Institute of Management.

Rao, C.A. *et al.* 1977. *Issues in Contemporary Malaysia*, Kuala Lumpur: Heinemann.

Rashid, N.I. 1977. *Work Value Systems of Malaysian Managers; An Exploratory Study*, Ph.D. Thesis, University of Kentucky.

Sabri, T. 1995. *Work Value Systems of Malaysian Engineers*, Unpublished MBA Dissertation, University of Malaya, Kuala Lumpur.
Schein, E.H. 1985. *Organization Culture and Leadership.* San Francisco, CA: Josey-Dass.
Scott, J.C. 1968. *Political Ideology in Malaysia: Reality and the Beliefs of an Elite*, New Haven: Yale University Press.
Sendut, Tan Sri Datuk Hamzah and Thong, Gregory T.S. 1989. *Managing Plural Society*, Kuala Lumpur: Longman.

C H A P T E R   S E V E N

Conflict Management in Thailand

SIRIYUPA ROONGRENGSUKE and DARYL CHANSUTHUS
Susin Graduate Institute of Business Administration, Chulalongkorn University, Thailand

Thailand has become known around the world as 'The Land of Smiles,' a name that reflects the social harmony that is so valued within the Thai culture. Because of their omnipresent smile, Thais are often perceived by outsiders as members of a cohesive, collectivist group who are friendly, cooperative, and passive. Yet, as many non-Thais have discovered, hidden behind the collective smile that appears so accommodating lies an intricately designed social fabric that is tightly interwoven with sturdy strands of individualism. The resulting behavior has been the source of much confusion and conflict for non-Thais who have attempted to develop business relationships with them.

> "A British manager, upset about the continued unauthorized borrowing of equipment between departments, burst in upon a meeting being held by his Thai subordinates and loudly berated the responsible person in front of his peers. Unwilling to dignify this insulting behavior with a response, the Thais remained silent, smiling grimly, until the offending manager left. The incident was followed, however, by a work slow-down and a spate of resignations of key personnel."

Although the Thais may appear placid and complaisant as they uncomplainingly conform to social and group behavioral norms, this behavior is more pragmatic than collectivist. Beneath the smooth, gentle surface are hidden independence, pride and dignity that are rarely sacrificed for a group or even for another individual. If a Thai feels that his personal freedom is in jeopardy or that his pride has been hurt or his dignity threatened, he *will* seek revenge. Sometimes, this is done openly and violently, but more often, revenge is carried out covertly and quietly in ways that will do no further damage to the individual's freedom, his dignity, or his pride.

To avoid such unpleasantness, the Thais smile. The Thai smile is not only for happy situations, but for stressful, potentially conflict-causing ones as well. In such situations, the smile may have one or more of the following meanings:

- there is a problem that requires patience, understanding, and assistance that the person who is smiling is too polite to ask for directly;
- there is such strong potential for serious conflict that the person smiling would much rather avoid it altogether so as to maintain a smooth relationship with one or more of those involved;
- the other party has come dangerously close to insulting the person smiling, and the smile is a subtle warning that, if the issue is pursued, trouble will most definitely result;
- the person smiling has already been insulted, and the smile is an attempt to maintain dignity in spite of the insult as well as a mask to conceal a counter-attack already being planned.

To provide a clearer understanding of the Thai behind the smile and thus of conflict behavior in Thailand, the following key areas will be explored within the context of Thai cultural norms, beliefs, and values:

1. Conflict and Culture
2. Behavioral Implications (A Situation Analysis)
3. Recommendations for the Non-Thai

The discussion of these three areas is aimed at assisting the non-Thai in gaining an appreciation and understanding of Thai attitudes towards conflict and their resulting conflict behaviors. This will aid the non-Thai significantly in developing appropriate strategies for minimizing and/or constructively managing conflict in Thailand so as to foster more cooperative business relationships.

CONFLICT AND CULTURE

If conflict situations are to be managed effectively within a specific socio-cultural context, understanding how conflict is *perceived* within that context is critical to the formulation of appropriate strategies for minimizing conflict and/or managing conflict more constructively within that particular context, as Jandt and Pederson (1996) point out:

> "Culture defines the values and interests that are at the core of conflicts, shaping perceptions, shaping alternatives, and defining outcomes as positive or negative. Communication about conflict is culturally mediated, and for that reason constructive conflict management strategies depend on cultural resources to define the common ground." (p.4)

To 'define a common ground' for a deeper exploration of conflict behavior in Thailand, this section will discuss the following:

1. Differing Perceptions of Conflict
2. The Thai Social System

An analysis of these areas will reveal not only how Thais perceive conflict, but also how various socio-cultural elements have contributed to that perception.

Differing Perceptions of Conflict

> "Have you learned lessons only of
> those who admired you, and were tender
> with you, and stood aside for you?
>
> Have you not learned great lessons
> from those who brace themselves
> against you, and disputed the passage
> with you?"
>
> Walt Whitman (1860)

Criticism, as defined in the West, has a dual nature. It is destructive when differing perceptions, beliefs, values and goals lead to hostility and infighting (Northcraft and Neale 1990, 221–222). It is generally believed that this kind of conflict leads to myopic environments of self-interest that encourage manipulation and dependency as well as foster feelings of helplessness.

Conflict in the West, however, also has a positive side. It is constructive when the open airing of differences (confrontation) focuses on issues, minimizes face-saving, combines personal advocacy of a position with public testing (debate) of the position, allows for free and informed choice, and leads to the development of a series of feasible alternatives (creative synergy) from which the relevant parties may choose for current and/or future action (resolution) (Lewicki *et al.* 1988, 212–214).

From the western viewpoint, some conflict within groups is desired because, if managed appropriately, it results in higher levels of productivity and significant increases in performance quality and employee satisfaction. Too little conflict, on the other hand, or the suppression of conflict to maintain superficial harmony is often believed to be a sign of serious organizational or group problems.

Underlying these western perceptions of conflict as *constructive* are a few basic assumptions. These assumptions include:

- productivity should be the primary concern of any work group;
- conflict, if well-managed, increases productivity and motivation;
- superficial harmony is not *meaningful* harmony and is, therefore, counter-productive;
- meaningful harmony (collaboration) supports and encourages the open, constructive expression of differences (confrontation);
- confrontation (public testing) of information and ideas creates a high level of psychological satisfaction with, and thus internal commitment to, decisions made among group members;
- face-saving and other conflict avoiding or withdrawing behaviors usually preclude effective conflict resolution;
- open confrontation in conflict situations is necessary if one is to discover 'truth' (valid data), effectively resolve conflict, and attain meaningful harmony.

The validity of these assumptions, however, is relative to the socio-cultural contexts of the western world from which the assumptions emerged, and the models for managing conflict arising from these beliefs are often ineffective in non-western nations, as Rabbie (1994) explains:

> "The importance of culture and cultural symbols in facilitating or hindering cross-cultural communications dictates a need to incorporate cultural attitudes and perceptions into models and theories of

> conflict analysis and conflict resolution. Models that were produced by Western specialists have continued to lack the proper tools to deal with non-Western nations, and thus they have remained largely irrelevant to those people." (p.37)

In Thailand, for example, conflict management techniques that are grounded in one or more of the assumptions outlined above could have disastrous effects. A fundamental reason for this is because, in Thailand, conflict is rarely, if ever, viewed as positive or constructive, even by many of the increasing number of graduates from western management programs.

> "In Thailand, forget all you have come to believe about constructive criticism. Almost all criticism is destructive. ...Criticism is not only disliked, it is also regarded as destructive to the social system."
>
> Cooper and Cooper 1982, 136

The Thais' low tolerance for conflict reflects a socio-cultural context that Hofstede (1984) identifies as collectivist and associates with high power distance and strong uncertainty avoidance. Hofstede's labels are a convenient short-hand for more complex traditional Thai assumptions and beliefs about conflict that include the following:

- harmony with one's environment is a virtue;
- maintaining 'face' of self and others is essential to maintaining harmony;
- surface loyalty to, and harmony with, one's patron or one's group is essential to an individual's well-being;
- maintaining good relationships is more important than completing tasks;
- inequality is natural and 'right';
- criticizing superiors publicly is unnatural and evil;
- latent conflict between ranks is normal;
- confrontation is rude, damaging, and undesirable;
- overt conflict within organizations is disruptive and damaging to the organization and to the individual employees;

- overt, aggressive competition among peers within the same social and/or organizational group is evil;
- unwillingness to conform to group behavioral norms is evil;
- expressing ambitions openly is inappropriate and undesirable.

These assumptions have emerged from a social system that has been centuries in the making. A brief review of some of the major components of that system will enhance the non-Thai's appreciation of why Thais prefer avoidance, withdrawal, and behind-the-scenes strategizing to open confrontation in seeking to resolve most conflict situations.

The Thai Social System

A western photographer visiting Thailand in the late 19th century was invited to photograph King Rama IV. Just as he was about to take the photograph, the King abruptly left, 'without a word to anyone,' leaving the poor photographer worried that he had, perhaps, done something to offend:

> "I thought this a strange proceeding, and fancied I must have given him some offense....I appealed to the Prince, but his reply was simply that 'the King does everything right, and if I were to accost him now he might conclude his morning's work by cutting off my head.'"
>
> J. Thomson (1875)

Thailand's first unified kingdom, the kingdom of Sukhothai (*circa* 1238–1438 A.D.), is believed to have been somewhat horizontally stratified (Wyatt 1993, p. 71). However, since the Ayudhya period (*circa* 1350–1767 A.D.), the Thai social system has been organized based on a strict vertical structure, with the King at the sacred apex of a complex hierarchy of superiors and subordinates. Within this system, open conflict between levels within the hierarchy has been avoided due to the emergence of a very important norm for Thai social behavior when interacting with superiors: *Never openly or directly challenge the authority or the 'rightness' of the actions of a superior.* Despite the country's change in the early part of this century from an absolute to a constitutional monarchy based on democratic principles, the vertical system adopted in the Ayudhya period remains largely in place today, and the belief that one's social superiors must be obeyed also remains a strong norm in Thai society.

The result is an almost inborn unwillingness to challenge directly and/or publicly anyone regarded as one's superior, whether that superiority be based on socio-economic status, age, or position within an organizational hierarchy.

An expatriate (expat) manager from Germany complained during a conversation with other foreign colleagues that his Thai staff refused to debate issues in an open meeting:

> "I throw an idea out to the group, and they just sit there looking at me like I've grown horns or something. I want to know what they think, I tell them. They know this environment better than I do, and they also know better than I do what will work and what won't. I practically beg them to point out the possible weaknesses of the idea, but the most I can get out of them is a vague assurance that if I think the idea is good, then it must be good. Yet, I can see them talking furiously to each other in Thai the moment they leave the meeting room. I just know that they're discussing the weak points of my idea among themselves, probably even making fun of my stupidity—or maybe this place is just making me paranoid."

What the expat in the example above did not understand was that, for the Thai, directly and openly challenging a superior, even in a mild suggestion form, would be to disrupt a social system and to break a social norm that have been in practice and a part of the collective Thai subconscious for approximately 600 years. This is a breach of decorum not easily or readily tolerated, regardless of changes in the internal and external environments.

In addition to the vertical social structure with its built-in system of superior/inferior relationships, Thai assumptions about and behaviors in conflict situations in general have been molded over the centuries by a variety of external and internal forces that have been gradually assimilated and accepted as 'truth.' Some of these forces and the assumptions and behaviors they have engendered relative to conflict are summarized by the historical period in Table 7.1 on the next page. The vertical arrows on the chart reflect the Thais' successful blending of different influences, such as the integration of Buddhist and animist beliefs, to build a coherent, cohesive national perspective and personality.

Since a discussion of each of the influences outlined in the chart would be impractical for the purposes of this chapter, only those most relevant to the modern Thais' behavior in conflict situations will be covered.

Table 7.1 Historical Summary of Influences on Thai Conflict Assumptions and Behavior

Historical Period	Influence Source	Influence Type	Assumptions Formed	Behaviors Practiced
Sukhothai	Khmer	Animism	• Our parents are benevolent creators; we owe them our lives and our obedience. • All things in nature, animate and inanimate, are spiritual and worthy of respect. • Our well-being is dependent upon the spirits of nature. • We must live in harmony with the natural world.	• Honoring parents by seeking their advice and obeying their commands • Appeasing or appealing to natural spirits, especially in times of trouble.
	Ceylonese	Buddhism	• The individual is the only source of truth. • Life is suffering–a continuous, futile cycle of birth, death, and rebirth until 'truth' is discovered. • Each individual is at a different level with respect to being aware of and understanding truth. • Extreme emotional states prevent the discovery of truth and increase suffering. • Neutrality and complaisance enhance the quest for truth and promote peace and harmony. • An individual's current lot in life must be accepted as the natural and appropriate result of his Karma–his past good and bad deeds. • Karma can be influenced by present and future actions, both good and bad.	• Relying on self–on personal, internal instincts–in matters having a significant impact on one's current or future state of being • Developing strong personal relationships with individuals rather than strong attachments to any particular group • Avoiding extreme emotional states and/or emotional displays • Accommodating others • Avoiding or withdrawing from situations with conflict potential • Maintaining neutrality and accepting one's 'fate' –the 'wait and see' approach to conflict resolution

Ayudhya	Indian	Brahmanism	• Inequality is the natural order and, therefore, is 'right.' • The higher one is in the natural order, the closer one is to divinity and the greater one's virtue. • Superiors lead and their inferiors follow. • Disobeying or challenging a superior is unnatural and evil. • All human beings in the natural order have dignity, differing only in degree.	• Accepting and accommodating the demands and desires of social superiors, whether in agreement or not and without asking questions or offering opinions • Expressing discontent or seeking revenge in indirect ways when interacting with superiors if unable to accept a situation or if dignity is attacked • Offering favors to superiors and reciprocating favors granted by superiors to gain merit and protection
↓	↓	↓	↓	↓
Thonburi/ Ratanakosin	Chinese	Confucianism	• Man exists through and is defined by his relationships to others; those relationships are structured hierarchically. • Harmony is ensured if each party honors the requirements of role relationships. • Projecting a good image of self in public is virtuous.	• Placing more importance on form (appearances) than on substance; enhancing face of self and of significant others • Saving face of self and others • Encouraging loyalty to the group (social or organizational) • Enhancing face through material wealth
Modern	American/ Western	Results Orientation	• Productivity is more important than relationships; results should not be sacrificed to maintain the appearance of harmony. • Conflict can be constructive and creative. • Confrontation is an effective tool in conflict resolution • Face-saving and enhancing are counterproductive	• Seeking English language and assertiveness training; keeping written records of business transactions; neglecting personal relationships in favor of results • Competing to move up the career ladder; switching jobs to facilitate career moves • Compromising to soothe feelings and achieve personal objectives in conflict situations

These include:

- *The Ayudhya Period: The Emergence of Elitism*
- *Buddhism: Winning is Losing*
- *Thai Individualism: The Conflict Within*
- *Confucianism: Face Saving and Collective Harmony*
- *Westernization: Competing and Confronting*

A more in-depth look at each of these areas will, for the non-Thai, shed light on the following conflict-related issues:

- *why Thais are extremely reluctant to criticize, either constructively or otherwise, those perceived to be social superiors;*
- *how reciprocity works to avoid conflict situations;*
- *how Thais view leadership roles and the use of power/authority;*
- *why social harmony and face are so highly valued;*
- *how individualism is expressed and its role in conflict situations; and*
- *how western management concepts are affecting Thai beliefs and values in urban centers.*

The Ayudhya Period: The Emergence of Elitism

In the Ayudhya period, the, personal, horizontally structured, free-trade environment of the Sukhothai period was replaced with trade and resource monopolies as well as with a vertical patron-client structure that was a modified version of the Khmer-Indian impersonal, master-servant system. The concept of kingship changed from king as father to king as god, a carryover of strong Indian and Ceylonese influences during the Sukhothai era (Samudavanij 1987, 27), and the government assumed the form of an absolute monarchy. The king became the sole owner of the nation's properties and resources, forcing a dependence on the monarchy that had not been necessary in the autonomous, self-sustaining agrarian villages of the Sukhothai era (Vatikiotis, 1996, 65). A court language was devised to refer to the king and his possessions as well as to sharpen the distinction between the nobility and the peasantry. A strict protocol governing proper behavior—posture, facial expression, eye contact, and gestures—between ranks was also developed, and specific parts of the body were designated as 'sacred' (top of the head) and 'profane' (soles of the feet).

The king, at the top of the social hierarchy, had absolute power over all those below him and his orders were to be obeyed without question. Failure to conform meant death, unless otherwise ordered by the king. The creation of the *sakdina* system during this period also gave the nobility, who were court officials and representatives of the king, similar power over commoners, and thus court nobles were given strict obeisance and a high outward show of respect. As a result, Thai society soon became firmly elitist, with a vast power gap erupting between the noble and the peasant classes.

Sakdina

In 1454 a law was enacted that established the *sakdina* system. *Sakdina* was a system of social stratification that gave each person a rank or 'degree of power' and a portion of land based on that rank (Keyes 1989, 29–30). In the *sakdina* system, all residents were ranked into a hierarchy and were graded in terms of bureaucratic distance from the king. Those with a high *sakdina* rank had the right to control large areas of land and large numbers of people, a scarce resource in those times.

Because the king and those closest to him were considered to be either divine or on intimate terms with the divine, they were not only believed to be the highest in status, but also the most virtuous. This gave rise to the belief that the higher one's rank was in the accepted social order, the better suited one was to lead, since the inherent virtue of those in higher ranks ensured the 'rightness' of the decisions made and of the orders given. Given this environment, challenging the authority of a superior was not merely a challenge to the established social order but to the divine order as well. The result was, as Michael Vatikiotis (1996) explains, 'a synergy between the spiritual and real world functions of the ruler' that made it 'difficult to question the leader's wisdom or right to rule on spiritual grounds' and 'hard to match his command of resources'. (p. 63)

Although the king and his nobles were believed to be the highest in rank, in dignity and in virtue it is important to note that *all* people within the *sakdina* system were given a rank. All were also accorded a certain measure of dignity, differing only in degree. Each person within the *sakdina* hierarchy was expected to respect the dignity (status) of others in the system, whether higher or lower, in a manner and measure appropriate to their rank. Thus, even those at the lowest rung of the ladder were accorded at least a modicum of respect from those at higher levels. This was usually accomplished then, as it is now, by a superior's acknowledging an inferior's greeting, or by extending an unsolicited kindness, or by handling reprimands and/or punishment for some misdeed in private. This public show of respect between ranks was mutually beneficial, since it enhanced the dignity of both the giver and the receiver in the eyes of onlookers.

Although the *sakdina* system has been compared to the feudal system of Europe, Keyes points out that the *sakdina* system differed from feudalism in that it was not associated with a fragmentation of power via land grants as feudalism would imply. On the contrary, power was concentrated in the hands of the monarchy, since '*sakdi*' (power) could only be parceled out to others by an act of a king and the '*na*' (fields) held by each individual were regarded as a portion of the total land owned by the king (Keyes 1989, 31). Consequently, the king's relatives and those appointed to high positions in court became powerful 'patrons' who had land and people under their control, but ownership of land and other resources remained solely in the hands of the king.

Despite the changes made in government administration after the 1932 revolution, the vertical hierarchy of fifteenth century Ayudhya as well as the beliefs and behaviors it engendered are still operative today, although to a lessening degree in urban centers. And the patron-client relationships that were formalized with the introduction of *sakdina* and emerged in almost every area of Thai social life are still widely evident.

The Patron-Client System

As in the *sakdina* system, the ideal patron is one who protects, assists, or rewards those whose status is inferior. In return, the client is expected to perform tasks efficiently and with the least amount of trouble to his patron. Additionally, as in the *sakdina* system, the client accepts the superiority of his patron. Two additional principles underlying patron-client relationships are: 1) the voluntary nature of the relationship; and 2) the implicit understanding that the relationship will last for only as long as it is mutually beneficial. Both parties, inferior and superior, are free to look elsewhere if they feel that their needs are no longer being met (Hanks 1962, 1247–1261).

Generally, these relationships have been strongest in the government sector, where the pursuit of self-serving interests rather than the public good has often been the focus of activity, as Jacobs observes:

> "Officials, decision-makers, and staff alike [in government service] continue to consider themselves above and apart from the public

> and in no way accountable to it, free to pursue their own interests as they see fit... In sum, the non-official Thai, although hardly subject to a despotic authority, is certainly subject to an often arbitrary and capricious one, without, at the same time, having at his disposal either the moral right or any legitimate formal channel to challenge that authority. At best, a private individual who believes he has a political grievance or interest to pursue can only hope to establish some personal, individual (i.e., patrimonial) patron-client relationship with an official to insure that that authority will not operate to his disadvantage, especially at a time when he is least prepared to deal with it."
>
> Jacobs 1971, 47–48

The Thai bureaucrat, literally a 'servant of the king,' has traditionally held a high ranking in Thai society. This ranking has, over the years, been utilized to advance the bureaucrat's personal interests as well as those of his clique. This clique-based favoritism is widely practiced throughout the government sector and is particularly evident in the awarding of promotions or of financially rewarding assignments (Grindle 1981, 58). The result is a general understanding among the lower ranks that moving up means pleasing one's superiors. In Thai terms, this means never publicly, or even in some cases privately, challenging the authority of a superior.

This explains why information that could be critical to the success of a plan is often not communicated between ranks in the government sector. The holders of the information, who are often staff at the operations level, dare not share the information with their superiors, particularly if the information contradicts their superiors' prevailing opinion, for fear of upsetting their superiors. This behavior is based on two main assumptions: 1) a subordinate's job is to follow the orders given by his/her superiors; 2) if the information were that important, then the superiors, who are 'higher,' would already be aware of it or, if they needed it, would have already asked for it. The result is a general rule of thumb that advises: 'If they don't ask, don't tell them'. Volunteering information that has not been asked for could be perceived by one's peers and superiors as stepping outside one's socially prescribed role, which could be interpreted as antagonistic (aggressive) behavior and could result in punitive action being taken by either peers or superiors against the informer to silence him and to force him back into his proper subordinate role. Taking the initiative and being assertive in an environment such as this is a dangerous undertaking indeed, for it could prevent a promotion or lead to a transfer to one of the country's most remote regions.

The impact of the patron-client system on relationships in Thai society has not been limited to the government sector. It has also influenced patterns of behavior in the private sector. From ancient to recent times, business owners or those high in the organizational hierarchy have been regarded by employees as patrons to whom respect must be paid and a satisfactory service performed (i.e., orders followed). In return, employees expect their bosses provide them with rewards, promotions, and protection. The result is a leadership style known among older Thais as *phradet-phrakhun*.

Phradet phrakhun

Phradet phrakhun prescribes a leadership style that is both autocratic (*phradet*) and benevolent (*phrakhun*), rather like a leader who cracks a whip with one hand while distributing money with the other. *Phradet* calls for tough leadership that demands loyalty and service, establishes direction, makes decisions, delegates tasks, and dispenses justice. *Phrakhun*, on the other hand, ensures faithful service by providing desired rewards, protection, prestige (by association), and personal care that extends to the employee's family members (Holmes 1996, 62–63). It is a leadership style that, at least until this decade, satisfied both employer and employee, as both had a crystal clear understanding of their reciprocal roles and responsibilities. And because those roles and responsibilities, which were based on patron-client relationships, were so clearly delineated, both superiors and subordinates enjoyed a secure, stable, harmonious environment. Each knew with certainty what was needed to extract what was wanted from the other.

Given the Thais' centuries-old orientation towards deference, inequality, submission to bureaucratic rules, and highly personalized and centralized decision-making (Gohlert 1991, 77), it should come as no surprise that even today many leading local companies have tall hierarchies, autocratic leadership, top-down communication, and centralized decision-making processes. However, in Bangkok at least, the impact of the patron-client legacy is diminishing in intensity as more and more young people are exposed to western egalitarianism via university education abroad as well as in reformed local educational systems that place greater emphasis on independent thinking and creativity. Businesses, faced with increasingly fierce competition, are also investing heavily in training programs and management strategies, such as re-engineering, that are aimed at flattening the organizational structure and at developing skills in assertiveness, leadership, creative-thinking, and empowerment. Nevertheless, for most Thais, the proverb that encourages one 'to walk behind a superior so as to avoid being bitten by dogs' still holds true, as the example below illustrates.

The western-educated Thai CEO and part-owner of a local Thai company hired a consulting group to find out why her employees lacked initiative and creativity in problem-solving. In an interview with a group of operations-level staff, a senior member had the following to say:

> "The senior managers create policies and pass them down to us. They don't ask for our ideas or opinions, but they expect us to carry out the policies to the best of our ability. We try very hard to do this because it's our job. Sometimes, though, we know before we start that the policies won't work. We don't say anything to the higher-ups because they didn't ask us and because they wouldn't listen to us anyway if we did tell them. They'd just think we were being trouble-makers and we'd pay for it in the end. They made the policies, so they must believe that their ideas are right. They tell us what to do, and we try to do it. If it fails, they will find out for themselves."

Although senior management claimed that they wanted to encourage their employees to participate in decision-making processes, the perceptions of this employee demonstrate quite clearly that old habits die hard. This is not merely due to the employees' reluctance to accept decision-making power and responsibility, but also to the unwillingness of the senior managers to share decision-making power with their subordinates, as revealed in one manager's complaint: 'Our employees aren't ready to make decisions for themselves. They need direction, because they can't see the big picture. And besides, if we didn't make decisions and control our subordinates, what would we do?' Despite their 'westernization,' the senior managers still viewed themselves as 'patrons' and expected their subordinates to maintain their subservient 'client' roles. That any other paradigm existed was beyond their ken. Employees who were good clients and obeyed orders were rewarded (*phrakhun*) with raises or promotions; those who actually took some initiative without first receiving the blessing of the appropriate superior or who challenged a policy publicly were punished (*phradet*), as yet another employee pointed out:

> "Just last month three people were fired. I knew one of those people. She was very aggressive. If she thought a policy was bad, she'd tell

the boss straight out at a meeting. I tried to warn her to keep quiet and just do what she was told, but she wouldn't listen. And now, see? She's gone. I guess she spoke up once too often to the wrong boss."

In promoting those who abide by the rules of the patron-client system and ostracizing or firing those who break those rules, the senior managers of this company are perpetuating the behavior they claim they wish to change. This is true for many Thai organizations and shows that, despite the onslaught of western management models and theories, long-established traditions governing appropriate behavior between ranks maintain a strong hold on the psyche of most Thais. For many Thais, that old adage, 'when the boss is right, he's right; and when the boss is wrong, he's right' remains a strong rule for survival and, if the right networks are formed, success in the organization. The smart Thai learns at a very early age that it's best to follow the leader.

Buddhism: Winning is Losing

The highly stratified Thai social structure with its patron-client networks is both tempered and complemented by Buddhism, the national religion since the 13th century. While the social system encourages dependence on one's superiors for protection and advancement, Buddhist philosophy encourages the opposite, as the Lord Buddha's final instructions to his faithful disciple, Ananda, reveal:

> "Therefore, O Ananda, be ye lamps unto yourselves. Be ye a refuge to yourselves. Betake yourselves to no external refuge. Hold fast to the truth as a lamp. Hold fast as a refuge to the truth. Look not for refuge to any one besides yourselves."
>
> Lester 1973, 21

However, despite this emphasis on the individual as a source of truth, the practice of Theravada Buddhism in Thailand does much to support interdependent relationships based upon mutual obligation and to encourage an attitude of tolerance that some non-Thais have unfortunately mistaken for apathy. Buddhism, as it is practiced in Thailand, offers a pragmatic appeal to human emotions, teaching temperance and patience in the face of change and urging compassion for all living things, as Kulick and Wilson (1996) point out:

> "Compassion is an exhortation in the Christian book, but Buddhism makes it something you can use with meaning. Its teaching ranks

> second to none. ... [H]ow supremely relevant, in this age of economic development and political corruption, is the jewel-like answer given to the greedy question, 'If you catch a big fish, how can you make it provide for you throughout the year?' The possible solutions flash through the mind. Dry it? Salt it? Sell it for money to buy other things? No, the answer is much simpler. Share it with neighbours, so that they will share with you when they catch one." (p.97)

In urging the practice of temperance, tolerance and compassion, Buddhism has long acknowledged the interrelationships and interdependencies of all things, something that western management gurus have only just recently begun to preach. The source of these interrelationships for the Buddhist is found in the law of Karma.

Karma

Under the law of Karma, every thought, word or deed has a consequence. These consequences must be borne by the perpetrator of the action in either this life or another, resulting in a Karmic cycle of birth, death, and rebirth that will continue until such time as one can experience Nirvana and transcend the effects of Karma. In Karmic law, then, every action has a reaction, with possible consequences that extend far beyond the present. The battle you fight and win today at another person's expense will come back to haunt you at another time or in another life, when you will be expected to pay for your victory. Thus, for the Thais, ultimately it is not possible to win if another must lose as a result. This does not mean, however, that good deeds will enable one to achieve Nirvana. Any deliberate act, whether good or evil, will result in a reaction and necessitate the continuance of the cycle. Karma is rather like a bank account that records an individual's debits and credits. The ideal is Nirvana—a zero balance, which can only be achieved by means of non-attachment.

For the pragmatic Thai, however, the short-term ideal is not Nirvana, which is too nebulous a state to ponder, but improved social standing and material well-being—the reaction that can be expected if one acts in virtuous ways. Viewed in this light, Karma becomes a vehicle for social mobility; and merit acts serve as the fuel that ensures one reaches the intended destination. More importantly, Karmic law serves as a constant reminder to the Thai that the kind of negative behavior associated with conflict situations must be avoided. If avoidance is not possible, then compromise, through the offering of favors and the return of favors granted, becomes the preferred alternative. These beliefs have given rise to several values in Thai culture that encourage harmonious relationships and discourage open conflict of any kind.

Bunkhun

Bunkhun is among the most important of these values in terms of its influence on the pattern of relationships among the Thais. *Bunkhun* refers to a strong sense of moral obligation that supports close interpersonal relationships. *Bunkhun* is the feeling that an individual has, for example, for her parents for giving her life. It is a gift so great that it cannot easily be repaid, but yet the recipient is ever-ready to reciprocate in whatever way possible. It is, as Henry Holmes explains,

> "...a psychological bond between someone who, out of sheer kindness and sincerity, renders another person the needed help and favor, and the latter's remembering of the goodness done and his ever-readiness to reciprocate the kindness."
>
> Holmes 1995, 30

Unlike the transitory nature of the patron-client relationship, relationships based on *bunkhun* are enduring and stable, and, as a result, highly valued. The results of Komin's study on Thai values and behavioral patterns revealed that *bunkhun* was regarded by the Thais participating in her 1978 national survey as one of their most important values, with both men and women ranking it 4th among 23 instrumental values (Komin 1990, 53).

Katanyu Katawethi

The great virtues of social life, *Katanyu Katawethi* are also Buddhist-based values and differ from *bunkhun* only in degree. *Katanyu* means to feel gratitude for any merciful favor provided by others, and *katawethi* means to return the favor (Mizuno 1976, 21) The principles of *katanyu katawethi* reinforce the psychological bond (*bunkhun*) between parents and children as well as between teachers (the great givers of knowledge) and students. *Katanyu katawethi* also support the reciprocal nature of the patron-client relationships between superiors and subordinates. They serve to maintain the social equilibrium by ensuring that favors received are returned in kind, that proper respect is given to the dignity of all, and that conflict between ranks, if it exists, is not given a chance to surface.

Kreng Jai and Jai Yen

Two other uniquely Thai values that strongly encourage conflict avoidance are *kreng jai* and *jai yen. Kreng jai* is perhaps one of the most difficult Thai values for non-Thais to understand. Some have explained the concept as 'a combination of deference and consideration,' while others have defined it as 'being reluctant to impose upon' someone or to 'have consideration for' another (Klausner 1993, 258). Perhaps the best explanation is that provided by Komin, who defines *kreng jai* as 'to be considerate, to feel reluctant to impose upon another person, to take another person's feelings (and ego) into account, or to take every measure not to cause discomfort or inconvenience for another person' (Komin 1990, 164).

The practice of *kreng jai* can be observed in both social and work relationships when an individual refrains from asking the assistance of others. *Kreng jai* becomes particularly important in direct interpersonal interactions where differences of opinion could lead to destructive conflict. In such situations, *kreng jai* allows for a harmonious resolution of differences, as the parties involved soften opinions, restrain emotions, and refrain from strong direct criticism in order to accommodate differing points of view. In this way, win-win solutions can be achieved and cooperative relationships maintained. To succeed in practicing *kreng jai*, however, one must first master yet another Thai virtue—*jai yen.*

Central to Buddhism is the Eightfold Path or the 'Middle Way,' which, in a very practical way, focuses on the human condition in the here and now and teaches one how to deal with this condition by avoiding extreme actions, emotions, and desires. The Thai concept of *jai yen*, literally meaning 'cool heart,' arose from this Buddhist ideal and has become a very effective mechanism for ensuring that social harmony is maintained and that the 'face' of the individual is preserved.

For the Thai, direct public confrontations that result in an overt display of anger, hatred, dissatisfaction, or impatience are destructive and self-defeating. Such confrontations erode the foundation of trust upon which a relationship of mutual obligation, whether personal or professional, is built. Thais do not avoid all conflict, as some may believe, but they do have a strong sense of decorum that demands that personal problems or grievances be discussed in private and that extreme emotions be held in check.

For the Thai, becoming overly emotional, particularly in a public setting, reflects a serious lack of self-discipline and results in a loss of status, prestige and/or dignity (*face*). Thais have thus been schooled almost from birth to avoid such lose-lose situations by keeping their emotions neutral and their problems private. An admonishment to *jai yen* is a gentle reminder that one should be mindful of self and of others and should not allow run-away emotions to disrupt the social balance.

Animism and Harmony with Nature

One final area needing attention before leaving the Thai belief system is that of the supernatural. In the daily struggle to improve their lot in life many Thais, despite Buddhist teachings to the contrary, seek assistance from the supernatural. The activities of many practicing Thai Buddhists at all levels of the social hierarchy are based on an animistic belief in spirits and are characterized by what westerners would call irrational, superstitious behaviors. Such a characterization, however, prevents one from understanding the role that the belief in spirits plays in the Thai Buddhist's way of life.

As Lester (1973) points out, this 'animistic orientation' to the world serves a similar function to that of a rational or scientific orientation in that both are concerned with an attempt to

> "...understand and manipulate man and his environment. ...The Buddhist sees the entire universe as alive, animated; so as to deal more directly and effectively with such a universe he personifies the various forces at work, collects data on their activities and when needful employs this understanding in manipulating these forces to his own welfare." (p.135)

Indeed, there are textbooks devoted to explaining the intricacies of the supernatural and the rituals that must be performed if one is to achieve the desired results.

On at least one level, the Thais' relationship with the spirits is contractual and parallels the social relationships previously discussed; one appeals to a particular spirit (as though to a patron) for a favor, such as a winning number in the lottery, success in a business venture, or the resolution of a problem or conflict, and promises to reciprocate should the favor be granted. Thus, one sees dances being performed at popular shrines or sacred trees decorated with gaily colored ribbons or donations being made to temples—merit acts that are also often the return of favors granted by spirits.

Paying respect to the appropriate spirits is a necessity at such auspicious events as the laying of a foundation stone for a new building or the opening of a new company. Failure to do so could have dire results, as one unfortunate expat manager discovered when one of his employees became 'possessed' by the spirit of the land upon which his new company was located.

> "Without fail, every single day for a month after we opened, this girl would fall down on the floor and start frothing at the mouth and jerking uncontrollably. Then she'd start screaming stuff that I couldn't understand. My other employees told me that she'd been possessed by the spirit of the land who was angry because we hadn't paid him respect. Of course, I thought that this was silly, and ignored it. When the girl continued to have these convulsive attacks, I put her on sick leave. But then, we started having accidents and things started going missing and machinery started breaking down for no apparent reason. I finally gave in and let my employees arrange a blessing ritual. After we did that, everything returned to normal. I still don't know if it really was a spirit causing all that trouble or if it was the workers themselves getting back at me because I'd ignored a custom that they felt was important."

In yet another example, the employee of a well-known subsidiary of a multi-national manufacturing operation had a dream in which the spirit of the land on which the company was located warned her that there would be a fire at the company. The next day, she shared her dream with colleagues and, eventually, through the company grapevine, top management, mostly westerners, also learned of the warning. They ignored it. Tensions rose within the company as employees, who took the warning very seriously, began to fear for their lives. Absences increased and work slowed down due to the employees' inability to concentrate. Word started to circulate throughout the company that management had little concern for the welfare of employees. This resulted in a mood of hostility that threatened to halt all work. Hearing that a possible strike was in the making, top management consulted a senior Thai outsider who advised that a Buddhist ceremony be performed to prevent any possible disaster and to raise the morale of the employees. The ceremony was performed, the employees felt that their superiors had acknowledged and respected their needs, and peace and harmony were restored to the workplace.

Despite the centuries that separate today's Thai from the Thai of Sukhothai, most still firmly believe that all living things in nature—whether plant, animal, human, or spirit—are connected by the law of karma. The function of human beings is to understand, accept, and respect the place of all things in the great cosmic order in a way that is complementary to universal harmony.

Thai Individualism: A Particularist Approach to Life

The term *individualistic* was originally coined by Alexis de Tocqueville in the early part of the 19th century to describe American behavior, which has since been generally characterized as being self-reliant, pragmatic, confrontational, rational, ambitious, and self-actualizing. Collectivists, on the other hand, tend to place more importance on the group than on self and thus behave in ways that maintain social harmony, avoid direct confrontation, promote loyalty, and protect 'face.' Hofstede (1991) provides a broader working definition of the terms:

> "Individualism pertains to societies in which the ties between individuals are loose: everyone is expected to look after himself or herself and his or her immediate family. Collectivism as its opposite pertains to societies in which people from birth onwards are integrated into strong cohesive ingroups, which throughout people's lifetime continue to protect them in exchange for unquestioning loyalty." (p.51)

At first glance, Thailand seems to fit the collectivist mold quite nicely. Yet, if one digs deeply enough beneath the surface layer of Thai culture, one will discover artifacts such as self-reliance, a love of freedom, and pragmatism that are highly individualistic in nature and that have their roots in Buddhism as well as in the cultural history of the Thai people.

In keeping with the Buddhist precept that encourages reliance on self in the search for truth, Thais generally believe that 'people should look to themselves, to their own intellectual and material resources, to solve a problem,' for to do otherwise would be 'weak and foolish' (Fieg 1989, 33). Or as the missionary Dr. Dan Bradley explained more than a century ago, in Thailand:

> "You are responsible for yourself, and you must take responsibility for your own life and your own decisions. This is a form of enlightened self-interest. On the other hand, you have a sensitivity to the other person which is usually lacking in our Western culture. You know Christians and Jews are taught that, 'you are your brother's keeper,' and this is taken for granted as a very good thing. Here they are taught that you are not your brother's keeper and there must be some social distance between you and the other person, and you

preserve his right to be free from your interests, from your prying concern, from being seen by you. So there is this notion of forbearance. You do not interfere with another person, not because you are not interested in him, but because you have no business interfering with him. It is for him, not you, to make his decision."

Mole 1973, 67

Thus, for Thais, there is a clear distinction between self and others—between one's own interests and those of others, and one is free to pursue one's own interests in whatever way one thinks best as long as those interests (and the pursuit thereof) do not interfere with the interests of others. This is a philosophy that has been given a great deal of lip service in the West, but that has been developed to a fine art in Thailand, giving rise to such other-focused values as *bunkhun, katanyu katawethi, kreng jai*, and *jai yen.*

It is also a philosophy that has aided Thailand in its successful assimilation of people from a variety of ethnic groups. Far from being homogenous, the origins of the modern-day Thai consist mainly of a mix of Chinese, Lao, Malay, Khmer, Mon, Shan, Lao Phuan, So, Song Dam, Thai Yai, and Phu Tai peoples (Phongpaichit and Baker 1996, 171). Up until this century, Thailand's only really scarce resource was its people. To combat this problem and create a strong nation state, the country's leaders, at around the turn of this century, proclaimed all native ethnic groups 'Thai', bestowed Thai citizenship upon the mostly Chinese immigrants, and ordered compulsory education in the Thai language and the essentials of 'Thai' culture (Phongpaichit and Baker 1996, 171–172).

At about the same time, surnames were introduced. Prior to that, people were known only by their first names, and there was no strong sense of lineage or ancestry that would bind one to an extended family group such as those found, for example, among the Chinese. Traditionally, the Thais' orientation has been more towards the immediate family, although the Thai definition of 'immediate' is a bit broader than that of western cultures. Thus, among Thais, there is not as 'binding a system of obligation to extended family or community as might exist in more communal or group-centered societies' (Fieg 1989, 32).

As a result, the concept of 'Thai' as a cohesive cultural group with a distinct cultural identity is a fairly modern one. This suggests a lack of deeply-rooted cultural ties that would bind the individual to the group and that would encourage the individual to place the interests of the group above his own. Thais do observe the social formalities required by the hierarchical social structure, but while personal interests may be hidden from the group to maintain the appearance of harmony, they are rarely sacrificed for the group. This is most clearly evident in the party-hopping that has long been popular among Thai politicians. Loyalty to the principles of a particular political party most definitely takes second place to the pursuit of personal interests. This is also true in patron-client relationships, which are binding only for as long as the personal interests of each party are served. Should either feel that he is 'giving' more than he is 'receiving', he is free to withdraw from the relationship and seek another that is more personally rewarding.

This reflects the pragmatic nature of Thai individualism, which places a higher value on flexibility than on rigid adherence to any particular ideology. Situations and people tend to be more important determinants of an individual's behavioral response than laws, principles or agreements, as Kulick and Wilson (1996) observe:

> "The Thai starts by seeing the human world as a world of particular individual persons—not at all sentimentally, but rather in a wholly practical down-to-earth sense. As a Buddhist, he does not see them as a totality, but is aware of them individually, one by one, as they impinge on his consciousness and enter his life, each in a different way with a different purpose and attributes." (p. 60)

Thais organize their world vertically. They develop relationships with particular individuals on the vertical scale with whom mutual obligations are formed that are mutually beneficial. There is no need to bundle people into groups or to attach themselves to horizontal groupings. A Thai's behavior towards another is often determined by the history of mutual services and obligations between them, which is why an acknowledged social superior may be, from a western viewpoint, fawned over excessively while a stranger in need may be ignored.

This particularist approach to relationships has led to a belief by some that Thais are unreliable and selfish. Yet, if this behavior is viewed from within a Buddhist context, a clearer explanation is revealed. Buddhism focuses on the cultivation of self—not on curing the ills of society. This, coupled with the law of Karma and loosely structured horizontal groups, has created a high context environment in which the average Thai works diligently to ensure that his relationships with significant others are smooth and harmonious. And this has resulted in an uncanny ability to assess the opportunities and threats of a given situation and to take appropriate action. Such action has usually involved deference and indirect but skillful machinations that have enabled Thais to assimilate a wide range of external influences with minimum conflict while maintaining their independence and their cultural integrity.

Unlike many of its neighbors, Thailand has enjoyed a long history of uninterrupted independence, a fact of which Thais are very proud. Traditional authority in Thailand has never been threatened or undermined by external or internal powers. The 'revolution' in 1932 that changed the absolute monarchy to a constitutional monarchy is no exception to this rule. The monarchy, which had already agreed to give up absolute power, continued to be revered as the nation's spiritual head, with the moral right to intervene in affairs of state. This, along with the evolution of political parties, prevented the armed forces from gaining the kind of power that nationalist forces won in other Asian countries when fighting against colonialism. As a result, the Thai social system has been able to develop naturally and organically from the absolutist tradition inherited from the Ayudhya era while selecting and absorbing freely from the world outside elements complementary to Thai tradition and culture (Kulick and Wilson 1996, 170–172).

Since its beginning, the Thai nation has demonstrated an exceptional ability to integrate the customs, cultures and belief systems of the people of other nations. Buddhist beliefs were imported from South Asia as were beliefs concerning the nature of kingship and the relationship between the king and his subjects in the Ayudhyan period. Animistic beliefs came largely from the indigenous Khmer and Mon tribes, whose own written language also served as the foundation upon which the Thai script was created. However, the greatest influence on Thailand's modern culture, particularly that found in the country's urban centers, has come from China in the east and from the U.S. in the west.

Confucianism: Face Saving and Collective Harmony

When they immigrated to Thailand, the Chinese brought with them a familial system that was based on a Confucian personal ethic, the basic tenets of which were:

a) man exists through, and is defined by, his relationships to others;
b) those relationships are structured hierarchically; and
c) social order is ensured through each party's honoring the requirements in the role relationship (Bond and Hwang 1991, 216).

This ethic, with its emphasis on social harmony via clearly defined hierarchical relationships blended quite nicely into the Thai patron-client social structure, and, over the centuries, the Chinese in Thailand have prospered due not only to their industriousness but also to the patronage they have enjoyed in royal and bureaucratic circles.

However, Chinese familism and the Thai patron-client structure do differ in one very important respect. In Chinese familism, the interests of the family are placed firmly above those of society and other groups within it. The family or *jia* is the supreme social relationship, transcending all other sources of authority—whether temporal or divine. Within this system, parental authority is absolute and rebellion against it is unthinkable.

Thais, on the other hand, although certainly taught to defer to their parents' authority, were not taught to do so above all else. In keeping with a main tenet of Buddhism, an individual's primary responsibility is to himself; he must take full responsibility for his own life and bear alone the consequences of his own decisions. Thus, although family ties are important, they must compete with other social relationships that are of interest and/or benefit to the individual. Thai social bonds, whether with kin or non-kin, are fundamentally voluntary—freely entered into and freely left.

Despite this difference however, both the Thais and the Chinese have shared, as a result of their belief systems, an ascription orientation that bases the distribution of rewards and favors on personal alliances rather than on achievement. In the social systems of each, the patron exerts his power to benefit his clients who reciprocate with loyal service. Consequently, the value placed on personal relationships inherent in both the Chinese and Thai social systems were mutually reinforcing and served to strengthen the practice of nepotism and the formation of cliques in both the public and the private sectors.

Another important aspect of Chinese culture that has been integrated into Thai culture is the more intricate concept of 'face,' which has been defined by Goffman (1955) as 'the positive social value a person effectively claims for himself by the line others assume he has taken during a particular contact. Face is an image of self delineated in terms of approved social attributes' (Bond and Hwang 1991, 244). In traditional Thai society, saving face basically meant avoiding conflict situations that could cause shame and embarrassment. The Chinese expanded this definition by adding the notion of face-enhancing to face-saving and by dividing the behaviors attributed to both into six categories:

1. Enhancing one's own face through the cultivation and demonstration of qualities admired by society;

2. Enhancing another's face through such tactics as ingratiating oneself to another in the hope that the other will reciprocate in a way that will benefit the ingratiator;
3. Losing one's own face damages one's social status and prestige and, thus, must be avoided;
4. Hurting another's face, resulting in the other's anger and/or dissatisfaction and could result in retaliatory action—a situation that must also be avoided;
5. Saving one's own face, can be achieved in one of three ways: a) compensating another for having caused him to lose face by, for example, terminating the face-losing behavior or by reinterpreting the situation; b) retaliating against another for having caused a loss of face by either directly or indirectly expressing dissatisfaction; and c) when either compensatory or retaliatory actions are inappropriate, defending oneself against a loss of face by maintaining silence or by attributing the face-losing behavior to an external cause.
6. Saving the face of another, particularly the face of superiors, by restraining from offering comments or criticism or, if forced to venture an opinion, by giving vague or moderate feedback (Bond and Hwang 1991, 246–248).

Behaviors from all of these categories are practiced by many Thais today, reflecting a high power distance society in which conflict-avoiding behavior is valued as a means of maintaining social order and, at least superficially, harmonious relationships. The impact of these values on today's urban Thai society, however, is decreasing due to an influx of western values imported by way of economic development efforts, modern education and technology, and the globalization of trade and business.

Westernization: Competing and Confronting

Although westerners have had contact with Thailand for several centuries, it was not until the 19th century and the reign of King Mongkut (King Rama IV) that Thailand started a program of modernization that was heavily influenced by the West. King Mongkut, upon his accession to the throne at the age of 47, inaugurated a policy for modernizing the country along Western lines, beginning with the signing of a new set of treaties with Western powers. In so doing, he opened the land to foreign commerce and opened the people's minds to new ideas. His accomplishments included administrative reform, the building of roads and canals, issuance of the first modern currency, the setting-up of printing presses, the hiring of foreign advisors to the government, and the establishment of a police force (The Publicity Committee 1959, 6).

The descendants of King Mongkut continued his policy of opening the country to western influence, and the western influences welcomed with open arms in the 19th century would, in the 20th century, give rise to a new political state. By the time King Prajadhipok (King Rama VII, 1925–1935) came to the throne, a number of Thailand's elite had been educated in France and Germany and, upon their return to Thailand, had urged the establishment of a constitutional monarchy. In 1932, King Prajadhipok issued first a provisional and then a permanent constitution. On December 10, 1932, Thailand's first Prime Minister was appointed.

Although the change from an absolute to a constitutional monarchy in 1932 laid the foundation for the Thais' appreciation of such concepts as democracy, equality, and public participation in government, these concepts were still alien to all but the elite few who had received their educations abroad, and thus had little impact on the social reality of day-to-day life in Thailand. The absolute monarchy was exchanged for bureaucratic absolutism, 'a form of rule by a mandarin-aristocracy, created under absolute kingship, embellished by colonial systems, and strengthened with modern American technology' (Phongpaichit and Baker 1996, 171). The seeds of change began to take root, however, in the 1960s, a period when the U.S. provided substantial aid for the development of tertiary education in Thailand.

In the early 1970s, fewer than 150,000 Thais had university educations, and the majority of these pursued careers in government service. U.S. development aid, the rise of industrialization, and rapid economic growth would change this in little more than a decade. The business sector's demand for an increasingly large number of white-collar workers coupled with the mushrooming of vocational/technical colleges and universities saw the number of university graduates in the workforce increase ten-fold by the early 1990s. A rising tide of young Thais from the growing ranks of the prosperous were also going abroad, many as early as in their high school years, for their (western) education, with the U.S. being the favored destination. These young people, quite a few with western spouses in tow, would return to their homeland several years later to high paying jobs and a way of viewing the world that, in some cases, contrasted sharply with that of their parents.

Higher education, foreign aid and investment, the economic boom, consumerism, telecommunications growth, and technological advancements have all combined to result in the emergence of a new urban culture that is unlike anything Thailand has experienced before. In the 1960s, white collar workers in Thailand numbered only about half a million. In the 1980s, this figure jumped to around four and a half million (Phongpaichit and Baker 1996, 184). The opportunities for tertiary education during the same period expanded with the establishment of open universities and an increase in the number of private universities. Graduates from these universities have eschewed the public sector, opting instead for jobs in the private sector with companies willing to pay high prices for their skills and talents. In Thailand's major cities, Bangkok in particular, a new generation of Thais, members of a burgeoning middle class, have come of age; and, exposed to western business practices, they are aggressively climbing the socio-economic ladder.

The West has also played a role in reshaping Thai organizations and the ways in which Thais conduct business. Faced with increasingly fierce competition both locally and abroad, businesses have had to take a more aggressive approach, resulting in a flattening of organizations and a decentralization of decision-making power. Achieving results has gained in importance, often at the expense of relationships. Individuals are strongly encouraged to confront problems and discuss issues openly in team settings in order to develop innovative solutions that will help the company maintain its competitive edge. Communication is becoming more multi-directional via a wider range of channels.

In this dynamic environment, the quiet, self-effacing, conflict-avoiding Thai may seem in danger of becoming an anachronism. And yet, the beliefs that gave rise to such traditional conflict-avoidance values as *kreng jai* and *jai yen* are still too strong to permit the confrontational behavior favored in the West to take firm hold.

BEHAVIORAL IMPLICATIONS (A SITUATION ANALYSIS)

Thailand has, over the past few decades undergone dramatic changes. Much of the conflict that arises among Thais in business today is a direct result of the modernization that was begun in earnest in the 19th century and that picked up tremendous speed in the latter half of this century. Exposed to western management practices in business schools and international companies and coming of age during the economic boom of the 80s, the young urban Thai today is much more ambitious, assertive, and achievement-oriented than many of his older colleagues are, often resulting in a schism between old and new. The village society is being rapidly replaced by a growing urban economy, and many of the underlying assumptions that sustained the village culture of old are being challenged by urban youth.

Yet the Thai smile, an integral part of the Thai personality, is still ubiquitous and continues to rank second to none as a defense mechanism in conflict situations. The traditions established centuries ago are buried too deeply within the collective Thai subconscious to be easily or completely uprooted, as the following example illustrates:

Max Sumler, the American senior manager of an American-Thai manufacturing joint-venture complained that his western-educated production manager, *Khun* Pichai, was not cooperating with him in implementing the new management-by-objectives system that the American was trying to set up company-wide:

> "Most of the office staff seem to understand the new system, and, even though what they've produced so far is practically useless garbage, they are at least trying to follow through. But my production people seem to be going nowhere with it. I've met with my production manager, Pichai, and his staff several times to discuss the system and to make certain they understand it. The staff say nothing and Pichai just smiles and assures me that they do understand. Yet, when I ask him for the objectives statements for his department, he continually puts me off with one lame excuse or another. When I call him on it, he just smiles and tells me that the statements are forthcoming—he needs a little more time. It's infuriating. I've got a deadline to meet and he knows it. I'm going to have the head office on my back if I don't show them some results very soon. Short of going down to the Production Department and bull-dozing the system through myself, I don't know what to do. I thought Pichai would be perfect for this job when I hired him a year ago. He's spent more than ten years in the States, you know, and he's been really good at helping me communicate with the others. But now I'm beginning to wonder."

An analysis of this predicament from Pichai's perspective will paint a clearer picture of the kinds of conflict situations that are occurring in Thai business today as modernization struggles against tradition. It will also highlight some of the more common strategies used by Thais in dealing with those conflicts among themselves and with non-Thais.

A follow-up interview with Pichai to get his side of the story revealed that he *did* understand the new system *and* strongly supported it, as he explained:

> "I worked for a company that used MBO in the States, and I really liked it. It provided a clear direction and concrete goals, but it was also flexible enough to accommodate the unexpected. I think a system like that would be perfect for my production people, and I am as eager to get the ball rolling as Max is. But what I can't seem to get Max to understand is that you can't just push something like that through here overnight. It's totally outside my people's experience, and they're a little afraid of it.
>
> Max arranged an orientation on MBO for all company personnel shortly after the new policy was announced. I thought the orientation provided a good overview of the system's philosophy, but it didn't really explain exactly how the system would be applied here or how, specifically, it would benefit the employees. Opportunities were given for people to ask questions, but nobody did, because, I guess, nobody knew enough about the system to know what to ask, and because Max was there and nobody wanted him to think that they didn't really understand.
>
> I know that the office staff have already started working on setting up departmental and individual objectives, but from what I've heard, people are not happy about it. Seems they think that Max's MBO policy is just a poorly disguised attempt to try to gain more control over them and to try to force them to do more work for the same amount of pay. I've heard that several of them are already looking for jobs elsewhere. Max doesn't have a clue.
>
> I've met with the same resistance among my people, especially my supervisors. Shortly after that orientation, rumors started spreading around the plant that the new system was going to be used to get rid of people and other such things. Productivity and quality dropped while absences went up. I realized pretty fast that if I couldn't recruit the supervisors to the cause, the system would never be successfully implemented. So, I've spent a lot of time talking informally with them about it to try to find out what the problems are. I've

been taking small groups of them out for dinner after work, and, after talking about topics of interest to them for a while, we gradually move into work related issues and to the MBO system. More than half of them are clear now on what the system is, how it works, and how it will benefit them, and I'm sure that, with their help, I can win the other half over within the month. Once that happens, I'll have a committed supervisory staff who will be able to help me communicate the same message to the workers, and then we'll be able to implement the system smoothly and successfully.

I've tried to explain all this to Max several times, but, like so many Americans I've known, he's not interested in listening when he thinks he's right. He wants this thing done yesterday. He has practically screamed this at me at our last few meetings—once in front of a few of my employees. He's not making my job any easier, and if he doesn't calm down a bit, I might be looking elsewhere for a job myself. He's only been here two years. He doesn't speak or understand a word of Thai. He is not aware of his staff's feelings or of the mass confusion about the new system. But, because I'm the only one who's actually tried to confront him with the problems, he thinks I'm the trouble-maker. I've stopped trying to explain things to him, and I've stopped arguing with him—I just waste time and end up making him and myself look bad in front of my workers."

Pichai's perception of the problem reveals that

1. the problem is far more serious than Max realizes, and
2. a number of factors related to socio-cultural norms and traditions of which Max is unaware are exacerbating the problem.

The factors that are directly contributing to the conflict situation involving Max, Pichai, and their employees are the primary catalysts of most conflict situations in Thailand (and elsewhere), especially those involving Thais and non-Thais. How and why these factors cause conflict will be discussed in the remainder of this section. The factors identified reflect the socio-cultural features covered earlier in this chapter and include:

- Perception and Cultural Diversity
- Power Distance, Status, Leadership and Face-Saving
- Uncertainty Avoidance versus Individual Freedom and Relationships

Perception and Cultural Diversity

At its most basic level, perception is 'the process of making sense out of experience—of inputing meaning to experience' (Haney 1967, 52); it is the means by which 'people select, organize, and interpret sensory stimulation into a meaningful and coherent picture of the world' (Berelson and Steiner 1964, 88). Interpretation is the act of giving 'meaning to observations and their relationships; it is the process of making sense out of perceptions' (Adler 1991, 70). Interpretation molds our assumptions and guides our responses to various stimuli in different situations. Our exposure to differing environments, which precludes our receiving the same stimuli, contributes greatly to unnecessary and destructive conflict. This is because of our unwillingness to acknowledge and accept differences—differences between our perceptions and reality as well as differences between our perceptions and those of others. Our behavior is determined by a perceptual framework that may be vastly different from that of those with whom we are interacting. Conflict results when we either do not acknowledge or accept this difference and when we assume that our perception of reality is the only 'right' one.

In the case described, the conflict between the principal players, Max and Pichai, arose in part due to their differing perceptual frameworks. Max viewed the situation as one requiring coercion, since Pichai was not producing the concrete results he expected. Pichai viewed the situation first as one requiring collaboration and later as one requiring withdrawal. The problem he was experiencing in the plant was also a problem in the office, although Max was not aware of it, and the only way to overcome it company-wide was through collaboration with Max. Because this did not seem possible, Pichai withdrew.

Max's perception of Pichai's performance was grounded in an American cultural focus on activity and achievement. Pichai's perception of the situation in general was based upon his knowledge of the Thai culture's emphasis on the present and on simply being—not necessarily achieving. He knew that, in general, Thais were far less results-oriented and far more relationship-oriented than most Americans. Also, Pichai was aware that conflict was viewed and managed differently in Thailand than it was in the States.

In this particular situation, Max was under pressure from his head office to implement an MBO system within a specific time-frame. This time-frame did not take into consideration possible socio-cultural differences that could—and did—become obstacles to successful implementation.

Because Pichai had more or less sheltered Max from these differences in the past, Max's knowledge of them, despite his two years in the country, was basically limited to the 'do's and don'ts' provided by the average tourist guidebook. Thus, when Max was under pressure to get something done fast, he expected Pichai's full cooperation, which, in Max's terms, meant immediate concrete results. Pichai's attempts to explain the problems from a cultural viewpoint came at the wrong time and were interpreted as excuses for weak leadership.

Max felt that Pichai was over-accommodating his employees rather than confronting them with the problem head-on. Max believed, as a result of his American cultural background, that the best way to solve the problem was to hold a meeting so that grievances could be openly aired and firmly addressed, and decisive, immediate action could be taken. Because he had done this with his staff and his staff appeared to be cooperating with their submission of objectives, his belief in the 'rightness' of this approach was reinforced, and he attributed the lack of similar results in the plant to Pichai's ineptitude.

On the other hand, Pichai felt that Max was moving much too quickly and applying too much pressure to get results while spending too little time on laying the groundwork necessary for employee understanding and acceptance of the new system. He was acutely aware that, in Thailand, appearances can most definitely be deceiving. His knowledge of the complaints being communicated with quiet ferocity through the company grapevine confirmed his belief that any seeming compliance was mere subterfuge, masking discontent while counter measures were being planned. Pichai knew that it would take more than one formal orientation meeting to implement the new system successfully. For reasons relating to status and face, the Thai staff would not open up in such a setting. Only personal lobbying of key personnel would elicit the concerns that needed to be addressed. Once these concerns had been aired in informal, non-threatening environments, they could be worked out in an easy-going, friendly manner. Moreover, in so doing, relationships between ranks would be enhanced, the communication and trust networks of key personnel could be mobilized to win over lower level employees, and real results could be achieved. Pichai's success with his supervisors convinced him of the 'rightness' of his approach.

Max, in keeping with his cultural orientation, viewed the situation linearly:

- Effect: Office staff are not complaining and have produced statements of objectives, but plant staff have not;

- Cause: I provide strong, effective leadership, but Pichai does not.

Using his own culture as a self-reference criterion, Max assumed that there was only one way to view the world—his way, and he perceived the behaviors of his office staff and of Pichai in reference to himself and to his American version of reality.

He assumed that the office staff, like their counterpart Americans, would confront him freely and openly with any complaints they might have about the new system. Since the staff did not confront him, he truly believed that all was well. This belief was strengthened by the staff's production of objectives, despite their poor quality.

Max, in projecting similarity between Thais and Americans, had fallen prey to an illusion of understanding that made him oblivious to his gross misinterpretation of the situation. His attachment to this illusion also led him to perceive Pichai in a negative light when Pichai's attempts to explain the situation from a Thai perspective contradicted Max's own.

Pichai, however, took a cyclical view of the situation in keeping with his Thai cultural orientation and his insight into the behavioral patterns of both Thais and Americans:

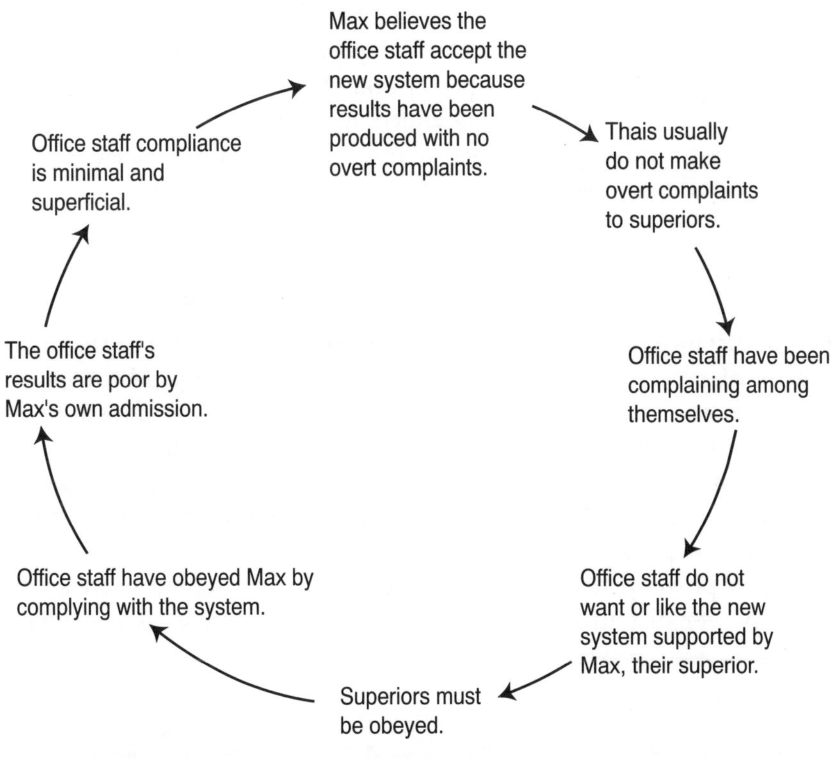

Although aware of Max's cultural blinders and of how they were exacerbating the problem that Max denied existed, Pichai did not realize, at first, that he, too, had become a victim of Max's cultural blindness. He also did not realize that his earlier efforts to shield Max from the realities of Thai culture had contributed significantly to that blindness and to the way Max interpreted the behaviors of those around him. Thus, when Max refused to listen to Pichai's analysis of the situation, Pichai assumed that Max's resistance was intentional—an American power play, and he attributed Max's aggression to his American cultural background. In so doing, Pichai shifted his focus from his and Max's management similarities to the cultural differences that began, in Pichai's mind, to loom large between them. This stereotyping led Pichai to believe that any further discussion with Max would be useless, a prophecy that was on its way to achieving fulfillment as Pichai withdrew behind a non-committal smile and a non-confrontational manner in his dealings with Max.

Both Max and Pichai started out by sharing the same goal—the successful and timely implementation of an MBO system company-wide, but their inability to manage cultural diversity due to perceptual barriers caused them to lose sight of this goal. Max believed that he had already achieved success in the office and that Pichai had failed in the plant. Pichai believed that Max had failed in the office and that he, Pichai, was succeeding in the plant. Approaching the situation from opposing patterns of thinking, both men firmly believed that their perception of reality was 'right,' and each man, in his own way, ultimately ended up competing with the other to try to force the other's acceptance of his version of reality while the MBO problem in the company continued to fester.

Power Distance, Status, Leadership and Face-Saving

Power distance refers generally to the degree of sensitivity to the distribution of power within a specific socio-cultural group. More specifically, it is 'the extent to which the less powerful members of institutions and organizations within a country expect and accept that power is distributed unequally' (Hofstede 1991, 28). In low power distance countries, people are considered 'existentially equal' while in high power distance countries people are 'existentially unequal'.

In low power distance countries like the United States, where an unequal power distribution in organizational hierarchies is considered merely a convenience, publicly challenging those in authority is an accepted behavioral norm that is encouraged and even admired. In high power distance countries such as Thailand, where unequal power distribution is believed to be based—and rightly so—upon an inherent inequality, the public confrontation of authority is viewed as socially disruptive insubordination and is strongly discouraged. For this reason, Max's office staff would not openly air their grievances with him about the MBO system. This was also true with Pichai's plant staff. Pichai became aware of his staff's discontent via increased absenteeism and decreased productivity. His employees did not confront him directly with their confusion and unhappiness over the new system. As explained in the first section of this chapter, the high power distance between ranks in Thailand and the Thais' aversion to confronting acknowledged superiors are related to the their understanding of status and the rights of status-holders, their beliefs about the nature of leadership, and their need to save face—their own and others.

Status

In Max's world, meaningful status is usually *earned* through hard work, experience, and publicly recognized achievement. Because status is earned—and is not an inherent right or virtue, status holders can be and *are* challenged. In Pichai's world, however, status is bestowed upon an individual by virtue of his seniority and/or his socio-economic standing within a community. In keeping with the law of Karma, high-status holders in Thai society are believed to be reaping the rewards of past meritorious acts. Their rank is high because, as elaborated earlier in this chapter, they are believed to be inherently virtuous. Publicly challenging the 'rightness' of their actions is an act in violation of nature and is thus sinful.

As a citizen of the United States, a country acknowledged by his Thai employees as being wealthier and more powerful than their own nation and thus of higher world status, Max's own personal status is already reasonably high on the social scale. Max's being sent to Thailand as CEO of the joint-venture firm places him even higher in the social order. Similarly, Pichai, who spent many years in the U.S., also has a reasonably high rank. Since substantial funds would have been needed to support his education abroad, his employees would assume that he came from a wealthy (i.e., high-status) family. His ability to speak English fluently, his high position within the company, and his past close relationship with Max all would have increased his status in the eyes of his employees. To their employees, Max and Pichai are quite literally and inherently *superior*, which means that their employees have a moral duty to comply with their policies and practices. Thus, the employees do comply, and they do so without openly complaining or protesting. Compliance, however, does *not* mean acceptance nor does it mean that unacceptable situations will be tolerated indefinitely.

Since direct confrontation at the outset of a problem is not an option for most Thais, the initial steps taken to alert a superior to a subordinate's dissatisfaction usually include absence from work, repetitive tardiness, extended lunch periods, a subdued, quiet demeanor, monosyllabic responses to questions, rumor-monging, and an overall reduction of performance efficiency. If the superior is insensitive to these indirect hints of dissent, the subordinate will be forced to take further action. Usually this involves withdrawing from the situation altogether by resigning from the organization, giving as an excuse a reason unrelated to the real problem. Sometimes, if truly pushed beyond endurance and left with no other feasible option, more drastic, direct action is taken, as in the case recently experienced by the executives of a foreign manufacturing firm in Bangkok. Employees, who were upset over the last minute reduction of an annual bonus, burned down one of the company's factories.

In the case of Pichai and Max, Pichai's sensitivity to the indirect tactics used by his employees to signal their discontent alerted him to the need to lobby his people for acceptance of the new system before pushing them any further with implementation. Oblivious to these same signals among his office staff, Max continued to push his subordinates, resulting in increased dissatisfaction and resentment.

Just as Max viewed Pichai's personal attention to the plant employees as overly accommodating and a sign of weak leadership, Max's office employees viewed Max's insensitivity to their plight and his impatience with Pichai as overly aggressive and a sign of poor leadership.

Leadership and Face Saving

Although economic development and the rise of the middle class has narrowed the power gap between levels in the social hierarchy, the power distance in Thailand is still much greater than that of countries such as the U.S. This does not mean, however, that an authoritarian management style is viewed with favor by Thais. Indeed, most of the conflicts between Thais and non-Thais occur as the result of non-Thai behavior that is perceived as being aggressively (and insultingly) authoritarian.

A case in point is an incident that occurred at a local Thai-Japanese joint-venture company. The Japanese supervisors at this company had management styles that were viewed as being stricter and more authoritarian than those of their Thai counterparts. They frequently criticized their Thai employees in the presence of others, causing the employees to lose face. This behavior was tolerated for a time, but the continued assault to their pride went beyond the Thais' considerable capacity for endurance, resulting eventually in a strike. The Japanese were astounded by this, explaining that their behavior was the norm in Japan and would not be taken so personally. Japan and Thailand have similarly high power distances, but, as this incident reveals, the ways in which that power is used and expressed in superior-subordinate relationships are very different.

Thai employees want and respect supervisors who *ru jai* (know their employees' hearts) and who treat them with kindness, respect and consideration. Such supervisors develop relationships with their subordinates that are based on trust and friendship, and for such supervisors, the Thais will indeed 'open their hearts.'

Because Max failed to differentiate between Thai and American patterns of behavior, he fell in the same cultural trap that many non-Thais before him have encountered. His cultural orientation caused him to react in ways considered inappropriate by his Thai employees. His employees, as a result, came to see his leadership behavior as far more *phradet* than *phrakhun*; that is, he was viewed as being insensitive, aggressive, and intolerant. All three adjectives are serious words of condemnation for most Thais, who are highly demotivated by such behavior in a superior. This is particularly true if the subordinate's relationship with the superior is distant, and there has been little or no history of benevolence *(phrakhun)*.

Because Max is a non-Thai and a superior, the distance between Max and his office staff is so great as to negate, in light of his current behavior, any past kindnesses he might have extended to them. Moreover, Max's public, negative behavior toward Pichai, whom employees had believed was Max's good friend, was greatly disturbing, for if Max could behave so shamefully (i.e., aggressively) in his interactions with a man of high position and of previous high regard, then what might such a man do to the employees, who were of much lower status and who felt a much greater power distance. In berating Pichai in front of subordinates, Max had caused Pichai to lose face, forcing Pichai to retreat behind a smile in an attempt to protect himself from any further damage. More importantly though, in his treatment of Pichai, Max caused himself to lose much more face, since, as a leader, he was expected to set an example for his subordinates, behaving with kindness, understanding, and charity. The employees felt that Max had betrayed one of his own, abusing the patron-client relationship they shared, and traitors are not viewed kindly in Thai organizations. In Max's case, both office and plant employees came to the conclusion that Max could not be trusted and did not merit their loyalty.

On the other hand, Pichai's personal concern for and attention to his employees' needs when he sensed their discontent made him, in the eyes of his employees, a leader who dispensed far more *phrakhun* (mercy, kindness, benevolence) than *phradet* (punishment). Pichai was seen as a leader who *ru jai* (understood), who had *nam jai* (generosity of spirit), and who was *jai dee* (kind, or literally 'good hearted'). Thai employees are highly motivated by attributes such as these and will usually respond in kind. Pichai also enhanced face for himself in the eyes of his employees in his non-aggressive handling of Max's inappropriate behavior, for, as most Thais know, in situations such as these, losing *is* winning. Max shamed himself and Pichai and the employees who were the unfortunate observers of Max's frustrated outbursts. He caused himself to lose honor and dignity by behaving inappropriately. Pichai, however, restored honor and dignity to himself and to his fellow Thais by withdrawing from the fray with a smile and showing sincere concern for the well-being of his employees.

As members of a shame-oriented society who place a high value on relationships, most Thais believe that behavior such as Pichai's *must* be rewarded with loyalty and devotion. Refusing to do so, particularly if the other party is a superior, brings shame to the dissident and to the group of which he is a part. Few Thais would refuse, since the penalty for such behavior could involve ostracizing the offender from his group, putting him at risk of being rejected by the members, not only of whatever current personal network he might have, but also of any future network he might try to build; and that, for a Thai, could very well mean a ruined future. Word spreads very, very quickly along the interconnected strands of the tightly woven web of Thai society, and violations of that society's norms are neither quickly nor easily forgotten, despite appearances to the contrary.

Uncertainty Avoidance versus Individual Freedom and Relationships

Uncertainty Avoidance

Uncertainty avoidance is the 'extent to which the members of a culture feel threatened by uncertain or unknown situations' (Hofstede 1991, 113). Although located in the 'strong' quadrant for uncertainty avoidance (Hofstede 1991, 123), Thailand is on the weak end of strong. While it is true that most Thais both need and enjoy structure, they will balk if they believe that their personal freedom is in danger of being restricted.

In these days of restructuring, down-sizing, and flattening, Thais at many companies complain about the lack of structure, which for them means the absence of specific job descriptions and a clear hierarchy. Removing or changing these important elements of Thai social and organizational life often causes acute anxiety, with statements such as 'I don't know what I'm supposed to be responsible for anymore' or 'I have a problem and I don't know who to take it to anymore' being common. As members of a vertical, rigidly structured society, Thais do not take well to structural changes. They are confused and upset when systems they have grown accustomed to and have learned how to maneuver are changed. For the Thai, this is equivalent to changing the rules in the middle of a game that one has played and enjoyed since birth. Consequently, the change to a management by objectives system that Max tried to implement was quite naturally resisted by the Thai employees, even though the system had been designed to provide a clearer direction (and thus reduced ambiguity) for job performance than the old system had provided.

The resistance in this case, however, was not merely due to uncertainty over the new. It was also due to a general feeling that the goals Max was aiming for would be *too* specific and, therefore, confining.

The goals were viewed as confining because the employees believed, and accurately so, that Max expected them to make achieving those goals the primary focus of their activity on the job. Goal-setting is a western import and is based on the achievement-oriented assumption that employees will most value and be most motivated by interesting and challenging work. Indeed, a study of Eastman Kodak employees in Australia and Thailand conducted by Philip Hughes and Brian Sheehan (1993) revealed that Australian employees *did* place a high value on interesting and challenging work; however, the responses of their Thai counterparts, who valued work primarily for the friends with whom they worked, suggested that western assumptions about what motivates people most are not necessarily universal.

Individual Freedom and Relationships

For the average Thai, relationship building and the pursuit of personal pleasure (*sanuk*) are given high priority. If, at work, one is expected to devote most of one's time to goal achievement, the time one has free to spend on building and nurturing relationships and on other personal priorities is limited. The more challenging the goals, the less freedom one perceives that one has; and the less freedom one believes one has, the more restricted and confined one feels. In her book *Mai Pen Rai Means Never Mind* (1965), Carol Hollinger, in reflecting back on her conversation with a 'high-status' Thai lady, captured the essence of personal freedom Thai-style as it contrasts with the highly regulated, achievement-oriented American lifestyle:

> "'Also,' added Khun Chern, 'there is no freedom in America.' The flat statement dumped a hemisphere between us. Even in the short time I had been in Thailand I had been sensitive to the ravages of dictatorship and I was dumbfounded that she could have found America wanting in comparison. 'Everywhere,' continued my hostess, 'Americans are told what to do, what not to do—worry, worry—always rules. Even signs saying DO NOT SPIT. I am scared to move. No freedom at all.' ...I remember thinking passionately at the time, how can she be so oblivious to the real meaning of freedom? By the end of our tour I knew, and sadly, that I agreed with her. ...Now, back home in America, I often stare at my fellow Americans pressed upon by thousands of rules, laws, deadlines and absurd conformities and I can see in their tense shapes and publicized ulcers the scars of a cruel regimentation. ...I find myself muttering, 'No freedom to spit! No freedom to spit!'" (pp. 62–63)

The management by objectives system that Max tried to implement in the joint-venture company he managed was perceived by employees as an attempt to regiment them and to rob them of their personal freedom. Because of this perception, they could not see any of the advantages such a system might offer, and they did not understand when the advantages were pointed out to them and explained in the orientation session Max arranged. All that they understood was that a new system that restricted their personal freedom on the job was going to be implemented. They felt that they were being forced by Max to shift their priorities. Force is a strong word and not one that Max would have agreed with, but an appropriate one here for four main reasons:

1. Confronting Max, a superior, with this concern at the meeting Max arranged was out of the question, since, from the employees' point of view, confronting Max publicly would be tantamount to questioning the wisdom of their leader and in violation of a very strong social behavioral norm guiding superior-subordinate relationships.
2. Because Max was their superior—their patron, he had to be obeyed. Obeying him was their duty as clients, even if they did so only superficially.
3. Because Max's relationship with his employees was job-centered, the distance between Max and his employees was too great for an individual employee to feel comfortable approaching him about the problem on a private, personal basis.
4. Max did not pick up on his employees' non-verbal signals of anxiety and discontent. He even praised their half-hearted attempts at goal-setting, which distressed rather than pleased the office staff. His approval of their below standard work meant that he was not getting the message they were trying desperately to send.

The Thai staff felt that they were being pushed into a corner—forced to sacrifice relationships for results, and they were quietly planning a counter-attack. By the time Max realized that something was, indeed, wrong and sought help, three senior members of the office staff had resigned, taking five junior members with them, and the fourth draft of the objectives of the office staff remaining were as useless as those written for the first draft.

Much of the trouble Max experienced was the result of his ignorance of Thai socio-cultural behavioral norms and his insistence on managing Thais based upon his own socio-cultural frame of reference. The first section of this chapter aimed at providing the non-Thai with an understanding of some of the more important Thai socio-cultural norms. This section has attempted to show how those norms influence Thai behavior and contribute to conflict in the workplace. The last section will offer some practical advice for non-Thais in managing conflict situations when interacting with Thais in both social and work settings.

RECOMMENDATIONS FOR NON-THAIS

The recommendations offered herein are based on the Thai proverb '*Kan wai dee kwa kae*,' which means—prevention is better than correction. Recommendations to prevent or minimize conflict situations will be provided for non-Thais seeking to establish social and/or business relationships with the Thais on either a short- or long-term basis. However, since, despite the best preventive efforts, conflicts do occur, strategies for managing conflict when it does occur will also be provided. Finally, approaches for introducing change in organizations in a Thai context will be suggested.

Social Relationships

Age and Status

In socializing with Thais on a short-term basis in any social situation, age and status play major roles in directing 'appropriate protocol' to cultivate 'social harmony.' Nationality may also determine how a non-Thai will be treated by Thais. However, individuals of certain nationalities who seem to benefit from this assumption cannot ignore the roles of age and status in socializing with Thais.

Foreigners accustomed to travel abroad have learned the importance of observation and good manners in creating a positive first impression and in gaining acceptance among the locals of the culture visited. 'Good manners' in Thai culture require the younger and lower in status to initiate greetings and introductions when meeting seniors. It is quite uncommon for *pu yai* (seniors, elders) to greet *dek* (juniors) first. There is no exception for gender.

If you happen to be the younger person of the pair and the senior is interested having a conversation with you, the senior will start the dialogue. During the conversation, you should be careful to note the topics/areas of interest to the senior and pursue those topics in a non-combative manner. That is, do not offer contradictory opinions that could be interpreted as criticism. Contradicting or criticizing the opinions of Thais, particularly Thais who are senior to you, may cause them to feel that they have lost face. This is especially true if there are witnesses to the event.

This does not mean, however, that you must let what you believe to be inaccurate information pass. Thais have learned to offer correction of this sort in an impersonal, diplomatic manner, beginning their sentences with clauses such as 'I heard that...,' or 'someone told me that...,' and then following up with the correction. In direct interaction, Thais generally avoid stating that they, personally, are in disagreement with another. They prefer to refer to a (sometimes non-existant) third-party who does not share their conversation partner's opinions.

Sacred Institutions

Next, never criticize the 'three pillars/institutions' that are held sacred by most Thais. These are the nation (*Chart*), Buddhism (*Sassana*), and the Monarchy (*Phra Mahakasat*). You should note that the pillars of Buddhism also include the rituals performed by Buddhist monks or Brahmans on occasions such as a company's opening ceremony, birthday parties, weddings, and funerals. Although you may perceive some of these rituals to be highly superstitious and an unnecessary bother, you should withhold your criticism, keeping in mind the admonition of one 17th century Thai Buddhist monk to a self-righteous westerner: 'Since I have had the complaisance to approve your religion, why do you not approve of mine?' It may be several centuries later, but the sentiment among Thais remains the same.

Informal Manner

Even in short-term social relationships, non-Thais are advised to be friendly and informal. In general, Thais tend to prefer to form informal relationships even with strangers. After a few minutes of conversation, if the parties feel at ease with one another, informal familial terms such as *pee* (elder sister or brother), *nong* (younger sister/brother), *khun lung* (uncle), *khun pa* (aunt) are often used, even among brief acquaintances, in lieu of the formal *Khun* (Mister/Ms./Mrs.). Therefore, when conversing with a Thai, you should take note of the level of formality to gauge how well you have been accepted. If the level of formality is high, acceptance is low or nil. If formality is low, then acceptance is high. And when dealing with senior Thais, if you behave very politely and humbly, as the young are expected to behave to the elders in their own family, you will most probably be warmly welcomed and accepted.

Sanuk or Fun-loving

In dealing with Thais who are of common age and status, being polite, humble, and informal are still good strategies to rely upon, although with a lesser degree of rigidity. If you are endowed with a sense of humor and fun, you can also use this to your advantage in creating relationships with Thais, because being *sanuk* or fun-loving is an attribute admired and enjoyed by most Thais. This explains why non-Thais who are willing to participate in activities the Thais view as 'fun' and who are able to contribute to the fun themselves are easily accepted and often well-liked by Thais. Given the immense pressure to conform to social norms and the economic pressures Thais face today, *sanuk* is an absolute necessity for many, as Kulick and Wilson (1996) explain:

> "Modernization increases the tensions in the Thai psyche, leading to a surprisingly high incidence of neurosis as well as murder. Their strong sense of individuality makes the Thais yearn for self-expression and open communication, but this is stifled in a society which insists on identifying them by their outward appearance rather than their inner qualities, so psychological tension is generated. The consequence is that they avoid becoming involved in other people's problems....To escape from all these problems, Thais have a legitimate outlet of relaxation in what is called *sanuk* or 'fun.' ...Having fun and deriving pleasure from carefree amusement with congenial friends or companions has a positive value in the code of behavior: no one indulging in *sanuk* would expect to be blamed or criticized." (p.63)

This explains why those who appear to be carefree and relaxed and who like having fun are easily accepted by Thais. Starting a conversation in an informal, relaxing tone and manner with a liberal dose of fun is therefore highly recommended.

Jaidee and Bun khun

Another preferred/admired personality trait among Thais is *jai dee* (having a good/kind heart). Thais are attracted to those who show that they have good heart and are helpful to others. In social functions, those who help pass the food, take plates of food to others, and generally offer whatever help may be needed are usually praised by Thais as having good manners and a good heart. This *jai dee* behavior is related to *bunkhun* in the sense that it starts the 'reciprocating cycle' in which a person who has received a 'favor' from another is expected to return the favor (*bunkhun*), if needed, in the future. This does not mean, however, that you should never accept any favor or any help from Thais for fear that they will expect a return on the favor from you. In such short-term situations, offering help is perceived by Thais as an act of friendliness.

Thus, when you accept a gesture of friendliness from a Thai, your acceptance of the act symbolizes your acceptance of the person. And if you can return a similar gesture in the future, the 'tie' between you and the Thai will be strengthened.

Body Contact

Even in short-term relationships, non-Thais should be aware of the level and nature of body contact permitted between people in public in Thai society. Western culture seems to allow more 'body contact' between genders than Thai culture does whereas Thai culture allows more contact among members of the same gender than is seen in the West. In general, it is best to avoid touching Thais of the opposite sex. Also, since the head is deemed the highest part of the body and the home of the spirit, you should never, for any reason, touch another person's head. Even in barber shops and beauty salons, hairdressers ask permission to touch their patron's head before beginning their work. Similarly, since the foot is deemed the lowest part of the body, it is improper to use it for anything except that for which it was designed—moving the body around. Also, when seated and facing another person, especially if that person is a senior or a monk or any other high-status person, or when seated and facing an image of the Buddha, you should make certain that your feet are pointed away from the person or the image. Failure to do this could anger the Thais nearby since pointing one's feet, even unintentionally, at something or someone sacred, is considered a serious insult to the dignity of Thais as a whole.

At this stage, it can be seen that even in a short acquaintance, behaving appropriately requires a reasonably high level of sensitivity. To create harmonious relationships with Thais in the workplace, the advice given above holds true, but to a much greater degree.

Working Relationships

There seems little doubt that almost all of the principle values of the Thais concern the cultivation of smooth interpersonal relationships that are based on trust, kindness, respect, and consideration. This is also true for working relationships between superiors and subordinates and among peers. For non-Thais aiming to effectively achieve their business goals within a Thai context, the following recommendations should be of significant value.

Preparing a Platform for Effective Working Relationships

For non-Thais wishing to do business with Thais, perhaps the most practical advice was that offered 66 years ago by Reginald le May:

> "Trust them as a friend, as an equal, and they will open their hearts. Come among them as an official with stern, unbending mien, and they will close their mouths like oysters at the touch."
>
> Fieg 1989, 12

Modern management practice normally divides up the work of managers into four major functions: planning, organizing, directing, and evaluating. Nevertheless, in a Thai context, carrying out these functions effectively requires that one first develop strong informal/personal relationships with employees at all levels. Organizations may have a formal organization chart outlining the responsibilities of each department and each individual. It may also depict the chain of command as well as the span of control of each person or position within the hierarchy. Without a strong personal network in place, however, these formal charts are often meaningless.

Problems that non-Thais often experience with Thais and that often give rise to conflict are problems such as failing to meet deadlines, unwilling to be responsible or accountable for work assigned, giving inaccurate or late information, providing poor service, and generally not cooperating. Problems such as these are symptoms of a deeper problem that the non-Thai must resolve if he intends to get things done. The deeper problem is his absence of a personal network within the organization upon which he can rely to ensure that the right people are doing the right things in the right way and at the right time.

As already mentioned in this chapter, Thais are more relationship-oriented than results-oriented. Therefore, in order to get results, non-Thais need to spend a substantial portion of their time identifying and developing strong reciprocal (i.e., patron-client) relationships with the key players, at all levels, within their organization. These relationships will form the network upon which the non-Thai must depend if he is to achieve performance goals.

It is common among Thais to create a 'family-like' environment in the workplace. Based on the patron-client model, subordinates anticipate protection and rewards from their bosses in return for their loyalty, first, and then their devotion to the task at hand. Similarly, in the spirit of *bunkhun,* co-workers are supposed to help each other. Supervisors are usually regarded (and called) as *pee* (elder sister or elder brother) and are expected to provide support and protection for their *nong* (younger sister or younger brother). Among peers, relationships are formulated to create a personal network or clique that is called in Thai *pak puak* and that serves as the individual's support group. Thais work hard at creating *pak puak* in as many departments as possible so that they will receive support and cooperation from other departments when it is needed.

In creating such networks in the workplace, *bunkhun* and *katanyu katawethi* assume key roles. By offering assistance or favors to supervisors/peers/subordinates, a reciprocal cycle of mutually beneficial acts is begun. It is a cycle that westerners more commonly refer to as friendship on one level and as good politics on another.

A second element of importance to network building is *mee sen* (pulling strings, having connections). This means that if you are able to include people of high-status as a part of your personal network—one of your *pak puak*, you can ask them directly for their assistance or simply refer to them by name to get assistance from one of their *pak puak*. In this way, bureaucratic red tape is made to disappear, service is timely, information is accurate, deadlines are met, and cooperation is on its best behavior.

Asking about and getting to know the family of supervisors, peers, and subordinates, joining social functions such as birthday parties, visiting employees at the hospital, going to the funeral of an employee's relative, and dining out with employees after work are just some of the activities that Thais participate in to assist them in developing and strengthening their *pak puak*. The non-Thai business manager or partner hoping to achieve relatively painless success in a Thai business context would be wise to follow suit.

Seeking Ideas/Advice and Commitment/Cooperation from Thais

In order to develop any plan, to make decisions, to divide up the work, and to coordinate, ideas and cooperation must be sought either from peers, subordinates or supervisors. In Western culture, ideas/advice and cooperation can usually be generated in meetings where people actively participate in brainstorming and/or criticizing/debating each other's ideas. Meetings in a Thai environment, however, portray a different scene. Since Thais value relationships and give much importance to status and face saving, they avoid directly criticizing or challenging others' ideas in public, particularly those of their seniors.

Given these norms, the senior member of an assembled Thai group will serve as discussion leader while the less senior members listen quietly. If the junior members are asked for their opinion, they will respond in a very humble and polite manner, toning down and de-personalizing ideas that might appear to contradict those of the senior (who may be a senior in terms of age and/or position). If the meetings are among people of similar status, a larger number of people will participate in a discussion, but criticism, if there is any, will be light and often presented in a humorous way. Usually, any serious criticism would be reserved for the topic of an informal discussion with one's own *pak puak* after the formal meeting ends.

In a western framework, meetings are perceived as an effective mechanism for generating ideas and resolving problems. Meetings for Thais, however, are usually information sessions in which superiors pass down and/or explain policies while subordinates listen respectfully. Lobbying before and after meetings is the strategy most often used by Thais to ensure acceptance of an idea or policy and its successful implementation. Holding informal discussions over lunch or dinner (or even in the restrooms during meeting breaks) is the most common strategy used to gauge feelings and gather information about the acceptance of a new proposal or the handling of a problem.

In order to find out what their Thai superiors, peers, or subordinates think about any issue, non-Thais should engage employees in informal conversations, preferably, in informal environments. It is through such conversations that the non-Thai will be able to determine the degree to which an idea or proposal or policy will be accepted or resisted by Thais. It is also in this manner that possible objections can be addressed and conflict can be prevented. Similarly, via informal conversation, Thais can be asked for assistance and cooperation. Pre-meeting talks with key people before a meeting is strongly advised. Doing so will help to ensure cooperation not only because the key people have been identified and lobbied, but also because consulting these people beforehand shows respect for them that will enhance their face.

Supervising (Directing)

Although the Thai administrative system has been heavily influenced by patron-client relationships that support an autocratic leadership style,

Thais have never responded well to repression or authoritarianism. The definite preference is for a benevolent, paternalistic autocrat, although more participative, democratic leadership styles are rapidly gaining favor among young urban employees.

If a non-Thai supervisor is older, he tends to benefit from his age and status because Thais will automatically respect and obey him. However, he should not exercise (or abuse) his legitimate authority by ignoring the importance of relationship-building. The non-Thai supervisor who acts as his subordinates' parent or elder sibling and who coaches and directs subordinates with kindness and understanding (demonstrating *phrakhun* or benevolence) will gain the loyalty and devotion of his subordinates. These benefits will be further reinforced if performance feedback that involves correcting behavior is given in private rather than in public, since public reprisals cause a loss of face for all involved and have a serious negative impact on morale.

In general, a relationship-oriented leadership style, whether autocratic or democratic in nature, is recommended for non-Thai supervisors during the initial phase of their work in Thai-staffed organizations. After strong relationships have been established, a more results-oriented approach can be introduced.

Managing Conflict in the Workplace

Within Thailand's urban centers, there is a growing preference for a collaborative approach to conflict management, as a preliminary study on attitudes toward conflict management revealed.

The preliminary study was based on Rahim's Organizational Conflict Inventory II, Forms A, B, and C (1983b), which was distributed to 400 Thais in 30 local and international organizations in Bangkok's private business sector. Rahim's Inventory was translated into Thai and cross-translated into English by different translators to eliminate possible inconsistencies. Participants in the survey were provided with both the Thai and the English versions of the Inventory. The purpose of the study was to assess the attitudes of urban Thai business professionals toward conflict management. Of the 240 questionnaires returned, 225 were valid. The results indicated a strong preference for a collaborative approach to conflict management in all three dimensions (with peers, with subordinates, and with superiors), regardless of age group, gender, position, or years of experience. Although a more formal, in-depth study must be conducted to validate these results, the preliminary results seem to support the interdependence orientation and the preference for collaboration observed by Komin in her formal study of Thai values (Komin 1990, 231) as well as the behavior observed in various training sessions conducted by the writers. The results also make sense when one considers the cultural context and the behavioral norms of the Thais.

Although Thais have borrowed the English word 'compromise' to describe the approach they use for the successful management of conflict situations, their interpretation of the word in Thai as *karn ruam meu ruam jai* (joining hands, joining hearts) is the meaning inherent in the word 'collaboration'. In collaboration, Thais have found an acceptable balance of behavior that is centered not only on the interests of self but on the interests of others as well. This approach suits the Thais' need for independence as well as their need to maintain interdependent, cooperative relationships. It has proven to be the most effective approach for Thais who want to have a voice in management decisions and who also want to preserve relationships with others, whether they be peers, subordinates or superiors.

Collaboration, the 'middle way' of conflict management strategies, permits the practice of *kreng jai* and *jai yen* in the truest sense, which involve maintaining one's own self-esteem while at the same time showing sensitivity to, and respect for, the feelings and ideas of others.

Despite these findings, Thais in general remain reluctant to engage in the direct, constructive confrontation that is necessary for collaboration, in the western sense, to occur. Thus, when conflict occurs, the most common strategy used for managing it is the use of a mutally respected third party as mediator. Although Thais work very hard to avoid conflict-provoking situations, there are times when misunderstandings do occur, sometimes due to a remark that was misinterpreted, sometimes due to offending rumors that have reached the ears of one of the parties concerned, and occasionally due to a stress-related outburst. When such conflict situations occur, Thais find it very difficult to confront each other with the problem in an effort to resolve the dispute. Thus, in most cases, a mutual friend or respected elder will, on his own initiative or at the request of one of the parties, intervene to assist in resolving the conflict. This is usually accomplished by the mediator having private conversations with each of the parties involved in the conflict first. These private conversations are then followed by a meeting between the parties themselves, sometimes with and sometimes without the mediator, depending upon the outcome of the private conversations.

In conflict situations, it is unwise for non-Thais to try to confront Thais with the issue. If asked directly about their feelings or perceptions, most Thais, to avoid conflict, tend to reply that they feel nothing or that they have no opinion. Because of this, uninformed non-Thais may be deluded into thinking that the conflict has been resolved. Non-Thais should find someone whom the Thais trust and respect to mediate the dispute. By asking a mediator to find out how the Thais really feel and/or what they really think about an issue, non-Thais can gain important information that will guide them in developing appropriate strategies for managing any conflict that may arise.

Also, to determine if an issue has conflict potential, non-Thais need to pay special attention to any changes in behavior or performance after an issue has been introduced, whether formally or informally. Should absences or tardiness increase or productivity drop, the help of a respected third-party should be immediately sought.

Success Thai-style

In sum, to succeed in Thailand, the non-Thai must remember to maintain his composure, avoid open criticism, and actively demonstrate a concern for the feelings of his Thai counterparts, regardless of their status within the organization. An enthusiastic people-centered management approach that recognizes and respects the individual and that responds to the Thai employee's need to *enjoy* his work and to establish mutually rewarding relationships with his colleagues will increase the Thai employee's willingness to communicate openly and cooperate wholeheartedly.

REFERENCES

Adler, N.J. 1991. *International Dimensions of Organizational Behavior*, (Second edition) Boston, MA: PWS-KENT Publishing Company.

Berelson, B. and Steiner, G.A. 1964. *Human Behavior: An Inventory of Scientific Findings.* New York: Harcourt, Brace, and World, Inc., 88.

Bond, M.H. and Hwang, K.-K. 1991. 'The Social Psychology of Chinese People.' In Michael H. Bond. (ed.), *The Psychology of the Chinese People*. Hong Kong: Oxford University Press, 213–66.

Cooper, R. and Nanthapa C. 1982. *Culture Shock Thailand.* Singapore: Times Books International.

Fieg, J.P. 1989. *Thais and North Americans: A Common Core*. Revised by Elizabeth Mortlock. Yarmouth, ME: Intercultural Press.

Goffman, E. 1955. 'On Face Work: An Analysis of Ritual Elements in Social Interaction.' *Psychiatry*, **18**, 213–31.

Gohlert, E.N. 1991. *Power and Culture: The Struggle Against Poverty in Thailand*. Bangkok, Thailand: White Lotus.

Grindle, M.S. 1981. 'Anticipating Failure: The Implementation of Rural Development Programs.' *Public Policy*, **29** (1) (Winter), 51–74.

Haney, W.V. 1967. *Communication and Organizational Behavior Text and Cases.* Homewood, IL: Richard D. Irwin, Inc.

Hanks, L. 1962. 'Merit and Power in the Thai Social Order.' *American Anthropologist*, **64** (6), 1247–61.

Hofstede, G. 1991. *Cultures and Organizations: Software of the Mind.* London: McGraw Hill Book Company Europe.

Hollinger, C. 1965. *Mai Pen Rai Means Never Mind.* Tokyo: John Weatherhill, Inc.

Holmes, H. and Tangtongtavy, S. 1995. *Working with the Thais: A Guide to Managing in Thailand*. Bangkok: White Lotus Co., Ltd.

Hughes, P. and Sheehan, B. 1993. 'Business Across Cultures: The Comparison of Some Business Practices in Thailand and Australia.' *Asian Review.* Institute of Asian Studies, Chulalongkorn University, Bangkok: 263.

Jacobs, N. 1971. *Modernization Without Development: Thailand as an Asian Case Study.* New York: Praeger Publishers.

Jandt, F.E. and Pedersen, P.B. 1996. *Constructive Conflict Management: Asia-Pacific Cases.* Thousand Oaks, CA: Sage Publications, Inc.

Keyes, C.F. 1989. *Thailand: Buddhist Kingdom as Modern Nation-State.* Bangkok,Thailand: D.K. Printing House.

Klausner, W.J. 1993. *Reflections on Thai Culture: Collected Writings.* Bangkok: The Siam Society.

Komin, S. 1990. *Psychology of the Thai People: Values and Behavioral Patterns.* Bangkok: Research Center, National Institute of Development Administration.

Kulick, E. and Wilson, D. 1996. *Time for Thailand: Profile of a New Success.* Bangkok: White Lotus Co., Ltd.

Lester, R.C. 1973. *Theravada Buddhism in Southeast Asia.* Ann Arbor, MI: University of Michigan Press.

Lewicki, R.J. *et al.* 1988. *Experiences in Management and Organizational Behavior,* (Third edition). New York: John Wiley & Sons.

Mizuno, K. 1976. 'Thai Pattern of Social Organization.' In *Southeast Asia: Nature, Society, and Development.* (ed.), Shinichi Ichimura. Honolulu: The University Press of Hawaii.
Mole, R.L. 1973. *Thai Values and Behavior Patterns.* Tokyo: Charles E. Tuttle Company.
Northcraft, G.B. and Neale, M.A. 1990. *Organizational Behavior: A Management Challenge.* Chicago: The Dryden Press.
Phongpaichit, P. and Baker, C. 1996. *Thailand's Boom!* Chiang Mai, Thailand: Silkworm Books.
Rabbie, M. 1994. *Conflict Resolution and Ethnicity.* Westport, Connecticut, Praeger.
Samudavanij, C.-A. 1987. 'Political History.' In *Government and Politics of Thailand.* (ed.), Somsakdi Xuto. Singapore: Oxford University Press, 1–40.
Vatikiotis, M.R.J. 1996. *Political Change in Southeast Asia: Trimming the Banyan Tree.* London: Routledge.
Wyatt, D.K. 1993. *Studies in Thai History.* Bangkok: Silkworm Books.

CHAPTER EIGHT

Mediation and Conflict Management in Indonesia

STEPHEN BENTON
School of Behavioral Sciences, University of Westminister

and

BERNADETTE N. SETIADI
Department of Psychology, University of Indonesia

INTRODUCTION

In a discussion with a company director who is used to working with people from different regions in Indonesia, we heard the following story.

Case 1

'I have two employees, one from Central Java and the other from Tapanuli (North Sumatra). Given an assignment which demands a very tight schedule, they give very different responses. The person from Java will say 'yes' without any argument. Quite often however, the assignment is not completed on time. When this happens, he will produce various excuses/reasons as to why the job was not finished on time. On the other hand, the person from Tapanuli will argue at the beginning that the schedule is too tight and try to negotiate for an adjustment in the time scale. Given a revised time scale that he is happy with, he usually meets the deadline. When this pattern had occurred repeatedly,

I realised that I could not use the same approach with the two employees. With the Javanese I have to be specific and go into the plan in detail so as to unearth any concerns from his part, because I know that he will never express his disagreement voluntarily and that he will avoid any confrontation as far as possible. With the employee from Tapanuli, this approach is not necessary as he will never hesitate to let me know what is in his mind even to the extent of disagreeing with me openly.'

Indonesia and Diversity

The above story has given us a glimpse as to what may take place when two Indonesians who come from different regions have to work together. The largest country in the Asia Pacific, Indonesia, consisting of more than 17,000 islands has a population of approximately 200 million people who belong to more than 300 ethnic groups and speak more than 500 languages and dialects. The national language, Bahasa Indonesia, is spoken throughout the country, but each ethnic group maintains its own language, culture, and preferred way of doing things, including how they react to conflict. Within this context, one can imagine the range of 'habits' or 'customs' that a non-Indonesian working in Indonesia may face. These certainly need to be considered when conflicts occur—and ways to resolve them are needed. Even though 6000 of the islands of Indonesia are inhabited, more than 60% of the population live in Java, and the majority of these live within the Javanese tradition. Therefore, for the purpose of this chapter it is sufficient to say that while one needs to be aware of the rich variation within Indonesia, this chapter will only discuss what is commonly observed in Indonesia relative to the Javanese tradition.

Traditionally, Indonesia was an agricultural country. During its first 25-year Long Term Development program, it has enjoyed rapid economic growth averaging 7% a year (Indonesia 1996). Along with the economic growth, there has been a rapidly expanding industrial base and internationalization of the market place. The Indonesian Business Community (IBC) has moved from a regulated domestic market initially dependent on oil revenues toward a more deregulated and diversified market characterized by increasing international competition. This has led to growth in the demand for quality and competitiveness in all business sectors with an associated growth in large scale organizational development. As a consequence, traditional negotiation and conflict management strategies which have been successful in the past can no longer meet the present needs of the business community, especially when moving towards an international business platform.

Attempts have been made to bridge the gap between traditional core skills and those required by the new organizational demands through management training and Human Resources (HR) consultancy services, as well as the importation of HR programmes. At the surface level, a non-Indonesian businessman entering the IBC for the first time may think that his HR training practices are as familiar to his Indonesian counter-part. In reality, many find difficulties because traditional values and customs still play a dominant role in shaping business practices and interpersonal expectations, including negotiation and conflict resolution. The following story from an Indonesian business man helps to illustrate this point.

Case 2

'I met quite often with a non-Indonesian business man who, after an initial meeting with a potential Indonesian partner, would confidently tell me that the meeting had gone very well. Everybody was apparently happy, there were no disagreements and it was almost certain he would get the deal. However, subsequent meetings with these potential partners did not result in the expected outcome. The non-Indonesian returns home without understanding why he failed. In fact, if he knew Indonesians, he would have understood that for an Indonesian, nodding, smiling, and showing no disagreement does not mean that he actually agrees with what is being proposed. It is only a way to maintain a good interpersonal relationship, something which is considered very important.'

In order to understand the difficulties encountered, it is necessary to look at the traditional values which underlie the attitudes and behavior of Indonesian negotiators and other Indonesians faced with conflict situations. The process of discussion and negotiation for Indonesians takes a longer time than is expected by a non-Indonesian.

This chapter will first discuss factors relating to conflict from an Indonesian perspective, such as the role of *musyawarah* and *mufakat* which reflect a century-old tradition, as mentioned in the state philosophy, *Pancasila*. It is followed by a description of the most common and acceptable practice in conflict management namely the *consensually validated* approach. The chapter will then discuss how this traditional approach is used in a modern economic environment, which will provide a better understanding of current and potential difficulties in negotiation processes.

CONFLICT AND RELATED CONCEPTS: THE INDONESIAN PERSPECTIVE

Conflict is commonly defined as two parties behaving in such a way that the actions of one party make another party's actions less effective. It can occur in both cooperative and competitive settings. According to Suseno (1985), conflict is seen as the disturbance of harmony. Even though this definition does not contradict the generally acceptable definition of conflict, it is necessary to look at the concepts of: harmony, hierarchy, *musyawarah* and *mufakat* in order to understand the Indonesian perspective on conflict.

Harmony

Harmony is very important, especially in socially framed relationships. It is expected to be maintained in all forms of social relationships, in the family, the neighbourhood, and the village, as well as in work groups. Social harmony is a fundamental norm from which other values will stem. Thus, an individual is expected to always behave harmoniously in order not to disturb the existing social harmony. We can readily see that social harmony will be threatened by any conflict, especially an open one. That is why in every social situation any expressions of conflict are usually concealed, even though underneath one can sense the tension. This pursuit of harmony underlines the importance of maintaining working relationships and cooperative behaviors.

According to Suseno (1985) in Javanese society there are several ways to prevent conflict, and hence maintain harmony. One way deals with social expectations. When conflict occurs as a result of opposing interests, prevailing social norms require that an individual be prepared to take second place, and if necessary, to let go of personal interest and to foster a joint agreement in order to maintain harmony.

At the emotional level, a Javanese is expected to maintain constant introspection and emotional control, always paying attention to the reactions of all those present, in such a way that it is impossible for any conflict to emerge. Reactions which indicate an inner disturbance or lack of control are felt to be improper. People must be especially careful in situations in which the interests of the opposing parties are in conflict. A request, or an offer that is not favorable, should not be refused directly; answers must be prepared and sugar-coated. At the same time, one's request should not be made directly less a rejection will cause an open conflict. Instead, one should first make an assessment of the interpersonal situation to feel or gauge its likely reception.

Hierarchy

Indonesian society has traditionally been characterized by, and still retains, a highly structured hierarchy where behavioral codes of practice are expected to reflect the established values according to the positions of the individuals in the social system. In the Javanese culture, the basic tenet is that all social relationships are ordered hierarchically and this hierarchical order is a value that should be respected in itself. Everyone has an appropriate place which determines his rights and obligations in the social order (Mulder 1992). In everyday life people express their social behavior following *tatakrama* (etiquette) which has four principles: (a) to have an attitude appropriate for one's position, (b) to adopt indirect approaches in expressing one's wishes, (c) not to give true information regarding unimportant or personal issues (dissimulation), and (d) to prevent any self expression that may show inner disturbance or lack of self-control.

Introduction to the concept of *Musyawarah* and *Mufakat*

Musyawarah is a decision making process through consultation. According to Mulder (1992), *musyawarah* is a procedure in which, ideally, all voices and opinions are heard. Everything that is put forward is considered equally correct, and is used in solving the problem faced. After listening to all parties using a non-confrontational form of dialogue, *musyawarah* attempts to achieve unanimity of desires which guarantees that the final decision will be accepted as appropriate by all parties. To achieve this goal, everybody in the *musyawarah* is expected to be ready to acquiesce to something.

The environment within which the process of *musyawarah* operates is typically a close agricultural village community, with a well-defined role for community leaders. The community has traditionally been responsible for much of its own decision-making in areas such as: the allocation of resources (usually land), changes of land use (farming to building), and personal disputes (marital problems, inter-community issues). This environment has seen the growth of behavioral expectations and protocol norms that have been adapted to the practical priorities of the community. Without an active investment in this process, diverse pressures (environmental as well as personal) would probably result in less community effectiveness, and increased personal perspectives, leading to a disruption of the social harmony which is integral to the sense of a community-led identity that is highly valued by all. The objective of *musyawarah* is to achieve *mufakat* (consensus). *Mufakat* is considered to have been achieved if all parties to a conflict can accept the solution.

In spite of the rapid Indonesian economic and social development, the above traditional values are still observed in the socio-cultural practices of present-day Indonesian communities, including those in the work place. This approach to traditional values is consistent with government policy which seeks to reaffirm Indonesian identity through the support of essentially Indonesian values. Another example of the application of traditional practices and values in response to developmental needs is *Pancasila* (the Five Principles), which is based on centuries old traditions and has been adopted as the state philosophy. The five principles are: (1) Belief in the one and only God, (2) A just and civilised humanity, (3) The unity of Indonesia, (4) Democracy guided by the inner wisdom in the unanimity arising out of deliberations amongst representatives, and (5) Social justice for the whole of the people of Indonesia. (Department of Information, Republic of Indonesia 1996.)

The influence of traditional values in the present socio-cultural practices can also be seen in the respect for status-based authority that is still fundamental to Indonesian social behavior and which is also a characteristic one meets in the work place. Individuals develop an acute awareness of their role boundaries within this hierarchy and expectations for their own preferred outcome are mediated through their role-based obligations. The hierarchy has developed into a series of behavioral checks and balances that traditionally served the maintenance of communal cohesion by actively promoting the avoidance of direct conflict and adherence to rules of collective responsibility. It represents a confirmation that everyone in the hierarchy has their own role and the rights and obligations that come with it. A father in a family has his own place, one that cannot be taken by others. By the same token, in an age-based organization, the role of the most senior person cannot be fulfilled by a younger person, even if he has all the necessary expertise, because it is not his place to do so. Whether it will change in the future depends on the likelihood of developing an expert-based organization that is acceptable by most without disturbing the harmony in the social relationships.

Thus the Indonesian experience of conflict management cannot be separated from the traditional social and behavioral norms that endorse the focus upon the interpersonal domain for the resolution of conflict. Whatever the cause of conflict and no matter at which organizational level it occurs, its behavioral consequences will affect the interpersonal environment. If the opportunity exists for a resolution of such conflict then the resolution will need to be worked through in a dynamic context as exists between accepted behavioral norms and personal needs. Individuals will only gain social support if, in the act of identifying, communicating and addressing conflict, they observe the cultural norms designed to preserve the cultural imperative of interpersonal order. Failure to process grounds for conflict within this context closes an opportunity for resolution of differences. As with any system of control and release, behavior becomes less predictable and more vulnerable to external conditions. This is in line with the Indonesian socio-cultural values which expect individuals to conduct any interpersonal exchange in keeping with the values of harmony and hierarchy.

Traditional Conflict Resolution Process: *Musyawarah* and *Mufakat* in Practice

In broad terms, conflict resolution practices in Indonesia can be classified as: (a) administrative or judicial procedures in which a respected or officially appointed third party makes a decision and (b) consensually validated processes in which parties work together to produce mutually acceptable solutions (Moore and Santosa 1995). The judicial procedure is the product of both the former sultanate-court administered rule and the Dutch colonial administration, while the consensually validated approach has evolved from self-governing communities. It is this latter approach that is taken to characterize the conflict resolution style considered to be integral to Indonesian culture and representative of a preferred behavioral style. The objective of the consensually validated approach is to achieve *mufakat* (consensus) by using a collectively endorsed procedure known as *musyawarah* (collective deliberation). In the following section the process inherent to this approach will be discussed.

The process is initiated when a community or its members are required to make a decision which requires that a problem be solved. The problem will become the property of all the members but before this occurs the elder or chief is required to create the appropriate decision-making environment. This environment will be founded upon a fundamental commitment to the development of dialogue, but successful dialogue will only be achieved if the socio-cultural requirements are met. Moreover, individuals will seek a collective view on a problem as a prerequisite to attaining an appropriate and personally satisfying outcome. Let us assume that a party feels aggrieved in some way and that they have brought this to the attention of the community elder. We will discuss the four behavioral categories central to this process: framing the problem, preparation for dialogue, features of dialogue, and the emergence of *mufakat*.

Framing the problem

The elder will proceed to identify all the parties involved by meeting them and listening to their points of view. These meetings could take the form of private meetings with the elder or a joint meeting with all parties present. The private meeting would take place in their homes, informal and completely non-judgmental, while the joint meeting may be considered to be a precursor to the formal environment within which full resolution of disputes may be attained. At this stage, points of clarification are raised only to make sure that all issues are being brought forward. At no time would the information collected be used to confront parties in order to clarify a matter of fact or principle. The information is gathered by open receptivity and serves the dual function of (a) building a framework for representing issues that is capable of holding all points of view with equality and (b) allowing individuals to benefit from running through their arguments with a respected person as this begins the process of open dialogue and consensual validation. Emotions can be expressed by the speaker without running the risk of direct confrontation and the consequent risk of irredeemable open conflict and its associated loss of social status (losing face). The process further supports the principle of commitment through participation by registering that the first steps in a system that is valued as effective have been taken, and that all parties concerned have taken those same steps.

Having collected together sufficient information the elder will decide when the problem solving process should begin. No direct or issue-specific questioning would have been done at this stage but the elder would have ascertained that all parties were comfortable enough with the opportunities that they have had to 'tell all', and also with the level of detail available, to move the process forward. The full background to the issue is established; where the boundaries are and what the focus is, making it is less likely that the parties will shift ground later. This lessens the risk of an expansion of the conflict in response to increased pressure for justification, which emerges at a later point in this process. So far no direct exchanges have occurred between those party to the dispute, however their views have gradually been refined and clarified in their own terms through the work of the elder. Now the next stage requires that these views be communicated to the larger group and submitted to the influence of a broader-based dialogue.

Preparation for dialogue

This next stage and its associated change of environment means that a new round of preparation is required in order not to corrupt a sense of continuity in the process. It also demonstrates that all parties are again receiving the same degree of opportunity and support. The leader will direct the sequence of events and will start by avoiding anything to do with the substantive issues in question. This reflects the view that it will be impossible to attain cultural norms designed to maintain interpersonal relationships without first allowing individuals to experience something in common. Usually the procedure involves the leader welcoming everyone followed by some communal activity such as the taking of refreshments.

In this way the meeting will communicate to the disputants that normal social protocol is working and that any elevation of situation-specific anxiety can be relieved. The leader will initiate the next stage by describing why they are meeting, outlining what will happen and what issues will be discussed. Again this helps to devolve participative responsibility back to the group while committing all to the structure as defined by the leader, with the achievement of a *mufakat* as the overriding objective.

Features of dialogue

Disputants are then invited to outline the problem. The dialogue environment is low on structural requirements and high on receptivity. All present may contribute to the discussion of points and opinions and this is conducted within a relatively unstructured framework in that discussion may range across issues as each participant makes a contribution. Indeed this low emphasis on structure is a prerequisite for an environment that is non-judgmental yet which seeks to foster problem-solving and shared ownership of outcomes.

The consequence of this approach is that participants are able to elaborate ideas and to explore different points of reference such as: previous custom-based practices, personal expertise and community precedent. As points of view are being considered in terms of merit and relevance, the dialogue will seek to avoid direct disagreement with any particular person's view. Instead, disagreements would typically be voiced through indirect questions. The leader will allow as much time as participants need in order for them to explore and elaborate options but under some conditions of over-wordiness the leader will impose a time constraint in fairness to others. This may be particularly useful as some communities may prefer to structure participation in these meetings along lines of seniority and younger participants may feel less comfortable speaking for longer than a 'senior'.

Throughout, the role of the leader will be to listen and to guide the process along by encouraging contributions from all quarters, creating openings for speakers, and when appropriate testing out possible solutions for group consensus. The disputants are seen as contributors to the group process and are not assigned a special role or position simply because they have brought the problem to the meeting. They are now participating in the shaping of how they see the problem in response to the collective view. When appropriate the leader will act as referee and may legitimately interject his views, identifying the most promising of options. This is a key aspect of *musyawarah* where the environment enables individuals to explore options and experiment with reasoning under conditions of high-receptivity. The harmony is maintained by avoiding direct conflict and by allowing argument and counter-argument to be filtered through a dialogue process based upon rapport designed to emphasize the value of relationships rather than debating skill. The collective nature of the process acts to enforce the equality of opportunity that is open to all disputants regardless of their particular level of articulateness and/or ability to persuade. Collectivity, under the operational conditions of openness, serves to support the best outcome rather than the best proponent of an outcome.

The emergence of mufakat (consensus)

Mufakat appears to emerge in different ways. One of the participants may suggest a solution with associated outcomes to the whole meeting, and this could be endorsed through collective assent. Or, someone may take components from different solutions and synthesize them into a solution with the support of others who may help through the elaboration of details. The solutions would be subjected to the group process and tested against a range of views, and if acceptable to all, then a *mufakat* is attained.

The leader's role is to nurture the whole process of *musyawarah* by (a) impartiality, (b) limiting the interjection of opinions, and (c) recognizing the 'convergence' of a group consensus. In other words, the whole process revolves around the adherence to protocols that are initiated and then guided by a leader. This leader is able to exercise control through the identification of common interests and the recognition and open articulation of individual's rights while exercising power (in a form governed by his position) to engender *mufakat*. Thus, the primary test of a successful *musyawarah* process is whether or not the compromise of the outcome meets the need to produce some form of workable solution and is also able to maintain harmony in the relationships involved. The hierarchy and the range of role-specific behaviors involved represent an almost tangible cultural need to avoid any issue-specific conflict which may place participants in a point by point exchange and locks them into a win-lose outcome which elevates the risks of disturbed harmony in the relationships. Direct confrontation and a display of differences are viewed as the result of poor sensitivity to context and failed interpersonal skills, rather than the necessary precursors to a solution or agreement as is commonly observed in the western style of negotiation.

Like any statement of cultural preference the preceding description of the traditional Indonesian approach to conflict resolution must now be seen within the cultural realities of the present situation. The rapid growth of the Indonesian economy is the most significant factor exerting pressure for the changing of traditional values to meet the new performance demands of the current economic environment.

The Impact of Economic Growth on the Current Business Environment

The Indonesian economy has experienced significant growth in its first 25-year Long Term Development Programme, averaging 7.6% per year in the last ten years. With the repetition of the collapse in oil prices during the 1970s and 1980s, Indonesia had to stimulate its non-traditional exports by introducing some reforms in trade sectors, beginning in 1985. The result can be seen in the growth of non-oil exports from about US$5.9 billion in 1985 to about US$30.4 billion in 1994. (Financial reforms in 1988 and 1989 which eased restrictions on the operation of foreign banks, permitting foreign shareholders to own 49% of the shares in listed companies, and the promotion of the stock market has resulted in the growth of the stock exchange value from US$249 million in 1988 to over US$75 billion before the financial crisis in 1997.) Foreign investment has increased from US$0.4 billion in 1987 to nearly US$40 billion in 1995 (Wardhana, 1996).

Since the late 1980s the Indonesian Business Community (IBC) has progressed from working within a regulated, domestic market towards competing internationally from a diversified economic base operating within a deregulated domestic market. The socio-cultural influences associated with these changes have impacted on traditional values and the individual's level of material expectation. Perhaps more particularly, for a labour intensive economy, the impact of these changes has meant that market utilization has occurred at such a rapid pace that the translation of traditional working practices and socio-cultural values into the modern environment has been uneven. Some sectors which are based upon labour-intensive traditional skills and in relatively small industrial units are still able to operate within the range of traditional skills and therefore have no serious need to adapt to the demands of modern work place. At the same time, there are important sectors which are based on high technology skills such as heavy industry, manufacturing, and the service industries (e.g., banking, real estate) where the existing pool of individuals with appropriate core skills is under pressure to meet rapidly changing performance demands.

One area that is regarded as being in need of rapid change is management. The established management attitudes and behaviors have evolved under a set of relatively docile domestic market conditions operating with strong guidance from government ministries. In the last few years the government has stressed the importance of continual economic growth, a dominant economic role in the region and a place in the global market. However, the traditional socio-cultural values have remained a constant and central feature of many government policies. The problem that appears to have emerged is that while adherence to the code (and practice) of interpersonal respect has been preserved and transferred into the modern organizations they have not been equipped with suitable managerial practices to make it work. Instead it encourages the growth of bureaucratic and inflexible commercial organizations, permitting little room for the development of new, much-needed management core skills. As a result, there is a shortage of managers with the skills necessary to meet the higher quality and efficiency criteria required by rapidly changing market conditions. Thus, managers, who are quite often themselves without the appropriate core skills, are under pressure not only to meet their main responsibility of getting the company into better shape, but also to develop in others the new behaviors required to meet the new demands.

Problems of Translation: Problems of Building Consensus

Attempts to overcome the problems that come with this new organizational environment can be seen in the growth of management training courses, consultancy agencies, and selection and development services. The importation of high profile HR programmes was, and still is, a major feature of the IBC's approach to the problem of meeting urgent training and development needs. Even though most Indonesian managers have studied bargaining and negotiation techniques, or assertiveness training, the social structure within the Indonesian organization may well prevent or limit their effectiveness when applied in practice. So, although a non-Indonesian businessman, entering the IBC for the first time, and his Indonesian counterpart may have similar previous HR training, this of course in no way ensures that there will be common behavioral ground. So what kind of environment would the non-Indonesian be expected to work within?

The Working Environment

Even though the government has made a strong commitment to increase its economic development in line with the globalization strategy for the next 25-year Long Term Development Plan (1993–2018), the role of traditional socio-cultural values still remains a constant feature of government policy, with an emphasis on respect for elders and leaders. Consequently, many organizations that try to maintain these values have adopted rigid, vertical line management. Most decision-making is carried out by the CEO, who is often the owner of the company, and there are minimal participatory roles for managers. The format and behavior during discussions between leader and subordinates conforms to requirements derived from the wider social context. Subordinates are expected to refrain from dissent and disagreement as the display of either would represent disrespectful behavior. The structure of hierarchy serves to consolidate behaviors within roles and does not foster constructive exploration and elaboration of different opinions.

Collectivity exists in the form of passive assent rather than an active process of participation through sharing. When a dispute arises, the same position-dependent hierarchy would be maintained and the dispute is dealt with under the same structural terms. The objective of agreement remains the same, yet the traditional process for eliciting and building a consensually validated resolution is inhibited. Traditionally, the position-dependent behaviors of respect and conflict avoidance were highly effective in coping with communal disputes because they were responsive to changes through the active information-seeking process of *musyawarah*. Without that process of information gathering the capacity of the position-dependent approach to meet new organizational demands is weakened. At the same time, the participatory practices associated with modern management techniques have not been effectively adapted and applied. In terms specific to negotiation, the structural procedure may declare that a 'resolution' is the objective but in practice the 'process' necessary to achieve this is missing.

Indonesians who understand position-role dependence as part of their cultural education at home, at school, and at community level function fairly well within this type of organization. But, for non-Indonesians (NIs) it is a different story. The NIs will find that their Indonesian counterparts are knowledgeable about the HR practices the NIs are familiar with, but the application of that knowledge will still be filtered through the position-dependent structures within their company and within themselves. When it comes to the Indonesian's business/management practice, social protocol and positional behavior will take over and they remain sensitized to the protocol of relationships. This way of behaving will very likely be entirely new to the NIs. The pressures imposing this change upon the translation of theory and new skills to the work place may not be apparent to the NI, who finds few clues as to why the behavioral environment has changed.

Factors Influencing Effective Conflict Management with Non-Indonesians

The growth of multi-national ventures in Indonesia over the last 10 years has provided a rich source of information concerning difficulties experienced by mixed management teams within the Indonesian context (Benton, 1995). The following case provides a good illustration.

Case 3

Conflict had occurred in the mixed management team of a joint-venture company producing electrical and electronic appliances which was also responsible for the marketing and distribution of its products. In the last few years there had been many disputes between the Indonesian and the non-Indonesian managers which caused a lot of dissatisfaction on both sides. The NI managers were unhappy because they believed that the Indonesian managers were not honest and not open in their working attitude. According to them, the Indonesians often took actions that were contrary to the decisions that had been agreed upon during joint meetings. The NIs said that the Indonesians were unreliable and not dependable. The NIs were frustrated and so far there had been no sign that the Indonesians were going to change their behavior. On the other hand, the Indonesians complained that the NIs were domineering and impolite. They always imposed their opinions in meetings as well as in everyday interactions. In meetings they tended to dominate, be overly critical and showed no respect for people's feelings. They directly expressed their criticism, hurting people's dignity.

During the last three months the situation had worsened to the extent that physical fights were narrowly avoided. The NI managers complained to the Head Office in their home country with the request that the Head Office should re-evaluate its policies concerning the placement of Indonesians at managerial level.

The Head Office asked the country Managing Director to find a solution. He asked an HR consultant to study the problems. According to the consultant, the main cause was that neither party understood the communication pattern of the other. The NIs had what he called a 'low context' pattern, where the content of the message is more important than the way of presenting it. Therefore they tended to present the message directly, and no special effort was made to adjust the style of presentation in a way that matched content to context needs. On the contrary the Indonesians used a 'high context' pattern, where the way of presenting a message is more important. A message, especially a criticism, should not be presented directly. It needs to be done indirectly, with full consideration of the person's feelings. Direct criticism is considered a personal attack that is shameful for the receiver, so criticism is expressed indirectly. For example disagreement with a decision in a meeting is expressed indirectly by ignoring or not implementing the agreed actions, because direct disagreement during the meeting will hurt the person involved and cause him to lose face. After a series of communication training sessions both parties were able to find ways to improve communication and the conflicts decreased.

In the above illustration, the socio-cultural values that stress the importance of interpersonal relations were directly applied to the working situation by the Indonesians, but the NIs were not aware of them.

It has often been the case that a common source of misperception originates from an initial impression of competency in the English language. The tendency is for NIs to be persuaded by the apparent ease of communication, which is reinforced by an abundant signalling of agreement and the absence of dissent, that a set of familiar, if not common, operational ground rules exists between the parties. The higher the degree of language compatibility the easier it is to believe that with good communication there would naturally follow a ready access to a functional rapport, from which business protocols familiar to the NIs would follow.

Moreover, as no apparent communication barrier exists, even those culturally-aware NIs may move towards setting the framework for discussions by employing concepts and practices which register so naturally within their business language (e.g., goal-oriented, objective verification, solution oriented and even consensus) and in so doing generate behavior that is unwanted and viewed as stereotypically NI.

Sketch of the Dynamics of Change: Dissonance and Attitude Change

It has been argued that attitudes are subject to change when an inconsistency exists between cognitions. Inconsistency acts as a motivation for change (Festinger 1957; Fiske and Taylor 1994). Individuals usually organize their behavior in a way that is consistent with their beliefs and cognitions. When we are faced with an inconsistency which requires us to behave in a way that is inconsistent with our established belief system, we may experience dissonance which may be relieved by either changing our cognitions or our behavior. Each cultural set will be sensitive to its own form of tension/release and the result of inappropriate leadership will be to raise the tension, and yet not facilitate shifts in cognition, until an avoidance response takes over. Perhaps successful conflict resolution is essentially concerned with a leader's capacity to create a constructive tension between an individuals behavior and his attitudes and to then facilitate shifts of cognition through a group process.

Dissonance may be considered to underly any form of personal conflict, as an individual's personal view and behavioral preferences come into contact with individuals who are equipped with different views and preferences. In this final section we will try to outline some of the behaviors that make up this interactive/interpersonal environment, as found within the IBC. It is intended that readers should gain a practical perspective of areas of likely misunderstanding based upon concrete examples.

Sketch of Behaviors: Primacy of the Interpersonal

There are a number of features that are fundamental to the way in which conflict resolution and the related need for attitudinal change (and shift of position) seem to be accomplished. The importance of reconciling interpersonal imperatives with personal objectives is a central theme when seeking to achieve acceptable and workable negotiated outcomes. Conflict resolution and agreements founded upon an imbalance between these objectives may lead to a reduction in the effective implementation of the outcome or to debilitating cost upon longer term relationships, perhaps both. We will outline some of the behavioral features of importance which may beset attempts at working towards acceptable outcomes and review their application within the personal, interpersonal cultural constraints set out above.

Specific Features: The Indonesia Joint Venture (IJV)

It may be the case that the core management tasks found within an IJV will reflect the market place realities and produce a framework for the pursuit of management objectives which is recognizable to the NI. However, the process, operating at the interface between the organizational and personal domains, will very likely be based upon different perceptions of what this framework means in practice and which effective behaviors should be associated with it. The approach here will be to characterize how people address tasks and interpersonal relationships, in other words, the day-to-day working environment. This practice of 'making sense of others' behavior' is an active ingredient of daily working life. In order to flesh out some of the components of these ingredients we will consider some of the more predominant stereotypes found within the IJV organization and how they are derived from a behavioral perspective.

Indonesian Perspective

a) NIs and Apparent Abrasiveness

NIs (in this case, Westerners) are seen to be abrasive in their manner and this can lead to this being seen as impolite. It is important to note that politeness is viewed as an essential part of social competence rather than some form of social nicety. The display of appropriate and polite behavior signals an understanding of the Indonesian rules and grammar of effective communication. Without this display, NIs will tend to be viewed as adversarial and inclined to pursue their point of view without real or demonstrable regard for improving the quality of interpersonal working relationships. The route towards gaining such an understanding, and hence better practical working relationships is through the appreciation of the values of mutuality of respect, equality and 'face'. In short, Indonesians require demonstrations of understanding of these values as a precursor to trust and the practical correlate of mutual respect.

Barriers to Effective Behaviors: Social Behavior

Appropriate social behavior is not optional

NIs working with Indonesians should not:

- talk emotionally or loudly.
- be dismissive.
- use personal criticism.
- interrupt or override: Indonesians may approach a problem from a different perspective, one that is sensitive to cultural imperatives. They may sound 'off' the point, but they rarely are; they are usually 'flagging' issues that will need to be worked through in order to achieve a successful agreement.
- use metaphors: plain English based upon reference to specific behaviors/events reduces the risk of misunderstanding. [1]

NIs should try to:

- actively demonstrate patience.

---

[1] Although day-to-day Indonesian is full of metaphors, it should not be assumed that the application of metaphors as used in the English language will have the same impact.

- encourage further clarification of views in order to facilitate **your** understanding of the emerging issues and views.
- recap and review your understanding without direct questioning.
- show commitment to the importance of the group's contribution by incorporating both task and process needs into the group's operational style.

b) NIs and Trust

There is also the view that an individual's inability to display the behavioral aspects of mutuality, equality and a sensitivity towards another's 'esteem' (face), the basic components of trust building, raises questions as to whether he is capable of behaving in a trustworthy manner. The consequence of these doubts may often be a weak working relationship that has a trust-like veneer, yet has few, if any, underpinning strengths. Moreover, this veneer may be able to support basic work interactions but will be unable to generate the more significant advantages associated with trust such as: open exchanges and confidence in the joint building of new perspectives. Typically, until the working relationship encounters a problem the NI may well feel that both relationship and understanding are off to a good start.

Trust, and a demonstrable mutuality of respect, is essential for Indonesians but apparently NIs, working in 'expatriate mode', apply less emphasis on it. They prefer to concentrate upon identifying tasks to be done and how they should be handed out or communicated to those responsible for their completion. Trust may be seen by them as an unreliable variable and, as such, business should not be impeded by its absence. While the Indonesians might see this behavior as rational and matter of fact, it may not necessarily be appropriate. It may well be the case that proposals from NIs may be viewed as plain wrong, but when a lack of grounds for trust is combined with the cultural preference for the avoidance of open conflict, the open exchanges designed to tackle the problem will be difficult to conduct.

Barriers to Effective Behaviors: Trust

Trust is built upon a demonstrable mutuality of respect

NIs working with Indonesians should not:

- frame a problem in personal terms.
- subject individuals to group censure.
- assign, during a group session, responsibility to an individual for an error.
- challenge or question an individual, in direct terms.
- display open criticism.

NIs should try to:

- be supportive of individuals as an attribute of group membership.
- concentrate upon the need to develop a solution rather than to attach blame.
- acknowledge that all members are on a learning curve as membership under the IJV operation raises new demands for all.

Without an overt commitment to the support of 'face' based upon an ability to engender consensus within the group, there would be small hope of establishing and maintaining a credible profile of commitment to all members.

c) NIs and Confrontation

NIs are likely to be perceived as working to an agenda which is based on confrontation and holding a pragmatic view of negotiation which is based on the premise that negotiations are to be won. Their approach will be to focus upon an issue or problem and to be reluctant to be flexible in both their diagnoses and solutions. Therefore they may be labelled by Indonesians as stubborn, argumentative, likely to impose their opinions in an aggressive manner, good talkers but poor listeners. This view may be enhanced by the standard practice of managers trained in the West of actively seeking dissent/conflict in order to test the strength of any solution/decision. Clearly, Indonesians who take the view that conflict is evidence of a failure in the interaction/exchange process, would see the NI's behavior as impolite, arrogant, pushy, and fundamentally wrong-headed.

Barriers to Effective Behaviors: Pursuit of Consensus

The pursuit of consensus: an act of commitment to equality

NIs working with Indonesians should not:

- use accusatory language.
- polarize issues and views.
- focus upon differences.
- expect fully resolved points of views to be readily expressed.
- expect resolution within the meeting's agenda.

NIs should try to:

- plan for a series of meetings. This will allow for the Indonesian preference to work towards issues of conflict from a well understood common ground of concern and evolving a range of possible outcomes and options. In fact, this approach reflects current group process recommendations which recognize the importance of building outcomes upon a blend of diverse options rather than rejecting, at an early stage, all but one option. The greater the mix and blend of views and perspectives the less likely will be the perception of confrontation and arrogance. Indonesians are more likely to participate in an environment that works towards the generation and blending of options than one that moves towards outcomes based upon selectivity **and** rejection.

d) Behaviors: Pace and Patience

Indonesians are usually surprised at how impatient NIs become and how readily they display such feelings. Impatience may be symptomatic of the NI's response to a lack of what may be referred to as a congruent response from the Indonesians, typically in group meetings. Frustration with an apparent lack of constructive disagreement and a sense of talking to an unresponsive, apparently apathetic, meeting can lead the NIs to become exasperated.

For example, given the failed implementation of a management group decision (Case 3) they may ask 'Why is it that we are back to square one? If there is no problem then why do I have a problem?' Unfortunately, the most likely interpretation of impatience from an NI will be that of arrogant superiority. This largely results from the direct and personal form that expression of such attitudes would take. In seeking to get straight to the problem, NIs are often seen to impose their opinions and to ignore vital interpersonal codes.

Without consolidation of interpersonal respect it is likely that moves to address any specific issues will be perceived as ill-paced and a signal of impatience. The Indonesians may feel the meeting is going too fast, largely because of the superficial nature of the process, i.e., the handling of content has been separated from the 'personal'. The sense of personal affront and/or shame experienced by an Indonesian denied the proper behavioral options (as previously outlined) during an exchange within a group (in public view), would deem the party responsible to be incompetent.

Barriers to Effective Behaviors: Displays of Anger

Self-displays of anger signal that you are not among equals

NIs working with Indonesians should not:

- ignore requests for more time.
- limit time for elaboration.
- override a pause with a specific query: a pause indicates that further exploration may be needed, not that people are not following points being made.
- use an emotional high-stakes approach.
- apply direct and personal pressure in an attempt to force a contribution.

NI's should try to:

- scale the issue/problem down into smaller stages. Agreement about the stage components may be easier to work through than the whole problem. If stages are agreed then the problem of pace may be alleviated, as each stage will act as a pause and buffer against any elevation in anxiety levels.

In General:

It should be noted that if an option or solution has not been subjected to the heat of interpersonal obligations, it will probably be viewed as suspect, if not deficient by default, by Indonesians. These interpersonal requirements are not facile forms of nicety, but rather tried and tested practical codes of behavior capable of fostering a workable behavioral interface between policy and practice in the work place. What use is a suggestion for work place change if its content or style of implementation leads to unresolvable conflict between an individual's personal values and work place role?

NI's perspective: Some observations and typical difficulties

a) Politeness

The most common initial impression formed about working with Indonesians is that they are polite. Indonesians seem to be very patient and good listeners, they appear attentive, but are not good at implementation. Also, particularly within a group environment, Indonesians seem to be shy. This is one of the most telling misperceptions, as the group environment is a second home to most Indonesians and participation poses few difficulties, if the other participants understand the procedures.

NIs repeatedly note that, try as they may to get Indonesians to participate in group meetings, the Indonesians do not 'open up' and participate in the discussions. This situation seems to lead onto one of the most difficult problems described by the NI, namely that of unreliability. The problem is encountered after meetings, when the NIs believe that an agreement has been worked out and that the consequence will be a measurable/demonstrable application. In practice, the application, to the immense frustration of NIs, is somehow modified or ignored. Associated with this situation is a feeling that the Indonesians have behaved dishonestly and that agreements had been broken. The working relationships may deteriorate as this problem may be repeated and can soon become the focus of much disillusionment and perplexity for NIs. In the worst cases this can lead to a breakdown in professional trust and etiquette with the NIs resorting to pushing their opinions through with increasing impatience in an attempt to motivate the Indonesians. The Indonesians have a different perspective, one that becomes equally negative, particularly as NIs may be seen to start to avoid consultation and to behave in an apparently increasingly authoritarian/superior manner.

The Indonesians appear unreliable and unpredictable, a powerful blend of ingredients capable of derailing the best intentions held by all parties involved.

Barriers to Effective Behaviors: Politeness

Politeness: the foundation for dissent

NIs working with Indonesians should:

- establish interpersonal support in preparation for group (problem solving) work. This demonstrates an understanding of the importance attached to interpersonal harmony as a concept and practice.

- encourage Indonesians to help identify interpersonal codes of conduct within the work place. Task groups to address tension/anxieties. Indonesians will excel within such an environment especially if role boundaries become flexible.
- actively listen with time and interpersonal space for reflection.

NIs should try to:

- develop the practice of re-presenting what you believe has been said and reflect upon any priorities from a neutral or organizational framework. This can allow time for the Indonesians to view how much 'you' have listened and understood.
- recognise that politeness is functional and that associated behaviors are designed to minimize direct confrontation while maximizing the chances of a workable and mutually accepted outcome.

Non-compliance may be the only form of disagreement open to Indonesians. The problems arise from the absence of an environment within which Indonesians are able to apply their codes of behavior. Following is a guide, intended to aid those involved in IJV operations, to identify some of the symptoms of failing management behavior with some practical suggestions about what to do.

The Right Environment for Conflict Resolution: A Guide

Given the life-long exposure of Indonesians to the social training and experience of **how to avoid** the causes of conflict and the display of dissent it is not surprising that, for Indonesians to have a chance of participating fully within a mixed organizational environment (NI and Indonesian), careful preparation of that environment is necessary. As most of the decisions need to be implemented for and by Indonesians it is essential that companies address this issue otherwise decisions fail and organizational objectives will, in practice, be split between the Indonesians and NIs. NIs and Indonesian managers can, and do, work effectively together on a whole range of other matters (e.g., technical assessment, financial planning, etc.). However, when it comes to situations that require the joint construction of diagnoses and interventions, which for the NIs may reasonably lead to the generation of different priorities, opinions and options, for Indonesians it is in practice likely to be experienced as an interpersonal obstacle course. Importantly, if IJV companies want to produce the best possible organizational practices then they need to make them cross-cultural. The problems currently encountered seem to reflect a situation where IJVs tend to simply accommodate two separate cultures without investing in the building of a synthesis. Without the 'right' environment, it is unlikely that any conflicting issues will surface or become subject to open assessment and proper resolution.

Let us break the problem of misperception and misunderstanding into manageable parts and examine them from the perspective of two key components: **meeting place** and **leadership**.

The Meeting Place

Assumptions and Behavior

When a problem needs to be dealt with, the management team is assembled and all the relevant information is made available to members. The environment is well defined, in that the general objectives have already been set and the specific details are expected to follow. The NI team will have as their objective a decision on what should be done, and the justification of any action should conform to the exigencies of the problem environment. The nature of the problem should determine the nature of the intervention!

a) Behavior in the group: symptoms observed ?

In the absence of disagreement, and the failure to provoke any by reality testing of solutions against the group's assessment of disadvantages, the NIs may perceive that the group is unified and conduct themselves accordingly. Much of the background training for business professionals working in this environment originates from research into 'group think' and the conditions for flawed decision-making. Consequently, the procedures employed by the professionals to avoid such problems, will be based upon many of the same assumptions found within this area of study. For example, Janis and Mann (1977) identified group cohesion as a major factor in the occurrence of group think. The research of Callaway and Esser (1985) further suggested that the best decisions were produced by groups operating at an intermediate level of cohesiveness, while highly cohesive groups, without effective decision-making protocols (e.g., the generation and testing of alternatives and encouragement in the use of and reference to expertise and expert data bases from outside the group), tended to adopt the worst decisions. This is in keeping with a field survey on studies of group think by Park (1990) which showed that the presence of group think was characterized by attributes including a low level of disagreement and a high degree of confidence in the group decision-making process, both of which served to fuel a high sense of insularity. It is suggested, by the authors, that it is precisely these attributes that can lead NIs to make the assumption of uniformity of understanding within a IJV group, while at the same time, the process engenders in the Indonesians a sense of frustation and isolation.

Barriers to Effective Behaviors: Group Cohesion

Accommodation of differences is insufficient grounds for a synthesis

NIs working with Indonesians should not:

- exercise premature judgement of group agreement.
- attempt to reduce risk of 'group think': reality testing.
- attempt to probe for agreement through direct generation of alternatives.
- ignore the importance of any relative seniority, especially within the Indonesian members.

NIs should try to:

- establish a list of key issues and stages as a form of topic-specific data base. Group members can respond to the issue by contributing to the data base. Competing priorities may be represented within a neutral framework. Once the information has been organized it can be structured into a form (e.g., hierarchy) that is neutral and then subjected to group scrutiny.
- establish a 'mentor' approach, where a senior member of staff follows through with group members, elaborating issues and details outside the scrutiny of the group. The mentor may have responsibility for presenting a framework/profile of 'extra' detail to the group. This improves on the initial chances of building a

wider information base for consideration without a strong risk of direct confrontation.

General Observation:

It seems there are two separate group processes which overlap within the behavioral domain where the behaviors are exchanged yet originate from different group identities. As a result of not gaining access to the ebb and flow of the group process, the Indonesians may perceive the group environment as: low in participation, poor in risk assessment of options and open to external sanction. Under these conditions the Indonesians would feel no justification in applying the resulting solution/decision in any direct manner. To the NI's puzzlement, the 'agreed solution' may not have been tried and found wanting but simply found wanting to be tried!

We note that in practice, within both joint venture and Indonesian business organizations, effective *musyawarah* is largely assumed rather than actively cultivated. One of the major problems in transferring *musyawarah* to the work place context is that its success revolves around an effective leader.

b) Group leadership: the Rogue variable

The overriding practical need for management teams in any IJV is to be able to deal effectively with those complex issues which require a full professional analysis and to benefit from different viewpoints and perspectives.

The capacity to resolve conflict using the Indonesian approach is essentially determined by the quality of the leader in the group or environment. This problem is currently challenging modern Indonesian and IJV organizations that are unable to demonstrate synergy in negotiation and conflict resolution.

Leadership skills and setting the scene

Features: Fundamental antagonism between NI and Indonesian approach

Indonesians will seek resolution of disputes within the limits of positional-dependent roles (as described above). Behaviors, type and range and outcome parameters are subject to the hierarchy of roles. Most Indonesian leaders would expect their position to be validated by others' behavior and most subordinates would be sensitive to ways in which this validation could be achieved.

- NIs are comfortable with the leader ignoring positional-based restrictions in order to achieve a specific objective, e.g., solution, new protocol, organizational change.
- It is essential to understand regional differences in behavioral and cultural values and preferences which characterize Indonesia.

NIs should try to:

- gain recognition of the tasks that are before the management team as part of a strategy of preparedness. The use of workshops, team tasks and role/position change exercises can help to build a workable degree of confidence in the leaders approach to issues by creating an appropriate environment for role flexibility.
- foster confidence in leadership through active support of contributions based upon a gradual and on-going move towards personal and task specific portfolios of responsibility. This would encourage individuals to voice opinions from within an agreed and legitimate framework of responsibility.

Any effective team work, problem-solving and decision-making is underwritten by a working and creative negotiation process, and all of these activities, particularly in the Indonesian arena, are enhanced by appropriate leadership. What this 'appropriate leadership' seems to have in common with general management themes, are three core competencies. Firstly, using Hersey and Blanchard's 1988 categories, it is the capacity to diagnose a problem situation in terms of what the problem looks like now, what the situation should look like in the future and instigate change in order to secure the new position. Second is the ability to lead managers towards adapting their skill-behaviors in order to meet the needs of the new situation. Third is a flexible communication style so that all participants are catered for.

The underlying fact is that leaders are there to influence people and to change their attitudes and behaviors, maybe even help them to change their minds. The established view is that without these skills or ingredients of leadership actively working on the organization and management team(s), the chance of current organizational competitiveness is minimal, and if achieved probably not sustainable. It is suggested that in order for leadership roles to be effective the individual needs to tap into the skills associated with the traditional leadership style. The question is what these skills might look like within the IJV environment.

The primary difficulty here is that the traditional role depends upon the group members investing respect in the leader. This legitimizes the suspension of established role protocol in order to achieve the 'greater good'. Traditionally, respect for a leader is formed from a blend of social referent power and personal respect. Without the skill base underpinning the respect, a dependency upon referent power is likely to lead to position-dependent limitations. This may well be one of the fundamental constraints causing many problems of communication between Indonesians and NIs as noted in the preceding case studies.

It is here that both Indonesian and NIs appear to find difficulties in assuming the 'leadership role' in a manner that does not neutralize the process necessary for beneficial conflict resolution and group performance. It is possible that a modern equivalent could be forged within the current organizational climate. This equivalent form would have to address interpersonal needs, such as establishing a basis for respect, and personal needs, such as confidence. The replication of core leadership values and authority may be obtained after the traditional structure has been translated into the environment of today's organizational 'community'. The demonstration of highly valued skills (derived from the behavioral process of *musyawarah*) could act as a basis for respect, a fundamental requirement for occupying a leadership 'role' in the traditional environment of conflict resolution. In today's terms these skills would amount to a necessary yet not sufficient set of performance criteria. Of equal importance would be the ability of the leader to communicate seniority through appropriate and conducive behaviors which also reflected process needs (those aspects of group environment and practice that address, in this case, the pertinent social context/beliefs of group members). If individuals combined both sets of skills they would then have both positional power (authority) and be able to establish 'credibility'. Within this environment, expertise (e.g., technical, managerial) alone would be unlikely to translate into effective conflict management if knowledge and judgement fail to find expression within the interpersonal dynamic of the process. It is noted that, under these conditions, individuals would appraise the risk associated with meeting the declared aims of the group.

Accordingly, and in keeping with the degree of risk perceived (dissonance), individuals would be sensitive to behavioral cues which either meet their criteria for 'encouraging' or are assessed as being dissociated from individuals' expectations. The interesting aspect here is that although the traditional leader's role cannot be easily reconstructed in modern Indonesian organizations (especially for NIs) it is possible to develop a leadership role, based upon credibility and founded upon quantifiable (and learned) skills, that could deliver the quality of conflict resolution and decision-making evidenced by traditional collective methods. The cultivation of confidence can only occur if the leader is able to instigate the interpersonal dynamics considered necessary for group process (Schein 1987).

Preferred forms of conflict mediation and resolution have evolved under specific pressures which may be taken to characterize a society, its values and behavioral priorities. In order to be effective, this process must be capable of accommodating traditional behavioral values and environmental priorities, while also demonstrating an ability to assimilate new challenges requiring the tackling of new organizational (environmental), interpersonal and resource pressures. To achieve this the process must be able to maintain a viable link between traditional priorities and current demands.

The flexible and participative nature of the information gathering and representation aspects built into *musyawarah* have enabled it to meet changing environmental demands over many generations. It has been able to achieve this through the development of core behavioral values (skills) which guide the process towards outcomes that are calibrated to relevant environmental priorities. For the individual this process has been responsible for providing context for the production and assessment of acceptable behaviors and enabled him to gauge interpersonal demands and expectations. In short, the process prepared participants to expect and to display particular behaviors which, on the basis of consensus, were considered to be appropriate. This set of behavioral codes and values has acted as a guide for handling old and new situations. In this sense, the traditional Indonesian approach to mediation offers a tremendously rich source of guidelines for the development of practical skills and approaches for today's organizational (environmental) needs.

ACKNOWLEDGEMENTS

The authors wish to thank Ayleen Wisudha of Wiston Associates (UK) and Qipra Galang Kualita (Indonesia) for reading, and making many helpful comments upon, the draft version of this chapter.

REFERENCES

Bentley, T. 1994. *Facilitation: Providing Opportunities for Learning.* McGraw-Hill.

Benton, S. and Setiadi, B.N. 1996. *Case Study-based Analyses of Indonesian Business Meeting Protocols.* Human Factors Research Group. Oct. Report.

Benton, S. 1995. *Joint Venture Management Teams in Indonesia: Problems, what Problems?* Human Factors Research Group. Jan. Report.

Callaway, M.R. and Esser, J.K. 1984. Groupthink: Effects of Cohesiveness and Problem-Solving on Group Decision Making, *Social Behavior and Personality*, **12**, 157–64.

Festinger, L. 1957. *A Theory of Cognitive Dissonance.* Stanford, CA: Stanford University Press.

Fiske, S.T. and Taylor, S.E. 1994. *Social Cognition.* New York: Random House.

Hersey, P. and Blanchard, K. 1993. *Management of Organizational Behavior*, (Sixth edition). Englewood Cliffs, NJ: Prentice Hall.

Janis, I.L. and Mann, L. 1977. *Decision Making: A Psychological Analysis of Conflict, Choice and Commitment.* New York: Free Press.

Moore, C. and Santosa, A. 1995. Developing Appropriate Environmental Conflict Management Procedures in Indonesia. Integrating Traditional and New Approaches. *Cultural Survival Quarterly* (**Fall**), 23–9.

Mulder, N. 1992. *Individual and Society in Java: A Cultural Analysis* (Second Rev. edition). Yogyakarta: Gajah Mada University Press.

Park, W-W. 1990. A Review of Research on Groupthink. *Journal of Behavioral Decision-Making*, **3**, 229–45. Wiley.

Schein, E.H. 1987. *Process Consultation. Volume II: Lessons for Managers and Consultants.* Addison-Wesley Publishing Company.

Suseno, F.M. 1984. *Etika Jawa: Sebuah Analisa Filsafi Tentang Kebijaksanaan Hidup Jawa.* Jakarta, P.T. Gramedia.

Suseno, F.M. 1985. Conflict and Harmony: From the Indonesian Perspective. *Prisma*, **36** (2), 69–84.

Wardhana, A. 1996. Economic Reform in Indonesia: The transition from Resource Dependence to International Competitiveness. *The Indonesian Quarterly*, **XXIV**, 3, 257–72.

C H A P T E R N I N E

Conflict Management in the Philippines

LYDIA BALATBAT-ECHAUZ
Graduate School of Business, De La Salle University Professional Schools, Inc. Philippines

INTRODUCTION

Not much has been written on how conflict, specifically conflict between a foreign superior and a Filipino subordinate, is managed in the Philippine organizational setting. What is much written about is the history and culture of the Filipino and their effect on his attitudes and behavior.

In this chapter we will start with some background on the Philippines: a brief history of its people and their heritage. We will then look at the results of a survey focused on the conflict that arises between a foreign superior and a Filipino subordinate, its causes and types, and the manner of managing such conflict. The survey sample was 50 foreign managers in the Philippines and 50 of their Filipino subordinates. It is a small sample, thus the survey results should be viewed with caution and taken for what they are—a possible indication of the bigger picture. We shall then end with some practical guidelines on how to optimize the working relationship between them in light of this issue of conflict in the workplace, citing the findings of some authors who have written about the Filipino and Philippine culture to help us begin to understand the average Filipino's behavior at work in business and industry.

This study does not include many foreign managers whose Filipino subordinates are in top managerial positions, who are most likely very highly educated locally or overseas, coming from higher social strata, and having much better exposure to or even assimilation of the western culture. The results may be different for them.

Filipino heritage

The Philippines is a cluster of 7,107 tropical islands with an area of 300,000 square kilometers, situated in the typhoon belt and 'ring of fire' of Southeast Asia. It has traditionally been an agricultural country, with the land and the sea as basic sources of livelihood. Its culture is Malay, but foreign elements, mainly Chinese, Spanish and American, have given it strong Eastern and Western influences.

Still a developing country with 35% of its people below the poverty line, the Philippines aspires to move towards globalization, having achieved recently, though precariously, the status of an 'emerging tiger' in the Asian group of economic tigers. Population has increased from 17 million in 1946, to 61.5 million in 1987, reaching 71.8 million in 1997. The Philippines was under Spanish, Catholic rule for over 300 years, from 1521 when the Spaniards conquered the islands to 1896. It then came under American, Protestant rule for almost 50 years.

Filipinos, upon their conquest by the Spanish, were Christianized, thus it is said that Christianity was somehow imposed by the sword. Christianity was for the most part only superficial, as the Filipinos, for centuries had their own pagan culture and deities. A kind of 'Folk Catholicism' became prevalent, especially in the countryside. This the institutional Church at various times tolerated, disapproved, or condemned. Scholars described Philippine Christianity, particularly Catholicism, as split-level Christianity.

Together with the religion, Filipinos adopted the Christian rituals, including the numerous concomitant religious festivities and traditional merry-making. These Christian rituals were in addition to their pagan-animist rituals and celebrations, the popular forms of which included drinking and dancing. However, as the nation and its people have matured, so has their spirituality and their practice of religion.

Under the governance of the Spaniards who ruled with overwhelming power and resources, Filipinos learned to be subservient and self-sacrificing, becoming wise in the ways of conflict-avoidance for fear of severe punishment such as incarceration or death. They learned to work for smooth relationships, especially with superiors, often at great cost to themselves. They pooled their familial relationships—by blood, affinity, or religious kinship—and strength to protect themselves from oppressive elements. Only a chosen few were allowed to own property, have access to education and consequently access to the Spanish language, the medium of instruction. That kept the majority or the masses 'in their place'. Oppression, mainly related to land ownership, was common among lowly farmers. Filipinos, whether landed or not, aspired for a better life, one like that of the Spanish. They also aspired to have the trappings of the good life, to look good and behave 'properly' as these were part of being accomplished.

Under American rule and during the period of preparation for Philippine independence from it, Filipinos gradually experienced the freedom that came with American democracy. Democracy and education were the main legacy of the Americans. Education was available to anyone who wanted it and could afford it, as was the English language, then the new medium of instruction and now one of the two major languages used in the Philippines. The Philippines has one of the highest literacy rates in Asia. Its first university was founded in 1611. It had 52 universities in 1986, and now has 220. Higher education is given priority by all Filipino families, and the number of university graduates is way above what can be absorbed by the Philippine economy. Thus, some four million Filipinos work overseas, remitting currently some US$7 billion yearly.

After the second World War, American corporations enjoyed special economic privileges as provided by certain U.S.-Philippine agreements. Evidence of Americanization in the Philippines came in the democratic form of government, the proliferation of schools, and commercial and consumer goods such as the automobile, the Hollywood movies, soda pop, cigarettes, and a whole array of goods and services, books and reading materials included. Filipinos, traditionally engaged in agriculture, fishing, and handicrafts, but not in manufacturing, were a huge and rapidly growing market for U.S. goods. A colonial mentality was reflected in the Filipino preference not for Spanish or European goods, which were in any case not abundant locally, but for American goods, which had flooded the market after the Second World War, and concededly had far superior quality compared to Asian and local goods. During these years, the economic domination of American firms was a given. Filipinos once again were economically inferior.

Over three centuries of colonization by Spain and half a century under the U.S. more than sufficed to prejudice the Filipino against his own country, countrymen, and culture. To the Filipino, anything Philippine-made was inferior to imported goods. The Filipinos perceived themselves a notch or two less than the foreigners, especially the whites. Almost anything Philippine, whether customs or culture, was a potential source of embarrassment in the presence of foreigners. It was in the 1960s that the spirit of nationalism was reawakened. The Filipino wanted and needed an identity distinct from those of its former colonizers. Philippine history books, long used and taken as absolute truth, were reviewed and re-thought in light of the nationalist struggle against Spanish and American cultural domination. For decades after colonization, the Filipino faced the many problems of nation-rebuilding and the crisis of identity confusion.

The double colonization should explain the western veneer of the Filipino, who is Malay in origin. It should also explain the oversensitivity of Filipinos to foreign domination and to oppression of any kind.

Prior to the colonization of the Filipinos, they were non-Christians, but they believed in higher forces who determined the life and the fate of every living being. The Filipinos, visited every year by a long series of typhoons, many devastating, respected nature and to some degree worshipped it, too. Living in 7,107 islands with some 120 identified ethnic cultures and tribes and speaking 120 languages and some 180 dialects, Filipinos are said to be still in the process of crystallizing their identity.

Deep within, the Filipino is a person all his own, Christian by name yet not Christian in many ways, Asian, specifically Malay, with generous traces of Chinese and Spanish blood, but also American, especially in adopted manners and veneer—all at once.

From the post-American period to the present (1946–1997), Filipinos have enjoyed a nascent democracy with all its inefficiency and slowness. In the era of President Ferdinand Marcos, a charismatic and brilliant leader, Filipinos took pride in the fact that their President could hold his own on the international scene. However, they suffered when they came under his eventual dictatorship. To stay in power when he could no longer legally hold on to the presidency (as his two terms, a total of eight years would end in 1973) he brought the situation in the country to a point where he could justify the declaration of Martial Law in 1972. At the start of the extension of his stay in office, the Martial Law years, Filipinos were lulled into thinking that that the arrangement was in their best interest. As the excesses of his administration and his family and cronies became both worse and clearer to the public, the Filipinos' memory of earlier oppression came alive once more. At the famous bloodless uprising, known as the EDSA revolution, in Metro Manila in 1986, the Filipinos' long-festering resentment of oppression and anger at the dictatorship came to a head, driving the First Family out of the country. Since then the Filipinos have become vigilant of their rights and their liberty, more patriotic, and more caring of their country and their people. President Marcos has since died, but the rest of the family is back in Philippine society. That in itself says much about the Filipino psyche, culture, strong sense of family, and religion, including the Christian values of love and forgiveness.

The Philippine Revolution Centennial in 1996 was also the 100th anniversary of the martyrdom of the Philippines' foremost national hero, Dr. Jose Rizal. This year, 1998, is the Philippines' centennial of independence from Spanish rule. Filipinos, now discovering their identity, seek to model themselves after Dr. Rizal, an educated, global Malay, who proved himself equal to the Spaniards whom he fought through his written work.

It is important to note that the Philippines is thought to have been peopled by waves of immigrants from Indonesia and inhabited for more than 30,000 years. It had had extensive trade with India, Indonesia, China, and Japan even before the Spaniards came. Other immigrants came from south China and settled in great numbers in the Philippines, intermarrying with Filipinos. Thus, many Filipinos have Chinese blood. Unlike in other Southeast Asian countries, the overseas Chinese in the Philippines are not resented by Philippine society. In fact, they are well assimilated. Considering the fact that they make up only one percent of the population, yet control some 70% of national sales, this may seem surprising. But the Chinese have had a very long history in the Philippines. They have worked hard for many centuries at trading and services, and at many lowly jobs Filipinos were not willing to do. The sentiment is that whatever the ethnic Chinese enjoy now is deemed deserved fruit of their labors and sacrifices. Moreover, the ethnic Chinese, much like the other overseas Chinese in the rest of the world, have not shown interest in political domination. They have taken care not to slight in any way the natives of their host countries. On the contrary, the Chinese have exerted effort to make friends with Filipinos; hence, the open acceptance of the ethnic Chinese into Philippine society. In fact, Filipinos look up to the Chinese in the field of business, and are now following in their footsteps to achieve the same kind of economic prosperity that the latter have achieved through the years.

Given this background of the long years of the Filipinos' long colonization and subordination to foreign rule, we seek now to understand how present-day Filipinos as subordinates interface with foreigners as superiors in the workplace. More specifically, we will look at the conflict aspect of their relationship. What brings about the conflict between them? What types of conflict arise between them? How do they view these conflicts? Do they have the same perceptions of the conflict situations? How do they manage them?

Fifty foreign managers and 50 Filipino subordinates participated in the survey to give us their views on their relationship and its conflict aspect. Both groups were asked the same questions.

The Survey

Overview of the responses of the foreign managers and the Filipino subordinates

In the survey of foreign managers and Filipino subordinates, both groups are agreed that conflict in the workplace is something that is manageable and can be handled professionally. They also believe that conflict is inevitable just as it is inevitable in other areas of life.

Foreigners cite the Filipino subordinates' lack of discipline, as shown by the latter's carefree attitude and lack of promptness, among other things, as the main cause of conflict between superiors and subordinates.

The Filipino subordinates, on the other hand, say that differences in management style and cultural values are the main causes of such conflict. Foreign superiors observe that Filipinos avoid conflict at all cost. This avoidance must be a source of puzzlement to the foreigners. Filipino subordinates, on the other hand, seem pleased with their superiors who they think have an open mind on the matter of resolving differences, and, in fact, encourage discussion and resolution of issues at hand. They think, however, that their Filipino co-subordinates need to be studied, understood, and adjusted to because their background differs from that of their foreign superiors. They think that Filipinos are wonderful and easy to work with. They are in effect saying that they themselves are so—wonderful and easy to work with.

Curiously, both foreign superiors and Filipino subordinates say that they get along well and that their relationship is professional and generally positive in that it is enjoyable, pleasant and educational. Most say that they seldom have any conflict between them. Foreigners recognize their differences with their subordinates and accept such differences. Superiors and subordinates think that each group is able to manage their relationship with each other very well. The subordinates are self-confident enough to be able to win their superiors over.

Foreigners have mostly objective cultural norms that they consider important in resolving conflict. Their responses include respecting opinions, keeping cool and objective, and giving clear instructions to subordinates. On the other hand, Filipinos have mostly person-oriented values that they consider important in resolving conflicts with their foreign superiors. These values include hospitality to foreigners, getting along with them, and their loyalty to their superiors.

Both parties are one in recognizing the fact that they need to know more about each other as they have differing concepts of management processes. By observing, listening, asking, reading, and getting advice from others, the foreign superiors believe that they could actually manage whatever conflict arises between them. Both superiors and subordinates are agreed that their conflicts are rooted mainly in their cultural differences. Both parties also say that conflicts are handled and settled professionally on the whole. There is generally an agreement between the foreign managers and the Filipino subordinates on the different aspects of the issue of conflict and conflict management. The two parties say that to resolve conflict with one another, they bring up the matter for discussion in a professional and respectful manner. Foreign superiors observe that Filipinos prefer to avoid conflict and confrontation. Filipino subordinates, on the other hand, say that their superiors prefer that when there is a conflict between them and their superiors, the subordinates raise the matter for discussion in order to resolve the problem.

To the question of what are the most difficult barriers that hinder conflict resolution with each other, the two groups have very different responses. The foreign superiors count the honesty problem and rule-bending as difficult barriers in conflict resolution, while the Filipino subordinates say that their superiors are mostly not aware of their (superiors') wider role in the work place, and that the foreigners are direct and blunt in their ways and in their words. This disparity leads to the main problems or conflicts between the two groups.

Guidelines for Foreign Managers coming to work in the Philippines

The following guidelines should help foreign managers coming to work in the Philippines to understand the Filipinos and thereby work more smoothly with them:

1. **Prepare by studying and understanding Filipino culture and values.** Previous experience working in another developing country

is an advantage as there is a great difference between the expectations of and standards in a developed country and a developing one.

Author Tomas Andres (1990) identified the following as items that motivate Filipino workers, or can prevent conflict at work: a personalistic family atmosphere in the company; attention to the emotional aspect of organization life, such as individual self-esteem, reciprocity between management and employees, respect for their human dignity; egalitarian treatment; flexibility in work assignment, schedules and deadlines; supportive role on the part of the officers; open communications and complete, genuine information; a cooperative and fraternal reward and promotion system. Other values he deems important to the Filipino are social acceptance by people of high social status who can be of financial aid, economic security, or the ability to meet ordinary material needs through one's family or group, and social mobility or advancement up the social scale to another class or higher position.

Filipino anthropologist and author F. Landa Jocano (1990) explained that it is easy to understand that when managers and workers come from the same culture, there should be negligible difficulty in understanding each other. Naturally, the situation is very different for management in a cross-cultural setting, especially in developing countries which have undergone colonization, as in the case of the Philippines. Westerners, for instance, value individualism, independence, free enterprise, and human rights. These are the values they have in their society and in their corporations. Superiors and subordinates from the same culture and level of economic development do not have difficulty relating to each other since they have common values in the different facets of their life. Any difficulties between them in the workplace will be in the areas of racial prejudice and social class discrimination, the same problems they have had throughout their history. However, in the Philippines, a colonized nation, the situation is different. Community values are indigenous, while corporate values are derived from the values of the educational system, which is that of the American colonizers. Thus, the structures of management, its philosophy, content, and practices are all American. Those schooled in these educational institutions logically acquire an orientation different from those educated differently. As a result of these derived, external corporate values, there exist differences in and conflict between the Filipino social and workplace value systems.

The problem becomes even more pronounced in multinational corporations where management is composed of foreign superiors whose community values and educational experience are different from those of subordinates of another nationality. Their mindset and value systems are just so completely different from each other's that a great effort is needed to begin to understand the dynamics between them.

It is, therefore, understandable that both foreign expatriates and Filipino employees have their own frustrations over their relationships, both in and out of the corporate setting.

To Filipinos, who are naturally sensitive to criticism, the foreigners' frankness is seen as arrogance, rudeness or discrimination. These differences seem rooted in differences in culture and the Filipinos' history of colonization and oppression.

Jocano (1990) says that if managers and workers have a common definition of corporate goals and share the same work ethics, then there will be no conflict. But when they do not, then unnecessary conflicts arise, causing factionalism, bureaucracy and low productivity. The Filipino is described as sensitive, highly personal in his ways, family-oriented, dependent on his elders for guidance, care and attention. Also he is known to be generally averse to confrontation, or a natural advocate of the 'win-win' approach.

To subordinates, the manager is 'superior' and people look up to him for guidance, direction, decisions, and assistance in fulfilling their dreams in life. He, therefore, must be credible as a role model, both as a leader (theirs) and a follower (of his superior). He is expected naturally to be firm and consistent.

Writer Ernesto Franco (1986) enumerates seven weaknesses of Filipino workers. These, he says, are the following: (1) Lack of self-confidence which can be traced to poverty and long-standing subservience to colonizers; (2) Colonial mentality which makes the Filipino look up to anything foreign, and look down on anything local or native; (3) Casual, semi-lethargic and overly relaxed general attitude which Franco attributes to the comfortable tropical weather and the rich natural resources and the easy life they afford the population; (4) Weakness in perseverance and sustained effort, for reasons similar to those cited in the previous item; (5) Holiday mentality due to the Sundays and many religious (Christian) holidays, days on which, for centuries, any kind of work or exertion of effort was forbidden; (6) Poor organizational and managerial effectiveness, resulting from the fact that the Filipinos are very personalistic by nature and culture and the fact that the Filipinos' wide exposure to corporate structures is a 20th century phenomenon; (7) Lack of self-reliant tenacity, due to the extended family system, the rich natural resources, the feudal, and political patronage, and Divine Providence.

2. **Earn points fast with Filipinos by making friends with them,** reaching out to them, and socializing with them. Filipinos are receptive to such relationships, being good-natured, warm and willing to please others. The majority of Filipinos are still very hospitable to North Americans and Europeans, almost in awe of them, and they exert extra effort to please them.
3. **Be sensitive to Filipinos and what they hold dear,** especially their person, their family, their traditions, and their country.

The issue of honesty is important to discuss at this point. To the foreigner, rules on punctuality, accounting of funds or supplies or time or telephone use, and others, are to be followed strictly. To the subordinate, rules are to be honored, yes, but they may be superseded by other considerations which they deem more important and therefore valid, such as family emergencies, personal relationships, or religious reasons. Subordinates, therefore, feel rules may be suspended, bent or stretched. To them, such behavior is not deemed a case of dishonesty, but as showing care or concern for others, usually family, friends or compatriots. Moreover, they expect their superiors to fully understand the Filipino behavior, psyche, and cultural values.

To the foreigner, rules set the procedures in the office. To the Filipino, the personal relationship between the superior and the subordinate should count for much more than rules in the course of business, but especially in times of need, usually the subordinate's need. Thus, a superior is expected to behave much like a patriarch whose role it is to understand the subordinate's needs and, in fact, help provide solutions to the latter's problems. An uncaring superior is likely to be resented by subordinates.

This expectation has much of its roots in the Filipinos' colonial past where the landowners saw to the needs of every tenant and his family, at all times. The landowners or fishpond owners always provided the farm's or fishpond's and the farmers' and fishermen's needs: financing, seedlings/fish fry, irrigation, fertilizer/fish feed, transportation, post-harvest facilities. They also provided funds for all of the farmers' family needs: tuition fees, medicine, hospitalization, and for religious milestones in families, such as baptism, weddings, religious festivities. Especially during times of emergency, the expectations are even greater. This dependence on the landlord continued even when the land ownership transferred from the hands of the colonizers to those of Filipinos. Land reform, which only recently broke up massive land holdings and distributed small tracts to ordinary farmers, ended this dependence on the landlord. However, the tradition of reliance on superiors for life's basic needs continues.

Andres (1981), writing on honesty, says that the Filipino is inherently good, honest, respectful and socially conscious, but that he lost his genuine values with the coming of western influences. While the Filipino welcomed the foreigners, the foreigners were seen to abuse his trust. Resentment grew, especially when the foreigners eventually became the owners of his land, life and property.

4. **Give the Filipino a gracious way out**, even if he/she is wrong, and agree on a policy for the next time around. The Filipino's sense of pride is as dear to them as life itself. Losing face can cost someone else's life.

The issue of loss of face is best discussed at this point. The Filipino, like most Asians, believes in saving his honor and face as much as those of the other person.

The foreign manager, on the one hand, thinks the Filipino subordinate is 'onion-skinned'. One who takes offense and gets humiliated easily, both situations made much worse by the presence of others, and who is inclined to slow anger. On the other hand, the Filipino subordinate thinks the foreigner is much too blunt with his/her words or manners. The Filipino sees this bluntness in the foreigner as a lack of understanding of cultural sensibilities, an air of superiority, or just throwing his weight around.

This sensitivity to slight comes from a number of root causes—the reawakening of a sense of the historical dominion of colonizers over the locals, the resentment of the same, the economic inequities, the feeling of inferiority to foreigners, the ignorance of European languages or inadequate facility in English, often the language of the superior. Also it springs from even the failed expectation that the foreign manager would care for the welfare of the Filipino subordinate's or his/her family, or from a disregard for what Filipinos' hold dear, such as religious traditions that have to do with family. These religious traditions include baptism, confirmation, weddings, funerals, town fiestas or festivals and rituals, and many others.

Still on the issue of face, Andres (Positive Filipino Values, 1989) says of the Filipino value of shame, or *hiya*, in the Filipino language, '*Hiya* is a Filipino trait with emphasis on fear of losing face. It is also fear of rejection. It is an emotion arising from a relationship with a person of authority or with society, inhibiting self-assertion in a situation which is perceived as dangerous to one's ego. It can be fear of losing self-respect. *Hiya* sums up the Filipinos' long-standing complex brought about by years of submission to foreign rule, mainly Spanish and American'.

Note that the Chinese, who were much earlier settlers in the Philippines than the Spanish, unlike the Spanish and the Americans, never aspired to political domination. The overseas Chinese, given their history, have generally not aspired to political domination in whatever host country they were settled. This is due to the history of the overseas Chinese being the object of oppression or discrimination, making them prefer to stay as low-key as possible. Thus, Filipinos do not have the same sense of *hiya*, or the same feeling of inferiority to the Chinese as they do with the Spanish and the Americans, even if the Chinese are economically dominant in the country.

The issue of face, however, is far from limited to Filipinos. In fact it is a universal issue. Doctoral student Covarrubias (unpublished thesis) cites several foreign sources who have written on the topic. Conflict situations are said to be strongly influenced by the concept of 'face,' which is a person's attempt to present himself, and to be accepted, as a particular kind of person. Acts which threaten face or can cause the loss of face also tend to bring about behavior to save face or re-establish face. This type of behavior very likely worsens conflict situations. Contending parties may resort to taking hard positions or altogether suppressing conflict issues.

The issue of face to the Filipino seems exacerbated both by his country's economic underdevelopment and his past colonization.

5. **Never criticize their family or their country**. They may do so themselves, but they take great offense when foreigners do. They can hold grudges for a long time, as shown in their past.
6. **Be especially tactful with countryside Filipinos**, who are generally kinder, gentler, and more leisurely and gracious, but also more sensitive to overbearing foreign visitors.
7. **Be professional in the workplace**. Filipinos like to look up to their superiors for competence, information, know-how and other 'superior' qualities.
8. **Be clean and well-groomed at all times**. Filipinos value personal hygiene and physical appearance.
9. **Be prepared to have to discipline Filipino subordinates** with regard to punctuality. Life in the Philippines is leisurely as there is no great need to rush. With a tropical climate, which necessitates no preparation for harsh winters, rich natural resources, which yield farm products and seafood generously, and the extended family system, which usually acts as a safety net for an individual in any kind of need, life is easy, or at least manageable.
10. **Understand their *bahala na* attitude** also expressed as, '*Bathala* (God/Nature) will provide' or 'It is God's (nature's) will' or 'It is fate (nature)'. The Philippines is in the typhoon belt, and farms and fishponds that have been worked on for months and are now ready to harvest can be wiped out by one strong typhoon. Farmers and fishermen live with this possibility and simply start anew if disaster strikes. They don't starve, as the country's soil and seas are rich. Some 20 typhoons visit the country every year. In addition, the country is on the 'rim of fire'. It has had its share of world-renowned volcanic eruptions and earthquakes, with devastating results to life and property.

'It is fate,' Filipinos will say. Like the true survivors that they are, they simply start anew. And they have survived, even lived well, for generations. Their ancient gods, nature, and the Christian God have been their source of hope. 'It is fate' has extended to other aspects of their daily life, such as at work.

REFERENCES

Andres, T. 1981. *Understanding Filipino Values*, Quezon City, Philippines: New Day Publishers.

Andres, T. 1985. *Management by Filipino Values*, Quezon City, Philippines: New Day Publishers.

Andres, T. 1989. *Positive Filipino Values*, Philippines: New Day Publishers.

Bolasco, M. 1994. *Points of Departure*, Manila, St. Scholastica's College.

Covarrubias, M.A. 1995. *Conflict Management in a School Organization*, De La Salle University.

Franco, E.A. 1986. *Pinoy Management*, Philippines: National Book Store, Inc.

Jocano, F.L. 1975. *Philippine Prehistory, An Anthropological Overview of the Beginnings of Filipino Society and Culture*, Quezon City, Philippines: Philippine Center for Advanced Studies, University of the Philippines System.

Jocano, F.L. 1990. *Management by Culture — Fine-Tuning Management to Filipino Culture*, Quezon City, Philippines: Punlad Research House.

Lexicon Universal Encyclopedia, 1988. NY: Lexicon Publications, Inc.

Rediscovery, 1983. Quezon City, Philippines: Golden Art Printing Corp.

Seagrave, Sterling; 1995. *Lords of the Rim: The Invisible Empire of the Overseas Chinese*, Bantam Press.

APPENDIX A

Profile of sample respondent foreign managers in the Philippines

Nationality:	%
American	30
Canadian	20
British	14
Korean	6
Australian	6
Japanese	4
Singaporean, Malaysian, Chinese, Indian, Iranian, Lebanese, Spanish, Swiss, Danish, Finnish	20

Gender:	%
Male	80
Female	20

Religion:	%
Catholic	26
Protestant	18
Methodist	16
Baptist	8
Mormon	4
Islam	4
Buddhist, Church of England, Hindu, Presbyterian	10

Civil Status:	%
Married	70
Single	20
Divorced/No response	10

Country of Birth:	%
US and Canada	47
UK	12
Korea	6
Australia	4
Malaysia, China, Japan, India, Iran, Lebanon, Spain, Switzerland, Denmark, Finland	20

Nature of Business:

Consumer product sales, woodcraft and antiques, telecommunications, information technology, management consultancy, research studies, automotive service, export of wooden furniture, carpet sales, communications, insurance, export/import, forwarding, banking and financial services, wires and cables installation, aluminum fabrication, cigarette distribution, general merchandizing, shipping, heavy machinery trading, metal craft manufacturing and exporting, travel, luxury resort, hotel, restaurants and food business, resort time-sharing, transport, manufacturing, real estate and joint venture construction.

APPENDIX B

Profile of the sample of the Filipino subordinates:

Religion:	%
Christian:	100
Catholic	88
Iglesia ni Cristo	8
Protestant	4
Gender:	%
Female	66
Male	34
Civil Status	%
Married	48
Single	48
Widowed/No response	4
Position at work:	%
Executive secretaries	29
Sales representatives	6
Assistant managers	4
Executive assistants	4
Accounting heads	4
Assistant senior managers	4
Assistant secretaries	4
Others*	38

Notes: 1) It is important to cite the religion of the Filipino respondents because their Christianity is intertwined with their long history of colonization, which in turn mostly explains their values and attitudes. 2) The survey was done in Metro Manila, and this explains the absence of Muslims (most of whom live in the southern Philippines) who make up the next largest religious group (8%) after the Catholics (84%) and non-Catholic Christians (8%).
**Others: Account manager, MIS manager, program analyst, export manager, assistant to the general manager, surveyor, head cook, administrative assistant, finance and administrative manager, assistant personnel manager, merchandiser, export marketing coordinator, marketing director, senior chief, beverage manager, executive secretary, marketing executive, secretary, branch manager*

APPENDIX C

Responses of Foreign Managers and Filipino Subordinates

Legend: FE: Asked of Foreign Executives
S: Asked of Subordinates

Note: Responses may exceed 100% because of multiple responses.

FE 1. How do you view conflict in general?

We have a lot to learn about conflict management in the Philippines.	68%
Conflict is inevitable, it being a part of life.	46%

FE 1a. How do your compatriots view conflict?

It can be avoided.	80%
I don't know.	12%
It can be handled professionally.	8%

S 1. How do you view conflict in a business organization in general?

Something manageable	*46%*
Avoidable	*40%*

FE 2. What are the common causes of conflict in your dealings with Filipino subordinates? Please list as many sources of conflict as you can remember and expound further to show the situation clearly.

Lack of discipline	60%
Lack of promptness	26%
Attitude of *bahala na* or fatalistic attitude	22%
Poor English communication skills	22%
Poor communication channels	6%
Different culture	4%

Note: *Bahala na*, originating from *bathala* meaning the Almighty, refers to the attitude of leaving it to God or nature or fate to take over the course of life.

S 2. What are the common causes of conflict in your dealings with your foreign superior? Please list as many sources of conflict as you can remember and expound further to show the situation clearly.

Mainly differences in management style	*66%*
Differences in cultural values	*44%*

Unclear or vague instructions from the foreign superiors	*32%*
Miscommunication or the language barrier	*8%*

FE 3. What is your assessment of how Filipinos view conflict at the workplace? What is the basis of this view?

Filipino subordinates avoid conflict at all costs.	96%

S 3. What is your assessment of how foreign superiors view conflict at the workplace? What is the basis of this view?

Superiors have an open mind and encourage discussion of the issue at hand.	*64%*
They use their position of authority and power to assert themselves.	*16%*
They think that conflict is a normal element of the workplace.	*16%*
They are able to sort out problems in the workplace.	*8%*

How do you perceive your Filipino subordinates as co-workers?

Filipinos have to be studied and understood.	70%
Filipinos have to be adjusted to because of differing backgrounds.	30%
Filipinos are wonderful people to work with.	28%
Filipinos are easy to work with.	27%

FE 4. How would you describe your relationship with your Filipino subordinates?

We get along well.	56%
We learn to accept our differences.	34%
We enjoy the nice side of our relationship.	16%
My subordinates know when to take me seriously.	14%

S 4. How would you describe your relationship with your foreign superior?

The relationship is professional, formal and business-like.	*66%*
It is pleasant and educational	*36%*
It is one of equals	*36%*
It is one of tension	*4%*

FE 5. What is your perception of your style of dealing with your workers?

Very well	90%
Well	8%

S 5. What is your perception of your style of dealing with your foreign superior?

Our style is accommodating, cordial, and respectful.	*66%*
Foreign superiors should be more open to other cultures.	*26%*
We are persuasive enough to convince our superiors to our side.	*18%*
Our superiors are bull-headed.	*2%*
Our superiors are flexible and adaptable to change.	*2%*

F 6. In your home country, what cultural norms do you consider important in resolving conflicts?

Understanding and respecting others' opinions	76%
Keeping cool	38%
Being objective	26%
Clear statement of instructions	2%

S 6. What Filipino values are important in dealing with conflict with foreign superiors?

Hospitality	*48%*
Perseverance	*44%*
Their ability to get along with others	*21%*
Loyalty	*17%*
Capacity for hard work, patience and understanding	*4%*

FE 7. What do you find as very critical factors for foreign managers in the Philippines during the first stage of alliance and relationship development with Filipinos?

Listen, observe, read, ask, get advice.	76%
Note that Filipinos can adopt and imitate styles.	22%
Do not push Filipinos.	4%
The language barrier is a problem.	4%

S 7. What do you find as very critical factors for foreign superiors in the Philippines during the first stage of alliances and relationship development with Filipino subordinates?

Understanding and adapting to local culture	*78%*
Ease of communication	*34%*
Preparedness to treat Filipinos well	*10%*
Encouragement of common interest	*6%*
Openness to suggestions	*2%*

FE 8. How often does conflict occur between you and your Filipino subordinates?

Seldom	46%
Not at all	36%
Often	18%

S 8. How often does conflict occur between you and your foreign superior?

Never had any conflict	*32%*
Off and on conflict	*28%*
Rarely had any conflict	*30%*
Often	*2%*

FE 9. What is your style of resolving conflict with your Filipino subordinates? You may indicate sources of conflict and identify management approaches you feel are appropriate in each situation.

Allow them to explain their side	84%
Talk to them softly and slowly	62%
Apologize when wrong	28%
Give them importance	4%
Use a third party for arbitration	2%
Be professional, not personal	2%

S 9. What is your style of resolving conflict with your foreign superior? You may indicate sources of conflict and identify management approaches you feel are appropriate in each situation.

We have no conflict.	*58%*
Approach superiors directly and open up the discussion of the problem	*38%*
Accept shortcomings at work, whether their superiors' or theirs	2%

FE 10. What are your observations/views about the conflict management style preferred by Filipino subordinates?

Filipinos avoid conflict at all cost.	52%
Filipinos are non-confrontational.	48%

S 10. What are your observations/views about the conflict management style preferred by your foreign superior?

That I raise the issue at hand, but without being personal about it	*90%*
That I recognize that he is the superior and I respect his decision	*18%*
That I choose to ignore the conflict and not repeat the deed	*2%*

FE 11. In your opinion, what are the most difficult barriers in the Philippines that hinder conflict resolution?

Honesty problem	44%
Inability to separate person from action	30%
Rule-bending	20%
Issue of 'loss of face'	18%
Silence about the problem	4%
Filipinos have to air their side.	4%

S 11. In your opinion, what are the most difficult barriers in the Philippines that hinder conflict resolution with foreign superiors?

Lack of awareness of the role of each one in the workplace	*52%*
The directness or bluntness of superiors	*32%*
The subordinates' fear of expressing themselves	*12%*

S 11 a. Do you think foreigners from a particular country have difficulty working with Filipinos? If yes, in what way? Please give a specific example.

Not really, if they adjust well, fine and effective.	*46%*
Yes, if they are of another culture (Not Spanish or American).	*34%*
We agree with what they think of us Filipinos.	*16%*
Some foreigners tended to show some superiority complex.	*6%*
We have communication barriers.	*6%*
No difficulty because Filipinos are adaptable, flexible, easy to please, hospitable, and proficient communication.	*6%*

S 11 b. How do your co-Filipinos handle conflict with their foreign superior?

Non-articulation of feelings and thoughts	*42%*
Non-confrontational	*32%*
General lack of assertiveness	*18%*

S 11 c. *What are the usual consequences?*

Fellow subordinates would prefer to keep quiet, becoming demoralized and unproductive in the process.	*70%*
They would just leave the work place.	*14%*
They become confrontational, with misguided nationalism, often in a misguided sense, and sometimes losing their jobs in the process.	*12%*

CHAPTER TEN

Negotiating with Australia: The Individualist Among Us

MARA OLEKALNS
Department of Management, University of Melbourne, Australia

Negotiation is a process of social exchange and, during this process, we establish a psychological contract with the other party. That contract has both a relational and a transactional component (e.g., Robinson, Rousseau, and Kraatz 1994). Each party has expectations about how negotiations will proceed, the type of relationship that will be created and how the negotiation will be resolved. Departures from these expectations will appear to be violations of the psychological contract in one of two domains. Relational violations will occur when the negotiation process is incongruent with expectations; such violations will influence perceptions of procedural justice. Transactional violations will occur when resource distribution does not meet expectations and these violations will influence the perception of distributive justice. Although such violations may occur in any negotiation, their likelihood is increased when the negotiating parties have different cultural backgrounds. If not recognized for what they are, these script violations have the potential to worsen relationships and encourage more competitive responses.

In this chapter I use the two dimensions of power and affinity to provide a unifying theme for considering relationships between cultural differences, the process through which negotiating relationships are built, strategy selection and interpretation, and outcome preferences. Cultural factors that orient individuals to group outcomes or reduce the importance of status emphasize the relational aspects of negotiation (affinity), and are linked to procedural justice and concerns about equality in resource allocation. Conversely, cultural factors that encourage individual outcomes and status differences emphasize the distributive aspects of negotiation (power) and are linked to distributive justice and a concern for equity in resource distribution.

CULTURE AND CONFLICT: A GENERAL FRAMEWORK

How we represent negotiations influences the strategies that we choose and the outcomes that we expect to obtain (Putnam and Holmer 1992). More importantly, our representation of negotiations provides a means for assessing our opponents' expectations and interpreting their behavior. Even in the same culture, individuals bring very different perspectives to a negotiation. As a result, settlement can be made difficult: unless negotiators are able to find a common understanding of the task that they face, they are unlikely to reach agreement (Pinkley and Northcraft 1994).

Many researchers have argued that not only culture, but also variables such as gender and personality, impact on how we interpret the communication and behavior of others (Kelley and Stahelski 1970; Tannen 1995; Triandis 1995). For individuals, culture provides a powerful set of norms for shaping behavior and expectations, while also influencing the interpretation of other individuals' behavior. Culture influences how we represent negotiations, the strategies that we prefer and our criteria for assessing outcomes. When two cultures meet, they no longer have the advantage of shared norms and values to provide a guide for representing negotiations. Consequently, expectations, communication and behaviors are all open to misinterpretation.

One of our tasks is to understand barriers to the development of shared meanings. To do this, I will consider two dimensions along which individuals categorize behavior, and further consider how these link to dimensions used for describing cultural differences. These two dimensions—power and affinity—influence how we judge others; they play a key role in the negotiation process; and they are central to descriptions of cultural 'personalities'.

Two dimensions of behavior

A dominant theme in negotiation research centers around the distinction between cooperative and competitive styles of bargaining (Deutsch 1973; Lewicki and Litterer 1985). Individuals are typically assumed to adopt either a cooperative or competitive orientation (Carroll and Payne 1991; Putnam 1990; Wilson and Putnam 1990), with accordingly different outcome, strategic and relational preferences. Cooperation is associated with a preference for high joint gain, a focus on information exchange and a problem-solving orientation (e.g., Lewicki and Litterer 1985; Carnevale and Pruitt 1992). Trust, rather than power, characterizes such relationships and negotiations emphasize affinity and equality (Deutsch 1982; Larrick and Blount 1995). Conversely, competition is typically associated with a preference for high individual gain, positional arguing, threats and minimal information exchange (e.g., Lewicki and Litterer 1981; Carnevale and Pruitt 1992). Power provides the dominant negotiating dynamic and negotiations emphasize power differences and equity (Deutsch 1982; Larrick and Blount 1995).

This distinction between cooperation (affinity) and competition (power) creates two dimensions for assessing communication and behavior. It becomes especially important in negotiations which are characterized by considerable uncertainty and require negotiators to extract meaning from ambiguous cues. Several examples of such ambiguity are apparent in the literature: threats, which are usually associated with competitive bargaining, can lead to cooperation and high quality settlements; information seeking can provide a means of control when used within a competitive context, but facilitate problem-solving in cooperative context; and suggestions of procedural change can be a means of controlling interactions rather than facilitating collaboration (Putnam and Wilson 1989; Wilson and Putnam 1990). How such strategies are interpreted will be determined by the expectations that individuals bring to the negotiation. These include cultural norms and values.

Two dimensions of culture

Two recurrent themes in the classification of cultural 'personalities' are the extent to which cultural norms encourage a focus on individual or group outcomes, and the extent to which they recognize and accept status or power differences. This dichotomy surfaces in two well-known examinations of culture, one at the organizational level, the other at the individual level.

Research in Organizations

The best known classification of cultural differences derives from Hofstede's (1991) work in organizations around the world. On the basis of his research, Hofstede differentiated cultures on the basis of several dimensions. Two are relevant here. The first, collectivism-individualism, distinguishes between cultures that value group membership and group outcomes from those more focused on the individual and his or her outcomes. The second, power distance, captures the degree to which hierarchical relationships and status differences are accepted as the norm within a culture.

Research with Individuals

Similarly, researchers have classified individuals along two, orthogonal dimensions: horizontal-vertical (power distance) and individualistic-collectivist (e.g., Triandis 1995). To date, research examining cross-cultural differences in conflict resolution has focused on the impact of the first dimension, individualism-collectivism. However, both differences in power and individualistic orientations are known to affect how people bargain. Research has shown that unequal power and an orientation towards own gains creates win-lose expectancies and leads to more contentious and competitive behavior than does equal power or a more collaborative orientation (e.g., McAlister, Bazerman and Fader 1986; Weingart, Bennett and Brett 1993).

Culture and the Individual

There are strong parallels between the dimensions that Hofstede uses to categorize countries, and those used by Triandis and others to categorize individuals. The best way of integrating these is to view culture as placing some broad constraints on the behavior of its members: describing a country as individualistic does not imply that its members will not display collectivism. We would simply expect, on average, to observe a more individualistic or competitive style in day-to-day interactions. Situations that accentuate collectivism may well evoke a strategic shift towards more cooperative behavior. However, that shift will result in less intense collaboration than we would expect to observe in members of a collectivist culture.

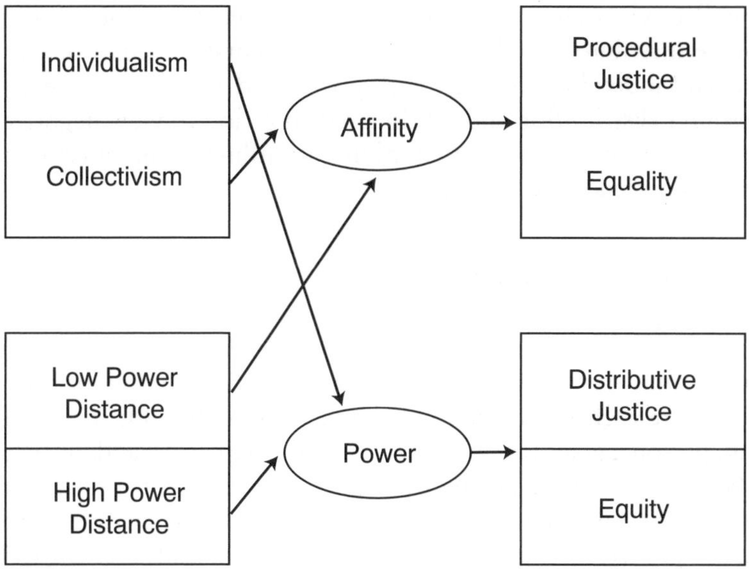

Figure 10.1 A framework for examining relationships between culture, behavior and outcome preferences

Implications for Negotiation

There are clear links between the dimensions of individualism-collectivism and horizontal-vertical relationships, on the one hand, and affinity and power on the other. Both collectivism and an emphasis on horizontal relationships imply a preference for collaborative bargaining: collectivism, because of the high value placed on group outcomes; a horizontal orientation, because of the emphasis on equality and relationship-building. Because it relies on trust, collaboration cannot occur without a good bargaining relationship. Consequently, a collectivist or horizontal orientation will align with a concern for relationship-building or affinity. Conversely, individualism and an emphasis on vertical relationships imply a preference for competitive bargaining. Valuing individual outcomes or emphasizing status differences creates a barrier to building good relationships, instead emphasizing the need to strengthen a negotiator's own position. As a result, these dimensions align more strongly with power.

In the following sections, I go on to consider the Australian negotiating style in more detail. Two assumptions underlie my discussion of this style (see Fig. 10.1): (a) a horizontal orientation (low power distance)

and collectivism align with affinity and a preference for equality in resource distribution, whereas a vertical orientation (high power distance) and individualism align with power and a preference for equity in resource distribution and (b) the predisposition to view negotiations from an affinity or power orientation will influence the interpretation of ambiguous cues and messages.

AUSTRALIA IN CONTEXT

Within the Hofstede and Triandis frameworks, Australians are described as horizontal (low power distance) individualists. Individuals in this category are highly autonomous: they remain independent from their group, personal goals take precedence over group goals, and, in their social behavior, they are guided by 'rights' and 'contracts'; relationships are (or are not) maintained as the result of cost-benefit analyses. In addition, this group places emphasis on similarity, especially striving to level status differences. In counterpoint, Asians are variously classified as collectivistic with high power distance, or as vertical collectivists, emphasizing interdependence, group goals, obligations and duties.

Taking this representation at face value, it seems that Australian negotiators face competing pressures not only in their goals, but in the expectations that they have of negotiating partners. For Australians, individualism creates a strong drive to maximize individual outcomes and increases competitive behavior. Simultaneously, their horizontal nature pushes Australians towards equality and relationship building.

Stories about Australia

There is little direct evidence about how culture affects Australian negotiators. In the following sections, I take as my starting point the assumption that—as a group—Australians are oriented towards individual outcomes and are relatively insensitive to status or power differences. However, before considering how these dimensions affect Australian negotiators, we can look for anecdotal evidence to support this characterization of Australian culture.

A Horizontal Australia

Australia and Australians are essentially egalitarian. This does not mean that they fail to recognize the markers of status and hierarchy; it does, however, mean that such markers carry less weight. This egalitarianism is fundamental to relationship building within Australian society: although status is recognized, individuals are taken at face value, and are treated the same no matter who they are. This egalitarianism captures what Graham and Sano (1989) describe as a 'Just call me John' style. Like the Americans described in Graham and Sano's (1989) book, Australians tend to downplay status differences and to emphasize informality.

In recent years, a memorable example of this trait was provided by the former Prime Minister, Paul Keating: newspapers around the world carried a photograph of Prime Minister Keating touching the Queen of England's back to guide her through a crowd! A courteous and acceptable gesture in Australia, interpreted as disrespectful elsewhere. This same egalitarianism is evident in what has been labeled the 'tall poppy syndrome'—an intolerance of high achievers (Feather 1993).

An Individualistic Australia

Simultaneously, Australia is described as individualistic, reflecting a concern for own (rather than collective) outcomes. A relevant example of this trait can be seen in recent changes to the industrial relations system, including the introduction of employment contracts[1] and a steady decline in Union membership. Both are consistent with a strong drive towards individualism.

Horizontal Individualists

Interestingly, the strong drive to individualism motivates collective action. The individualist's focus on rights and justice, combined with egalitarian sentiments, often sends Australians to the streets. When rights are violated, protests follow. The most recent example of this is the series of protests, some violent, organized in response to proposed changes to the Industrial Relations legislation. But such collective action is not confined to issues of employment. Some decades ago, action groups

[1] The Australian Industrial Relations system is highly regulated. At the level of the Commonwealth, several commisions act to interpret and enforce awards, review unfair contracts and dismissals, resolve disputes between employers and unions, and provide a framework for award protection and fair bargaining. Recent reforms have enabled the negotiation of enterprise agreements, which aim to increase flexibility in the workplace. A major difference between these and more traditional agreements is that they do not require union participation in the negotiation process. Similar systems exist in each state and deal with those sectors of the workforce governed by State rather than Commonwealth law (Nankervis, Compton and McCarthy 1996).

took to the streets in protest over the location of the Franklin Dam in a wilderness area of Tasmania. Since then there have been protests against the location of the Melbourne Grand Prix around public parklands; the proposed felling of 100-year-old trees to make way for freeway extensions; the closure of inner-city schools and swimming pools; and many other local and environmental issues.

These anecdotes can help us to understand the Australian conflict management style. Expect a concern with rights and justice which will most likely be sparked when others' outcomes appear better (the individualist streak!) Expect an attempt to level any apparent differences between individuals and groups. Lastly, expect relatively direct action in response to perceived unfairness.

RELATIONSHIPS, POWER AND CULTURE

The two components of Australian style exist in a state of tension. While individualism emphasizes achievement and individual contributions (equity), a horizontal orientation emphasizes fairness and an equal distribution of resources. One way of reconciling these tensions is provided by Deutsch (1975). Deutsch suggests that concerns for fairness, because they are linked to concerns about equality, dominate relationship-building, whereas concerns about equity dominate task completion, in this case how negotiations are settled. Based on the characterization of Australians as horizontal individualists, two assumptions are possible: (a) for Australians, issues of status leveling are more important in the process of relationship building and (b) issues of equity become more important in settlement. Drawing on these assumptions, I will make some suggestions about how culture influences attributions about the other party, strategy management, and preferences for resource allocation.

Attributions about Negotiating Partners

There is considerable evidence that individualistic and competitive orientations affect how we interpret the behavior of others. Several authors (e.g., Kelley and Stahelski 1970ab) have argued that an individualistic orientation predisposes negotiators to interpret an opponent's moves in terms of power, whereas a cooperative orientation predisposes negotiators to make moral judgements about an opponent's behavior. This means that cooperatively- and individualistically-motivated individuals make quite different attributions about the use of competitive and cooperative strategies. Whereas individualistically-oriented individuals perceive strategic moves in terms of power, equating cooperation with powerlessness, cooperatively-oriented individuals perceive strategic moves in terms of morality, describing competition as bad or wrong (e.g., Kelly and Stahelski 1970ab).

More recently, researchers have argued that differences in orientation affect not only the broad judgments that we make but also how we interpret communication. For example, Tannen (1995) argues that men and women—because of 'cultural differences'—give quite different meanings to the same speech patterns: whereas women use questions to establish and build relationships, for men questions signal a lack of power. One inference from Tannen's (1995) arguments is that individualistically-oriented negotiators are more likely to interpret questions as reflecting power differences.

This analysis identifies one obstacle to collaborative negotiating. It is well-established, in negotiation theory, that information exchange about needs, values and priorities is vital to optimal outcomes. To exchange information requires that at least one negotiator is willing to ask relevant questions (Thompson 1991; Thompson and Hastie 1990). However, in so doing, that person exposes him- or herself to misunderstanding: if an opponent interprets these questions within a power-frame and assumes an advantage, the dynamics of the negotiation are fundamentally altered.

If Australian negotiators see questions as signalling powerlessness, they are less likely to use them. When they do use them, they are more likely to be used as a means for advancing a preferred position, rather than as a means for obtaining information. Furthermore, in interpreting an opponent's use of questions, Australian negotiators may mistakenly conclude that they are more powerful and hold the upper-hand, a perception that will encourage further contentiousness.

Strategy Management

In any negotiation, individuals must balance the need to develop collaborative relationships with the need to divide resources (e.g., Lax and Sebenius 1985). In terms of the framework that I have proposed, negotiators must manage both affinity and power. Some insight into how these dimensions are managed can be gained from stage models of negotiations (Holmes 1992) which identify relationship building (affinity) as critical in the early stages of the negotiation and an outcome focus (power) as gaining importance in the later stages of the negotiation (see Singelis, Triandis, Bhawuk and Gelfand (1995) for a similar argument concerning contextual effects). As the relative weighting of power and affinity shift through the negotiation, a cross-over effect will become evident: as the importance of the vertical-horizontal (power distance) dimension decreases for Australians, it will increase for Asians; simultaneously, as the importance of the individualist-collectivist dimension increases for Australians, it will decrease for Asians.

The implication for cross-cultural negotiations is that each country will be looking for different cues when attempting to interpret the developing relationship. Consequently, the relevant cues are likely to be overlooked or misinterpreted. For example, early in the negotiation, Australians will be searching for status leveling cues as an indication of how their relationship is developing. If, at this stage, Asian negotiators emphasize status or power difference, they are likely to violate Australian relational norms. As a result, they can expect the defensiveness of Australian negotiators to increase.

A second, empirical observation is that individualistically- or competitively-oriented individuals are less sensitive—and consequently less responsive—to strategic differences in their opponents (Kelley and Stahelski 1970ab). In practical terms, this means that individualists are strategically flat: unlike cooperatively-motivated individuals who alter their level of competition in response to opponents' strategies, individualists respond competitively no matter what strategy is adopted by their partners. Again, the implication for cross-cultural negotiations is clear. Because individualists behave contentiously they effectively cause collectivists to shift to contention, thereby escalating conflicts.

While competition has a place in negotiation (e.g., Fisher and Ury 1981; Pruitt 1981), it also has the potential to escalate conflicts, leading to impasse. It becomes especially problematic if the strategic flatness of Australians violates norms of reciprocity, in this case in relation to collaboration. Individualists are unlikely to recognize their strategic flatness. However, Asian negotiators can facilitate a shift to collaboration at two levels. First, they can alter the underlying dynamics of the negotiation. This will be achieved if reciprocal competitiveness is also avoided: do not adopt a tit-for-tat strategy in which positional arguments are made, attacked and defended. Second, in the absence of reciprocal contentiousness, following contentious responses such as positional arguments and demands with priority information or a rejection of the demands will improve joint outcomes (Olekalns and Smith 1996).

Justice and Resource Allocation

Triandis (1995) and others (Singelis *et al.* 1995) link Fiske's (1992) analysis of social relationships to preferences for how resources are divided. Of relevance here is Triandis' argument that horizontal individualism is linked to equality matching and market pricing. *Equality matching*, which prescribes the equal distribution of resources and emphasizes fairness, captures the horizontal orientation of Australian negotiators; *market pricing*, which results in an emphasis on achievement and the distribution of resources according to individual contributions, captures their individualistic nature. Again, we have evidence of the competing pressures faced by Australian negotiators.

Earlier, I proposed that an affinity orientation aligns with a preference for equality, and a power orientation aligns with a preference for equity; I also suggested that for Australian negotiators affinity and equality are major concerns in the relationship building process, whereas power and equity become issues during resource distribution. I would now like to further link these concepts to issues of justice and fairness. For Australians, perceptions of procedural justice will be linked to perceived equality, whereas perceptions of distributive justice will be linked to perceived equity.

First, this means that for Australian negotiators the assessment of procedural fairness will be linked to issues surrounding status and power. Specifically, they will view the negotiation process as fair if these issues are not emphasized. Strategies and communication aimed at status leveling will increase Australian negotiators' satisfaction with the negotiation process. Strategies that emphasize status or power differences will be interpreted as relational violations and may serve to increase contentiousness.

Second, this means that distributive justice will be judged against the criteria used for resource distribution. For Australian negotiators, equity reflects the preference for individual outcomes. Consequently, in the assessment of distributive justice, individual factors such as skills and resources will weigh more heavily than factors associated with power and status. Outcomes will be judged as fair if they reflect these individual differences.

From Theory to Practice

Cultural differences in conflict resolution preferences and negotiating styles have long been a subject for research. To date, however, research has focused on identifying differences between American and Japanese, Asian, South American and European styles of negotiating, or on more fine-grained analyses of differences between Asian countries (e.g., Drake 1995; Elsayed-Ekhouly and Buda 1996; Graham and Sano 1989; Natlandsmyr and Rognes 1995; Tse, Francis, and Walls 1991). Comparisons with Australia are conspicuous by their absence. Given the increasingly frequent interactions between Australia and Asian countries, this seems a major oversight and one which has recently been addressed.

A recent survey of undergraduate students provided a comparison of the conflict resolution preferences of Asian[2] students studying in Australia with those of Australian students. First, consistent with the characterization of Asian cultures as more collectivist than the Australian culture, for Asian students in this sample the least preferred strategy was competing and the two most preferred strategies were avoiding and compromising. For Australian students, a somewhat different pattern emerged: accommodating was the least preferred strategy, while collaborating and compromising were the two most favored strategies (Fletcher 1997).

Comparing the two groups, the results suggested that overall there were more similarities than differences: the groups did not differ in their preferences for accommodating, collaborating, or compromising. This seems like good news for negotiators on both sides of the Pacific. However, two informative differences did emerge: in comparison to the Asian sample, the Australians showed a stronger preference for competing and a lower preference for avoidance (Fletcher 1997). Overall, this pattern suggests that Australian negotiators will adopt a more direct and confrontational approach than their Asian counterparts. Consequently, they may run the risk of damaging the negotiating relationship.

THE AUSTRALIAN NEGOTIATOR

Because of their tendency to focus on their own outcomes, individualists are highly competitive. They are outcome oriented and predisposed to using active or dominating conflict management strategies. Like individualists elsewhere, Australian negotiators will exhibit a fixed-pie bias—the belief that they can gain only at the expense of their opponent. Australian research shows that negotiators are subject to a range of

[2] This survey sampled a group of second-year students at the University of Melbourne. Although it was possible to distinguish between Asian and Australian students, the sample size was too small to allow finer-grained distinctions among Asian countries.

systematic biases that distort their perception of both the available resources and the most appropriate negotiating style.[3]

External Determinants of Negotiated Outcomes

Several factors will exacerbate the view that interests are mutually opposed: when individual negotiators are focused on what they stand to lose, when they are explicitly encouraged to compete, or when they hold more power in the negotiation (Olekalns 1994, 1997; Olekalns and Frey 1994). Under these circumstances, negotiators obtain high outcomes only at the expense of their opponents. When faced with like-minded (contentious) opponents, both parties do poorly, frequently settling for last minute compromises.

An obvious solution is to re-focus negotiators on what they stand to gain, to explicitly encourage cooperation or to redress apparent power imbalances. I would like to say that when this is done, Australian negotiators are transformed into problem-solving individuals, willing to work towards maximizing joint gain. However, the picture is far from clear. Research shows that as the situational factors encouraging cooperation increase, so the behavior of Australian negotiators becomes more unpredictable. More importantly, it becomes difficult to predict outcomes, which range from being extremely poor to being optimal. One conclusion is that in cooperative negotiations, Australian negotiators are confused. They have fewer norms to guide their behavior: once the setting is not congruent with the more competitive orientation that is typical of Australian negotiators, they have no clear 'script' to guide them.

Communication Processes in Negotiation

The extreme variability of negotiators' behavior under conditions of cooperation draws attention to the process by which outcomes are achieved. It suggests that we will better understand the role of situational factors when we understand how they influence communication between negotiators. In the context of conflict resolution, Triandis

[3] The experiments reported in this section are laboratory-based. All experiments employ a widely-used negotiation simulation as a tool for exploring the impact of contextual factors. The simulation requires participants to reach agreement on several issues. The value of these issues is defined by the points that participants earn; a key feature is that issues in the negotiation differ in their priority for the two negotiators.

(1995), along with other authors (Kirkbride, Tang, and Westwood 1991), suggests that individualists are more likely to use a dominating conflict resolution style, full of threats and arguments that highlight the negative consequences of failing to reach agreement. Research investigating how Australians use language in negotiations shows precisely this pattern. Their negotiations are dominated by positional arguing: arguments that support their position or attempt to weaken their opponents' positions, threats, promises, and insults (Olekalns, Smith and Walsh 1996; Olekalns and Smith 1996). In short, classic positional bargaining (Fisher and Ury 1981).

However, against this highly contentious background, more subtle patterns of communication are linked to the quality of negotiated outcomes (Olekalns *et al.* 1996; Olekalns and Smith 1996). Research shows that three factors are influential in determining outcome quality: the frequency with which either positional or priority information occurs; the extent to which it is reciprocated; and the way in which one negotiator responds to another's strategies. Not surprisingly, high levels of positional information result in poor outcomes, whereas high levels of priority information lead to optimal outcomes. Under these conditions, positional reciprocity is a predictor of impasse, and priority reciprocity is a predictor of outcomes that maximize joint gain (Olekalns and Smith 1996).

When four types of outcomes, varying in their quality, are examined, further differences become apparent. Impasse negotiations differ from those that end in distributive agreements in two ways: their access to priority information is greater and their use of concessions is lower. This leads to the conclusion that impasse negotiators are informed but unwilling, whereas win-lose negotiators are willing but uninformed (Olekalns and Smith 1996).

Even when negotiators seem better motivated, they don't always maximize joint gains. Again, two keys differences emerge between negotiators who maximize joint gains (optimizers) and those who fail to do so (sub-optimizers). Optimizers appear willing to take greater risks in their strategy choices, being more likely to use ambiguous and contentious strategies. Essentially, the high level of priority information reciprocity has created a safe environment in which these more ambiguous strategies can be used. Optimizers also appear better able to discriminate the informational value of priority and positional information, consequently showing higher levels of information exchange (Olekalns and Smith 1996).

TOWARDS COLLABORATION: UNDERSTANDING AND MOTIVATING THE AUSTRALIAN NEGOTIATOR

As well as specific effects such as differences in strategy selection, two more general differences between Australians and Asians will influence negotiations: their conversational norms and their underlying motivation for reaching settlement.

Communication and attribution

Remember the Australian tendency to bluntness

We tend to focus more on task-oriented activities and less on relationship-oriented activities (see also Graham and Sano 1989), especially in business settings. We are inclined to launch straight into business talk, without attending to the social niceties. Furthermore, we speak our mind, with little regard for relational consequences. Colloquially, this Australian speech pattern is often referred to as 'calling a spade a bloody shovel'. Australians are blunt, and to others we can appear to be so to the point of rudeness.

Remember that Australians use silence differently

It is perhaps more apt to say that we don't use it at all. We know that individualists find silences uncomfortable and embarrassing. In fact, whenever I undertake conflict management skills training, one of my hardest tasks is to get participants to be silent for a 60-second period! (Graham and Sano (1989) make a similar point in relation to American negotiators.) This means that Australian negotiators are unlikely to allow thinking space; they are much more likely to talk too much and fill in silences.

Meaning is in the message

Drawing on considerable research evidence, Triandis (1995) suggests that for individualists, the meaning is in the message. They focus far more on message content than on message context; consequently, for individualists, little additional meaning is conveyed by the situation in which the message is sent (Singelis and Brown 1995). This means that, in negotiations, Australians will pay little attention to who is present, or whether the negotiations are public or private. For them, the meaning inherent in the message will be the same. Conversely, when evaluating Australian communication, context will not add meaning. For example, a commitment is no less binding for having been made in private.

Status leveling

The more egalitarian approach of Australians will lead them to adopt what could be called status leveling strategies, being more informal and casual. In short, they will display a 'failure' to acknowledge status differences. For Asian negotiators, this may well appear as a relational violation. They should bear in mind two issues: do not look for cues that acknowledge status and do not interpret this lack of acknowledgement as a slight on the part of Australian negotiators. Recognize and accept the more casual and informal style of Australians for what it is.

Motivation and outcome preferences

Competition is important and status comes from achievements

For Australians, status accrues from getting a 'good deal', in order to save what has been described as self-face (Triandis 1995). Follow the prescriptions of Ury, Brett and Goldberg (1989) and assist in face-saving: make it clear what the negotiating team is gaining. For as long as negotiators are focused on their losses (profits, power, status) they will remain competitive to save face. Reframe the negotiation in terms of gains, literally.

Do not use persuasive arguments based on the need for cooperation

Persuasive arguments based on the need to maintain equity are more likely to appeal to Australians' motivation. This should not, however, be interpreted to mean that Australian negotiators cannot be shifted to cooperation. Rather, consider the framing of such messages. Do not make direct appeals to cooperation to shift negotiator perspective. Rather, in the spirit of a cost benefit analysis, demonstrate the advantages of cooperation and lead negotiators indirectly to collaboration by attending to the sequencing of strategies.

The Oz Psyche

There are several additional factors that are likely to shape the behavior of Australian negotiators. More importantly, these factors will affect how they interpret and react to their Asian negotiating partners.

The experienced negotiator

First, Australians are acutely aware that negotiation is far more a part of Asian culture than it is of Australian culture. Generally, this leaves us feeling disadvantaged—on the 'back foot'—and creates a level of defensiveness and guardedness. I have seen a similar phenomenon emerge repeatedly in my experimental work. Two negotiators 'discover' that on a particular issue, they are in complete agreement; they actually want the same thing! Rather than accepting this, each appears to believe that the other must be misrepresenting the situation to his or her own advantage. The result is a settlement that is less than optimal. The lesson for cross-cultural negotiations is that Australian negotiators will be less likely to take strategies, tactics, or proposals at face value; they will be alert to the possibility that seemingly good proposals somehow disadvantage or exploit them.

Second language is an issue

A further issue, raised by Graham (1996) in relation to Japanese-American negotiations, is the availability of a second language. Graham found that American negotiators, observing interchanges in Japanese, believed that those discussions centered around them. In fact, they were attempts to deal with translation difficulties, or discussions about the nature of the Japanese offers. Thus, according to Graham, this was a 'good' sign misinterpreted as a bad sign. These conditions can potentially give rise to what have been called paranoid cognitions (Kramer 1994), creating an escalation in mistrust—a bad outcome for negotiations

Time frames

Finally, Asia Pacific countries differ from Australia and New Zealand in their time perspective. Not only is there a widely-held, popular belief that Asia Pacific countries have a more long-term and less time-pressured approach to negotiations, but more recently Hofstede (1991) has shown that these countries do, indeed differ in their long-term orientation. This means that we are likely to encounter a difference in strategies that stems from a stronger task-focus on the part of Australian negotiators. I have already mentioned this trait in relation to the bluntness of Australians, which is one manifestation of their greater short-term task orientation.

AUSTRALIAN ORGANISATIONS: SHIFTING CULTURAL PERSONALITIES

Negotiations with Australian managers must be placed within the context of prevailing cultural norms, described earlier. It would, however, be remiss to ignore the moderating influence of organizational culture. As Graham and Sano (1989) point out, negotiating styles differ across Japanese industries. The same can be expected of Australian companies. Organizations are key stakeholders in any bargaining context and individuals negotiating on behalf of their organizations will need to bargain for organizationally-determined outcomes.

Paralleling a now familiar theme, power distribution and resource allocation rules can be used to construct a two-dimensional typology of organizations (Kabanoff 1991). This yields four types of organizations:

- *elite* organizations such as bureaucracies have unequal power distribution and support vertical relationships, favoring resource distribution based on equity;
- *leadership-focused* organizations such as the armed forces, are also characterized by the unequal distribution of power and favor equality;
- *meritocratic* organizations are characterized by the equal distribution of power, support horizontal relationships and favor equity allocation rules; and
- *collegial* organizations such as universities, are also characterized by the equal distribution of power but favor equality.

Of these, the most compatible with the Australian type (as I have described it) is the meritocratic organization. Like horizontal individualists, these organizations have equal power distribution and adopt equity-based allocation rules. Such organizations reinforce the prevailing cultural traits. The remaining three organizational types will either reinforce or balance some aspects of the Australian personality. For example, in

Table 10.1 The impact of organizational culture on the Australian 'personality'

Organizational Type	Definition		Impact on Personality	
	power balance	allocation rule	power distance	individualism
meritocratic	equal	equity	reinforce	reinforce
leader-focused	unequal	equality	balance	balance
elite	unequal	equity	balance	reinforce
collegial	equal	equality	reinforce	balance

collegial organizations the prevailing norms regarding status will be reinforced, while the drive towards maximizing individual outcomes will be lessened by organizational norms that emphasize equality (see also Table 10.1)

Each organizational type has different norms and values, implying that the argumentation and logic of negotiations must be adapted to match the messages organizations are most willing to 'hear'. Based on Kabanoff's (1991) analysis of these organizations, Australian negotiators placed in these organizations will be most responsive to the following arguments and strategies:

- *Elite organizations give additional importance to vertical relationships.* For these organizations status and hierarchy will dominate the assessment of equity. More than negotiators in other kinds of organizations, negotiators in these organizations should be responsive to power-based arguments.
- *Leadership-focused organizations reorient individuals to group outcomes and issues of status.* Consequently, individuals in these organizations should be more sensitive to power and status differences, as well as being more receptive to influence attempts that appeal to cooperation. Arguments appealing to a common vision, as well personal appeals, should be especially persuasive.
- *Meritocratic organizations reinforce the Australian characteristics of horizontal individualism.* These organizations stress core values. Persuasive arguments should be congruent with, rather than violating, those values. Such core values can be used to create a common vision and to establish the benefits of a proposed settlement. Because individual skills, attributes and contributions are dominant, individuals in meritocracies will be more responsive to rights-based arguments.

- *Collegial organizations highlight the importance of collective outcomes.* Of all the organizational types that I have considered, these are the most likely to offset the Australian trait of individualism and to foster an atmosphere of collaboration. A watchpoint in negotiating with negotiators from these organizations is that they may be less motivated to examine and expand available settlement options: the individualist's interpretation of collaboration is often compromise! More than any organizational type, the collegial organization should increase an individual negotiators' receptivity to arguments based on underlying needs, as well as the need for collaboration.

Bureaucracy in Conflict: Inside an Australian Organization

Little research has examined organizational conflict within Australia. One such study analyzed both the causes of and responses to conflicts within a large, Australia-wide public-sector organization (Gaylard 1994). Bureacracies, which are elite organizations, counterbalance the horizontal orientation of Australians. Instead, they reinforce power differences and a more competitive style of conflict resolution. This greater emphasis on power and status is apparent in organizational conflict management. Research investigating manager-employee disputes shows that employees prefer an obliging (yielding) strategy, even though they believe this to benefit managers. Managers believe that any action on their part will benefit their employees. However, they rate active styles as less harmful to themselves, and consequently prefer these over more passive styles of conflict management (Gaylard 1994). Both patterns are consistent with an unequal power structure in which most of the benefits flow to the more powerful party.

AUSSIES AND KIWIS: THE SAME BUT DIFFERENT?

Applying any of the classificatory schemes that I have already described would lead to the conclusion that Australians and New Zealanders are more alike than different. In comparison with the Asian countries discussed in other chapters, both are horizontal individualists. However, a closer look reveals subtle differences that should not be ignored. In comparison with Australians, New Zealanders are characterized by lower power distance and scored lower scores on the individualism dimension; that is to say, status and hierarchy are even less important and the emphasis on individual outcomes is lower for New Zealanders, than is the case for Australians; in addition, New Zealanders are less task-focused being the same as Australians only in that New Zealanders also adopt a short-term perspective.

The New Zealand conflict resolution style has been the subject of even less research than the Australian style.[4] Most empirical work has focused on Maori-Pakeha relationships and the resolution of race-related conflicts. It is unclear how much insight this provides into the conflict management styles of New Zealanders. We must bear in mind that a considerable proportion of these conflicts are resolved within a formal, legislative arena and center on the interpretation of Maori rights, as set out in the Treaty of Waitangi.

Having lived for several years in New Zealand, I can make some outsider observations about the conflict management style of New Zealanders. I should stress that these are highly personal observations, and may of course reflect cultural differences in the attributions made about the behaviors that I observed. With this qualification, I would say that my strongest impression of New Zealanders is their extreme individualism, Hofstede's classification notwithstanding. I would describe this individualism as passive, in that it manifests itself implicitly rather than explicitly.

The espoused cultural norm is one of cooperation. New Zealanders would certainly describe themselves as collaborative and focused on group goals—hence the lower score on Hofstede's individualism scale. There is a strong component of social desirability in this. In an experimental setting, my colleagues and I observed a similar phenomenon when we attempted to classify New Zealanders as belonging to one of three social motivational orientations: cooperators, competitors or individualists. Although an even larger than expected proportion of the group were classified as cooperators (people who value joint gain), their behavior said otherwise! For example, McClintock and Allison (1989) reported that, when asked how many additional hours they would

[4] Note that some of the research described in an earlier section was conducted by the author while she was at the University of Otago in New Zealand. This research suggests that, like individualists elsewhere, New Zealand negotiators fall prey to a range of cognitive biases.

participate in experiments, cooperators nominated significantly more than either competitors or individualists. We, however, found that our 'cooperators' were just as likely to forget about their experimental commitments as individualists and competitors; what's more, if they did participate in experiments, in general they behaved no more cooperatively than the other groups.

The lesson that I would like to draw from this is that, in negotiating with New Zealanders, you will experience apparent cooperation. Be aware that underlying this cooperation is a very strong streak of competitiveness. Cooperation emerges as the dominant strategy only to the extent that it is able to serve a competitive purpose—maximizing individual outcomes.

A FINAL WORD

In this chapter, I have explored how two dimensions—individualism-collectivism and horizontal-vertical social relationships—influence the Australian negotiating style. This exploration has considered the frame that these dimensions will create and how this frame will filter our perception of negotiation strategies and outcomes. In doing so, I have suggested that the two dimensions carry different meanings for Australians and Asians. Perhaps because it is an individualist's preoccupation, I have placed considerable emphasis on how these frames will affect the resource allocation procedure, treating strategies as a means to an end. This is not to say that procedural considerations are unimportant to Australian negotiators. The emphasis on fairness and justice that arises from their highly egalitarian nature means that how they are achieved will contribute to their assessment of the final outcome. Consequently, the *how* of negotiation cannot be neglected for the more tangible *what*.

ACKNOWLEDGEMENTS

This chapter was prepared while the author was on sabbatical at the Center for Decision Making Research at the University of Chicago, and the Department of Psychology at the University of Illinois at Urbana-Champaign. I would like to thank Josh Klayman and Peter Carnevale for their support during my visits to these universities.

REFERENCES

Carroll, J.S. and Payne, J.W. 1991. An information processing approach to two-party negotiations. In Sheppard, B.H., Bazerman, M.H. and Lewicki, R.J. (eds.), *Research on Negotiation in Organizations* (**vol. 3**). Greenwich, CT: JAI Press Inc.

Carnevale, P.J. and Pruitt, D.G. 1992. Negotiation and mediation, *Annual Review of Psychology*, **43**, 531–82.

Deutsch, M. 1975. Equity, equality and need: What determined which value will be used as the basis for distributive justice?, *Journal of Social Issues*, **31**, 137–49.

Deutsch, M. 1973. *The Resolution of Conflict*. New Haven, CT: Yale University Press.

Drake, L.E. 1995. Negotiation styles in intercultural communication, *The International Journal of Conflict Management*, **6**, 72–90.

Elysayed-Ekhouly, S.M. and Buda, R. 1996. Organizational conflict: A comparative analysis of conflict styles across cultures, *The International Journal of Conflict Management*, **7**, 71–81.

Feather, N.T. 1993. The rise and fall of political leaders: Attributions, deservingness, personality and affect, *Australian Journal of Psychology*, **45**, 61–8

Fisher, R.J. 1994. Generic principles for resolving intergroup conflict, *Journal of Social Issues*, **50**, 47–66.

Fisher, R. and Ury, W. 1981. *Getting to Yes: Negotiating Agreement without Giving In*, Britain: Arrow Press.

Fiske, A.P. 1992. The four elementary forms of sociality: Framework for a unified theory of social relations, *Psychological Review*, **99**, 689–723.

Fletcher, L. 1997. *Cross-cultural Differences in Conflict Resolution Styles: An Asian-Australian Comparison*. Unpublished Honors dissertation, University of Melbourne.

Gaylard, A. 1994. *Superior-subordinate Conflict Management: Predicting Process and Outcomes*. Unpublished Masters dissertation, University of Melbourne.

Graham, J.L. 1996. *Vis-a-vis. International Business Negotiations*. Unpublished manuscript. Graduate School of Management, University of California, Irvine.

Graham, J.L. and Sano, Y. 1989. *Smart Bargaining: Doing Business with the Japanese*. Los Angeles, CA: Sano Management Corporation.

Hofstede, G. 1991. *Culture and Organizations. Software of the Mind.* London: McGraw-Hill.

Holmes, M.E. 1992. Phase structures in negotiation, In Putnam, L.L. and Roloff M.E. (eds.), *Communication and Negotiation*, Newbury Park, CA: Sage Publications.

Kabanoff, B. 1991. Equity, equality, power and conflict, *Academy of Management Review*, **16**, 416–41.

Kelley, H.H. and Stahelski, A.J. 1970a. Social interaction basis of cooperators' and competitors' beliefs about others, *Journal of Personality and Social Psychology*, **7**, 401–19.

Kelley, H.H. and Stahelski, A.J. 1970b. Errors in perception of intentions in mixed-motive games, *Journal of Experimental Social Psychology*, **6**, 379–400.

Kirkbride, P.S., Tang, S.F.Y. and Westwood, R.I. 1991. Chinese conflict preferences and negotiating behavior: Cultural and psychological influences, *Organization Studies*, **12**, 365–85.

Kramer, R. 1994. The sinister attribution error: Paranoid cognition and collective dissent in organizations, *Motivation and Emotion*, **18**, 199–230.

Larrick, R.P. and Blount, S. 1995. Social context in tacit bargaining games. In Kramer, R. and Messick, D. (eds.), *Negotiation in its Social Context*. Thousand Oaks, Sage Publications.

Lax, D. and Sebenius, J. 1986. *The Manager as Negotiator*. New York: Free Press.

Lewicki, R.J. and Litterer, J.A. 1985. *Negotiation*. Homewood, IL: Irwin.

McAlister, L., Bazerman, M. and Fader, P. 1986. Power and goal setting in channel negotiations, *Journal of Marketing Research*, **23**, 228–36.

McClintock, C.G. and Allison, S.T. 1989. Social value orientations and helping behavior, *Journal of Applied Social Psychology*, **19**, 353–63.

Nankervis, A.R., Compton, R.L. and McCarthy, T.E. 1996. *Strategic Human Resource Management* (Second edition). Melbourne: Nelson Publishing Company.

Natslansmyr, J.H. and Rognes, J. 1995. Culture, behavior and negotiation outcomes: A comparative and cross-cultural study of Mexican and Norwegian negotiators, *The International Journal of Conflict Management*, **6**, 5–29.

Olekalns, M. 1994. Context, issues and frames as determinants of negotiated outcomes, *British Journal of Social Psychology*, **33**, 197–210.

Olekalns, M. 1997. Situational cues as moderators of the frame-outcome relationship, *British Journal of Social Psychology*, **36**, 191–209.
Olekalns, M. and Smith, P.L. 1996. Strategic sequences and outcome optimality in negotiation. *Paper Presented at the 1996 Academy of Management Meeting*, Cincinnati, Ohio.
Olekalns, M., Smith, P.L. and Walsh, T. 1996. The process of negotiating: Strategies and timing as predictors of outcome, *Organizational Behavior and Human Decision Processes*, **67**.
Olekalns, M. and Frey, B. 1994. Power, frame and negotiated outcomes, *European Journal of Social Psychology*, **24**, 403–16.
Pinkley, R.L. and Northcraft, G.B. 1994. Conflict frames of reference: Implications for dispute resolution and outcomes, *Academy of Management Journal*, **37**, 193–205.
Pruitt, D.G. 1981. *Negotiation Behavior*. New York: Academic Press, Ltd.
Putnam, L.L. 1990. Reframing integrative and distributive bargaining: A process perspective, *Research on Negotiation in Organizations*, **2**, 3–30.
Putnam, L.L. and Holmer, M. 1992. Framing and reframing in negotiations, In Putnam, L.L. and Roloff, M.E. (eds.), *Communication and Negotiation*, Newbury Park, CA: Sage Publications.
Putnam, L.L. and Wilson, S.R. 1989. Argumentation and bargaining strategies as discriminators of integrative outcomes, In Rahim, M.A.(ed.), *Managing Conflict: An Interdisciplinary Approach*, New York, Praeger.
Robinson, S.L., Kraatz, M.S. and Rousseau, D.M. 1994. Changing obligations and the psychological contract: A longitudinal study, *Academy of Management Journal*, **37**, 137–52.
Singelis, T.M. and Brown, W.J. 1995. Culture, self, and collectivist communication: Linking culture to individual behavior, *Human Communication Research*, **21**, 354–89.
Singelis, T.M., Triandis, H.C., Bhawuk, D.P.S. and Gelfand, M.J. 1995. Horizontal and vertical dimensions of individualism and collectivism: A theoretical and measurement refinement, *Cross-cultural Research*, **29**, 240–75.
Tannen, D. 1995. The power of talk: Who gets heard and why, *Harvard Business Review*, **73**, 138–48.
Thompson, L. 1991. Information exchange in negotiation, *Journal of Experimental Social Psychology*, **27**, 161–79.
Thompson, L. 1990. Negotiation behavior and outcomes: Empirical evidence and theoretical issues, *Psychological Bulletin*, **108**, 515–32.

Thompson, L. and Hastie, R. 1990. Social perception in negotiation, *Organizational Behavior and Human Decision Processes*, **47**, 98–123.
Triandis, H.C. 1995. *Individualism and Collectivism*. Boulder, CO: Westview Press.
Tse, D.K., Francis, J. and Walls, J. 1994. Cultural differences inconducting intra- and inter-cultural negotiations: A Sino-Canadian comparison, *Journal of International Business Studies*, 537–55.
Ury, W., Brett, J.M. and Goldberg, S.B. 1989. *Getting Disputes Resolved*. San Fransisco, CA, Jossey-Bass.
Weingart, L.R., Bennett, R.J. and Brett, J.M. 1993. The impact of consideration of issues and motivational orientation in group negotiation process and outcome, *Journal of Applied Psychology*, **78**, 504–17.
Wilson, S.R. and Putnam, L.L. 1990. Interaction goals in negotiation, *Communication Yearbook*, **13**, 374–406.

C H A P T E R   E L E V E N

North American Conflict Management

JAMES A. WALL, JR. and JOHN STARK
University of Missouri, USA

And God said unto them, 'Be fruitful and multiply, and replenish the earth and subdue it: and have dominion over the fish of the sea, and over the fowl of the air, and over every living thing that moveth upon the earth.'

Genesis 1:28

'Winning isn't everything; it's the only thing.'

Vince Lombardi

How do a people who embrace such ideas manage their conflicts? In this chapter we'll attempt to answer this question and when doing so we'll draw upon the process delineated in Fig. 11.1. North Americans, it will be noted, view and perceive conflict very favorably because of their 'competitive' norms and values. When they find themselves in conflict, Americans behave as if they are in a win-lose sporting event. And in their management of the conflict, they are very self-oriented and rational. When their self-management of the conflict fails they turn to formal adjudication (i.e., the courts). Third-party assistance is a continual option for the disputants—early as well as late in the conflict—yet, as the dashed arrows indicate, it is a road less traveled for conflict management.

Consider now the North Americans' competitive biases.

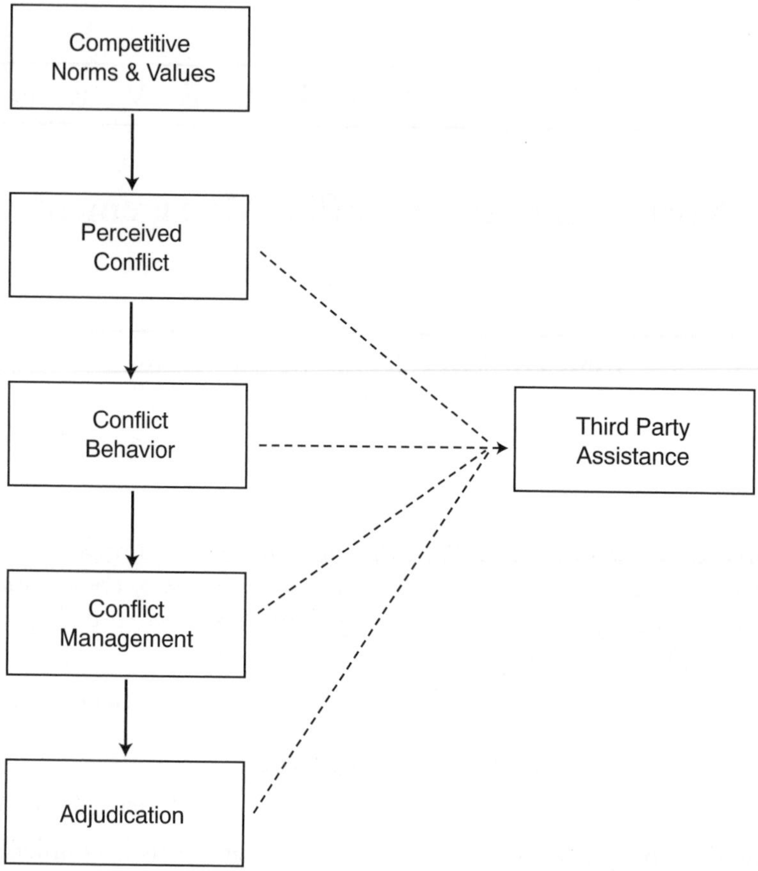

Figure 11.1 North American Conflict and its Management

COMPETITIVE NORMS AND VALUES

North Americans enjoy, value, and are comfortable with competition, which is spawned by a number of factors. One is the Judeo-Christian religion. Herein, God intends for man to subdue the earth and to be good. He is—in the process—expected to fight evil.

Another factor contributing to the North Americans' competitiveness is their pioneer heritage. Discovering, getting to, and settling North America was no easy task. And once settled, the land—which was here for the 'taking'—needed to be 'tamed'.

The successful taming of the wilderness perpetuated competition in three ways. First, competition was important in operationalizing freedom. For early settlers the capability to live completely as they wanted was not much of a challenge, as there was plenty of room in the new land and those small groups that did congregate tended to live by the same beliefs (the pilgrims in Virginia, the Quakers in Pennsylvania, etc.). However, as the population increased (especially in the prime areas along the coasts and along the main river routes) people of differing ideas came in contact with one another. These differences were quite often 'ironed out' in a competitive fashion (Zucker 1986).

A second interface is salient in the 'Do or Die' spirit of the pioneers. They believed it was their 'manifest destiny' to tame and control the new land; accordingly, they felt with enough hard work and persistence any obstacle could be overcome. This competitive spirit—overcoming the land—was strongly reinforced with success. Armed with the vision of a better life, the conviction that control was possible, and a determination to see any effort through, the settlers tamed the area which was to become the United States and Canada, becoming quite prosperous in the process.

Finally, as they tamed the wilderness, prairies, mountains, and woodlands the Americans also conquered the current inhabitants—beasts and Native Americans. At this last task, North Americans were quite successful (with substantial assistance from smallpox); consequently, this competitive behavior was well reinforced. And in the process of taming the land, its beasts, and its inhabitants, Americans developed an ample set of action-heros such as Daniel Boone and Buffalo Bill, who exemplified the payoffs from competition and violence.

Just as religion and the pioneer heritage have ingrained the value of competitiveness, so have America's wars. For the most part, war has been good to Americans and has socialized them to appreciate competition and conflict. The Revolutionary War gave the U.S. its beginning, and the War of 1812, like the Spanish-American War and War with Mexico, allowed the U.S. to defend (and expand) its borders and to develop national cohesion. The U.S. Civil War, which was costly in casualties, preserved the Union. In World Wars I and II and the Korean Police Action, the U.S. and Canada were able to achieve victory and generate heroes on other shores. Only in Vietnam did the U.S. question the value of war and probably, if the U.S. had won, it's citizens would be praising it and claiming William Westmoreland and Earl Wheeler (generals in that war) as heroes.

In addition to the influence of religion, history and war in generating an appreciation of competition, the North American economies have also encouraged competition. While neither is 'purely competitive' both, relative to most world economies, are perceived as 'competitive' (Samuelson 1985). For the most part, firms in these economies are allowed to compete with each other for customers, knowledge, capital, land, and labor. Likewise, customers are allowed to compete for goods and services in the open market. While various sectors of the economies are owned or strictly controlled by the government, most sectors are perceived as competitive arenas, wherein capitalists, managers, and workers get what they 'earn'. And in this arena, our folk heroes—Lee Iacocca, Bill Gates, Ross Perot—are those whose firms 'won' over the competitors.

Such an economy determines the winners or losers; here, risk and competition are expected and accepted. It is also anticipated that the 'best man will ultimately win'. In this arena, society takes steps to ensure that all involved know the rules by which the game will be played, that all involved will play fairly, and that unfair competition will be punished. The focus here is not to prevent competitive clashes, rather it is to make them as fair as possible.

As America's religion, history, war and economy have ingrained competition into its values, so have its sports. For North Americans, 'sports' are equated with 'competitions', without a second thought. It seems obvious to them, even if it is not so obvious to many other world citizens. This differential perception became obvious in a local recreational center. There were three on-going basketball games: one among American college students, one among a group of Korean college students, and a third among some American youngsters (10–12 years in age). What stood out was the 'play' on the Korean court. The ten players, together, moved from one end of the court to the other. There were no fast breaks; rather, lots of passes. When it became apparent that a player was prepared to shoot, his opponents let him do so. However, he was not allowed to take an uncontested short shot. If a shot was made, the entire team (and most of the opponents) clapped. Then the opposing team was allowed to bring the ball down court unmolested, to follow through with a similar ritual.

What was happening on the American students' court? Here the rules were different, and the 'play' was a competition. Everyone was out for himself, and sometimes out for his team. There was a lot of arguing about the rights a person had (e.g., to take a fast break without a foul) and violations of the rules (e.g., traveling). The score was always very important, for winning was the goal. And the loser paid the price of having to leave the floor so that the winner could take on the new challenger.

Having watched the two older student games—play versus competition—it was interesting to observe the American youngsters. Each was attempting to develop his individual talents, dribbling or shooting well. As a last resort a player passed to a teammate. In short, they were well on their way to becoming competitive individualists.

The characteristics and comparisons observed on two of those three courts are quite indicative of North American sports. North Americans expect their teams to be competitive, to win, to beat the other team. Winning, not cooperation is the goal, and 'players' are expected to strive forcefully toward this goal. When the team is winning—whipping the opponent—a major consideration is which individual is making the major contribution. Who is the top scorer, the most valuable player?

As religion, the pioneer heritage, history and sports have engendered North Americans' competitiveness, the system of government has further ingrained it within the society. Because Americans are wary of concentrated power, they divide government power into levels (federal, state/province, local) that have different, yet overlapping areas of influence. The overlap plays the levels against one another and allows each level to hold the others in check. Each level of government is further broken into branches (typically executive, legislative, and judicial sections), which offset and are offset by the others. Competition between these various levels and branches not only serves to prevent any one area from becoming too powerful; it also prevents policy from swinging radically to one extreme of the political spectrum.

Also in both Canada and the U.S., representatives to the governments are selected by competitive elections. The selections pit the aspirants to political office against one another so as to bring out their ideas and to produce government representatives who heed and reflect the desires of their constituents.

The competition in government does not end with the design of government and the selection of representatives. Continually, the United States and Canada use competition to form their government policy and laws. Through the legislative process—which involves voting on competing measures—competition provides debates on the relevant issues, and is intended to facilitate the selection of optimal laws and policies.

How effective is this system? Daily, Americans debate this question, especially when the government moves slowly or blunders visibly. Yet when a fault is detected in a government unit, or with a person or political party, the cause is often held to be an excessive concentration of power or the lack of oversight by another (countervailing) unit. And the cure is usually the creation and empowerment of a unit that will bring the offending segment into alignment.

PERCEIVED CONFLICT

Given their strong competitive biases, North Americans, it seems, might automatically slip from high levels of competitiveness into similar levels of conflict. This is not the case; rather, competition seems to seep sluggishly into conflict.

One reason for this 'sluggish seep' is that North Americans seldom draw a strong distinction between competition and conflict. To most North Americans, conflict is simply a heated form of competition and there is an ambiguous overlap between the processes, as depicted in Fig. 11.2.

By the same token, North Americans tend to rate interactions as competitions, rather than as conflicts. As depicted in Fig. 11.3, North Americans (versus East Asians) are more apt to locate various interactions (e.g., who is promoted, which firm gets the sale) on the left side of the competition/conflict continuum.

Not only do they distinguish vaguely between competition and conflict, and tend to rate interactions as competitions, North Americans also tend to perceive competition and conflict positively. Both are felt to be valuable. The exact representation of these ratings (versus those of East Asians) is somewhat inexact; yet we feel they resemble the pattern laid out in Fig. 11.4.

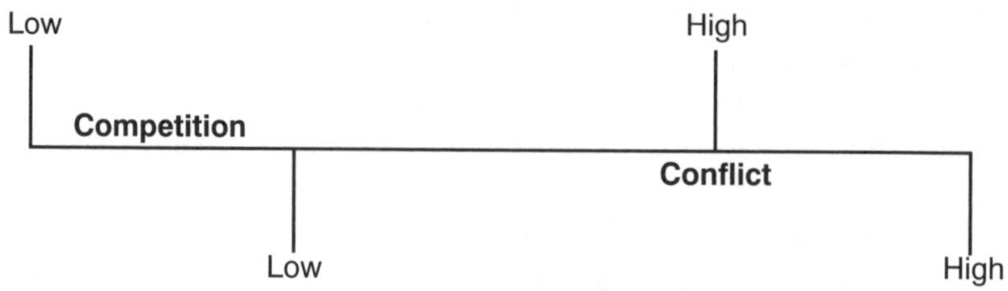

Figure 11.2 The Competition-Conflict Overlap

The bell-shaped curve graphically represents the notion that North Americans feel a moderate level of competition is better than no competition. And up to a point, the more competition, the better. The long zenith of the curve indicates the lack of distinction between competition and conflict as well as the opinion that rigorous competition (or a touch of conflict) is an asset. This opinion was reflected well in a recent statement by a U.S. Defense Department official who stated that without competition people naturally get lazy (Dupont 1997). By contrast, East Asians—as the negatively-sloped curve indicates—place much less value on competition and conflict. To them, harmony and cooperation are valued (for example, we found that Koreans place a very high value on mutual cooperation in the community and workplace; Kim, Wall, Sohn and Kim 1993; Sohn and Wall 1993). In general they feel that the greater the competition and conflict, the more deleterious the relationship.

A second reason for the 'sluggish seep' between competition and conflict is that North Americans have developed various legal techniques to control conflict (i.e., to keep it from becoming excessive). One is the modern contract. In contracts, the parties precisely lay out

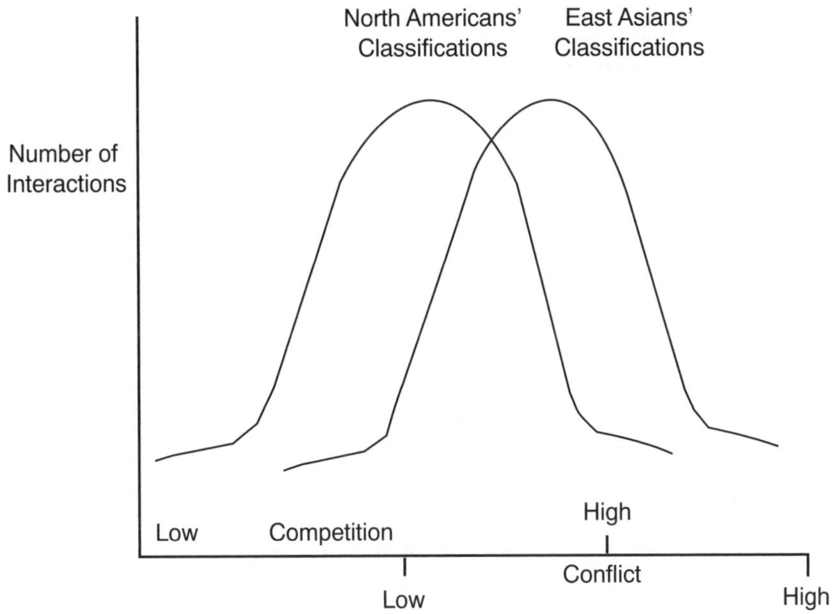

Figure 11.3 Ratings of Interactions

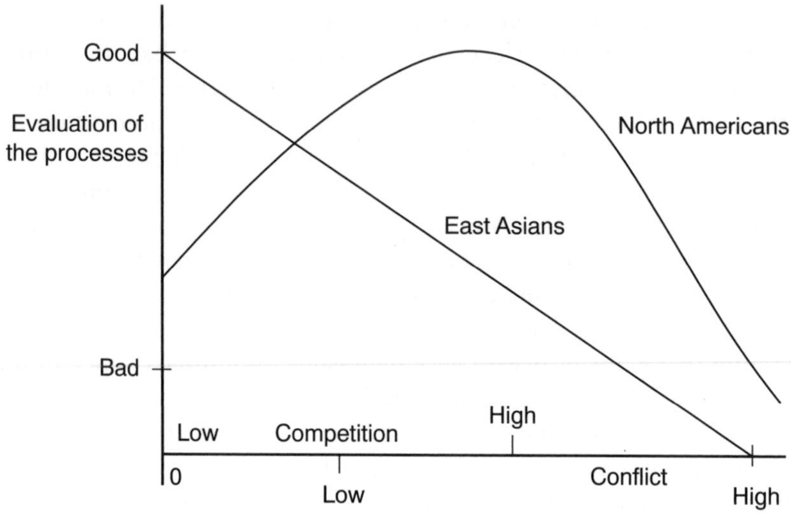

Figure 11.4 Evaluations of Competition and Conflict

the intent of their endeavor, how the duties and rewards of the effort are to be split, and how differences will be resolved, should they arise. The good faith and fair dealing basis of these modern contracts is seen similarly in both the U.S. and Canada (National Law Review 1995). Contracts help to ensure peace and justice by establishing the rules of conduct, so that the parties' behaviors do not degenerate into conflict.

Insurance is another tool for the control of conflict in the United States and Canada. While contracts attempt to provide a fair, stable competitive interaction, insurance has more of a 'do-over' focus. If a contract is not sufficient for controlling conflict, insurance can provide a way to reinstate the injured party. In this way conflict is controlled because any damages which would lead to conflict are prepaid by the insurance.

A third tool for the control of conflict in these two countries is the use of formal third parties in transactions. As opposed to the Japanese (Callister and Wall 1997; Jones 1995), North Americans formalize third party relationships. A formal intermediary not only helps to ensure fairness, it also reduces the need to trust the other party in the transaction. In this technique, a party outside of the original transaction (a bank, broker, expeditor, etc.) is used as a buffer between the dealing parties.

We have argued that North Americans move very hesitantly into the conflict arena; yet, once they are there, how do they behave?

CONFLICT BEHAVIOR

The answer has five components: first, when in conflict, Americans address their dispute *openly*. A disputant, Americans feel, should be forthright enough to say what is wrong, what he wants, and why he is disturbed. As opposed to their Japanese counterparts, North Americans do not place a high value on vagueness and subtlety. (Honna and Hoffer 1989.)

Secondly, a moderate amount of emotion will be displayed, because Americans feel they have a right to express themselves. Instead of being viewed as uncouth, emotional displays are held to be a valid mechanism for personal venting and an acceptable method of communication. The displays should not be excessive, because these would indicate a lack or loss of self-control. But it is felt that emotional displays can be used tactically not only to communicate with the opponent but also to put him on the defensive, or to embarrass him.

Thirdly, each disputant will *focus on him or herself* (not on either group) because they view themselves as individuals, rather than as a member of a larger collective (Triandis 1996). Americans perceive that a conflict exists because the opponent is blocking some personal goal or outcome. Consequently, Americans perceive the goal is to overcome or eliminate the obstacle and to acquire the outcome for themselves.

Fourth, because they are self-oriented and seek personal benefits from exchanges with others, North Americans focus on the facts in the conflict rather than on personal etiquette in the conflict (Moran and Abbott 1994). That is, they're concerned with the rules as well as with what they deserve, what they have, what they have given up, and what they have a right to receive.

Finally, because of their person orientation, North Americans assume private ownership of the conflict (Augsburg 1992) and maintain the right to deal with it, by themselves, and as they wish.

Given the above orientation to conflict and their own personal outcomes in it, what is the American attitude toward the opponents' outcomes? Many scholars maintain that the American disputant holds a win-loss perceptual frame in which a gain to self is felt to result in an equal loss to the opponent. A more realistic explanation, we feel, is that most American disputants give very little thought as to how their own gain affects the opponent's outcomes. For example, consider a dispute between a group of residents and the State Bureau of Corrections over the location of a half-way house. The residents do not want the half-way house located in their neighborhood, because it will reduce real estate values. In framing this dispute, no resident will conclude that not locating the half way house nearby so as to maintain existing house values will impose a cost on the Corrections Bureau. Probably the individual resident knows it will cost the Bureau somewhat more to locate elsewhere; however, she does not know how much more. Nor does she care.

This perception of or attitude toward the opponent's outcomes changes radically when the disputant reflects upon gains in the opponent's outcomes. Here she frames the relationship as (at least) win-lose. That is, she feels, or fears, the opponent's gain will result in an equal loss to herself.

Very rarely does the disputant perceive the relationship of her own outcomes and that of the opponent (other) to be independent as represented in Fig. 11.5. Rather, they tend to view the total outcomes in a relationship as interdependent such that an increase in one's outcomes

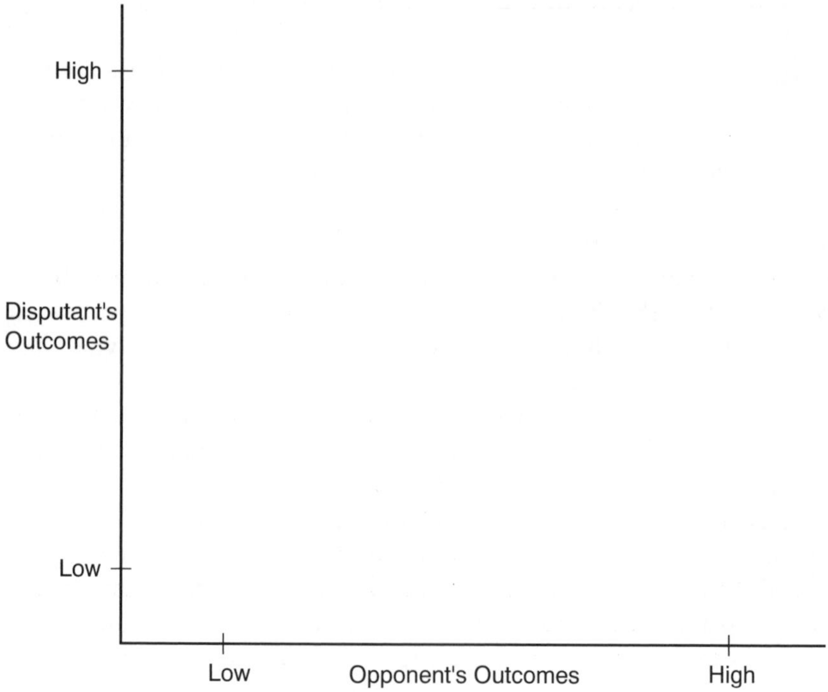

Figure 11.5 Independent Relationship Between Disputant's and Opponent's Outcomes, Indicated by the Right Angle Comparison

dictates some decrease in the other's. We emphasize this point because the development of Blake and Mouton's Grid (1984) along with Kilmann and Thomas' (e.g., 1977) work have perhaps conduced many scholars and practitioners into thinking that disputants visualize the world as we academics represent it.

Objectively delineated, the relationship between most disputants' outcomes and those of their respective opponents is independent and in this relationship (a) one disputant's increase does *not* come at an equal cost to the other, and herein (b) there is an opportunity to raise the joint outcomes. Yet disputants do not perceive the conflict relationship and process in this way. To them, it's 'my gain is perhaps some loss to you' and 'your gain is definitely an equal or worse loss to me.'

Because of this mind set Americans view conflict as an opportunity to beat the opponent. Beating the opponent not only allows Americans to raise their own outcomes, it simultaneously allows them to savor the victory.

CONFLICT MANAGEMENT

Once the disputant and opponent shift from conflict behavior to conflict management, how do they behave? Because they believe in 'heads-up', open competition and personal ownership of the conflict, they most often choose to handle it themselves. That is, disputants in North America, unlike their counterparts in China, (Wall and Blum 1991) typically do not turn to third parties unless they are *un*able to resolve/manage the conflict themselves or if the conflict is very costly.

As they attempt to resolve their 'own' conflict, how do the disputants proceed?

Specific Approaches

Because they are rationally oriented and think of conflict somewhat as a mechanical process—with causes and effects—North Americans frequently address the causes. In doing so, they rethink and perhaps modify their own goals so that they don't block those of the other.

A second, very rational, approach is to think through the core process. When they find themselves at loggerheads with each other, the disputants on occasion step back from the conflict and try to view it objectively (like a car that overheats). In doing so they often conclude that people and groups quite naturally have different goals, and it is only rational that they pursue those goals. With this rational conclusion in mind, the disputants each attempt to maintain self-control and seek to resolve or work around the conflict. Each tries to understand the opponent's goals and goal-oriented behavior.

Thirdly, the disputants often choose to deal with the results of the conflict. North Americans have a strong tendency to conclude that conflict (e.g., enhanced competition) is natural. It's like a machine that's running hard; it heats up. Therefore, they live with conflict, attempting to keep it from becoming too destructive. For instance, when a disputant finds the opponent is angry, he listens to her and coolly explains his own position, without giving in. Disputants meet openly to state their positions and clear the air. And, not unimportantly, opponents call upon each other to be 'good sports'.

As they take the above steps, disputants take open, obvious steps to show that they are playing fairly. Also, they emphasize the rules of the conflict (e.g., it's okay to get angry but not to hit) and attempt to keep communications open with the opponents.

The reader may note that the above approach is very 'fact-oriented' rather than emotion- or interpersonally-oriented. This is because North Americans, in their interactions and conflicts, like to compile facts and evidence that support their case and then rely on these to move the other/opponent in the desired direction. A very common phrase used in such cases is 'the facts speak for themselves'.

Concomitant with their use of facts, is the North Americans' attempt to use power in interactions and conflicts. Americans like to rely on power because it is efficient, quick, and rather unambiguous. In sum, Americans prefer to rely upon facts and power to manage their interactions and conflicts rather than to *negotiate.*

Why Americans eschew negotiation is an open question with manifold answers. To some extent it is the result of a structured economic system in which prices are set by the seller and are taken or passed up by the purchaser. To negotiate frequently is seen as very inefficient and time consuming.

For Americans, negotiation also implies weakness in that it indicates one party must 'give in' to (agree to negotiate with) the other in order to reach an agreement. The more preferred approach for Americans is to be strong and force the other party to behave as he or she should.

While they prefer not to negotiate, Americans, on occasion find they must. And when they do, Americans have a very distinctive approach. The first characteristic is an ambivalence toward continuing the negotiation/interaction. On the one hand, Americans prefer to terminate negotiations because they are perceived to be costly (especially in terms of time). Also, they—unlike their Eastern counterparts—do not place a high value on relationships. Nor do they fear creating a loss of face for the opponent by walking away from the negotiation.

On the other side of the coin, Americans tend to remain in negotiations because they are overly optimistic about raising their outcomes in the interaction/negotiation. A second, and more potent, reason for remaining in the negotiation is that Americans believe walking away from a negotiation is cowardly. And a third, related, explanation is that exiting the negotiation/conflict allows the other to win, while remaining is perceived as putting up 'a good fight'.

When he is in the negotiation, how does the American behave? In general, he holds to a reciprocity norm but applies it with a competitive bias. When an American makes a concession, he expects the opponent to return it, tit for tat. Yet, when *he* receives a concession, an American disputant feels it is acceptable to concede a little less, so as to challenge the opponent or to 'get one up on him.'

If the opponent punishes the disputant or attempts to reduce his outcomes in some way, the American feels justified in retaliating, even in *over*-retaliating to teach the opponent a lesson. (Forgiveness is not highly valued in North American negotiations.) On the other hand if the opponent over-retaliates, the American tends to become offended. Perhaps he then plans to even the score.

As he negotiates, the American tries to eliminate some of the opponent's alternatives, or the perception that the alternatives have high payoffs. Doing so gives the American an edge in the negotiation/dispute because it makes the opponent more dependent. 'Boxing in' the opponent in this manner is considered acceptable (even though it might generate embarrassment) because it allows one to win and because the opponent may otherwise have the opportunity to box in the American.

Americans take these assertive steps—reducing the opponent's alternatives and in general raising their own power—because they believe the opponent, if unconstrained, will seek to increase his own strength or outcomes and will use these to win the conflict/contest.

How does the opponent respond to these assertive negotiation tactics? Rather defiantly; that is, the opponent doesn't capitulate. Instead, he opposes the disputant (e.g., stands his ground) or responds strategically to obtain the best deal he can for himself. Such defiance of a powerful opponent takes place because North Americans hold to democratic ideals and values, one of these being that the person with power does not necessarily have the right to wield it.

As they pursue their individual goals, hold to the reciprocity norm, attempt to reduce the other's alternatives, seek to use their own power, and deter the more powerful party, the Americans negotiate under a set of well-understood rules of fair play.

Rule #1: Each person looks out for himself and his team.

Rule #2: The negotiation is rational. Each side must explain why it should receive an outcome or can deny it to the other side.

Rule #3: The negotiation is rights oriented, in that each side has the right to keep what it obtains in the agreement. Each also has the right to correct procedures (e.g., each side listens to the other's offer before making a counter-offer.)

Rule #4: Honesty. Each side is expected to tell the truth and to keep its commitments. Bluffs are okay; the truth can be stretched somewhat; one can sandbag (withhold information); and one can drag one's feet in fulfilling a contract. However, blatant lies are unacceptable.

Rule #5: The negotiators get to the point. They don't dwell on vague and peripheral issues.

Rule #6: Moderate embarrassment of the other side is acceptable. (That is, one is not expected to 'give face' to the opponent.) A negotiator is not to embarrass the other excessively, but moderate to high levels of embarrassment are permitted.

Rule #7: Each side can argue for outcomes it needs, but feelings and emotions are not usually 'put on the table'. That is, an American would seldom ask the opponent to give a concession so that their relationship would be improved or so that the American could feel better.

Of the above standards, Rule #2 is the most interesting because it creates a paradox for the North Americans. They want the negotiation to be rational, but they are irrational in bargaining. The first aspect of the irrationality is that they (as noted earlier) have a fixed-sum perception of the dispute/negotiation. That is, they believe that the other party's gain will come at an equal or greater cost to them.

A related irrational aspect is that North Americans overvalue winning in negotiations. Even though North Americans place a high value on individual payoffs, they will quite often sacrifice these to beat the opponent, to embarrass him, or to reduce his outcomes.

A third, powerful, aspect of the irrationality is that North Americans become overly committed to certain options and continue to incur costs that far exceed the payoffs from that option. This mistake, which is unfortunately shared with many cultures, stems from the inability to ignore sunk costs. The process underpinning this bias is quite understandable. As the American negotiates and becomes committed to a course of action, she develops a goal of having her total outcomes from the dispute/negotiation to exceed her total costs. Therefore as her costs in pursuing an option increase, she strives harder and harder to increase the outcomes of that option. These attempts most often raise the cost of the option, further motivating the American to increase her costs to it (as a gambler attempts to recover losses by gambling further)! Consequently, the disputant raises her commitment to a losing option. The rational approach would be to compare the cost of pursuing the option to the potential benefits of this pursuit. Yet as many of us know, the rational approach is easier to describe than to follow.

A final irrational bias is the North Americans' over-emphasis on the short run, the emphasis on winning the current negotiation/game. In an interaction, each course of action should be judged according to its total net outcome over an extended period of time. Objectively, North Americans know this; however, in their interactions/negotiations they focus excessively on the current payoff. This orientation motivates them to be hasty in their negotiation, to undervalue relationships with the opponents, and to hammer out short-term specific contracts.

With these biases, playing under these rules, and with the aforementioned norms and goals, the North American disputants, in one-on-one contests, attempt to manage/negotiate their conflict. If they fail, they abide by:

Rule #8: Send or take the dispute to adjudication (i.e., court).

A Short Detour

To this point we have discussed North Americans' competitive norms and values. Subsequently, we noted how North Americans perceive conflict, react to conflict and attempt to manage or negotiate within it. And, in the following section, we'll note how they behave in adjudication (i.e., court).

Before moving to that section, we need to discuss some Canadian-U.S. differences. For the most part, we have utilized the term 'North Americans', which tends to equate the citizens (along with their values) in the two countries. Yet there are some distinct differences.

Strictly speaking, North America is made up of three countries: Canada, the U.S., and Mexico. These countries, like siblings, began their modern histories at roughly the same time and share a common European heritage. They have experienced a cultural blending enhanced by relatively open borders and have economies that are being melded by joint trade agreements like the recent North American Free Trade Agreement (NAFTA). In spite of these similarities, the three countries have very unique cultural attributes.

The focus of this chapter is on the northern two siblings, Canada and the U.S., which are quite alike owing to their common history as English colonies. This similarity is to some extent limited, as there are some fundamental differences between these two cultures. While the United States developed as a melting pot, molding a multitude of immigrants into an English-speaking tradition; Canada developed around two distinct language traditions: English and French. Although some commentators suggest that English-speaking Canadians are fundamentally like their brothers to the south (Hartz 1964), others see cultural differences (such as the strength of socialism in Canada) that transcend the language similarities (Horowitz 1966). A basis for this difference is the divergence in the colonial period, with the United States choosing revolution and Canada choosing to remain in the Common-wealth (Lipset 1963). Despite two unique histories and traditions, the issue of concern in this chapter is to what extent the conflict management processes of the two countries differ.

The answer to the question of difference comes down to perspective. On the world stage, Canada and the United States are seen as distinct entities (Robbins and Stuart-Kotze 1994). And, until recently, it was generally accepted that the two countries approached business in different ways (Lipset 1968). However, recent studies have begun to question this assumption of differences. While citizens from Canada may use a different approach or process in working through a business situation from someone from the U.S., the outcomes envisioned by the two are very similar (Adler and Graham 1987). In fact, even the processes used by the majority of Canadians (those of the English-speaking tradition) are indistinguishable from those used in the United States (Baer, Grabb, and Johnston 1990). Possibly as a result of growing economic ties, the legal systems of the two countries are also becoming more similar with respect to business law (National Law Review 1995). The bottom line in a comparison of Canadian and U.S. citizens is that while the practical reality of difference is not great, the Canadians take great pride in their uniqueness (MacLeans 1988). As a result, while the analysis in this chapter will treat Canadians and U.S. citizens as interchangeable, the reader should remember to respect the perceptions of national difference in one-on-one dealings with citizens from each country.

Having drawn these distinctions, let's now describe how North Americans approach adjudication.

ADJUDICATION

North Americans enthusiastically enter, embrace, and battle within the adjudicative process. Perhaps the primary motivator for doing so is the perception that adjudication is a type of legal contest in which each disputant has an opportunity to prove she is right. There she can beat the opponent.

While one disputant's victory means the other's defeat this latter outcome is not viewed as a major concern by the Americans or their society. 'Defeat' in a North American contest is to be expected, and accepted. Americans tend to feel, 'you win some and lose some', 'You live to fight another day' or 'it's not whether you win or lose, but how you play the game.'

A somewhat related explanation for the use of adjudication is that North Americans do not mind openly admitting that harmony has been disrupted and that the two sides are involved in (and responsible for) disharmony. For Americans the disharmony/adjudication is viewed not as an embarrassment but more as a competition in which a person opposes and attempts to defeat an adversary.

In the court an impersonal authority (judge or jury) decides who is right (winner) and who is wrong (loser). It does so by permitting the disputing sides, armed with clear central, relevant, non-peripheral facts, to compete head-to- head. In this contest, each contestant relies on his or her confrontational skill, valid self-disclosure, assertiveness, and astuteness in attacking the opponent's position. After both sides have been given adequate opportunity to attack (with facts) each other and to defend their own positions, the court, which is expected to be neutral, decides the winner. It does so with the following process:

A detailed set of laws act as the gatekeeper, specifying how, when and where a legal dispute can be brought into the court (Anderson and Kumpf 1975). Once the adjudicative process is entered, it proceeds in these steps:

1. Commencement of Action: The process begins with the filing of a 'complaint' by an aggrieved party, known as the plaintiff;
2. Service of Process: The defendant, or the party being charged, is next legally informed that a court action is pending against him;
3. Pleadings: The plaintiff files a written statement of their claim and the defendant is given a chance to answer the charges in writing (also during this stage the defendant can ask the court to dismiss the charges, and/or the defendant can file a counter claim or cross-complaint against the plaintiff);
4. Pre-trial Procedure: At this stage either party can ask for a ruling on the issues as presented (known as a 'Motion for Judgement on the Pleadings'); or can bring in sworn testimony to indicate that the other side's action is based upon false or deceitful claims and should thus be ruled against (known as a 'Summary Judgement'); or the court can hold a Pre-trial Conference to narrow the issues; and then provide for Discovery (a process in which rules guide the exchange of information between the parties) and Depositions (a process in which sworn testimony is collected by either side);
5. Determination of Facts: In this stage the type of trial is determined (i.e., the witnesses are listed and subpoenas [orders to appear] are issued);
6. Conduct of the Trial: Finally the actual court process begins, involving the presentation of the plaintiff's case, followed by the defendant's case, followed by the charge to the jury (if applicable). All this leads to the deliberations of the jury, and finally the verdict

and determination of a judgement (Anderson and Kumpf 1975; Conry, Ferrera, and Fox 1986).

However, even with the final judgement, the process is not necessarily over as the appeals process may basically start the entire cycle over again, albeit in a higher court.

As they shift their personal conflicts to the adversarial procedural-bound, fact-based, rights-oriented court system, North American disputants play out a paradox: they relinquish control of the dispute, but concomitantly they retain control. As noted above the disputants, when turning to adjudication, do allow the court to decide the winner. However, at any point in the judicial process, the disputants can settle the dispute themselves; that is, they by mutual agreement can remove it from the court's control and negotiate an 'out of court' agreement.

THIRD PARTY ASSISTANCE

As noted in Fig. 11.1, the disputants at any point in the conflict management process (that is, at the perceived conflict, conflict, conflict management or adjudication stages) can seek third party assistance. One form of this, mediation, is being used increasingly in North America (Kressel and Pruitt 1989). Currently, we find formal mediation of divorces, small-claims cases, neighborhood feuds, landlord-tenant disputes, siting of garbage dumps, labor-management disputes, labor grievances, etc. Mediations of these disputes, as well as informal mediations unfold in a distinct American fashion.

Call for Mediation

The beginning point for the mediation is the disputants' conflict. Because of the North American emphasis on individual rights, mediation is seldom forced upon the disputants, as it might be in China or in rural Malaysia. Rather the disputants, after some attempt to resolve the conflict by themselves, or in court, ask or allow a third party to assist them.

As several authors have pointed out, a number of conditions determine whether this assistance is sought. Rubin (1980) for example, notes that when a conflict is of low intensity, the disputants feel they can manage the conflict by themselves. It also seems that extremely hostile disputants do not request assistance because they prefer confrontation to mediation. Or perhaps because of their hostile orientation they do not recognize the mediation option. Also, once the disputants have reached a hurting stalemate (e.g., they are deadlocked and their funds have been depleted by legal proceedings) in their conflict they are more apt to call for mediation.

The Mediator's Response: to Mediate or not

In North America, third parties are somewhat hesitant to mediate or assist in a dispute because they feel the conflict is a personal/private matter. Also, third parties do not feel a personal responsibility to maintain societal harmony. Given such hesitancy, under what circumstances does a third party overcome this inertia and agree to mediate? Some mediators are bound by agreement to assist 'when called', or assistance is a defined part of their job responsibility. Many such mediators are found in the ranks of the National Mediation Conciliation Service, alternative dispute resolution centers, or community mediation centers. Some mediators assist because that is their profession: mediation provides remuneration, a reputation and future business (Fisher 1986).

While prior agreements, job requirements and professional payoffs motivate mediation by some third parties, others intervene because they feel their assistance will be useful to the parties (Rogers 1991). However, since North Americans typically do not feel a major obligation to maintain societal harmony, most will not intervene unless they perceive specific benefits to the disputants, to themselves, or to their constituencies.

Techniques

Having entered the dispute, what techniques does the mediator employ? The literature indicates that North American mediators draw from about 100 techniques, which are applied to the disputants' relationship, the disputants themselves, and to the parties' relationship with others (Wall 1981; Wall and Lynn 1993).

When addressing the disputants' relationship, the mediator, if she has sufficient power, might establish and enforce a protocol for the negotiation. Then she can manage or alter the perceptions and communications in the relationship (Karambayya and Brett 1989; Schwebel, Schwebel and Schwebel 1985; Shapiro, Drieghe, and Brett 1985). She might also attempt to strike a power balance between the disputants, propose specific agreement points, separate the disputants, and develop ways to expand the negotiations so that the disputants will begin to explore options that have integrative potential.

When focusing on the disputants themselves, the mediator can determine which points are negotiable for each disputant, reframe the disagreement and options for each disputant, bring pressure to bear from other third parties, or, if she has it, use personal power to extract concessions from each disputant.

Determinants of Mediators' Approaches

Given that mediators have about 100 techniques at their disposal, what governs the mediator's choice? In North America this is determined by: (a) rules and standards, (b) the dispute characteristics, and (c) the mediation context.

Rules and Standards

For formal labor disputes, the labor mediators must abide by the rules established by the Federal Mediation and Conciliation service or the American Arbitration Association. These rules in general lay out the procedures the mediator should follow, and prescribe that the mediator should be thorough, accurate and impartial.

More informal standards come from scholars and practitioners, who advocate that mediators be rational and analytical. Barsky (1983) for example, holds that mediators should first determine the source of the conflict and then follow through with techniques that address that source. And in a similar analytic vein, Raiffa (1983) notes that mediators should be as analytical as the dispute is complex.

Dispute Characteristics

A major distinguishing characteristic of North American mediation is the prescription that it be tailored to the dispute. This standard operating procedure stems in part from an analytic, rational belief that most sorts of problems can be identified, isolated and addressed.

With this operating procedure in mind, North Americans, focusing on the current dispute and drawing upon their past experience, come to some rough conclusion as to the possible outcomes in the dispute. Then they apply the techniques they feel are most apt to yield these outcomes. For example, mediators use humor to lighten the atmosphere whenever they detect hostility. If too many issues emerge and the dispute becomes very congested, the mediators attempt to simplify the agenda, suggest trade-offs and hold long sessions that facilitate compromise or, when the disputants are found to lack experience, mediators educate the disputants, perhaps by noting procedures that have been used in the past.

Mediation Context

The setting for North American mediation which has been delineated previously, entails a general consensus that conflicts, between individuals, groups, companies, etc., are the responsibility of the disputants. Its resolution is up to the principals; they may choose to use a mediator and, if they so wish, they can dismiss him. This ideology places the mediator in a low power position, as does society's rather low evaluation of, and support, for the mediation process.

Consequently, most mediators in North America rely on low-power techniques. For example, they use logic, persuasion, personal favors, etc., rather than threats, strong calls for concessions, criticisms, etc.

RECAPITULATION

In summary, we find that North Americans are competitively oriented because of their religion, pioneer heritage, history, economy, and sports. This competitive bias—along with other forces—engenders their conflicts. In general, these conflicts are played out almost as heated sporting events. Specifically, the disputants claim control of the conflict and within it they are self-oriented and rational. In any culture the line between conflict behavior and conflict management is an opaque one, but this is especially true for North Americans, because they prefer to manage their own conflicts rather than relying on assistance from third parties. As they manage their conflicts, North Americans rationally analyze the conflict and address its causes and results. As they do so, they display anger, look out after themselves (and their own face) and attempt to exercise their power. As the disputants attempt to wield power over each other, their conflict management can evolve into a negotiation. Here each disputant attempts to increase his outcomes. While doing so, he adheres to a reciprocity norm, attempts to beat the opponent, uses his power and attempts to keep the negotiation rational. Ironically, while North Americans place a high value on rationality, they are quite irrational in their negotiations/conflict management. Evidence for this is found in their emphasis on winning as well as their fixed-sum perception of the conflict and preference for short-run payoffs.

When North Americans' self-management of the conflict fails, they typically turn to the courts. In this formal system, bound with its emphasis on facts, individual rights, consistency, and correct procedures, the disputants engage in an adversarial process wherein they attempt to 'win' their case.

With their emphasis on self-management of conflict, North Americans seldom rely on third parties for assistance. When they do turn to third parties, American disputants expect the third parties to be nonassertive, neutral, fair, rational, procedurally correct, and oriented toward the rights of the disputants. Since they hold to the same values and norms as the disputants, the mediators (or other neutral third parties) behave consistently with these expectations/requirements.

WHAT TO EXPECT FROM NORTH AMERICANS

Given that North Americans engage in and manage their conflicts as described above, what should foreigners, specifically, East Asians, expect in interactions with them? We predict (and explain) the following:

	Expected Behaviors	Explanation
1.	North Americans will be competitive in their interactions and conflicts.	North Americans live in a competitive environment, they like competition, and perceive relationships as competitive.
2.	North Americans frequently do not recognize that an interaction has turned into a conflict.	They do not distinguish clearly between competition and conflict.
3.	In the interaction/conflict, Americans assume that the other party will attempt to 'beat' them.	North Americans view relationships as competitive/win-lose and assume the other will try to win.
4.	North Americans will attempt to raise their own outcomes and will expect the other party to do the same.	Americans are individualists and assume others have the same orientation.
5.	Americans are polite in that they are open, honest, and sincere.	Americans place a great deal of emphasis on facts and the exchange of accurate information. Facts and information allow them to make progress on a task and to measure how well they have done.
	But	

6. Americans are rather unrestrained in showing anger and causing face-loss for others. At the same time they react strongly to losing face.	Americans feel that individuals have the right to display anger and to show how they feel. They place more emphasis on individual rights than on maintaining a harmonious relationship with others. In addition, they feel each person should look out after himself.
7. North Americans want to give a person what he 'deserves' rather than what he needs. Also they make concessions when the other does, or expect concessions in return for their own.	Americans hold strongly to equity and reciprocation norms.
8. Americans want the conflict resolution to be rational (e.g., addressing causes, setting up rules, addressing past wrongs).	Americans address industrial, mechanical, electrical, medical, financial, etc. problems rationally and extrapolate this approach to conflict management.
9. North Americans typically do not rely upon assistance from third parties.	Americans feel they own their dispute and have the right to manage it themselves.
10. When this assistance (e.g., mediation) is utilized, Americans expect it to be neutral, objective, and rather passive.	Americans believe the mediators have the same role as a referee at a sporting event.
11. North Americans are quick to take their disputes to court, where they are conducted in an adversarial fashion.	Americans have a long tradition of taking disputes to court. Herein is an open arena where the individual can claim his/her rights and defeat the other.
12. Americans want and expect agreements (e.g., contracts) to be detailed, clear, and enforceable.	Americans trust precision, clarity, and the law more than they do relationships.

Interacting/Managing Conflicts with North Americans

If North Americans behave in the above fashion, how should East Asians interface with them? We see three viable options, (a) adoption of the American approach, (b) conducing Americans to use an Eastern approach and (c) development of a hybrid form of interaction.

The American approach

The first option is a 'When in Rome, do as the Romans' approach. Herein, you can acknowledge that you, like the Americans, are engaged in a competitive encounter which may or may not be a conflict. In the interaction, each side will look at its own interests, trusting that the other side will do the same. Both sides will be allowed to be competitive trying to beat the other, but in so doing they can explore options and close upon those that provide acceptable benefits to each side.

When developing and exploring the various options, you, like the North Americans, can openly and quite candidly critique the North Americans' proposals. Likewise, you can precisely state what you expect from the Americans and what you feel they deserve, backing up these statements with trenchant facts and rational arguments.

As the Americans make concessions, you should likewise concede; whereas, if the Americans stand fast, so should you. Throughout the give-and-take, standing ground, reciprocal concessions, etc., you should very clearly state why you are taking various steps, clearly indicating the payoffs to yourself and the American side.

Perhaps most difficult, you will have to tolerate personal affronts as the Americans expect you to 'take it on the chin' (incur the discourtesy) and 'be a good sport' (tolerate and excuse the discourtesy). In turn, you should not be concerned with giving face to the North Americans, and on occasion can be brusque, proving you can 'dish it out as well as take it' (i.e., retaliate).

As complements to the above strategy, you should develop and use a slate of Western competitive, or sports-oriented terms such as:

- Slam-dunk: This means something is certain to happen. In basketball when a tall player jumps and pushes the ball down through the net with his hand(s), it is called a 'slam dunk'.
- Leveling the playing field: To level the field means to give no advantage to one side or the other. In (American) football or soccer if the field is not level, the side defending the higher side has an advantage.
- End run: This term indicates one party is avoiding a difficult party to find one who is easier to work with. It is borrowed from (American) football where it is the name of a play in which the player carrying the ball runs around the opposing players rather than through them.
- Penny-wise, pound foolish: Here is a British term that indicates one should have a broad perspective. To be penny-wise means to be frugal, usually on minor items in the short run. Adding 'pound

foolish' indicates that taking this approach often dictates failure on a major, long run outcome. For example, failure to grease a bearing does save money on grease; however, it could cause the bearing (and the machine) to fail.

- Live to fight another day: This indicates it is wise to give up if one is losing. The term seems to have been spawned by the military.
- Circle the wagons: A pioneer term, it relates how settlers would place their wagons in a circle when attacked by Indians. Consequently, it means to go on the defensive, usually in the face of aggressive opponent.
- Take to the hills: This means to flee in the face of danger or overwhelming odds.

The East Asian approach

Because North Americans have recently been inundated with primers on how to negotiate, do business with, understand, and get along with their Eastern neighbors, it is feasible that you may be able to interact with North Americans somewhat as you would with your compatriots. That is, you can follow your natural interaction/conflict management styles and expect the North Americans to follow suit, (that is, to adjust to you and to deviate from their normal behavior).

This interaction should be prefaced or interlarded with some explanations for the North Americans. The explanation must emphasize that East Asians value harmony and do not automatically view relationships as competitive. Likewise it should be noted that East Asians place a very high value on retaining face and giving face to others, even if it means bending the facts, appearing inconsistent or irrational, appearing vague or refusing to say 'no' when you mean 'no'.

In addition, Americans should be counseled so that they understand East Asians are group-oriented as opposed to individual-oriented. Therefore, you must explain that you will often delay decisions or answers until you have checked with, or built consensus with, your group (or home office).

It would also be useful to help Americans to be patient. And they must be convinced that the most tightly written contract is only as good as the relationship between the people who signed it.

Having educated the North Americans, you could invest considerable time in getting to know the Americans and into forcing the Americans to become familiar with you.

With this educational underpinning, you can turn to the task at hand, but always keep in mind that Americans will feel you are looking out for your own outcomes. Also keep in mind that many Americans will be unable to be flexible in their conflict management. When the two styles conflict, people tend to revert to old habits rather than being reflexible and responsive to others.

Integrative approach

An alternative to the above two approaches is one in which the North Americans and East Asians each adopt aspects of the other's style which are (a) very important to the other side but, (b) of low importance (or cost) to the conceding side. As a starting point for this approach, consider the attributes of North Americans and East Asians in Table 11.1.

With these attributes in mind, the Americans and East Asians need to indicate to each other which aspects are very important to them. Subsequently, they need to determine, by communicating with the other side, which of these the opposing side could provide at low cost to itself. To us, the writers, it seems that open, honest communications and a reliance on rationality and facts are very important to North

Table 11.1 North Americans' versus East Asians' Attributes and Preferences

North Americans' Attributes and Preferences	East Asians' Attributes and Preferences
Competitive	Value harmony
Slow to recognize conflict	Quickly recognize conflict
Seek personal outcomes	Seek personal and joint outcomes
Assume other will try to 'win'	Don't assume other will try to win
*Open, clear in conversation	Vague in conversation
Show anger	Do not show anger
Oriented toward what a party deserves	Oriented toward party's needs
Expect reciprocity	May expect reciprocity
*Want rationality and facts	Want general understanding
Don't prefer third-party assistance	Appreciate third-party assistance
Low concern for face	*High concern for face
Want detailed agreements	*Seek dependable relationship

*Tradeable items

Americans. As for East Asians, it appears that a dependable relationship and concern for face (self and others) are very important.

While these four attributes, two for the North Americans and two for the East Asians, are highly valued by their respective nationalities, it seems that each could be provided at rather low cost by the other side. This being the case it seems that non-North Americans, early in their interactions, could propose an integrative trade in bargaining tactics: The East Asians will be open in the interactions, saying exactly what they want and expect. Also, they will go the extra mile to provide and rely upon facts and rationality.

In turn, they will expect and appreciate the North Americans' investments in building a strong dependable relationship. Also the East Asians would appreciate self control from the Americans and concern for the East Asians' 'face'. This probably will require that the North Americans not reveal their anger or frustrations in the interactions. Likewise, supplying the East Asians with several alternatives (i.e., not cornering them) would be very much appreciated.

Perhaps the trades between these sets of preferences will not be the most productive. However, the outline for this procedure designates the manner in which East Asians can interact productively with North Americans. In addition to locating preferences (and tactics) that can be traded integratively, the charted procedure provides insights for each side into the other's orientation and preferences, thereby setting the groundwork for productive interactions.

A CLOSING CAUTION

The preceding pages have sketched a sweeping portrait of conflict management in North America. As with any broad generalization, there is much diversity underlying it; this is particularly true for the U.S. and Canada whose populations were formed by recent migrations from many countries.

While most Americans value competition, there are those who prefer cooperation. Likewise, some Americans favor subtlety when expressing and managing conflicts. Many of us choose to avoid the courts, a few are comfortable with informal third-party assistance. And, a growing number of Americans are attempting to interface with outsiders in an open, participative manner.

Given this variety, we offer a closing bit of advice to East Asians. Use our descriptions and ideas as rough gauges for probing the characteristics of the Americans you encounter. Do not allow our observations to generate rigid stereotypes. Then, interface with the person(s) you actually find and not just with the ones you expect to find.

REFERENCES

Adler, N.J. and Graham, J.L. 1987. Business negotiations: Canadians are not just like Americans. *Canadian Journal of Administrative Sciences*, Sept., 211–38.

Anderson, R.A. and Kumpf, W.A. 1975. *Business Law: Principles and Cases*. Cincinnati, OH: South-Western Publishing Co.

Augsburger, D.W. 1992. *Conflict Mediation Across Cultures: Pathways and Patterns*. Louisville, KY: Westminster/John Knox.

Baer, D., Grabb, E. and Johnston, W.A. 1990. The values of Canadians and Americans: A critical analysis and reassessment. *Social Forces*, **68**, 693–713.

Barsky, M. 1983. Emotional needs and dysfunctional communication as blocks to mediation. *Mediation Quarterly*, **2**, 55–66.

Bazerman, M. 1986. Why negotiations go wrong. *Psychology Today*, 48–54.

Blake, R.R. and Mouton, J.S. 1984. *Solving Costly Organizational Conflicts*. San Francisco, CA: Jossey-Bass.

Callister, R.R. and Wall, J.A. 1997. Japanese community and organizational mediation. *Journal of Conflict Resolution*, **41**, 311–28.

Conry, E.J., Ferrera, G.R. and Fox, K.H. 1986. *The Legal Environment of Business*. Dubuque, IA: Wm. C. Brown Publishers.

Dupont, D. 1997. Playing nice. *Scientific American*, April, 35–7.

Fisher, R. 1986. Why not contingent fee mediation? *Negotiation Journal*, **2**, 11–3.

Hartz, L. 1964. *The Founding of New Societies*. New York: Harcourt, Brace and World.

Honna, N. and Hoffer, B. 1989. *An English Dictionary of Japanese Ways of Thinking*. Tokyo: Yuhikoku.

Horowitz, G. 1966. Conservatism, liberalism, and socialism in Canada: An interpretation. *Canadian Journal of Economics and Political Science*, **32**, 143–71.

Jones, K. 1995. Masked negotiation in a Japanese work setting. In Firth, A. (ed.), *The Discourse of Negotiation*, 141–58. Tarrytown, NY: Elsevier.

Karambayya, R. and Brett, J.M. 1989. Managers handling disputes: Third party roles and perceptions of fairness. *Academy of Management Journal*, **32**, 687–704.

Kilmann, R.H. and Thomas, K.W. 1977. Developing a forced choice measure of conflict handling behavior. The 'Mode' instrument. *Educational and Psychological Measurement*, **37**, 309–25.

Kim, N-H., Wall, J.A., Sohn, D-W. and Kim, J.S. 1993. Community and industrial mediation in South Korea. *Journal of Conflict Resolution*, **37**, 361–81.

Kressel, K. and Pruitt, D.G. 1989. Conclusion: A research perspective on the mediation of social conflict. 394–435 in *Mediation Research: The Process and Effectiveness of Third Party Intervention*. San Francisco, CA: Jossey-Bass.

Lewis, C.S. 1960. *Mere Christianity*. New York: MacMillan Publishing Company.

Lipset, S.M. 1963. The value patterns of democracy: A case study in comparative analysis. *American Sociological Review*, **28**, 515–31.

Lipset, S.M. 1968. *Revolution and Counterrevolution*. Boston, MA: Basic Books.

Luther, M. 1967. *Selected Writings of Martin Luther*, (T.G. Tappert, ed.). Philadelphia, PA: Fortress Press.

Macleans, G. (Jan. 4, 1988). Defining identity. 44–45.

Moran, R.T. and Abbott, J. 1994. *NAFTA: Managing the Cultural Differences*. Houston, TX: Gulf Publishing.

Raiffa, H. 1983. Mediation of Conflicts. *American Behavioral Scientist*, **27**, 195–210.

Robbins, S.P. and Stuart-Kotze, R. 1994. *Management* (Fourth edition). Scarborough, Ontario: Prentice Hall.

Rogers, S.J. 1991. Ten ways to work more effectively with volunteer mediators. *Negotiation Journal*, **7**, 201–11.

Rubin, J. 1980. Experimental research on third-party intervention in conflict: Toward some generalizations. *Psychological Bulletin*, **87**, 379–91.

Samuelson, P.A. 1985. *Economics*. New York: McGraw-Hill.

Schwebel, R., Schwebel, A. and Schwebel, J. 1985. The psychological/ mediation intervention model. *Professional Psychology: Research and Practice*, **16**, 86–97.

Shapiro, D., Drieghe, R. and Brett, J. 1985. Mediator behavior and the outcome of mediation. *Journal of Social Issues*, **41**, 101–14.

Sohn, D-W. and Wall, J.A. 1993. Community mediation in South Korea, *Journal of Conflict Resolution*, **37**, 536–43.
Triandis, H. 1995. *Individualism and Collectivism*. Boulder, CO: Westview.
Triandis, H. 1996. The psychological measurement of cultural syndromes. *American Psychologist*, **51**, 407–15.
Wall, J.A. 1981. Mediation: An analysis, review, and proposed research. *Journal of Conflict Resolution*, **25**, 157–80.
Wall, J.A. and Blum, M.E. 1991. Community mediation in the People's Republic of China. *Journal of Conflict Management*, **35**, 3–20.
Wall, J.A. and Lynn, A. 1993. Mediation: A current review. *Journal of Conflict Resolution*, **37**, 160–94.
Zucker, L.G. 1986. Production of Trust: Institutional sources of economic structure, 1840–1920. *Research in Organizational Behavior*, **8**, 53–111.

C H A P T E R   T W E L V E

Conclusion: Conflict Management in the Asia Pacific

DEAN TJOSVOLD
Department of Management, Lingnan College, Tuen Mun, Hong Kong and Simon Fraser University, Canada

and

KWOK LEUNG
Department of Psychology, Chinese University of Hong Kong

Conflict is intellectually challenging to understand and highly significant for management practice. The authors of this book's chapters have suggested the wide-ranging issues over which Asia Pacific partners, managers, and employees contend and described the diverse ways they approach and handle their conflicts. How people manage conflict depends upon their traditional culture, their country's socio-economic development, and their organization's milieu as well as their individual abilities and personalities. Managing conflict requires a rich understanding of people and the context in which they work. Fortunately, managing conflict is a way to know and appreciate people and their situation. But managing conflict is a practical science. How can the chapter's ideas, knowledge, and guides be put to work?

Because conflict is so pervasive and yet so potentially valuable, Asia Pacific partners, managers, and employees must learn to manage it constructively. This chapter argues that constructive conflict management, especially between Asians and Westerners, requires an integration of their values so that conflicts are approached both to build relationships and to discuss issues open-mindedly. Asians and North Americans can, together, learn to manage their conflicts and develop supportive values, procedures, and skills. Developing these abilities not only contributes greatly to organizational success but helps us learn to work globally. Asia Pacific business provides an excellent forum for learning how to manage the intercultural conflict that occurs in our increasingly interdependent, diverse world.

The Conflict Management Imperative

Managing conflict is critical for doing business in the Asia Pacific. All organizations have conflict, but the book's chapters show that business in the Asia Pacific with its various values and customs requires a great deal of conflict managing savvy.

Take an Indonesian business person. Within Indonesia, he or she has to be highly flexible in managing conflict. Javanese employees will publicly agree to new demands without argument but then deliver excuses when they fail to deliver: Tapanuli employees will contest, challenge, and negotiate but, once they agree, fulfill their bargain. With a population of 200 million consisting of more than 300 ethnic groups who speak more than 500 languages scattered over 17,000 islands, the Indonesian encounters many different ways of working! Indonesians today must manage conflicts with Japanese joint venture partners and American and European customers, all of whom have their own expectations and stereotypes of how to negotiate with Indonesians. Managing in Indonesia is not dull.

Diversity within and between nations is the region's reality. In China, free market philosophy now contends with traditional Confucian values and socialist and communist ideology in business thinking. Korea is the Land of Morning Calm and the Land of Warriors; it is collectivist as well as dynamic and individualistic. The Thais are relationship-oriented but also self-seeking and fun-loving. In Malaysia, Malay, Chinese, and Indian managers have their own value systems, though the country's recent economic development has been moderating these differences.

There is no realistic alternative to conflict management. Too often managers and employees are surprised by the conflicts they encounter. They unrealistically expect interpersonal harmony and smooth operations. They ignore early warnings and, when the conflicts intensify, feel trapped. Ignoring the conflict and trying to impose one's will only further complicate and escalate the conflict. Especially when working in the diverse Asia Pacific business environment, considerable creativity and persistence are needed to deal with conflict.

Conflict as Window

Conflict is an opportunity to learn. By highlighting frustrations, conflict identifies issues and problems that need attention, conflict stimulates an examination of relationships and the intricacies of working together. Through discussing opposing positions, persons understand each other's perspective and feelings. Conflict helps them articulate their own values as they learn the values of others.

The authors have described how their country's values impact how their compatriots approach and manage conflict. Studying conflict highlights our cultural differences. The most powerful contrast, and one that should be understood as a generalization with many exceptions, is that in the Pacific Rim, Asian countries highly value relationships whereas Western ones focus on tasks and issues.

Contrasting Values

Japanese people, with a deep commitment for their ingroups, take a nonassertive approach to managing their conflict, although with outgroup members they can be aggressive. Filipinos are sensitive to violations of their harmonious culture that make them lose face. They value family and personal ties and, while emotional, do not take the initiative in resolving disputes. Malays are inclined to be humble, self-effacing, courteous, and indirect. They seek to uphold the reputation of their kampung community and are comfortable with their hierarchical society. The result is the 'It's all right, never mind' Malay style. Although the Chinese are highly committed to their immediate families and the Thais are more willing to pursue individual goals, both groups strive to maintain relationships and face.

In contrast, the Australians, New Zealanders, and North Americans are directive and competitive. The Australians are highly individualistic with an aggressive egalitarian streak. The New Zealanders espouse more relationship values, but are often as competitive in their negotiations as Australians. North Americans must both win and be right; they build up their power as they undermine the alternatives of others; they are calculating, unemotional, and forceful. Their Judaic-Christian traditions, pioneering experience, free market ideology, and winning (most!) wars reinforce these values.

Managers and employees on the Asian side of the Pacific are committed to interpersonal harmony whereas those in North America as well as Australia and New Zealand concentrate on getting the job done. Asian business people are sensitive and skilled at protecting face and building relationships; North Americans directly confront issues and hammer out solutions.

The contrasting emphases often frustrate conflict management. As described in the Thailand chapter, an American manager and his Thai subordinate who were both originally committed to a common goal ended up feeling fragmented and competitive. Under pressure from the head office, the American forced the office employees to accept a new Management by Objective program although in fact they were uncommitted. Highly sensitive and patient in understanding employee resistance in the factory, the Thai slowly explained the value of the new program and lowered resistance. However, the American blamed the Thai for delays; the Thai employees believed the American betrayed the loyalty of his Thai manager. The result was chaos and the Thai, the American, and the company all lost.

Compatibility in Approaches

Westerners and Asians must understand their contrasting emphases on problems and relationships. However, understanding their differences does not mean that they are to use them as a shield against each other and as a way to avoid conflict: 'You can't criticize me because my values are different,' 'That's your problem if you think I am too abrasive'. There is also the danger of taking the differences too literally and superficially, and concluding that they must adopt one or the other perspective because the two are irreconcilable. But this is not managing the conflict inherent in how to approach conflict constructively.

It is a myth that Asians are not prepared to discuss their conflicts openly and constructively, that Asians cannot and do not manage their conflicts, and that smoothing and avoiding conflict are the only viable solutions. Asian people have had to manage conflict for centuries. Filipinos, for example, have dealt with imperialist powers, colonization, significant immigration inflows, war, occupation and liberation, internal insurgency, religious differences, the geographical dispersion of 7,107 islands, and now the development of a robust democracy.

It is equally a myth that Americans do not understand the value of relationships, that they have a single-minded focus on getting the job done. Relationship building through golfing, fishing trips, and the exchange of presents are part of business in North America as well as Asia. Tom Peters advised American business, 'Read more novels and fewer business books: relationships really are all there is'.

Either emphasis by itself is incomplete, even dangerous. The rational, task orientation taken by many Americans can lead to a self-righteous, fixed-sum mentality where self-interest is sacrificed to make sure others do not 'win'. But a belief that direct discussion can affront social face may lead to avoiding issues which do not disappear, but fester and contaminate the relationship.

Too often cultural differences are examined to see whether the Asian or American style of conflict management is superior and which method the organization should adopt. But this examination makes the differences more difficult to manage. From a conflict management perspective, we need to create integrative solutions that combine the best of opposing positions. The challenge and the opportunity of Asia Pacific business is to develop conflict management methods that both build relationships and confront problems.

The Possibility of Integrating

Conflict management exposes the assumption that conflict is inevitably a test of competing wills to see whether it will be 'my way' or 'his way'. Conflict management can transcend such thinking to create mutual value, spurring the creation of new alternatives that promote the interests and incorporate the ideas of many. Managing conflict helps us break out of our simple trade-off thinking and appreciate our diversity as well as our commonality.

But managing conflict requires integration. Managers and employees are more able to manage their conflict when they feel part of the same team and have developed common values and procedures. How can Asian and American values be melded so that diverse people manage their conflicts productively?

Openness and Melding Relationships in Korea

Under the pressure to change and modernize, Koreans have made progress in openness and synthesizing relationships. Believing themselves to be collectivist, Koreans work to develop strong relationships and commonality, but they are prepared to take a stand and force issues in order to make decisions and pursue goals. Although uncomfortable in confronting differences face-to-face, they want to resolve issues, make decisions, and manage their conflicts cooperatively with in-group members.

Working outside the immediate situations, Koreans involve third parties and superiors to help them resolve disputes. Sensitive to feelings, they socialize and drink to release tensions and restore feelings and relationships that may have been bruised during the conflict management. Although their conflict management style is distinct, their aspirations to attain their goals and maintain relationships are not.

Building on Tradition in Indonesia

Although the global marketplace and intense demands on organizations have enlarged the scale of conflict, Asia Pacific peoples have been managing conflict for centuries. The challenge is to translate traditional procedures to the modern organization.

Indonesian villages traditionally used *musyawarah* where issues are jointly considered and disputes managed. The objective of *musyawarah* is to achieve *mufakat* (consensus) where all parties to the conflict accept the procedures used to reach a decision and believe they have worked together to develop a mutually acceptable solution.

Musyawarah is directed by a respected, often officially appointed person but it is also a consultative process. The elder has the protagonists share refreshments and encourages a relaxed, social climate. Each side is to feel that its opinions can be voiced and will be considered fully and that that they are working together to resolve their dispute.

Indonesians have a history of full consultation and guided conflict management where both sides speak their minds in a context of trying to strengthen the relationship and develop mutually useful solutions. However, translating this experience into the modern corporation has proved difficult. In many contemporary organizations in Indonesia, issues are resolved in an autocratic manner without the sensitive consultation and relationship building of *musyawarah*.

Integrated ways of managing conflict can be and are being forged in the Asia Pacific. Research from Asia as well as North America suggests that business people who build a strong relationship are much more prepared to discuss their opposing views openly and thereby manage their conflicts constructively. Strong relationships and open discussion are not only reconcilable but they strongly reinforce each other. Integration is not only possible but probable when strong relationships and confrontation of problems are the basis of constructive conflict.

Developing Conflict Abilities Together

The payoff for managing conflict is substantial for individuals and organizations but the challenges are formidable. It takes courage to break out of old habits and to integrate approaches with others, especially those with different cultural experiences and values. It takes two to manage conflict; one person cannot manage conflict alone. Fortunately, managers and employees can learn how to manage conflict together.

Becoming Motivated

In many conflicts, people not only disagree but suspect each other's motivation and conflict management style. They see others as too arrogant to listen or too conniving to say what is really on their mind. Yet they are unable to discuss these attitudes, or to focus on their conflict about how they manage conflict, for fear of making the conflict too probing and 'personal'. Rather, after fighting competitively, they move toward avoiding the issue and each other.

Conflict itself stimulates an interest in learning how to manage conflict. When conflicts have escalated, people wonder what went wrong and take stock of their relationships and ways of handling differences. But conflict can be an expensive, ineffective way to learn. An American partner in a Western restaurant chain in Asia tells of how he watches many North American managers psychologically deteriorate in the early months of their careers. The new manager expects to give orders to Asian employees without either building relationships or having an open discussion of issues. The employees counter this, not by fighting openly, but by uniting against the new manager, who soon feels isolated and ineffectual. These managers leave Asia without ever realizing what went wrong.

Fortunately, reading about conflict can help us get prepared. The chapters have described the need to manage conflict and shown the obstacles people confront as they deal with their conflicts. The chapters also provide ideas for understanding conflict styles and suggestions for how to manage conflict in Asia Pacific countries. You and your colleagues can use these ideas and guides to improve how you manage your conflicts.

Joint Discussion

Koreans and other Asia Pacific people want to learn how to manage conflict and other critical leadership and teamwork skills. The problem is not so much that people do not want to be more direct and honest in the workplace, but that they do not know how to proceed. A major stumbling block is that people are unsure whether others are interested in learning and changing. We often believe that we are open to strengthening our conflict management abilities but doubt that the other side is.

Reading the chapters of this book can help partners, managers, and employees from the Asia Pacific understand the value of improving how they manage conflict. The chapters show that conflict is natural and inevitable and can be highly useful when managed for mutual benefit. By discussing the chapters, managers and employees can begin a dialogue about the need for them to manage their conflict.

The chapters can also initiate an assessment of the present level of conflict management. Reflecting on one's own conflicts can be very useful; unfortunately, too often this reflection occurs only within one side. The Japanese managers get together to vent their frustration at the belligerent Americans; the Americans complain to each other about the coy Japanese. The responsibility for avoiding and escalating conflict lies with the other group and the solution is for others to change. The result is a painful standoff.

What is needed is a combined consideration of their conflicts in the context of how everyone can improve and contribute to the resolution of conflicts. An acknowledgement that they are all committed to the common, cooperative goal of learning to manage conflict and being able to use their conflicts productively enables them to move away from blaming and finding fault to helping each other learn the relationship, communication, and problem solving abilities needed to manage conflict.

Applying Ideas Together

The ideas and suggested guidelines for managing conflict given in the chapters are much more powerful when people apply them together. Managing conflict is a joint responsibility. When persons agree upon how they want to manage conflict, then they can all contribute to positive conflict and help each other develop skills.

Key to conflict management are building relationships and discussing issues directly and open-mindedly. Protagonists should communicate clearly the desire to manage the conflict for mutual benefit. The conflict management style is understood to be largely cooperative, with each side trying to help the other get what it really wants as it tries to reach its own goals.

They discuss issues in ways that convince both sides that they really do want to find mutually acceptable solutions. They express their opinions, develop their arguments, rebut weaknesses, and refute criticisms. However, they also stop presenting their positions to listen carefully to the other side and demonstrate that they understand its position. Rather than insist on doing it their way, they create alternative solutions and synthesize positions to reach a decision that, to the greatest extent possible helps both sides accomplish their goals.

To reinforce this open-minded, cooperative approach to conflict, managers and employees can use the specific ideas and guides in the chapters to develop their own norms and procedures. They can write in their own words the values that are to shape how they work together and manage conflict. They can develop specific procedures they can all use to manage their conflicts for mutual benefit. Throughout the process they are integrating so that the values and procedures are appropriate, acceptable, and effective for all the diverse groups in the organization. They do not have to adopt the Eastern or Western way to approach conflict; they can create their own way to manage.

Integrative Approaches

Managing conflict constructively integrates rational and emotional emphases. Managers and employees critique, question, and explore arguments, but they also feel a commitment to their positions and react emotionally to opposing arguments and strategies. Involvement, love, and anger all affect the dynamics and outcomes of conflict. Rather than ask people to be unemotional, managing conflict shows how feelings can be developed, expressed and integrated.

Managing conflict in the Asia Pacific requires both 'tough' and 'soft' approaches to form a contemporary style of working. Managing conflict requires confronting problems and struggling to work through them. But it is also 'soft' in that it requires people to be respectful and sensitive to each other and develop strong, trusting relationships.

Managing conflict shows how the Asian emphasis on groups can be integrated with the American emphasis on the individual. Organizations today require empowered, diverse teams built of independent-minded specialists. By combining their opposing views, ideas and perspectives, team members take effective action. With constructive conflict, individuality and freedom of expression very much contribute to the quality of group life and the productivity of the organization.

When partners, managers, and employees together adopt a common, cooperative approach to managing conflict, they see each other as open-minded and can focus directly on the specific conflict at hand. They are managing their conflicts not to embarrass others, but to identify frustrations and strengthen the relationship. They are operating on the same wavelength, not in the unrealistic sense that they will always agree with each other, but in the realistic sense that they agree on the approach they will use to deal with their differences.

Business for Learning to Manage International Conflict

Its diversity of people and perspectives is not an obstacle but a vital part of the richness of working in the Asia Pacific. There are many ways of working, not just one Western and one Eastern. Conflict is not a problem either: it is part of the solution. Through conflict, we create new solutions, appreciate our differences, and learn to work across national and cultural boundaries. Managing conflict is not a new challenge. What is new is to manage conflict in modern organizations that today face strong demands to perform globally.

The world is more clearly and intensely interdependent; currency and stock market fluctuations on one side of the Pacific Ocean affect those on the other side. But being more interdependent does not mean that we will manage our conflicts more successfully. Fragmentation within and between nations is a real possibility. Indeed, recent experience suggests that our ineffectiveness at dealing with intercultural ethnic conflict can have disastrous effects.

Managing conflict in business offers a way to learn to manage these complex conflicts more successfully. Every day in the Asia Pacific diverse people argue, debate, and develop solutions to the many issues which arise in the course of doing business. They can learn to use their conflicts to keep abreast of changes and reach their goals. However, they must become skilled in maintaining relationships and discussing issues openly, rationally, and respectfully to make their conflicts productive.

INDEX